The Complete
Nevada Traveler

ON THE COVER: *"Savage Mansion above the Pogonip, Virginia City"*
by Max Winthrop.

TITLE PAGE: *"Are We there Yet?"*
by Robin Cobbey
Photograph of the author near Warm Springs.

To everyone who helped with this 110,000 square mile project–
and especially to my favorite singer of my favorite songs–
Thank you!

A special thanks to Paul Cirac and White Sage Studios
for the maps, design, layouts, inspiration and patience.

Printed by Edwards Brothers Printers, Ann Arbor Michigan.

ISBN: 978-0-940936-17-1

GOLD HILL PUBLISHING COMPANY, INC.
PO Drawer F
Virginia City Nevada 89440
Tel—702-847-0222 Fax—702-847-0327
email—cnt@nevadaweb.com

The Complete Nevada Traveler

by David W. Toll

The Affectionate and Intimately Detailed Guidebook to the Most Interesting State in America

ALEXANDRA TOLL

Desert Venus at the Goldwell Open Air Museum at Rhyolite.

Introduction: Gains and Losses vi

Cowboy Country 1

Reno-Tahoe Territory 50

MAX WINTHROP

The Grosch brothers' wall is now nothing: just a pile of rocks.

Gains and Losses

As I prepared this new edition I was struck by the way the old Nevada is slowly — and not so slowly — vanishing. It's happening in big ways and small. In Reno and Las Vegas, landmark structures are being demolished. In Silver City a rock wall fell down.

Granted, both the Mapes Hotel in Reno and the Stardust on the Las Vegas Strip, the most recent properties to be scraped away, were beyond redemption as profit centers. They had become old and in the way, preventing the high-priced real estate they sat on from realizing its prime purpose, and so they had to go. Generations of memories went with them.

That rock wall in Silver City is a more complicated case. It had been built more than a century and a half ago by two brothers from Pennsylvania, Allen and Hosea Grosch, who had come west as '49ers. As they had packed their way across the Isthmus of Panama, they met a man who had ranged north from Mexico with a prospecting party. He told them about a region far to the north where silver abounded, and told them how to find it. After a season in the California placer mines they had crossed the Sierra to Nevada, following the directions of the man they'd met in Panama, and settled in Gold Canyon where a small population of prospectors were spread out along the little creek panning gold.

Like their neighbors they built a rough cabin, dry-stacking rock against the wall of American Canyon, where a tributary stream feeds into the main channel of Gold Creek, and building the other three walls and the roof of logs and limbs. In 1856 they wrote home, "Native silver is found in Gold Cañon; it resembles thin sheet-lead broken very fine, and lead the miners suppose it to be." Later they wrote, "One of these veins is a perfect monster."

But before they could record or develop their

claims, Hosea drove a pick through his foot and died of blood poisoning. Allen then struck out for California, but was caught on the Sierra by winter snows and died of exposure.

Their little cabin had been left in the care of Henry Comstock, generally recognised as "a lazy, drunken prospector" (as one historian put it), who took possession of their possessions, including a trunk containing documents and correspondence. These papers were never brought to light, and it was Comstock's name that was attached to the great discoveries of gold and silver that followed: the Comstock Lode.

As the mines were developed, Virginia City soon became into the greatest city between San Francisco and Denver, Gold Hill was renowned for its rich mines and Silver City, which took form just uphill from the Grosh brothers' crude cabin, attracted over 1000 residents. The little cabin, long abandoned, fell into disrepair. Its wooden parts were doubtless scavenged to burn for heat in a freezing winter. But through the years of bonanza, and the borrasca that followed, as the generations succeeded one another, the significance of the stacked rocks was forgotten. No placque, no-one left to remember. Yet the wall remained intact.

Until last spring, when it tumbled down into a heap, and the last remaining handiwork of the men who located the Comstock Lode became just a meaningless jumble of rocks.

Around the state there are many historic treasures that are being protected, restored and revived. But at the mouth of American Canyon a big piece of our history was lost when that little wall came down.

About the little ads...

You'll see that there are small ads at the end of many of the sections in this book. They represent the opportunity for local enterprises and organizations to extend their invitations to you when you visit their locales. These ads appear by invitation only, and they represent the best Nevada has to offer. They range from humble convenience stores like R-Place in Ash Springs to luxurious resorts like David Walley's in Genoa, from historical treasures like the Eureka Opera House in Eureka and The Way It Was Museum in Virginia City to the most contemporary of attractions like Tahoe Ridge Winery in Genoa and the Pahrump Valley Winery in Pahrump, from the prehistory of the Lost City Museum in Overton to the alternative history of the Alien Research Center in Hiko and the Little A'le' Inn in Rachel. We are glad to provide them space to expand upon their offerings, and pleased to recommend them to you when you become a Nevada traveler.

MAX WINTHROP

A neighbor's back cabin wall remains intact and unnoticed beside the highway.

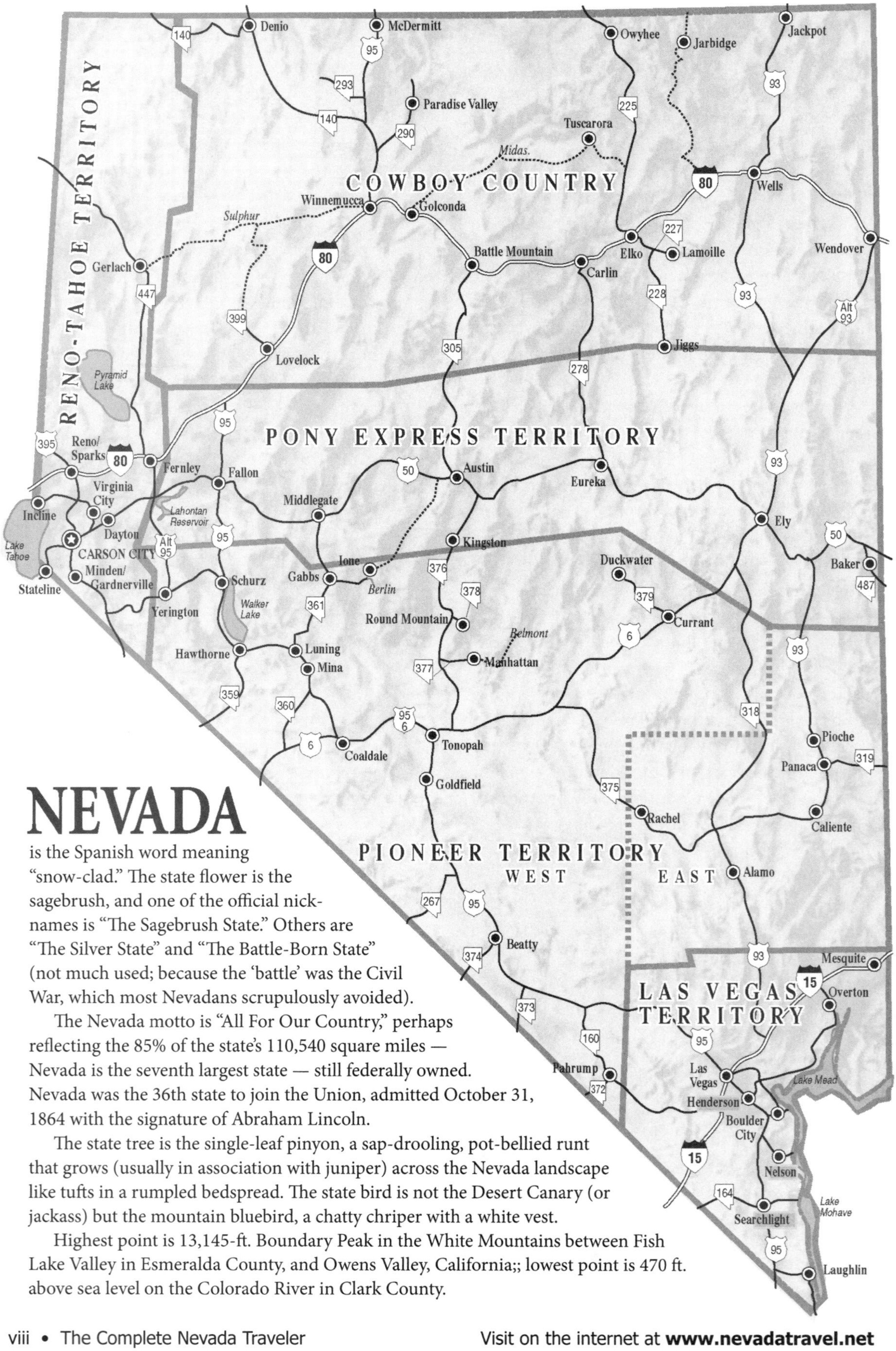

NEVADA

is the Spanish word meaning "snow-clad." The state flower is the sagebrush, and one of the official nick-names is "The Sagebrush State." Others are "The Silver State" and "The Battle-Born State" (not much used; because the 'battle' was the Civil War, which most Nevadans scrupulously avoided).

The Nevada motto is "All For Our Country," perhaps reflecting the 85% of the state's 110,540 square miles — Nevada is the seventh largest state — still federally owned. Nevada was the 36th state to join the Union, admitted October 31, 1864 with the signature of Abraham Lincoln.

The state tree is the single-leaf pinyon, a sap-drooling, pot-bellied runt that grows (usually in association with juniper) across the Nevada landscape like tufts in a rumpled bedspread. The state bird is not the Desert Canary (or jackass) but the mountain bluebird, a chatty chriper with a white vest.

Highest point is 13,145-ft. Boundary Peak in the White Mountains between Fish Lake Valley in Esmeralda County, and Owens Valley, California;; lowest point is 470 ft. above sea level on the Colorado River in Clark County.

Cowboy Country

Most of the travelers who whiz along the Interstate scarcely notice the Humboldt River. For them, it is a minor element in a monotonous landscape. Yet for twenty years, from 1848 to 1868, this slow surge of muddy water was one of the best-known and most important rivers in America.

It's a sluggish stream of no discernible distinction that runs through northern Nevada like a strip of gristle through a cheap cut of beefsteak. For three hundred miles it slithers through broad alkaline valleys, past the nub ends of scuffed and ribby mountain ridges.

It lay too far east, beyond the Sierra Nevada, and too far north, beyond the Colorado, for the Spaniards to discover from California or Arizona. It lay too far west, beyond the Rockies, for the French or the Americans to discover it from the Dakotas or the great plains. And it lay too far south, beyond the Columbia and the Snake, for the Astorians or their British successors to discover from the Oregon country.

And so the Humboldt was the last major American river to be discovered.

It was 1828 when Peter Skene Ogden led a party of Hudson's Bay Company trappers south out of the Nez Perce country of Idaho and followed one of the Humboldt's tributaries down to the river's big bend, about where the town of Winnemucca is today. Ogden trapped beaver there briefly, then went east into Utah for the winter before returning in the spring to what he had first named the Unknown River, and then Paul's River after one of the trappers who had died along its shore in the snows of late autumn. Ogden led his party slowly downriver, trapping as they went, until they reached the marshy bog in the shadow of the Stillwater Range where the river spread out into the desert sand and disappeared.

For ten years British and American trappers worked the river, which they called Mary's River then, or St. Mary's. By 1838 the beaver had been trapped out, but silk hats were already replacing beaver on the heads of fashionable eastern men, and the economy of the Far West was going through drastic change. Only three years later the first party of American immigrants to California dared the grueling overland desert journey.

On the advice of the mountain men, they followed the Humboldt west from near its source at

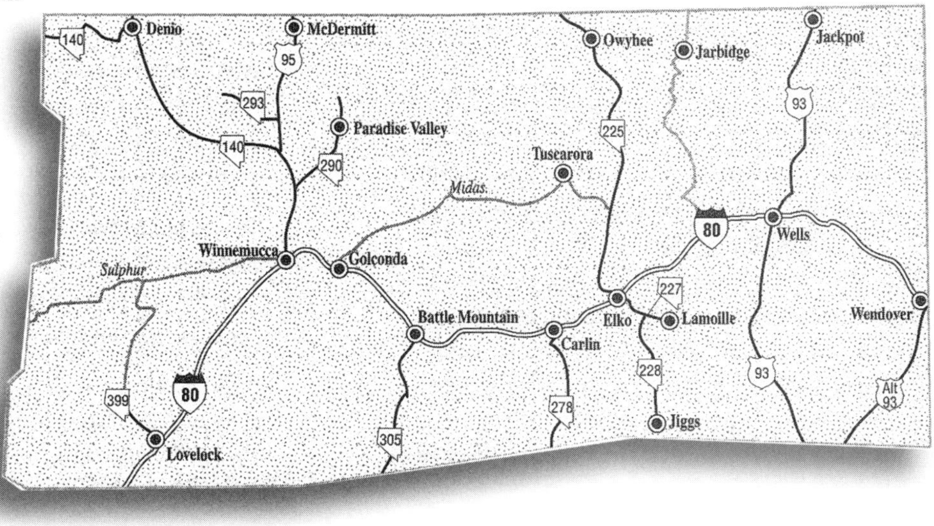

NEVADA STATE MUSEUM

Chief Winnemucca.

Humboldt Wells to its sink, then crossed the Forty-Mile Desert without water to the banks of the Carson, and with great hardship scaled the Sierra. They had been forced to abandon their wagons early, and they survived the ordeal of the mountain crossing by eating their oxen and most of their horses. But they reached California, and established the Humboldt Trail as a feasible overland route for all who would follow.

In 1845 Fremont began his explorations and, more important, his publicizing the desert country between the Rockies and the Sierra Nevada. It was he who named the river Humboldt. In 1846 the Donner party followed the Humboldt west to its rendezvous with horror. No traveler used the trail without learning to hate the river it follows, for except for providing a source of bitter, sometimes undrinkable water, the Humboldt did little to alleviate the exhausting difficulties of the trail.

After 1849 those difficulties were multiplied out of all expectation by the California gold rush. Within the space of a single season the scant forage along the river's course was grazed away. Reeds and willows were devoured by hungry animals, and parties that made the journey late in the season were devastated to find the river barren of grass for their oxen and horses, and destitute of game for themselves. More than that, the Indians, infuriated by the ceaseless intrusion of heedless strangers, began to resist the westward march. Outrage motivated their attacks, and avarice became a factor, too, when they learned what treasure the settlers carried with them: guns and tools and clothing and food as well as animals. The emigrants were weak, exhausted, and confused as they plodded west day after blistering day beside the naked banks of the sullen stream, easy prey to a carefully thought out attack. So the Humboldt meant adventure, hardship, despair, and death.

Meanest and muddiest, filthiest stream
most cordially I hate you;
Meaner and muddier still you seem
since the first day I met you

What mean these graves so fresh and new
along your banks on either side~
They've all been dug and filled by you,
thou guilty wretch, thou homicide.

Now fare thee well, we here shake hands
and part (I hope) to meet no more,
I'd rather die in happier lands
than longer live upon your shore.

The Iowa man who wrote the poem about the river in 1850 was the only one to express his loathing in meter and at leisure; most of

the survivors of the Humboldt Trail shouted their hatred at the tops of their lungs as their wagons mired down in mud, as their animals fell down dead from starvation, as their exhausted children screamed with hysteria and hunger.

In 1851 a group of enterprising Mormons from Salt Lake City established the first settlement along the Humboldt Trail, at Mormon Station (now Genoa) at the eastern base of the Sierra, and for a

NEVADA STATE MUSEUM

Tuscarora freighters on Weed Street.

few years after that, while the wagon traffic along the river continued strong, a few more trading posts appeared along its banks. These were crude, rough-built shanties offering a limited supply of staples at high prices, and most of them were temporary. A trader stayed just long enough to make a grubstake in that desperate country, and no longer.

The grandest of these outposts was located on a tributary of the Humboldt, near the west foot of the Ruby Mountains. It was established in 1852 by Peter Haws, an apostate Mormon slung out of Salt Lake City for manufacturing whiskey there. Haws farmed, and husbanded a few cattle, and bartered with the emigrants. He also traded with the Indians, providing them with a market for the goods they stole from the wagon trains and had no use for. He even organized attacks on wagon trains himself, attacks resulting in massacres, looting, and the driving off of livestock. He himself was driven out after two years, following the shooting of one of his Indian accomplices.

But even before Haws had taken over the south fork of the Humboldt, the Jackass Mail was using the Humboldt Trail to haul the U.S. mail between Salt Lake City and Sacramento. And the trail was used in trade. In 1852 Kit Carson herded thirteen thousand merino sheep from New Mexico to Wyoming, and then west to the California gold fields by way of the Humboldt. The sheep contributed to the devastation of the fragile desert ecology, but Carson realized $15,000 for himself at the mines and went home rich to Santa Fe.

Through the 1850s, wagon trains of every description trundled painfully along the meandering course of the Humboldt, their metal-rimmed wheels cutting tracks so deep into the rock at some places that they can still be seen today. Horace Greeley came west along the Humboldt in 1859, and was horrified by the river.

"The Humboldt," he wrote, "...is the meanest river of its length on earth... Though three hundred and fifty miles in length, it is never more than a decent millstream; I presume it is the only river of equal length that never even had a canoe launched upon its bosom... I thought I had seen barrenness before... Here, on the Humboldt, famine sits enthroned, and waves his scepter over a dominion made expressly for him... The sage-brush and grease-wood, which cover the high, parched plain on either side of the river's bottom, seems thinly set, with broad spaces of naked, shining, glaring, blinding clay between them; the hills beyond... seem even more naked. Not a tree, and hardly a shrub, anywhere relieves their sterility."

This repellent picture of the Humboldt was not Greeley's alone; since the early 1850s it had prompted attempts to find a more direct southerly route to the Sierra Nevada. In 1858 a route surveyed by Captain Simpson through the Ruby Valley (and many miles from the river), was adopted by the mail service, which was then making weekly departures between Salt Lake City and

Sacramento, and covering the route in the fast time of sixteen days.

The new route was also selected for use by the Pony Express when it galloped into operation in 1860. The Overland Telegraph Company selected the new route also, because of the lack of timber for stringing its lines along the Humboldt, and the Overland Stagecoach Company used it as well. In 1862 Fort Ruby was established on the Ruby marshes to police the trail. In the Ruby Valley the Overland Stagecoach Company and the Fort Ruby soldiers farmed to provide feed for their animals. Colonel Jeremiah Moore, who commanded Fort Ruby for a while, used soldiers under his command to develop a ranch for himself, and when they had finished, he resigned his commission and rode away to Texas, returning a few months later with a herd of 800 longhorns.

Longhorn cattle were selling cheap in Texas after the Civil War. Hundreds of Texas ranchers were bankrupted by the collapse of the Confederacy. Their herds were largely intact, but their markets were destroyed and their cash was worthless. Many sold out for whatever their animals would bring and started from scratch; others trailed their herds out of Texas for the grazing lands of Wyoming, Montana, Utah, and Nevada.

Other herds migrated into Nevada from the droughted, overgrazed, and increasingly fenced ranch lands of California and Oregon. Ranches were established everywhere in Nevada — everywhere there was water. But northeastern Nevada was the prime grazing land, and by the middle 1860s most of it had been appropriated to the use of the cattle ranchers, usually on the basis of a small freehold and unrestricted use of the adjacent public lands. The Indians were increasingly confined to reservations. Still there were few settlements, and those that existed were no better than way stations on the single stagecoach line that bisected the great empty spaces of the Humboldt.

Then came the railroad. Surveyors followed the course of the Humboldt from west to east in the fall of 1868. Grade building crews followed their markers early the following year, and rails were spoked to ties before winter was gone.When the intercontinental railroad was linked atPromontory, Utah, in May, 1869, the Overland Stage and the Army posts that guarded it became superfluous and the Humboldt River once again became the line of development in Nevada's Cowboy Country.

The railroad brought towns. Wells, Elko, Carlin, Winnemucca, Lovelock, odd desert hybrids combining the antique, hand-made qualities of the outlying ranches with the up-to-rate, highly mechanized character of the railroad. The towns prospered. In January of 1869, Elko was four sun-bleached, leaky canvas tents. Six months later, after silver strikes at Bullion to the south and Aura to the north, Elko was a thriving shipping center with a population of nearly 2,000 and more than a dozen permanent build-

NEVADA HISTORICAL SOCIETY

Pedro Altube on his Spanish Ranch, 1881.

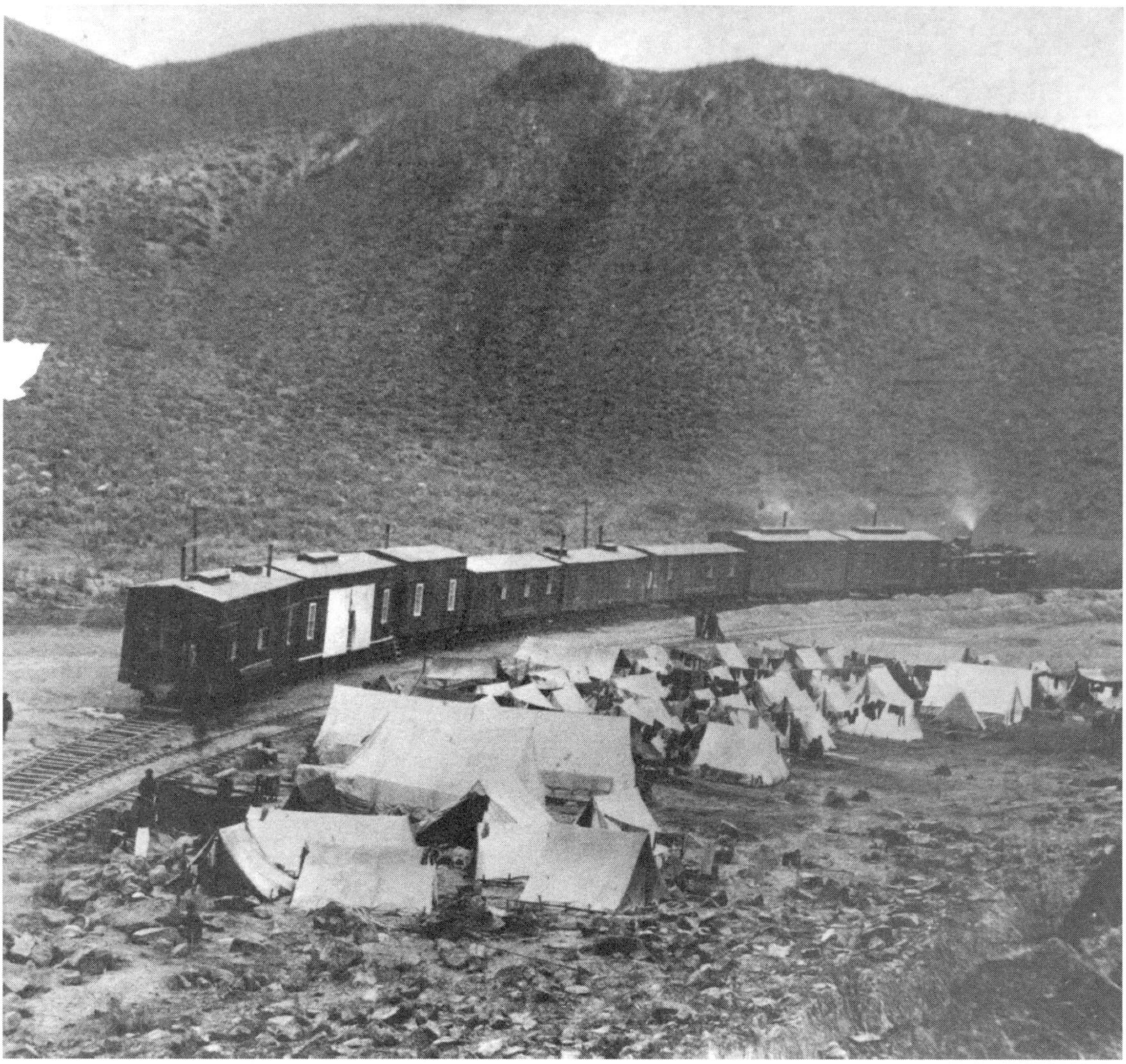

NEVADA HISTORICAL SOCIETY

Building the Central Pacific Railroad, 1868. Chinese section camp and headquarters.

ings of planed lumber. Ranchers continued to drive herds into the country. The Garat family sold out the San Joaquin Valley property they had ranched in California since 1852 and drove 1,000 head of cattle into Elko county; the Altube brothers, Basques who had built large dairy herds on theSan Francisco peninsula brought 1,000 animals to the Independence Valley and founded the Spanish Ranch.

Scottish herders had brought bands of sheep into western Nevada from California and Oregon in the 1860s. They were succeeded by the Chinese who had worked in the construction gangs that had built the railroad, and the Chinese were replaced in turn by Basques from the Pyrenees Mountain provinces of France and Spain. In the late 1880s and early 1890s, when the cattlemen of northeastern Nevada were staggering under the impact of the disasterous Winter of 1889-90, the sheepmen invaded.

They pushed in from the north and west, driving their bands onto the public grazing lands the cattlemen had come to think of as their own. The ranchers responded by posting armed guards at watering places, by scattering bands of sheep, and by sniping at the herders. But the sheepmen were as tough as the ranchers, and they stayed.

MAX WINTHROP

The railroad is still a big part of the Nevada landscape.

By the turn of the century Elko, Winnemucca and Lovelock were bustling provincial capitals for more than half of Nevada's cattle and two-thirds of its sheep. Headquarters for the huge cattle and sheep outfits, and railheads for the mines still producing in the far mountain ranges, these towns — county seats now — represented a much greater concentration of wealth and influence than their unprepossessing appearance suggested.

The same is true today; there is little about Nevada's Cowboy Country Territory to indicate its importance to the casual glance. The towns along the length of the Humboldt are only now beginning to concern themselves about the good opinion of travelers. When one of them — Battle Mountain — was singled out as "The Armpit of America" by the Washington Post, at least two of the others breathed a great sigh of relief. Yet these towns are the rarest kind of place. They are about the closest thing to the frontier western town that still remains. And once out of the barren trough which funnels the Humboldt west, the scenery and outdoor recreation — ranging from simple touring to backpacking into isolated mountain lakes of stunning beauty — are perfectly delightful.

Mining had fueled the local economies in northeastern Nevada until 2000, when they began cutting back and closing down., just as they had done in the 19th and 20th centuries. You can book a room online in the Cowboy Country of Nevada, but the trappings of the 21st century are only lightly, and awkwardly, laid over the very present past. And because that past encompasses the mountain men, the wagon trains, the Cavalry, renegades, Indians, Cattlemen vs. sheepmen, the railroads and the miners, it is a unique and flavorful present indeed.

GARY ELAM

Pershing County's unusual round courthouse, Lovelock.

Lovelock

THIS ATTRACTIVE community has been a comfortable stopping place for travelers since the days of the wagon trains. One of the hardy souls who braved the Humboldt Trail in 1849 jotted down impressions of the Big Meadow one August day:

LOVELOCK	
Reno	92
Winnemucca	72
Elko	197

"This marsh for three miles is certainly the liveliest place that one could witness in a lifetime. There is some 250 wagons here all the time. Trains going out and others coming in and taking their places is the constant order of the day. Cattle and mules by the hundreds are surrounding us, in grass to their knees, all discoursing sweet music with the grinding of their jaws. Men are seen hurrying in many different ways and everybody attending to his own business. Some mowing, some reaping, some packing the grass, others spreading it out to dry, or collecting that already dry and fixing it for transportation. In fact the joyous laugh and the familiar sound of the whetted scythe gives an air of happiness and content around that must carry the wearied travelers through to the 'Promised Land.' The scene reminds one much of a large encampment of the army, divided off into separate and distinct parties, everybody minding his own business and letting other people alone."

Lovelock, named for an early homesteader and storekeeper in the Big Meadows when the Central Pacific Railroad drove its rails this way in 1868, became a way station of some importance as mining strikes in the surrounding mountains and agricultural development in the valley combined to encourage the growth of a small settlement. By the turn of the century it had become a town of about a hundred homes, a school, two churches, and a business district of almost three dozen firms, all within a few steps of the railroad tracks.

Lovelock in those days was a part of Humboldt

GWEN CARTER

At the park, Lovelock

County, and in 1905, Allen Bragg, editor of the daily Silver State in Winnemucca, came to pay his respects. "Lovelock is 'on the trail' to be a city of considerable magnitude," he wrote. "I think if I could come back to this dusty ball 50 years hence I should see a city of at least 50,000 souls, for Lovelock Valley, if put to its highest uses, would support 50,000 or 75,000 busy men and women, and it would be an ideal spot to raise children and start them in life with bright prospects."

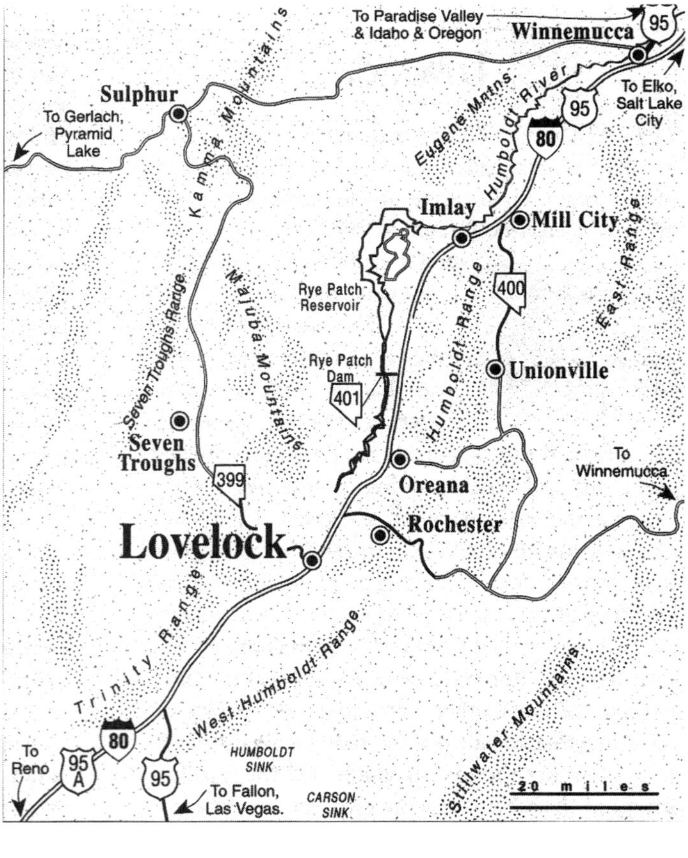

Editor Bragg had a severe case of Nevada optimism, but Lovelock did prosper from the nearby mining activity in the late 19th and early 20th centuries. It achieved 2,803 residents by 1920 but that's the high point so far. Lovelock incorporated as a city in 1917, but was so broke two years later that the City Council laid off the Indian Policeman and the night Jailer. They had the city's Teamster sleep in the jail, cut the Police Chief's salary in half to $25 a month, and instructed the City Clerk to see about turning off the street lights during moonlight nights.

Since then Lovelock's economy has become largely agricultural again. The conditions of soil and climate that produced the lush growth of grass for the pioneers is famous as Nevada's "Banana Belt." Lovelock boasts some 40,000 acres under irrigation in Upper and Lower valleys, most of it devoted to grain for feeding livestock, and to the alfalfa seed for which Lovelock is known around the world.

The country around Lovelock is a geological exhibit of extraordinary complexity, and provides a variety of outdoor enjoyments. Tufa formations, the rough-textured remnants from the bottom of the long-dried Lahontan sea, wart the desert floor at several places nearby. The largest and best-known of these coral-like eruptions are to the west seven and 20 miles, within sight of the highway. A smaller bed is easily accessible about a mile north of town on Western Avenue, covered with red and black lichen, and providing an interesting spot for a picnic lunch or simply for contemplating the eons.

Edna Purviance is Lovelock's only movie star so far, but the town has produced at least one semi-hero. Andrew Humbert Scott — Scotty the Assayer — was a familiar figure in Lovelock. In his little assay office near the railroad depot (now moved to the Marzen House Museum), he had analyzed the ore from countless discoveries in the region, including some of the biggest. But his claim to at least local fame is that he had made the first military parachute jump in history.

During World War I, when General Billy Mitchell proposed to a skeptical military establishment that aircraft could deliver fully armed troops to the battlefield by dropping them from airplanes, it was Lt. Scott, rifle, pack and parachute ready, who sat in the forward seat of the little biplane snarling across the soggy winter's sky above the Potomac River. Scotty's target was a small island in the Potomac, but he got tangled up in his seatbelt and was late getting out of the plane. He splashed down in the river, and Mitchell was court martialed for not sitting down and shutting up.

Pause for a moment to admire the single stoplight dangling over the intersection with Main street. It was once the last signal light to regulate traffic between San Francisco and New York — until the freeway bypassed Lovelock in 1983.

The Pershing County Court House is Lovelock's architectural jewel. It is round. Like all Nevada court houses, it is open to visitors during regular office hours, and county offices are located around the perimeter of the building, off the corridor that rings the round court room at its center. "My wife and I were divorced in Lovelock," a Winnemucca man told me, "and we're still going around in circles."

Nowadays the court house, or at least the small plaza behind it, is better-known for love. Borrowing a tradition from ancient China and drawing on the town's distinctive name, a series of short chains has been suspended from posts surrounding a rose garden where blissful couples to "lock their love" by

The Marzen House Musem

THE RESTORED Marzen home, now housing the Pershing County museum, is located at the west end of Lovelock. It would not, by today's standards, qualify as a mansion. However, if a man's castle is his home, Colonel Joseph Marzen built for his family and ultimately for posterity an edifice of enduring quality.

Joseph Marzen was born in Germany in 1824 and emigrated to America at 18. His first five years in this country were spent in New York, where he worked as a butcher.

In 1850 Marzen married his first wife, Margaret Bechtel, a native of Germany, and in 1851 he emigrated to Sacramento, where he continued to succeed as a butcher. Over 20 years Marzen broadened his endeavors and conducted business in Virginia City, Reno, and Truckee, California.

On a cattle buying trip in 18v73, Marzen visited Lovelock Valley. In 1876 he was back in the valley, not to buy cattle, but to purchase land. He had seen the promise of the country and envisioned what could become reality. Soon his 3,480 acres were producing record grain and hay crops. His livestock won consistently at exhibitions in western shows. He imported stock from Scotland to upgrade his prize animals. In addition to his Short-horn Hereford cattle, he bred Percheron, Clydesdale, and English Shire horses, all of which won blue ribbons at livestock shows. His 30 dairy cows and his presidency and part ownership of the Lovelock Creamery attested to his agricultural diversity.

Marzen served one term in the State Legislature, his political career ending when he severed his Silver Party affiliation. He was a Mason and a member of the Odd Fellows.

Marzen's 40-year Nevada residence left an imprint on the state and on this small community. The Big Meadow Ranch, as the Marzen holdings are now designated, has retained its productivity through several owners. The cluster of trees still sheltering the buildings, the broad fields of grain and alfalfa comprise the picture seen by uncomprehending travelers speeding along I-80.

— Eleanor Gottschalk

MAX WINTHROP

Lovers' Locks gleam in the sunshine in the small plaza behind the round courthouse.

attaching padlocks engraved with their names. You can bring your own padlock to add to the gleaming display, or you can buy one locally for a pittance.

The county library and the public swimming pool are only a few steps from the court house. You'll also find a pleasant park with picnic tables and a children's playground.

Broadway was the original business street that grew up along the railroad track in the 1870s. The old depot building is a classic, and the fancy-porched residences, the plain box of the (now roofless) Bernd Hotel, the bright blue Palace Club and the other original structures offer a glimpse, only slightly filtered through stucco and neon, of the frontier west.

Check at the Chamber of Commerce a half block south of the Court House for directions to the nearby historic sites of Vernon and Seven Troughs. The Cowpoke Cafe and La Casita are quite good restaurants, and there are half a dozen choices for lodging, RV hook-ups and automotive services. Sturgeon's is a classic small town full-service Nevada hotel-casino.

Unionville

THIS HISTORIC AND well-protected mining city is accessible from Lovelock and from Winnemucca via I-80 and Nevada Highway 400. This road is paved from Mill City to the mouth of Buena Vista Canyon, within three miles of Unionville, and generally has cows or sheep wandering on it or near it. It is unpaved the rest of the way back to I-80 at Oreana.

Unionville was established in May, 1861, by a party of southern-sympathizing prospectors from Silver City who named their camp Dixie. Their interest had been stimulated by the arrival on the Comstock of a group of Paiutes carrying lumps of rich ore, and by early July of that year dozens of claims had been established along Buena Vista Canyon, on the east side of the Humboldt Mountains. By autumn the little town, now renamed Unionville, consisted of "eleven cabins and a liberty pole" and was selected over the smaller Star City to be the first seat of Humboldt County.

ROGER LAVAKE

Unionville

By early 1863 Unionville was a substantial city of some 200 residences, a horse-drawn bus line, a newspaper, nearly 50 business houses of every description, and a schoolhouse already in need of repair. A slapdash approach to construction was characteristic of most mining camps, but Unionville was a champion in this regard. A visitor to the county offices during a summer rainshower found the County Clerk huddled with his records in the one corner of the room "where the rain didn't come any thicker than it did outside."

Construction difficulties largely stemmed from the scarcity of local lumber and the poor quality of materials shipped in. The subject excited the editorial interest of the Register, which noted in 1863 that about half the lumber shipped to Unionville was "just what it was cracked up to be" and the other half was "knot." The paper also commented ruefully that it was often difficult to distinguish between loads of firewood and hay, since some of the trees were so slender, and some of the hay so coarse.

Despite the town's rapid growth and the rich assay reports, development of the mines at Unionville proceeded slowly, the owners being more concerned with promoting stock than excavating ore. When Sam Clemens made a prospecting trip to the town in the winter of 1861-62, he took claims, but then succumbed to stock fever and abandoned the shaft at a depth of twelve feet in order to trade in shares of the district. He and his partners bought into the Columbiana, the Branch Mint, the Universe, the Grand Mogul, the Great Republic, the Root Hog Or Die, and more than a score of promising mines before departing after a stay of a few weeks.

Nevertheless, by 1864 a number of Unionville's mines had begun to produce substantial quantities of rich ore, and in 1868 the Arizona began to show signs of the ore which would ultimately bring nearly $6 million up in the skips. The Arizona, the National, the Manitowoc, and the Gem of the Sierra were all producing well in the late 1860s. But by 1881 Unionville had dwindled down to about 200 residents, most of whom were engaged in small-scale mining operations. By 1939 the tailing piles of the Arizona mine alone had been reworked fourteen times.

Unionville today is a slender chain of jutting ruins and foundations extending almost three miles up Buena Vista Canyon. Cattle browse among the rock ruins that mark the steep old streets, and poplars have matured and grown tall where wagons once clattered down to the stamp mills at the mouth of the canyon.

About a dozen residences remain tenanted, and the Old Pioneer Garden Bed & Breakfast welcomes guests. After a dusty desert drive, Unionville is a refreshing oasis of green. Remember, though, that aside from the B&B, the residents are not in the business of catering to tourists, so mind your manners.

Edna Purviance
Nevada's Forgotten Movie Star

YOU MIGHT THINK that a state with so few celebrities to brag about would make a big deal about a movie star who called Nevada home. But Edna Purviance, who starred with Charlie Chaplin in the pictures that elevated him into the first rank of Hollywood performers, is now almost forgotten here.

Born in Paradise Valley in October, 1896, Edna moved as a youngster to Lovelock where she and her sister Bessie helped their mother keep a boarding house, and where she finished high school in 1913. Except for Broadway Street and the railroad tracks, there is nothing left in Lovelock today harking back to the eager young girl who had made the beds and washed the sheets in the boarding house, tending to the needs of the bachelor railroad men and listening to the trains chuffing in and out of town.

When Bessie got a job in the show at the Pan Pacific Exposition in San Francisco as a diving belle, Edna decided she'd go too. Edna's girlhood friends remember her as vivacious and attractive, and she found a ready welcome in San Francisco. She shared an apartment with Bessie, took a business course, and worked in an office on Market Street while entering into the Bohemian life of the city.

Charlie Chaplin, meanwhile, had just signed a contract with the Essanay movie company at Niles, California. Chaplin was a promising young comedian from England Bronco Billy Anderson was taking a chance on. In the spring of 1914, Charlie and Bronco Billy drove over to San Francisco in search of a leading lady. This unlikely pair inspected every chorus girl in the city, but failed to find just the right combination of sexy nymphet, mature calm and zany eccentricity that Charlie especially liked.

Then another actor suggested Edna. She wasn't in show business, but she had a special quality. Perhaps it was her sweet smile, with its hint of mischief. Perhaps it was the duck she walked on a leash. Whatever it was that made Edna special, Charlie liked it.

COURTESY OF THE ACADEMY OF MOTION PICTURE ARTS AND SCIENCES

Our beautiful Edna.

"She was quiet and reserved, with large, beautiful eyes, beautiful teeth and a sensitive mouth," Charlie wrote in his autobiography. "I doubted whether she could act or had any humor, she looked so serious. Nevertheless, with these reservations, we engaged her. She would at least be decorative in my comedies."

They appeared in nearly 40 films together, beginning in February, 1915, with "His New Job." She was his leading lady in "The Tramp," in which he established the persona of the little fellow with the ragged clothes and heart of gold. Edna was the farmer's daughter Charlie rescued from the gang of thugs, and when they shot him, Edna nursed him back to life. In the bittersweet end, Charlie lost the girl as usual.

Offscreen he got the girl as usual, and during the ten years of their close association that followed, Chaplin's genius flowered. They were lovers during most of that time, but they did not marry.

"We were serious about each other," Chaplin wrote, "and at the back of my mind I had the idea we might marry, but I had reservations about Edna. I was uncertain of her, and for that matter uncertain of myself."

But not uncertain about 15-year-old Mildred Harris whom he married in 1917 and divorced in 1920, or Lita Grey, whom he married in 1924 and who divorced him in 1926, naming Edna as one of several contributing causes.

By then, though, their romantic passions had cooled. Edna had taken up drinking, and of course Charlie kept on getting married. "Although Edna and I were emotionally estranged," he recalled, "I was still interested in her career. But looking objectively at Edna, I realized she was growing rather matronly, which would not be suitable for the feminine confection necessary for my future pictures."

In Edna's place came such feminine confections as Paulette Goddard, Dawn Addams and Claire Bloom, among others. But give Charlie credit. In 1924 he tried to help Edna launch her solo career. He wrote, directed, and played a small part in "A Woman of Paris" in which she starred opposite Adolphe Menjou. It was a flop and Edna's career was over.

But her friendship with Chaplin continued, and in fact she received a small salary from Chaplin's film company until January 13, 1958, the day she died of cancer in Los Angeles.

"How could I forget Edna?" Chaplin responded to an interviewer after her death. "She was with me when it all began."

Indeed, our Edna was the farmer's daughter who nursed Chaplin's little tramp to life.

Yet, as the Lovelock Review-Miner mournfully pointed out a few years ago, there is no monument to Edna anywhere in town, no Purviance Street, not even an Edna Purviance Film Festival once a year.

Only in Winnemucca, where she spent summers as a girl, is there any memento of Edna and her fabulous career. The silk dress she wore about 70 years ago in "The Adventurer" is in a display case at the museum, pinned there like a butterfly, motionless and faded. Beside it, her photograph smiles brightly out through the glass, her face, once gazed upon raptly by millions, is now unfamiliar.

COURTESY OF THE ACADEMY OF MOTION PICTURE ARTS AND SCEENCES

Charlie and Edna in "Sunnyside" 1919.

Off the I-80 Freeway

INTERSTATE 80 CONNECTS all the major towns along the Humboldt Trail like a concrete dot-to-dot across the Nevada map. It's great for truck drivers hauling triples, for cross-country travelers intent on making fast time and for people with a lot on their minds. But for you and me, eager to experience the unknown (or at least not-quite-known), there is a better way, many ways, in fact, for detour, digression and deliverance from monotony. If you work at it, you can get all the way across the state with only a few miles on the freeway. It takes longer — measure it in days instead of hours —but it's a lot more fun.

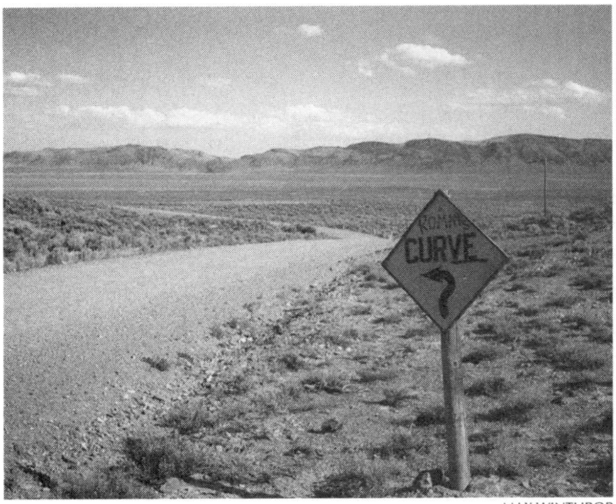

MAX WINTHROP

Roman's curve.

Here are some appealing off-the-freeway diversions, from west to east. They can all be accomplished in the family sedan, but you'll appreciate having something at least a degree more rugged, and 4-wheel drive is always a great idea.

Sparks to Lovelock

This is a big one: 236 miles through the Smoke Creek and Black Rock deserts

Start by taking Pyramid Way north from Sparks (it becomes Nevada 445) to Pyramid Lake. Go left past Sutcliffe and around the west shore of the lake — the lakeside warm springs at The Needles are closed now — through the Smoke Creek Desert (about 50 miles of graded gravel road) to Gerlach. If you start early in the morning and don't linger at the lake, you'll get to Gerlach by mid-afternoon

You can take a shortcut by turning right on Nevada 446 when you reach the lake. Continue through Nixon and then go north on Nevada 447 along the east shore of the lake 56 miles to Gerlach, pavement all the way. That is a very brief description of a whole lot of lonesome desert travel. Equip yourself so that annoying inconvenience doesn't become life-threatening disaster: water, food, blankets, flashlight, inflated spare tire, jack, shovel and a book to read if all else fails.

Three miles southeast of Gerlach a graded gravel road leads east. Take it 41 miles to the old railroad depot at Sulphur. From Sulphur continue south 65 miles to Lovelock, or continue east beside the railroad tracks 57 miles to Winnemucca.

Don't be in a hurry. If you are equipped with a normal degree of curiosity, a camera or simply a love of tranquility, this will take all of a long day, considerably more than the freeway time of an easy hour and a half to Lovelock or three hours to Winnemucca.

Oreana to Mill City

43 miles over the Humboldt Mountains to Union Canyon with a digression to the "ghost Vvtown" of Unionville.

At Oreana, eight miles northeast of Lovelock on I-80, turn southeast on the graded gravel road leading over the Humboldt Range and then north to the end of the paved part of Nevada 400. You'll see evidence of a century and more of mining, grazing cattle (and occasionally, sheep) and plenty of wildlife on land and in the air. Turn west into Union Canyon and drive three miles to Unionville.

Golconda to Elko

A long day's very satisfying drive through the sagebrush with stops at Midas and Tuscarora.

Two of Nevada's most interesting remote-but-accessible mining towns lie along this graded gravel road. They provide many pleasures but few

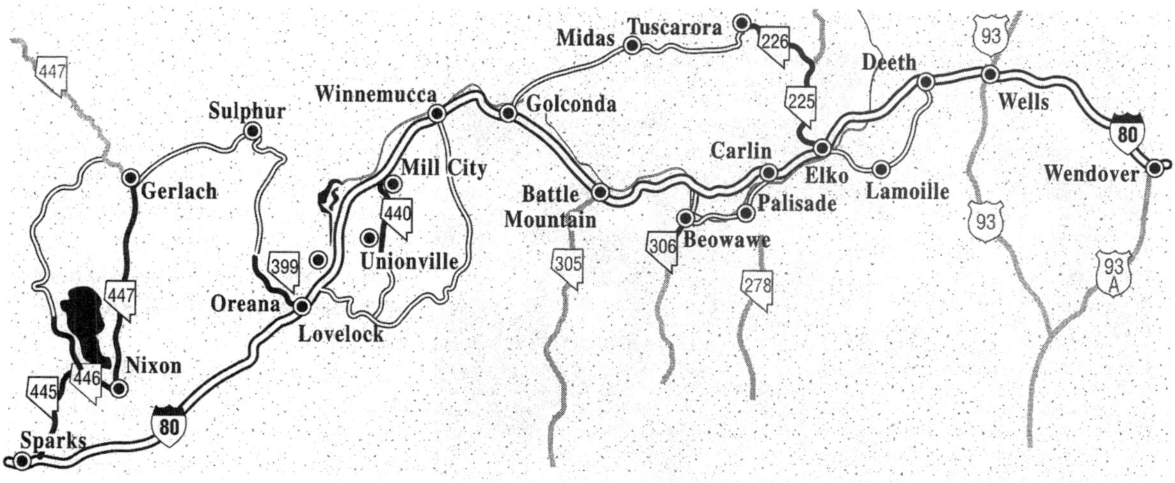

services, so provide yourself with the necessities before leaving Winnemucca or Golconda. The first leg (drive north from Water Hole #1) is paved part of the way and, when it turns to dirt (you take the middle road), leads past several of the large scale mining operations that have increased northern Nevada's gold production in recent years.

It is 45 miles from Golconda to Midas, a mining town that dates back to the first decade of the 20th Century, and 42 miles more from Midas to Tuscarora. The journey is like sailing a sagebrush sea, and carries you far, far from the freeway. My own most recent trip began toward dusk, so the last part of the drive was made in the dark. Unforgettably, I came around a corner to meet a group of enormous draft horses — Percherons or Clydesdales, some huge breed. These magnificent animals were scampering and cavorting together, enjoying one another's company in the warm summer's night, a happy family if ever there was one, and a grand sight capering around in the dark.

Tuscarora's old saloon is padlocked now, and

Out here you have the world to yourself.

MAX WINTHROP

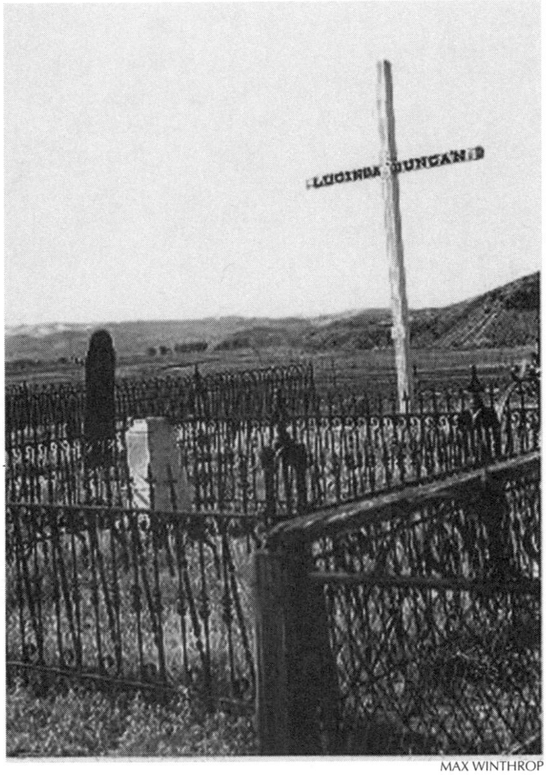

MAX WINTHROP

The Maiden's grave, near Beowawe.

its only active business is Dennis Parks' pottery gallery, so be sure to bring everything you'll need (other than pottery). The cemetery is always open, though, and as long as you carefully respect other people's property and privacy, you are welcome to stroll through town.

Beowawe to Carlin

45 miles along the Humboldt River, especially enjoyable for foamers, er, railroad enthusiasts.

This half-day trip is beautiful and exciting. The excitement comes from the fact that most of its 35 miles closely parallel the railroad tracks. As you pick your way along the gravelled road at one of the narrow places, with tracks on one side and a sheer cliff rising up on the other you'll find the sudden appearance of a hurtling freight train enormously exciting, especially if the engineer amuses himself by giving you a friendly blast with his huge horn. That's exciting! The traffic is fairly heavy, so there's never a shortage of trains — which is a part of the beauty of this side trip: seeing the trains in their natural habitat, curving along with the meandering river, powerful graceful and romantic all at once.

Begin by turning south off I-80 at Nevada 306 and drive to the far edge of Beowawe. Go across the railroad tracks and take the gravelled road east. About two miles along you'll see a large white cross on a little knoll. Railroad workers camping nearby discovered this site where a victim of the Humboldt Trail had been buried overlooking a peaceful bend in the river. A stone inscribed with the name Lucinda Duncan prompted the sentimental railroaders to christen it "the maiden's grave" and to maintain it over the years as a shrine to a departed child.

Subsequent research has determined that Lucinda Duncan was past 70 when she expired — whether that makes her fate more or less touching is for you to decide. Over the years Lucinda's grave has attracted other corpses from Beowawe and the nearby ranches, and there is now an attractive and individualistic collection of markers here beneath the great white cross.

As you continue east you'll encounter grazing cattle, and perhaps some cowboys out riding the range. You'll cross the river on a one-lane bridge, you'll find a sandy-beached swimming hole much favored by the local folks, and pass a coal mine conveniently located at trackside. Eventually you'll arrive at Palisade, an interesting settlement dating back to the 1860s. From here you'll need only a few minutes to reach Nevada 278, turn north ten miles to Carlin and return to the freeway.

Elko to Deeth

60-120 miles, depending on your route, through glorious mountains and valleys.

From Elko take Nevada 227 southeast toward Lamoille. If you are taking the long way around, turn south on Nevada 228 for 26 miles to Jiggs, where you can verify the passibility of Harrison Pass. Continue three miles more to the end of the pavement and turn left on the Harrison Pass Road 15 miles over the spine of the Rubies to the north end of Ruby Lake and the prized bass fishing of the Ruby marshes. Spend as long as you like here, and then turn north along the Ruby foothills about 26 miles to the end of the pavement on Nevada 229. Take the left fork over Secret Pass to Halleck (35 miles) or Deeth (38 miles); or take the right fork to US 93 (14 miles) and Wells.

MAX WINTHROP

The Rolling Thunder Monument to Native Americans at Imlay.

Imlay and Mill City

THE DOTS that represent these two historic communities on the map give no hint that thay have evolved into polar opposites, conflicting visions of reality along the roadside, as odd a pair of near neighbors as you'll find in the world.

IMLAY	
Reno	92
Lovelock	42
Winnemucca	72
Elko	197

Imlay was a railroad town, established in 1869 on the Central Pacific. It is now a wind-blown confusion of tattered roof shingles and swooning porches in a small cross-hatch of dirt streets. Diesel locomotives rush through, air horns blasting, to remind old Imlay of the long ago time when the railroad was king and hundreds of little settlements like Imlay were built to serve it. Now the Interstate is king, and Imlay all but invisible — except for the monument to the Native Americans on the north side of the freeway.

In 1968 a World War II vet from Oklahoma, terribly burned in a tank battle outside Leipzig, came to this out of the way place. He resumed using his

MAX WINTHROP

The incredible grunting man.

MAX WINTHROP

Rolling thunder's vision is still indelible.

Creek Indian name, Rolling Mountain Thunder, and he began building this astonishing collection of structures that catch your eye from the freeway. Built of desert flotsam and concrete, the monument is an astonishing work of art, as powerful and intriguing as the Watts Towers. During construction, a small population of kindred spirits joined in the effort, living here and there in the surrounding canyons and attempting to connect with the spirituality of the ancients. Quoting a Washoe prayerman he said: "'In order to be one with the power, you've got to get up every morning one with the power.' And this is essentially the only lesson we teach here." Variously described as a monster and a visionary, Rolling Thunder"s presence attracted a small community of spiritually directed residents all building, gardening and otherwise working to expand and maintain the shrine. "The only qualifications we've ever had is that they aspire to the pure and radiant heart."

Rolling Thunder is gone now, and his followers dispersed. The property is occupied and protected by his grown children who welcome visitors for self-guided tours. Do this. The strangeness of the place is somewhat daunting without Rolling Thunder's personal welcome, but even a brief visit is an unforgettable experience. The fantastic vision represented by the rock and concrete structures with their spidery arches, antic figures, stoic silences, buttresses, ladders, ramps, doorways, paths and the profusion of sculptures all combine to transport you…elsewhere.

On my last visit I didn't see the item that most represented Rolling Thunder's theme in my memory — a rusty pedestal (an ore car from a nearby mine? a safe? a stove?, with a heap of bleached bones and skulls piled on top and spilling off onto the ground) and the single word painted across it: Promises.

The compound has been cleaned up ("My dad spent 20 years hauling junk in there," says his son Dan, "and I've spent almost that long hauling junk out."), and the structures fenced off to prevent vandalism and injury. The paint, so vivid when it was splashed and daubed on, has faded and been worn away; the structures and figures are slowly crumbling, the television screens, railroad ties and roadside debris falling to earth, devolving back to junk again. Acknowledging the monument's artistic and historic value, the state has no intention of acquiring it. Too big a liability, costly to maintain, etc etc, all perfectly legitimate objections to spending public money. So Dan Van Zant, Frank's eldest son, is seeking a buyer or benefactor for the property.

Mill City, a hop, skip and a jump east of Imlay, was created to process the ores from nearby mines at a place with water and convenient to the railroad. It survives as a near twin to old Imlay: a frowsy exhibit of residential disrepair with a commercial center dominated by a boarded up grocery store.

Down Main Street (now renamed Frontage Road) a mile or so east, Burns Brothers Truck Stop is a bright nexus of man-made energy, drawing traffic off the freeway to rest and refuel. There is a restaurant, a motel, gas pumps, a store — a modern mini-city, all straight lines, square corners and designer color schemes — busy with the mundane tasks of the material world.

MAX WINTHROP

The entrance to the Burns Bros. travel complex at Mill City.

RICH MORENO

Winnemucca is a small city in the big country.

Winnemucca

WINNEMUCCA	
Reno	164
Elko	125
Austin	142
Denio	96

ALTHOUGH WINNEMUCCA has never laid claim to being the oldest settlement in the state, it could: its location has been more or less continuously occupied since about 1830 when beaver trappers like Peter Ogden established a camp here on what they called Mary's River. Twenty years later, when westward bound wagon trains began using the Humboldt Trail, the trading post on the southern bank of the river at Graveley Ford came to be called Frenchman's Ford and by 1863, when it was renamed for the last time, in honor of the principal Paiute chief of the region, a rough settlement had grown up along the river bank.

Twenty years later the transcontinental railroad had been built along the hillside to the south and a rival townsite was established upslope from the old village at the river's edge. For years, until they grew together around US 40, there was friction between the railroad-dominated Upper Town and Lower Town, where the farmers and ranchers carried the weight.

Despite its split personality in those early years, Winnemucca prospered as a shipping point and commercial center, and in 1872 the bustling young town had wrestled the county seat away from failing Unionville beyond the Humboldt Mountains. Brick buildings graced Winnemucca's streets in the middle 1870s as its population grew to 1,600 people. At the end of the decade, though, a historian has noted that the little city "in consequence of being situated on a line of extensive travel, where persons of all nations come in contact, has an extensive record of homicides."

The most exciting single moment in Winnemucca's mostly calm (except for the homicides) past fell just short of bloodshed, but it has been a source of controversy since the 19th day of September, 1900, when, as the story goes, Butch Cassidy and the Hole in the Wall Gang rode into town, put a knife to First National Bank president George Nixon's throat, and made him open the safe.

Butch and the boys got clean away, galloping out of town in a hail of bullets with $2,000 in gold coin. Later on, the story tells us, he added insult to injury by sending the bank a photograph of himself and the boys in fancy new suits, stiff collars and derby hats. With it was a mocking thank-you note expressing appreciation for all the Winnemucca money they were spending for their fun. It's a great story, a delicious story, and it has been told many times in many variations. In fact I have told it myself, in an earlier edition of this very book.

But perhaps it is not a true story. In fact, Butch Cassidy didn't send that famous photograph, and the evidence is not clear that he was ever in Winnemucca in his life.

The great robbery took place of course. Butch may have known about it — may even have planned it, or made arrangements for it. It is almost certain that Elzy Lay and some other of his larcenous friends in the Wild Bunch were involved — that knife to the throat was something Harvey Logan (Kid Curry) would do. But it's not clear that Butch himself was there that thrilling day.

The photograph was actually found by an alert detective in a photographer's display window at Fort Worth, Texas. The Pinkerton Detective Agency sent it to Winnemucca for banker George Nixon to identify. After studying the photo of the six dapper dudes in new suits and neckties, he wrote back: "While I am satisfied that Cassidy was interested in the robbery, he was not one of the men who entered the bank."

So, if he didn't enter the bank, according to an eye-witness with a vital reason to notice . . . was he there at all?

Plenty of people say he was, including Charles Kelly, author of a definitive history of Cassidy's career, and that's good enough for Winnemucca. Butch Cassidy has been absorbed into municipal history, and Butch Cassidy Days is a big celebration in the Winnemucca calendar, attended by thousands and enjoyed by all.

Winnemucca is placid, green, open and friendly. Its quiet neighborhoods are slowly spreading away from the railroad tracks, and the main street, Winnemucca Boulevard — once upon a time it was U.S. 40 — has become a bright strip of businesses catering to travelers, with new street lights extending from the cemetery at the west end of town. Motels, restaurants and auto services are available in abundance. The Griddle is a favorite breakfast stop, open at 6 am and crowded by 6:15. Modern casinos provide the familiar 24-hour casino ambience — games, food, drink and overnight lodging). The Chamber of Commerce information desk is in the East Hall of the convention center at the corner of Bridge street, which also contains The Buckaroo Hall of Fame and the Western Heritage Museum.

North across the river by Pioneer Park the Historical Society Museum occupies a former Episcopal Church and a new brick building constructed

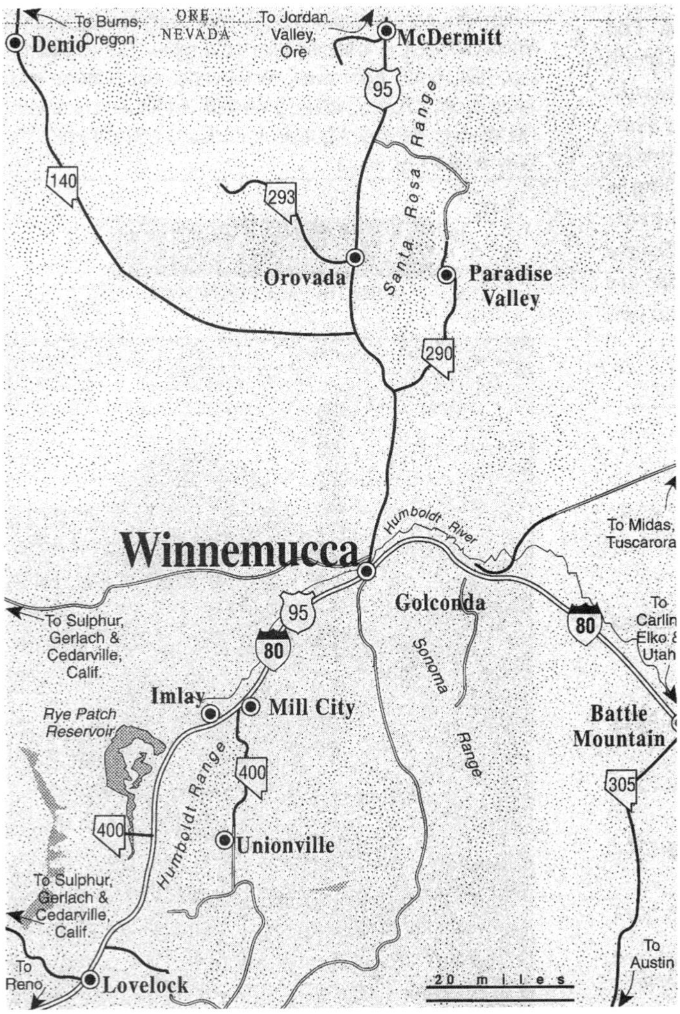

MAX WINTHROP

Winnemucca's most peaceful neighborhood.

to house and to exhibit the collection of the North Central Nevada Historical Society. This includes the Clarence Stoker Automobile Collection and antiquities collected from the Lovelock Caves, as well as mining and ranching memorabilia. The prize exhibit is on the second floor, the recreated skeleton — cast from the original — of a mammoth with great curving tusks.

Outdoors, you can enjoy Pioneer Park, overlooking the cemetery where many early settlers (presumably including the homicide victims) were planted. The view of the Humboldt gives an opportunity to consider the pioneer experience: they crossed the river with their wagons here.

Look back across the river to the south and you'll see the Winnemucca Hotel, built in 1863 in the original riverbank settlement. Basque meals are served here family style, and the back-bar is a fine example of the genre. Winnemucca's other Basque restaurant is in the Martin Hotel up on Railroad Street at Melarkey. This was Upper Town, and the center of commercial activity from 1869; across the street is what was the C.P. Hoskins flour and grain warehouse. The Martin is noteworthy not only for its wonderful family-style dinners and interiors covered with an amazing variety of pressed tin walls and ceilings, but for the superlative performances by nationally-known musicians staged here by Great Basin Arts & Entertainment.

Bridge Street offers the "Mile of Monuments" walking tour, a history of Winnemucca in bronze tablets placed in such locations as the Sweet Sixteen School, the Frenchman's Canal, the Chinese Joss House and the bank building at the corner of Fourth Street where the celebrated stick-up took place. The Golf Course is uphill from the railroad tracks, and there are lighted tennis courts, two swimming pools, and two parks and picnic facilities in town.

The big attraction, though, is still under construction as this book goes to press: America's Car Collection, a museum exhibiting about 75 famous movie, muscle and race cars, most of them from the '50s, '60s and '70s.

In the early and middle 1970s a high school kid named Ralph Whitworth built up a '65 GTO from parts he got from wrecking yards. When Ralph graduated in '73 he went to work at the golf course, and when the Parks & Rec Director's job came open, Ralph applied and was hired. He was 19. He wrote the grant for the new swimming pool while he was there, but after a couple of years a local dentist helped Ralph attend UNR, then on to law school at Georgetown. While in Washington he worked on the U.S. Senate Judiciary Committee staff of Senator Paul Laxalt and on the 1984 Reagan election campaign.

MAX WINTHROP

St. Paul's Catholic church is on the historic walking tour.

MAX WINTHROP

On of the many hot cars awaiting display at America's Car Collection.

When he left Washington he went to work for T. Boone Pickens and learned from the master about finance and managing investments. In the years since leaving Pickens Ralph's business enterprises have flourished. He is a partner in Relational Investors, a $3 billion investment fund with large holdings in major corporations and he is a director of some of America's largest corporations.

When Ralph came back to visit his home town after 15 years away, he donated $1 million to the Humboldt County school system because he attributes his success in large part to growing up in Winnemucca, and to the values he learned here. He also went to a car show with one of his old buddies, and saw a great car in sad condition — a '36 Ford roadster convertible — what a great project!

Ralph bought it. They went to an auction and Ralph bought another one. And almost before they knew it, he'd bought 190 cars. Movie cars, muscle cars, street rods, kustom kars, dragsters — almost all of them American cars of the '50s, '60s and '70s. Some of these cars are on loan to automobile museums elsewhere, but most of them are destined for display in Winnemucca where construction is underway for America's Car Collection on the site of the old Bulls' Head Motel at the east end of town. The Flying A Garage, where the collection's cars will be carefully restored and maintained, is already in place as architects make the final changes in the exhibit hall plans.

While construction proceeds toward a 2009 opening, the collection is being culled to fewer than 150 cars, with about half of them on exhibit on any given day. The Little Red Wagon is there, several Ed Roth cars, one of Elvis' limos and the Dodge Charger Daytona that Buddy Baker drove faster than 200 mph at Talladega, the first car ever to make that speed on a closed track. They'll be displayed in the new building, drawing visitors from all over the world — a goose that will lay golden eggs in Winnemucca as long as men love cars.

Welcome to Winnemucca

Area Information

WINNEMUCCA CONVENTION & VISITORS AUTHORITY
50 W. Winnemucca Blvd. 775-623-5071
WINNEMUCCA offers overnight accommodations and 24-hour casino action. It is a recreational paradise! Hunting, fishing, hiking, photography, biking, ATVing, just to name a few. WINNEMUCCA has a full calendar of events from rodeos, classic cars, motorcycles and mules. There is something here for everyone! We invite you to WINNEMUCCA for hospitality and fun! 800-962-2638

HUMBOLDT COUNTY CHAMBER OF COMMERCE
30 Winnemucca Blvd. 775-623-2225
Winnemucca is a great jumping-off point for outdoor recreation. Nearby are fabulous hiking, hunting and biking trails, as well as miles of ATV and off-road adventure trails. More than 1,000 hotel rooms, diverse restaurants, casino gaming, and plenty of other opportunities for fun. Visit us for all area information.

Lodgings

RED LION INN & CASINO
741 W. Winnemucca Boulevard 775-623-2565
We offer restful accommodations, luxury guest rooms, friendly staff, business center, fitness room, children,s arcade and a swimming pool. Enjoy exciting gaming Slots, Blackjack and our Sports Lounge. Offering family style dining from ham and eggs to steak and lobster in our Coffee Restaurant.

SCOTT SHADY COURT MOTEL
400 First Street at Pavilion, 775-623-3646
Located 4 quiet blocks from the downtown area. All rooms have cable television and telephones. Free local calls, free WiFi. Year 'round swimming pool and sauna, separate sundeck and patio and a children's playground. Large vehicle parking. Major credit cards. "Your Home Away From Home."

McDermitt

LT. COL. CHARLES MCDERMIT, 2nd Cavalry, California Volunteers, was in command of the Military District of Nevada at Fort Churchill on the Carson River in 1865. He sent soldiers to establish a military presence on the road to Boise City, nearly closed by Indian resistance. In August of that year Colonel McDermit himself was killed from ambush and the outpost was christened Camp McDermit a week later.

McDERMITT	
Winnemucca	71
Battle Mtn.	126
Oregon	1

McDermitt acquired an extra 't' somewhere over the years, and today is a modest little settlement straddling the Oregon line at the north end of the Quinn River Valley. Its people provide all basic needs for the traveler, including a friendly welcome.

Owyhee

HEADQUARTERS TOWN FOR THE DUCK Valley Indian Reservation. The trading post on the reservation carries a stock of Indian beadwork, but the main attraction for travelers at Owyhee is the four-day Rodeo and Pow Wow held on or about the Fourth of July, highlighted by competitive dancing, round dancing, hand games, junior and adult rodeos and an enormous free barbecue. A second Pow Wow in September is highlighted by the crowning of the new Shoshone Paiute Queen, with special singing and dancing performances, games and contests and another great barbecue.

OWYHEE	
Winnemucca	164
Battle Mtn.	125
Austin	142

Paradise Valley

40 MILES NORTH of Winnemucca via US 95 and Nevada 290, this enchanting community was established in 1864 by W.M. Gregg who had entered the valley to prospect the surrounding mountains. When he saw the rich soil of the valley floor, he traded in his miner's pick and shovel for a plow.

Paradise City, as it was known then, grew up in the 1860s as a hybrid town. Its immediate surroundings were crop and grazing lands, but in the early 1870s a number of mining strikes were made in the hills that Gregg had turned his back on, and Paradise prospered considerably from the mining operations.

The eventual failure of the mines reduced the town's population again, and it snoozed quietly for decades. By the 1960s it seemed nearly a ghost. Recently, though, life began to return to its tree-shaded streets, and now kids ride their bikes shouting through puddles again, and many of the old residences show recent repair and renovation. The Paradise Valley Saloon is welcoming customers as it has done for generations, but the small grocery down the block, which once provided staples like bread, beer and videos, is closed.

Adding to the attraction of this pleasant excursion from Winnemucca is the Stonehouse Country Inn just south of town, a fabulous three-story ranch house surrounded by a lush lawn and shaded by cottonwoods. It is now a bed-and-breakfast of considerable appeal.

The Paradise Valley Fathers Day Barbecue is famous in five counties and three states.

ROBIN COBBEY

Paradise Valley street scene.

MAX WINTHROP

Palace Saloon, Golconda.

Golconda

THE HOT springs at Golconda were well-known to western travelers, and Golconda was modestly famous as a spa even before the railroad built a small station here in 1868. Not until 1897 was a townsite actually platted, however, in conjunction with development of the copper mines at Adelaide and construction of the short line Golconda & Adelaide Railroad. The mines were only moderately profitable, and Golconda never grew much larger than 500 persons. The hot springs, though, inspired the construction of a half dozen hotels, including the Hot Springs Hotel, the Banquet, the Exchange and the Morning Star. After the turn of the century the hot springs provided the main economic resource to the village. In the '20s and '30s it was fashionable in sophisticated Reno circles to get aboard the Reno rattler on Friday afternoon for a weekend tryst at Golconda.

GOLDCONDA	
Winnemucca	16
Battle Mtn.	37
Midas	44

The Hot Springs Hotel burned years ago, and the hot water bathing pools have been filled in. Most of Golconda's elegance is long gone.

The town still has a sense of humor, though, as Mark Crowley demonstrated a few years back, when he was proprietor of Waterhole #1, one of modern Golconda's drinking establishments. Crowley had a pet pig named Waterhole Ike. When he heard that the champion racehorse Secretariat had been sold to a syndicate to be put out to stud, he decided to do the same with Ike .

He began selling shares in Ike's future revenues, and when the cigar box he put the money in began overflowing, he went to the bank to open an account. But the bankers told Crowley that he couldn't open an account in Ike's name without a social security number.

Crowley dutifully obtained an application for Ike's social security card and filled it out carefully. Mother's Maiden Name: Go-Pig-Go. Father's Name: Three Star. Date of Birth: May 1, 1974. He signed the application, "Waterhole Ike, by Mark Crowley" and in due course the federal machinery delivered Ike's registration card. His $25 stud fees began applying toward his retirement benefits as his savings account grew. The press learned about Ike's busy career and stories about Golconda's enterprising porker appeared in the national press. But success didn't spoil Ike. He still stopped by the bar every morning about 10:30 for a bucket of beer with his old friends from before he became rich and famous. All good things must come to an end, however, and Mark Crowley and Ike have departed from Golconda; Mark for new opportunities elsewhere and Ike, alas, for Hog Heaven.

The Golconda Strip now boasts two saloons, a store and post office, and an automotive repair garage. The old center of town, though, lies somewhat to the north. There, the Golconda Mercantile has long since sold its last mousetrap, and the old post office and the Palace Saloon buildings hark back many years to more prosperous times. In the low light of late afternoon, you can just see the faint letters that materialize on the old post office wall: MUG Root Beer 5¢.

The cemetery is a sandy patch of ground decorated with grave markers of wood and stone and dilapidated enclosures. Most of them are simple, but there are some more elaborate ones, including a monument to the memory of Gabrielle Silve, nee Michel, born April 11, 1872 in France, and died June 5, 1898, so far from home.

The most recent grave is that of Hughie Bain, who died in 1986 on the floor of Waterhole No. 1. As he felt himself slipping away, Hughie begged the proprietor to bury him in Golconda. "He truly didn't want to be caught dead in Winnemucca," he remembers. Hughie's dying wish went against the grain of the county bureaucracy, though, and the permit process extended into endless delay (burials had been suspended for years) so Hughie's friends simply borrowed a backhoe, found a likely spot, dug him a grave and fitted him into it to redeem the final promise, all without benefit of red tape.

Only the Volunteer Fire Department remains at what was once the thriving heart of a lively town, but it is the richest Volunteer Department in Nevada. It serves Gold Run Township, site of the Valmy power generation plant and half a dozen large mines in the mountains to the east of town. The facilities and resources to knock down fires in these industrial locales would make a small city proud.

Golconda is locally famous as the gateway to Midas, a former gold mining town 44 miles northeast via graded gravel road. From there you can continue along another 42 miles to Tuscarora, connecting there with Nevada 226 for an easy return to I-80 at Elko.

MAX WINTHROP

Downtown Midas.

Midas

45 MILES EAST of Golconda, 42 miles west of Tuscarora. The original discoverers wanted to call their town Gold Circle in the summer of 1907, but post office officials refused to allow another Nevada postmark with 'Gold' in it, so they settled for Midas. Two thousand people crowded into the camp the following year, which turned out to be about 1,750 more than the mines could support; they were gone when the snows fell. Production was small until 1915, when a cyanide mill was built and Midas prospered in a small way. Production ended suddenly when the mill burned in 1922, resuming spasmodically until 1942, when it ended for good.

After its few years of rich ore, barely surviving became Midas' specialty, and while other, gaudier camps have died, been abandoned and utterly obliterated, Midas today still barely survives. There is no active mining, and the population was recently dwindling down dangerously low, until a recent influx of retirees has brought it safely back up to a dozen again. Edith's Gold Circle Saloon is Midas' only business and civic center, complete with parking meter.

Early photographs of the crude camp show a ragged line of tents across a naked slope, but the camp's elderly remains are pleasantly shaded by mature cottonwoods. Electricity was extended to Midas in 1989, and there are threats to bring the telephone too. Except in hunting season, which is a big item on the Midas calendar, there's not much to do but day-dream: a lollygagger's paradise.

Commercial Row, after a century, still the center of activity in Battle Mountain.

Battle Mountain

THE ORIGIN OF ITS colorful name is uncertain, as it is situated on the valley floor and no battle is known to have occurred nearby. Livestock and agriculture have long been the basis for Battle Mountain's economy, and Battle Mountain has managed a rather staid existence since 1870 when the population of Argenta deserted their little mining settlement and re-established themselves at Battle Mountain Station on the Central Pacific Railroad. On the 4th of July, 1870, just months after its founding, Nevada's first Womens' Sufferage Convention was held here.

BATTLE MOUNTAIN	
Reno	217
Austin	89
Elko	72

The settlement depended for its prosperity on the railroad, and on the mines that blossomed and wilted along the slopes and side canyons of the Reese River Valley all the way to Austin, 90 miles to the south. Galena, Jersey City and Lewis were three of Nevada's most prominent mining camps in the 1870s, all of them served by the railroad at Battle Mountain, as was Pittsburgh in the 1880s and Dean in the 1890s. After the turn of the century the mines at Hilltop, Bannock, McCoy and Betty O'Neal all shipped by way of Battle Mountain.

Battle Mountain was the last stop for W.J. Forbes, a famous Nevada newspaperman of the l9th century. He was remembered by Carson City journalist Sam Davis: "Pioneers still laugh about his quips and fancies. Writing under his pen-name Semblins he discoursed on every subject known to man, and his shafts so often hit the mark that he became popular with all classes of readers." Forbes edited and published a dozen newspapers in California and Nevada, and in 1873 started the short-lived The New Endowment in Salt Lake City. "Returning to Nevada," Davis wrote, "he started Measure for Measure at Battle Mountain. It was a wonderful paper, but it did not pay, and a friend found him on the morning of October 30, 1875, lying stiff and cold across his shabby bed. He had fought a fight against all odds all his life, was one of the brightest geniuses the coast had ever seen, but he lacked the faculty of making and saving money and lived in communities where his mental brightness was more envied than appreciated."

In 1880 the Nevada Central Railroad was completed through the length of the Reese River Valley to the south, connecting Austin with the transcontinental line, and in the following year a short line was built to the mines at Lewis. One of the Nevada Central's officials was James H. Ledlie, a former Union officer in the Civil War whom Ulysses S. Grant called, "the greatest coward of the war." A siding near the southern end of the route through Reese River Valley was named in his honor, and Ledlie was a familiar visitor to the railroad.

Grant's scorn dated from the ghastly Battle of the Crater, a slaughter that ensued when a troop of Pennsylvania coal miners dug a tunnel beneath the Confederate lines protecting Fredericksburg, packed it with explosives, and blew it up. Ledlie was to have led his soldiers in the charge through the resulting crater, but instead got drunk in his dugout and refused to come out. The troops attacked without him and were shot down like deer as they struggled across the great hole. Interestingly, Ledlie was in Battle Mountain the day in 1879 that Grant came to town on his triumphal western speaking tour. No doubt he made sure to stay out of sight.

But the BM&L lasted less than a year, and the Nevada Central was only profitable as long as the mines at Austin were operating at full capacity. By the middle 1930s most of the mines that generated traffic at Battle Mountain had shut down and boarded up, and the NCRR had passed into receivership for the last time.

Battle Mountain's 30 year snooze by the side of US 40 ended abruptly in 1967 when the Duval Company invested more than $20 million in the development of large copper ore bodies in the mountains to the south. All at once Battle Mountain became a boomtown in its own right: the schools overflowed, the sewer system burst its seams, the municipal wells began pumping sand and the cost of policing the town doubled.

Things have quieted down in the years since. Duval gave up on copper and sold the mine, which then produced gold and has since closed down altogether, leaving Battle Mountain in slow times again. Which is how things stood when an article appeared in the Washington Post Magazine in the autumn of 2001, naming Battle Mountain the Armpit of America. The homely little burg had been minding its own business, and out of nowhere it had been blindsided, mugged in the national press as the nation's least attractive community.

Once the shock has passed, Battle Mountaineers began to recognize they'd been floored by the unfamiliar knock of opportunity. Within two weeks, Armpit t-shirts were available at the drug store, and, despite some mixed feelings, a "Festival in the Pit" was held in June. The Chamber of Commerce sent a blanket invitation to any community that has been considered an armpit: free booths at the festival if they'll just show up and man them. The Bakersfield Chamber of Commerce chartered a bus to bring members to Battle Mountain to see what they've got that Bakersfield doesn't.

Some other small Nevada communities which breathed huge sighs of relief when Battle Mountain was named the national armpit were soon envious of the attention the town received. Battle Mountain has been featured on CNN, "Good Morning America" and the BBC, and the phone in the Chamber of Commerce office never stopped ringing. More recently though, the local folks have tired of making light of the armpit designation and have taken down the billboards on I-80 urging travelers to make a "pit stop" in Battle Mountain, instead promoting the easy access to Nevada's back country.

Battle Mountain may be a pain in the eye, but if you like the friendly small town life this could be the armpit for you. A recent flurry of real estate sales on Commercial Row suggests a modest rennaissance is under way. For the traveler there are motels, restaurants, even shopping.

And, surprisingly in this slow-paced community, there is speed. In August the Pony Express 130, the longest Open Road Race in the USA, starts here. Cars ranging from 60's era muscle cars to European sports cars race against the clock south to Austin. After refreshments and a turnaround at the Austin High School, the cars re-grid and run 47 miles back toward Battle Mountain to the finish line, a total of 131.5 miles. There's a Saturday car show too.

In September Battle Mountain hosts bike races on the same straight, flat stretch of highway south of town. Not the bike you rode as a kid, though. These are streamlined kevlar pods designed purely for speed, and the event is known as the 'World Human Powered Speed Challenge'. In 2002 Sam Whittingham pedaled his two-wheeler at 81 mph over a 200 meter distance to establish himself as "the fastest man alive".

There is an Olympic sized swimming pool next to the Elquist Memorial Park on Nevada Route 305, which continues south to Austin. And, there is a lovely scenic view at the dump about three miles toward Austin. Come at sunup or sundown and park with your back to town. In the winter you're likely to see Bald Eagles, Golden Eagles and several species of hawks.

Welcome to Battle Mountain

Casinos

OWL CLUB CASINO

72 E. Front Street. 775-635-2444

The Owl Club has been Battle Mountain's favorite casino for three generations, with lots of the latest and greatest slots and video games, full bar and family-style restaurant serving a varied menu 24 hours a day. Our attentive staff will make your visit friendly and fun. Come visit us.

MAX WINTHROP

The railroad rolls along the Humboldt River outside Carlin.

Carlin

FOUNDED LATE in 1868 at the eastern terminus of the Central Pacific Railroad's Humboldt Division, Carlin grew quickly to accommodate the railroaders employed at the roundhouse and machine shops, and the crews manning the trains that rattled through in both directions. The business street at the south side of the tracks lengthened to include a hotel, a telegraph office and an express office along with two cafes, four stores and an indeterminate number of saloons. The railroad built a library and filled it with 1100 books, and the county built a jail. By the turn of the 20th century Carlin was a noisy, dirty little goiter of prosperity clinging to the iron rails, wholly the railroad's child.

CARLIN	
Eureka	90
Elko	23
Beowawe	33
Battle Mtn.	57

During five succeeding decades Carlin was subject to gentle, slow alternations of rise and decline in its municipal fortunes. In the early 1950s, however, those fortunes were cast violently down. Steam engines were replaced by diesel power, and Carlin's maintenance shops were closed. Refrigerated cars meant the end of Carlin's icing station. Families moved away. Carlin's business district began creeping away from the railroad tracks and toward U.S. 40. Even the opening of the enormous Carlin Gold Mine by the Newmont Mining Company in 1965 did relatively little to restore Carlin's old vitality, since so many of the workers employed at the mine and mill lived in Elko.

A few of the old facades attempt a spurious youthfulness, about as persuasive as grandma's rouged cheeks. The Overland, the State, the Humboldt Club, and other places with no names at all, as if the paint had faded away and never been missed -- the dim and homely buildings lean glumly against one another in a single row. It is an unromantic monument to all the railroad towns that fronted the Central Pacific across a thousand miles of western landscape, and even a brief pause here makes a fascinating detour from the freeway, although there are gaps now appearing in the line of structures.

To get across the tracks, drive south on Fourth Street. Once across all the tracks, turn left. A pedestrian walkway crosses above the switching yard, and provides an excellent view of the railroad activities that still account for most activity here.

It is an odd little town, lacking in any hint of the fantastic. Yet in January, 1889, the Carlin correspondent to the Elko Free Press wrote cheerfully about the ghost that shared the Carlin house into which she and her husband had just moved. "Sometimes he taps on the headboard of the bed. Other times he stalks across the kitchen floor, and he hammers away at the door but nobody is there.

But the gayest capers of all are cut up in the cellar. There he holds high revels, and upsets the pickles and carries on generally."

When the ghost persisted, the lady's husband went into the cellar and probed the earthen floor and walls. Behind the pickle shelves he found a partially burned and dismembered corpse. The husband and wife who formerly occupied the house were eventually tried and convicted of murder. Their hanging, a gruesome affair in the back yard of the Elko County Court House, was the first legal execution of a woman in the Pacific region, and the only one so far in Nevada history.

Carlin also provides convenient access to Palisade, once the connecting point with the Eureka and Palisade Railroad and now an inhabited "ghost town" with some interesting ruins. Take Nevada 278 south out of town; you'll see the Palisade turnoff about ten miles along.

A new casino and hotel occupy the site of the old Gearjammer's Cafe near the freeway offramp, and Chin's Chinese Restaurant is famous for miles around.

N.E. NEVADA MUSEUM

The Central Pacific in the Palisades, 1868.

Palisade

ESTABLISHED IN 1868 as a station on the Central Pacific Railroad, and named for the distinctive red-black rock formations enclosing the river to the east, palisade thrived as the shipping points for mining districts centered at Mineral Hill, Hamilton and Eureka. In 1874 it became the northern terminal of the Eureka & Palisade Railroad. At its peak, Palisade had a population of about 600, mostly employed by the railroads. Decline began as the output of the Eureka mines began to diminish, slowing activity on the E&P RR during the middle 1880s.

Local comedians sometimes entertained themselves by staging enormous gunfights on the station platform as the San Francisco-bound passenger trains pulled into the station from the east. The passengers crouched under their seats out of harm's way, and gave up their waiting suppers in the depot restaurant rather than risk the dangers of the wild west.

In 1908 the Western Pacific also laid tracks through the narrow canyon, and Palisade's prospects improved, but in 1910 heavy flooding swept much of the town downriver. The final collapse of the E&P in 1938 doomed Palisade and gradually the population moved away. The cemetery on the hill above, the dugout warehouses behind the foundations of the old business street and a few structural ruins give a sense of the old place.

For decades there were no residents at Palisade, but it was sold at auction a few years ago and is now inhabited again. Trains still burst around the bend in the river, thunder through the narrow canyon past the old ghost, and hurtle out of sight without stopping.

MAX WINTHRIOP

The remnants of Palisade invite exploration.

Nevada's Basques

HIGH-SPIRITED BASQUES from all over America converge on Elko, Ely and Winnemucca each year for uproarious, come-one, come-all celebrations that assure pleasure for spectators and participants alike.

These annual get-togethers help preserve the ancient traditions of the Pyrenees Mountain villagers who migrated to the American West after the turn of the century to become sheepherders and stockmen. Descendants have spread out into other areas and occupations, but they remember their homeland through these festivals.

The keen-featured, smiling men and women who throng to these celebrations seem anything but enigmatic, yet the Basques have always been a mysterious people. No link has been found to connect their complex language with any other European tongue, and the Basques themselves seem unrelated to any other European people with the possible exception of the prehistoric Celts.

Whoever they are, the Basques have long maintained a legendary taste for adventure and independence. They have managed to preserve their ancient language and customs despite unwilling absorption into the French and Spanish nations, and to establish themselves all over the world.

Columbus' navigator was a Basque, and so was Magellan's. St. Francis Xavier and St. Ignatius Loyola were Basques.

So was Pedro Altube, an unsuccessful California gold rusher who turned to cattle ranching in the wilds of central Nevada. As his ranch prospered, Altube, needing more hardworking wranglers, sent to his native village for friends and relatives. Many of these men took part of their pay in stock, branched out on their own, and in turn sent for more of their countrymen.

Eventually, non-Basque stockmen adopted the practice of hiring the tireless, dependable Basques as sheepherders, speaking only a few words of English, to follow the flocks on three-year contracts.

It is this heritage that they honor in their exuberant celebrations. In some of the communities the festivals are small, local affairs for Basques only.

N.E. NEVADA MUSEUM

Dutch oven bread experts.

But in Elko, Ely and Winnemucca each summer everyone is invited.

After a parade of costumed Basques through the center of town come the contests and competitions that have been standard fare at village fairs in the Pyrenees for a thousand years. Weight carrying, weight lifting and sheephooking (a reflection of the Basques' American experience) are open to all comers. If you were lucky enough to see Benito Goitandia lift the stone, you can tell your grandchildren you saw the master.

The biggest event is always the woodchopping. Contestants are provided with sections of fresh-cut Aspen logs and a supply of razor sharp short handled axes. They stand atop the logs and chop between their bare feet. The chips leap away like startled rabbits, to glisten on the ground. The crowded grandstand is a hurricane of cheering, and as the last log is parted, the winning woodchopper is lifted up on his helpers' shoulders like a heavyweight champion while around him thousands of dollars change hands among the bettors.

After the competitions, the streets fill with cheerful crowds. In the evening, a small Basque band bursts into a rollicking jota at the Armory and 80 youngsters in colorful costumes dance and sing melodies whose origins had been lost when Hannibal battled his way across their ancestral mountains on his way to Rome. After their performance, everybody dances. Ipa!

Sunday, a solemn Mass is followed by a mammoth family picnic. Goatskin bota bags are squeezed into open mouths, the band plays and refreshment stands serve up chilled soda pop and spicy chorizos — sizzling sausages made to exacting Basque recipes. And everyone dances.

After lunch, while the grown-ups snooze under the nodding trees, children compete in games and dances.

These warm-hearted, joyful celebrations by America's Basques are unmatched for sheer exuberance and high spirits. "Well," as one grinning man said hefting his bulging bota bag, "you can't dance on skimmed milk."

NEVADA COMMISSION ON TOURISM

Traditional Basque dancer.

The days of the great sheep outfits have faded and South American herders, many from Peru, have taken the places of the Basque herders from the Pyrenees.

MAX WINTHROP

Elko hosts the National Basque Festival.

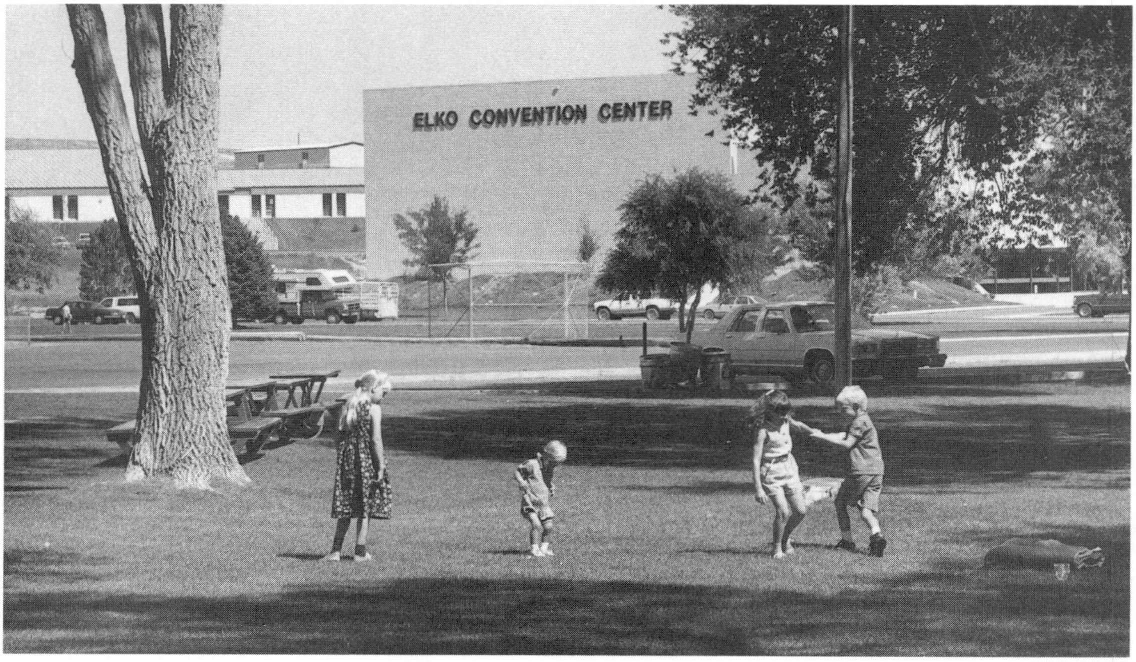

RICH MORENO

Elko's large city park is a traveling parent's dream come true. Picnickers welcome.

Elko

Founded as a railroad-promoted townsite and railhead for the White Pine mines in 1869, Elko has served for generations now as the provincial capital of an enormous cattle ranching empire embracing parts of four states.

ELKO	
Wells	150
Ely	115
Reno	289
Las Vegas	469

Sixty years ago Lowell Thomas called Elko "the last real cowtown in the American West," and until fairly recently that was still a good thumbnail description. But half a dozen large mining operations in the region now produce millions of ounces of gold a year, and they, along with the general westward migration, have helped transform the dusty old cowtown into a prosperous young city.

In the decade from 1980, when population stood at about 10,000 people (city size by Nevada standards) to 1990, the population nearly doubled, and in one hectic 12-month period beginning in July, 1986, Elko's population increased by 21 percent. Population within the city limits was 17,000 in 2000, and is about twice that in the township as a whole today. This growth is evident over many square miles of countryside to the south where Spring Creek was developed in the 1970s, but it is most visible on the east and west ends of the city. On the east a bright new business district is anchored by shopping centers and the Red Lion Casino. On the west another commercial nexus has materialized at the western freeway offramp, with supermarlets and bigbox chain stores predominating, and an actual Starbuck's. And the city center, built around the railroad switching yard nearly a century and a half ago, has undergone a renaissance.

You can experience this for yourself with a visit to the Duncan Littlecreek Wine Bar, next door to Capriola's on Commercial Street. Up until a few years ago this place was called Jack's Bar, and sported a buzzing neon sign, a cloud of cigaret smoke, and an elderly clientele sipping Budweisers. Now it's a combination art gallery and wine bar, offering a rich selection of tasty varietals and a vivaceous display of art, most of it from local and nearby artists. There's a Poetry Night once a month and what the customers are sipping comes from the Napa Valley or from France.

Walk across what was once the railroad switching yard (and is now a parking lot the size of Nye County), to the Western Folklife Center. It occupies the old Pioneer Hotel building which closed upon the passing of the Age of Cattle. The Center originated the Cowboy Poetry Gathering and other projects aimed at preserving and celebrating Western American traditions. An exhibit gallery displays ranch-made items, from leather chaps to meticulously braided horsehair ropes, all so finely made they might be sculptures or jewelry. A gift shop offers a wide selection of goods for sale, hand-made and otherwise. It's a living homage and memorial to the Elko that was, and which is lowly fading away.

Keep going north on 5th Street, to the Stray Dog for a micro-brew, to Cowboy Joe's for a latte, or to the Flying Fish, for . . . sushi! Yes, sushi in Elko. Lowell Thomas would be baffled. You don't get sushi in cow towns, Elko is a city now.

Elko — conflicting (and slightly absurd) stories are offered to explain the name — prospered rapidly after its founding as a station on the transcontinental railroad in 1868. By 1870 townsite lot prices had multiplied three and four times, the population had risen to 2,000 or more, and the place had begun to assume its character as the leading settlement of Nevada's great northeastern cattle country. By 1873 the mood in Elko was so soaring and optimistic, largely on account of new mining discoveries in the districts to the north and south, that it had bid for and won the State University. The university opened with seven students in 1874, and closed ten years later with 15, to be moved unceremoniously to Reno. As a freighting center, Elko was following the mining towns it served as into decline, and in the 1880s the population fell to less than 1,000.

In retrospect, one bright note appears in the history of Elko in the otherwise stagnant final years of the nineteenth century. In 1896 G.S. Garcia arrived in Elko to establish his celebrated saddle shop on Railroad Street. Garcia became one of the foremost western saddle makers of his time, and his famous American Eagle saddle, elaborately carved and decorated with patriotic motifs, worked in silver and gold, won gold medals at both the 1904 St. Louis World's Fair and the 1905 Lewis & Clark Exposition at Portland, Oregon. Will Rogers and Teddy Roosevelt rode on Garcia saddles, as did dozens of other western celebrities of the first three decades of the century, hundreds of international customers from Argentina, Australia, Mexico and France, and thousands of stockmen and buckaroos from around the west.

Despite the steady growth in size and importance of the livestock business in the valleys around Elko, the town's affairs did not brighten much until 1907. In that year the Western Pacific Railroad extend its rails to Elko, and mining activity revived in half a dozen camps that relied on Elko for freight and services. The price of beef went from three-and-a-half to eight cents a pound, and wool from four to 60 cents a pound. In ten years Elko's population had nudged up toward 3,000.

Prosperity continued until the devastating one-two of the failure of the Wingfield banking chain and the national Depression which followed immediately after. Caught in the machinery activated to sort out the bank failure and bled by the decline in livestock prices, many of the ranches around Elko were foreclosed. In 1931, the beef and wool economies in chaos, gambling was made legal by the state legislature. Elko, like towns everywhere in Nevada, had a new industry, and un-

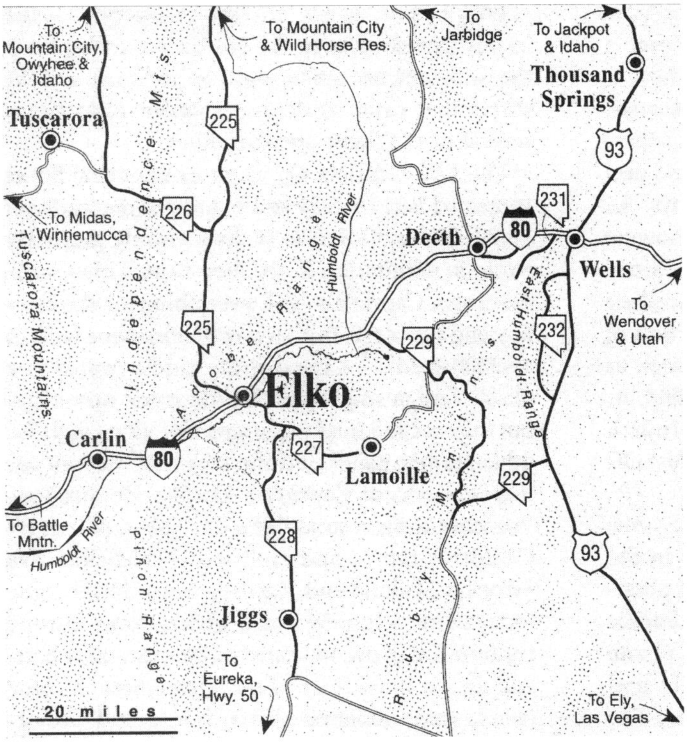

MAX WINTHROP

This gigantic polar bear has welcomed thousands of visitors to the Commercial—the original is inside.

like most, it had an entrepreneur to make the most of it. Newton Crumley had operated saloons and hotels in Tonopah, Goldfield, and Jarbidge before he settled in Elko in 1925 and bought the Commercial Hotel. He and his son, Newton Jr., operated the hotel with an eye toward the future.

By 1937 they had added a two-hundred-seat cocktail lounge to the Commercial, and in 1941 they hired Ted Lewis, the "High-Hatted Tragedian of Jazz", his orchestra, and his 21-person Rhythm Rhapsody Review for an eight-day engagement. After Lewis came Sophie Tucker, then Skinnay Ennis and his band. For drowsy little Elko, more than 250 miles from the nearest radio station, the situation was stunning. Even more impressive was the effect on automobile traffic along U.S. 40: few travelers passed through Elko without a detour into the Commercial.

In 1946 the Crumleys began "remodeling" a ten-foot wide root beer stand into the sixty-eight room Ranch Inn Motel-Casino (at that materials-short time after WWII, new construction was prohibited but remodeling was permitted). The Crumleys had the largest non-ranching payroll in Elko County after the railroads.

With ranching restored to prosperity, with gambling and big-name entertainment adding a cosmopolitan flavor, and with newcoming ranchers like Crosby, Joel McRae, and Jimmy Stewart providing glamor and sophistication, Elko entered a golden age at the end of the 1940s.

The Hollywood rancheros have died or sold their Elko spreads now, and the Crumleys are long gone from the scene. There is entertainment at the Commercial (no longer a hotel), and at the Stockmen's, but nothing as ambitious as in Newt Crumley's time.

You still see lots of broadbrimmed hats here. Elko is unmistakeably western, and it still wears its history out in plain sight; Capriola's Saddle Shop, Anacabe's Elko General Merchandise, and the Star Hotel are still going strong, but it's unmistakeably modern too, with Cucina Fresca around the corner on Idaho, and lattes everywhere. And the magnificent Ruby Mountains press up against the southern sky like Alps.

The traditional Basque hotels still flourish along the south side of Silver Street (south of the Stockmen's and much wider without the railroad tracks).

The Bil-Toki is a Basque dinner house and bar, The Nevada and The Star cater to a regular lodging clientele, but open their dining rooms to the general public at supper time. They offer hearty food and plenty of it, served family-style. The atmosphere is both homey and exotic, a pleasantly provocative combination.

The Commercial and the Stockmen's still preside

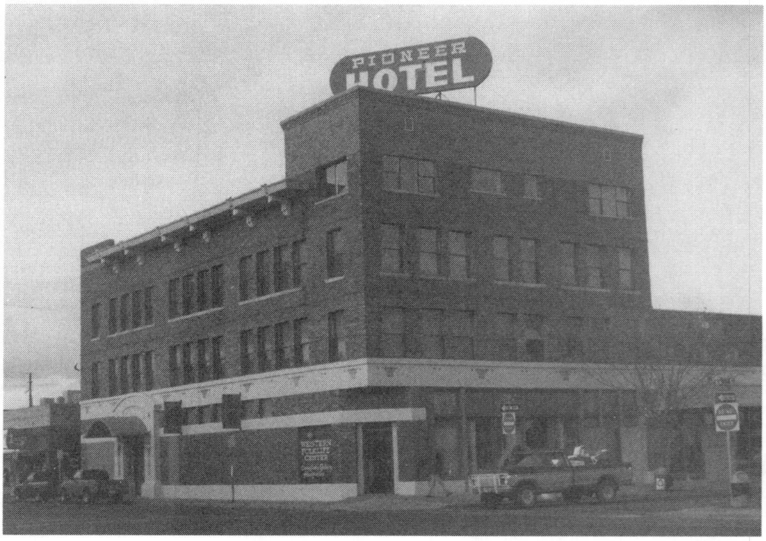

MAX WINTHROP

The Pioneer Hotel is now the home of the Western Folklife Center.

over the downtown, but one great landmark is gone now: the switching yard that spawned the city in the first place. It hasn't been missed. A few pessimists declared that moving the Western Pacific switching yard three miles east would eliminate the train whistles at all hours of the night and Elko's birth rate would decline (local joke). The community is delighted with the peace and quiet, and you'll appreciate all the free parking.

As the population figures suggest, Elko is a bustling little city, offering a wide variety of services and amenities to visitors. Don't expect to find a room at Basque Festival time or during the Cowboy Poetry Gathering unless you've booked well in advance, but at most other times of the year you'll find motel rooms readily available. Restaurants range from the homespun to the elegant.

Every kind of automotive service is available in Elko, from shade tree mechanics to new car dealers. I had no trouble getting a flat tire fixed on a Sunday morning during a recent visit.

Elko is still "town" for the buckaroos — the locally preferred term for cowboys — who work the cattle ranches out beyond the horizons, and the stores that cater to them are major attractions; several of the finest are downtown.

The J.M. Capriola Co. is on Commercial Street. It opened here in 1929 and maintains the tradition established by G.S. Garcia. As a visiting journalist wrote in admiration in the New York Times some years ago, Capriola's "sells everything for the cowboy and his horse, from a box of horseshoe nails to a $3,500 saddle." A hand-made saddle crafted to a classic design costs more than that nowadays, but they are still made right upstairs, along with the other leather goods and the tack that account for three-fourths of Capriola's world-wide business. President Reagan straddled a Capriola saddle at his California ranch, and other Hollywood celebrities do the same today. The volume of mail orders from Europe continues to grow, but most of the customers here, and on the main floor of the store where the blue jeans, snap-fastened shirts, boots and hats are displayed, are still working cowboys as they have always been.

Anacabe's equally venerable and welcoming Elko General Merchandise Store is on Idaho Street downtown. Here you can outfit yourself for a day's ride or a winter in a line shack, or just stop in to soak up the atmosphere.

MAX WINTHROP

Elko is home to the National Basque Festival.

Idaho Street was once U.S. 40 and it's still Elko's main commercial thoroughfare. It's a solid stream of traffic from the city center to the east side, a bright stripe of restaurants, motels and other visitor services.

More than 50 years ago, at what used to be the eastern edge of town before the age of asphalt and electricity, the city of Elko bought the China Ranch and created a magnificent City Park with broad lawns, towering shade trees and wide-ranging recreational facilities. It would be an ornament to cities many times Elko's size and is the venue for the annual Basque Festival, held each 4th of July weekend. On a sunny day in Elko the park is all you need.

There's more. The Northeastern Nevada Museum is located on the edge of the park, a professionally managed archive with exhibits of local historical items donated by local residents. One exception is the old saloon bar from Halleck. For this beloved relic the museum is required to pay rent in the form of one bottle of Beefeater's Gin

Welcome to Elko

Local Area Information

ELKO CONVENTION & VISITORS AUTHORITY
700 Moren Way. 775-738-4091
Come to Elko where the air and ideas are always fresh. The Elko Visitor Center is at 1601 Idaho St. Here at the Convention Center we provide comfortable meeting and banquet facilities plus the professional support staff to bring your event off without a hitch. 1-800-248-ELKO

Museums

NORTHEASTERN NEVADA MUSEUM
1515 Idaho Street. 775-738-3418
Exhibits in the 40,000 square-foot Northeastern Nevada Museum feature local and natural history, local cultures, world-wide wildlife in natural settings, and both permanent and rotating art. Research facilities include 40,000 photos, area newspapers from 1872, public records, and a 1,000-volume library. There is also a gift shop and 90-seat theater.

Night Life

DUNCAN LITTLECREEK GALLERY BAR
518 Commercial St. 775-738-3426
Visit us to savor fine wine, great martinis, microbrews and the contemporary work of local artists in a uniquely congenial atmosphere. The cosmopolitan Inn at DLC offers intimate overnight accommodations for individuals or small groups. Call us for details and availability.

Shopping

ANACABE'S ELKO GENERAL MERCHANDISE
416 Idaho Street. 775-738-3295
If you live within 150 miles of Elko working outdoors, you probably shop here already. Western and steel-toed boots, blue jeans, hats, cold weather gear: everything for the well turned out miner, buckaroo, construction worker, outdoorsman. Everything top quality. Stop in just to experience the old-time atmosphere. 800-821-3556.

MAX WINTHROP

Paul Dunbar serves up traditional Cornish pasties at B.J. Bull on the west side of town.

per year, served over the bar. Rent day began as a private ceremony, but has developed into an annual invitation-only affair of considerable eclat in the local community.

The exhibits range back into prehistory, and the gift shop offers an interesting combination of gifts and books. It also contains the Wannamaker Wing, a large room filled with stuffed animals, posed to appear alive in carefully crafted environments.

The museum is also noted for the variety and quality of its art exhibits, including its annual traveling show of Nevada photography which is easily the most-visited art exhibit in the state. One recent addition is the installation of the Spring Creek Mastodon exhibit. These two million year old bones, about 40% of the animal, were unearthed in 1994. Admission to the museum is $5, $3 for seniors and students, $1 for children 3-12, free for tykes 3 and under.

The Elko Chamber of Commerce is a near neighbor, in the historic Sherman Station building, a historic log structure brought from the Ruby Valley. There's an information desk and a gift shop with Elko items.

You can get current visitor information here and at Elko's Convention Center, also located at the park complex. The facility hosts meetings and conventions, and opened with a concert by the Utah Symphony.

You can take Nevada Route 225 north to Wild Horse Reservoir, Mountain City, and Owyhee.

Nevada Route 227 leads southwest to Spring Creek, South Fork State Park, Lamoille, and the magnificent Ruby Mountains.

Ruby Mountain Brewing Company

MAX WINTHROP

The Ruby Mountain Brewery.

ANGEL CREEK RANCH, Clover Valley, 10 miles south of Wells, Nevada take the Clover Valley Road and it's the first ranch on your right.

For almost 30 years Steve and Maggie Safford have raised cattle and cut hay on the Angel Creek Ranch, beneath the crags of that massive spur of the Rubies called the East Humboldt Range. It is exceptionally beautiful here, but an accumulation of drought years persuaded Steve and Maggie to diversify. More than anything else they wanted a revenue source not dependent on agricultural markets or the weather.

They decided on beer.

Steve had tasted English beer at pubs at 18, and thanks to his father's Air Force postings around Europe he had developed a sophisticated palate by the time he entered Cal Poly at San Luis Obispo. He was too young to buy beer in California, so he brewed a five-gallon batch in the German tradition he prefers. After he and Maggie were married in 1973 he continued making his distinctive home brew for themselves and their friends. His friends assured him it was as good as the best.

MAX WINTHROP

Steve Safford, Ruby Mountain's brewmaster and jack of all trades.

But could they actually develop a brewery in this out of the way place? Or should they go somewhere else — a city — and open a brewpub? The next winter was especially wet and they took it as an omen: they would stay.

"There is no reason we can't make beer right here that's as good or better than anywhere in the world," Steve says. "And we do."

They make three standard varieties, Angel Creek Amber Ale, Vienna style lager and Porter, which have taken Gold, Silver and Bronze awards at Beer competitions around the west. They also brew batches of special recipes, like the lively Buckaroo Beer they make for the Cowboy Poetry Gathering in Elko. You can find their brews at Trader Joe's and Raley's stores, and at other leading local grocers in northern Nevada. Over the bar it's all over the map — the Owl Club in Eureka stocks it, so does Red's in Carson City, the Northern in Goldfield, the Bucket of Blood in Virginia City, the Hotel Nevada in Ely, and other forward-thinking saloonkeepers around the state.

At the brewery you can buy a bottle, a case or a keg, but if you're planning to visit you should call ahead to be sure someone is on hand after bucking hay or moving cows to pour you a taste: 775-752-2337.

Elko Area Guides and Outfitters

Rugged trails offer unlimited opportunities for horse pack trips ranging from a few hours to several days. They offer endless vistas of craggy peaks to 10,500 feet, with glacial lakes, steep canyons and rushing streams.

Wildlife is plentiful. The hunting, fishing and photography are superb. You might see Rocky Mountain bighorn sheep, mountain goats, mule deer, elk, beaver, Himalyan snowcock and many other varieties of animals and birds.

The licensed Guides and Outfitters listed here are experts in all aspects of the great outdoors.

MAX WINTHROP

Elko area guide services bring visitors into Northeastern Nevada to hunt, fish and photograph.

BLACKROCK OUTFITTERS
Mike Hornberger
P.O. Box 1192
Winnemucca, NV 8946
775-623-5926

COTTONWOOD RANCH
Agee Smith
HC 62 Box 1300
Wells, NV 89835
775-755-2231
775-752-3604
www.cottonwoodguestranch.com

CURRENT CREEK OUTFITTERS
Riley Manzonie
P.O. Box 1994
Elko, NV 89803
775-761-3332
775-738-6206

ELKO GUIDE SERVICE
Bill Gibson
Ruby Crest Ranch
HC 30 Box 197
Lower South Fork
Elko, NV 89801
775-744-2277

HALL'S GUIDE SERVICE
Keven Hall
P.O. Box 399
Wells, NV 89835
775-752-3778

HIDDEN LAKE OUTFITTERS
Henry Krenka
HC 60 Box 515
Ruby Valley, NV 89833
775-779-2268

HUMBOLDT OUTFITTERS
Wilde or Sheryl Brough
HC 60 Box 160
Wells, NV 89835
775-752-3714

LIGHTNING CROSS OUTFITTERS
George Corner
HC 36, Box 461-16
Spring Creek, NV 89815
775-738-6077

NEVADA HIGH COUNTRY TOURS
Paul Bottari
P.O. Box 135
Wells, NV 89835
775-752-3040
775-752-3809

PRUNTY RANCH OUTFITTERS
Bill Gibson
2016 Ellis Way
Elko, NV 89801
775-738-7811

NEVADA HIGH DESERT OUTFITTERS
Mitch Buzzett
P.O. Box 28-1251
Lamoille, NV 89828
775-738-1408

RANGER'S GUIDE SERVICE
Carl Ranger
HC 30 Box 432-3
Spring Creek, NV 89815
775-744-4566

RUBY MOUNTAINS HELI-SKI GUIDES, INC.
Joe Royer
P. O. Box 1192
Lamoille, NV 89828
775-753-6867

RUBY MOUNTAIN OUTFITTERS & GUIDES
Frank Zaga
Unit 400 Box 22
Jiggs, NV 89815
775-744-4359

SECRET PASS OUTFITTERS
Steve and Joe Wines
HC 60 - 620
Ruby Valley, NV 89833
775-779-2226

TESTOLIN GUIDE SERVICE
Wayne Testolin
HC 30 Box 352-2
Spring Creek, NV 89815
775-744-4254

WESTERN FRONTIER ADVENTURES
Rich Hankings
P.O. Box 1420
McGill, NV 89318
775-591-0345

NEVADA HISTORICAL SOCIETY

Tuscarora Joss House, far right, circa 1880

Tuscarora

87 MILES northeast of Golconda via graded gravel road; 52 miles northwest of Elko via Nevada Routes 225, 226 and three miles of graded gravel road.

TUSCARORA	
Elko	52
Midas	42
Golconda	87

Discovered in 1867 and named for the Civil War gunboat on which one of the locators had served, Tuscarora was at first a placer camp where 300 miners staked out diggings around the adobe fort they built for protection from the Indians.

After completion of the Central Pacific through Elko in 1869, a large number of Chinese miners drifted to Tuscarora to sift through worked-over claims and work as laborers on the ditches supplying water to the placers. When silver lodes were discovered nearby in 1871, most of the placers were abandoned to the Chinese altogether, and a rush developed. By 1877 Tuscarora had a permanent population of nearly 4,000, not counting the Chinese who continued to work the placers and to cut the sagebrush used for fuel in the mills. Their settlements comprised one of the largest chinatowns east of San Francisco.

The citizens of Tuscarora were tireless joiners, and the social season was full with the doings of every conceivable organization from a National Guard company to a ballet society. In 1878 alone, more than a million dollars in bullion was hauled south to the railroad, but in the 1880s the mines began to falter. Production continued more or less regularly until 1900, then surged up again briefly in 1907. Activity has been practically nil since World War I.

Many of Tuscarora's old buildings remain, but

ELAINE PARKS

Fourth of July parade, Tuscarora.

MAX WINTHROP

Tuscarora in full decline.

they stand in contrast to the bright aluminum trailers and campers moored in empty lots all over town. There are 15 full-timet residents, enough to support the small post office. Many, maybe most of these residents are artists whose studios are open to the public every other Memorial Day weekend in odd-numbered years. In 2007 the Tuscarora Pottery School and 22 local artists participated in eight locations with music and other entertainment and the 4-H kids fixed box lunches for sale. It's good to remember that there are no stores in Tuscarora (15 full-time residents), nothing to buy except postage stamps, art and a 4-H lunch every other year.

The building that houses Dennis Parks' celebrated pottery shop is characteristic of the jumbled history of a Nevada mining camp. Built originally as a hotel in Gold Hill (more than 300 miles to the west) in 1859 or 1860, the structure had been moved to Cornucopia in the 1860s, where it was Mrs. Morton's Boarding House, and then to Tuscarora where Mrs. Zweifel operated it as a boarding house. It hadn't been in Tuscarora long when one of the upstairs tenants was shot through the window by the next-door neighbor. By the 1940s it was the Woods family residence, the post office, the telephone switchboard and the Justice Court combined. The building now houses pottery school students upstairs, and is surrounded by kilns and studios.

Jarbidge

JARBIDGE	
Tuscarora	99
Elko	102
Las Vegas	591

JARBIDGE IS THE MOST ISOLATED of all Nevada's prominent mining ghosts, and it occupies the most beautiful setting. To get there, drive 102 miles north of Elko, only 55 of them on pavement. Be sure you want to make this trip, and when you're sure, outfit yourself for the wild. Water, food, shovel, jack, rope, chains, blankets — all of it. Then take Nevada 225 north to 4-1/2 miles beyond North Fork where a dirt road leads east. Take it. 48 miles of dirt road later you'll be in Jarbidge.

A gold strike in 1909 prompted a rush the following spring when reports of the region's spectacular richness appeared in the press. Some 1,500 miners reached the deep canyon to stake claims on the snowdrifts covering the ground as deep as 18 feet, but when the snow melted it exposed the exaggeration of the newspaper reports, and most of the claims melted away with the snow. Further discoveries were made in 1910, however, and by the end of the year, Jarbidge was a long, narrow community of several hundred residents connected by stagecoach with its nearest neighbor, Rogerson, Idaho, some 65 miles away. The hold-up of this stage (and murder of its driver) at the outskirts of

BILL GEERMINO

Business district, Jarbidge.

N.E. NEVADA MUSEUM

Jarbidge, circa 1914, before the fire.

Jarbidge during a December blizzard in 1916 was last stagecoach robbery in the American West.

The population rose to about 1,200 and then began a fluctuating decline which continued despite the large scale mining which commenced in 1918, when the Guggenheim interests acquired the Jarbidge mines, and lasted until 1932. A dozen permanent residents remain, with two stores, a gas pump, two bars, a museum, modern lodgings, a cafe (sometimes two), and a post office.

Jarbidge Days is celebrated each August with a parade, barbecue, Dutch oven cooking, and music, and the Harvest Dance is held in September.

The Jarbidge River, splashing through the canyon in which the town is wedged, eventually squirms its way to the Snake, the Columbia and the sea. The wilderness area to the east is as God and nature made it. One July visitor counted more than 60 varieties of wildflowers in bloom on the way to Jarbidge and in the tightly woven maze of mountain canyons.

This wonderful old town has a curiously modern aspect these days. Fewer and fewer of the sway-backed old buildings remain unmodified and there are new structures sprinkled among the relics. Roscoe Fawcett's private hunting lodge is a B&B now, and his caretaker's 'cottage' was on the market recently for about $100,000. Jarbidge has been discovered.

It's worth discovering. Camp out or luxuriate indoors, you'll savor the wild beauty here.

Lamoille

THIS CHARMING VILLAGE at the foot of the Ruby Mountains is a little Shangri-la of family farms and country lanes that has become a popular destination with travelers from around Elko County and around the world. Apart from the pleasing atmosphere the main attraction is The Pine Lodge, a long-established dinner house (and 3-room hotel) with an astonishing display of game animals in the dining room. Mounted moose heads are just the beginning here — there are museum-quality diaramas with deer, mountain lions, even enormous bears at your elbow as you nibble your entrecote. O'Carroll's Bar & Grill serves a Sunday Brunch that attracts folks from Spring Creek, Elko

LAMOILLE	
Elko	20
Halleck	15
Deeth	18

and Jiggs. The Gallery at Lamoille presents art and antiques across from Swisher's General Store and gas pump.

Some of those visitors came to ski. Lamoille's long, quiet winters were the very model of rural isolation, but with the establishment of Ruby Mountain Heli-Ski, and the very elegant Red's Ranch accepting guests, Lamoille in winter is a miniature cosmopolis. Each morning just after daybreak, helicopters detach themselves from a cow pasture near the entrance to Red's Ranch and float up to the summits of the Rubies, where they pause to set a small group of skiers and their guides lightly down on the virgin powder snow. The view from there, of the vast white wilderness, is magic enough. The swift plunge down the mountainside: pure ecstasy. It's also expensive, which is why the apres-ski crowd tends to be well-heeled, and explains the conversations about skiing in New Zealand, Africa and South America. One group of skiers arrived from Texas, only to discover that one of them had left his ski boots at home. So they telephoned the pilot of their jet at the Elko airport and had him fly to Aspen to buy a pair. He was back with the boots in four hours.

Ruby Mountain is one of only two heli-ski operations in the west, and with 500 square miles of ski terrain in the Rubies alone (and two other mountain ranges available), it is by far the largest in the U.S. It attracts skiers from all over the world. "It was the best skiing of our lives," an earnest Marin County pediatrician told me during a winter visit to Lamoille. "Every run in fresh snow. No lift lines — no lifts, for that matter. It's an indescribable sensation to be the only skiers on the mountain."

The scenic Lamoille Canyon Road is one of the most beautiful in the west, one of Nevada's crown jewels, in fact: a smooth granite sluiceway created by slow flowing glaciers, and provides a full summer's day of picnicking, fishing, strolling or serious hiking in the pines.

Campsites in the canyon were washed out when Lamoille Creek went on a flooding rampage, but there are rest rooms at the upper end of the road, which is also the trailhead for the Ruby Crest Trail.

MAX WINTHROP

Lamoille Canyon is spectacular for its glacial origins and scenic beauty.

ROBIN COBBEY

Lamoille's Little Church of the Crossroads is at the foot of the Ruby Mountains.

Metropolis

BUILT AND FINANCED by the Pacific Reclamation Company beginning in 1911, Metropolis was to be a planned community of 7,500 residents in the center of more than 40,000 acres of intensely cultivated fields. A four-block business district with cement sidewalks and streetlights was built, containing the grandest three-story hotel between Salt Lake City and Reno, a wagon factory and the splendid Lincoln High School, as well as the usual collection of farm-town enterprises.

But an unfavorable court ruling on water rights in 1913 resulted in the failure of the parent company, and Metropolis did not flourish. In 1925 the railroad spur was abandoned. In 1936 the hotel burned. In 1946 the post office was closed, and in 1947 the school was closed as well.

Ranching continues in the region, but Metropolis itself is only a historic marker and the monumental arch — once the front entrance to the high school — rising out of the sagebrush like a 20th century Stonehenge. It is the only remaining structure of this ambitious city-to-be, and on my last visit was inhabited by an owl. The immense hotel ruins nearby also demonstrate the impressive ambitions of the city's founders.

To make the pleasant trip through the sagebrush, head north from the Burger Bar (closed at press time) on the west side of Wells, turn west on 8th street, and continue 13 miles through the scenic ranchlands of northeastern Nevada. Bring what you need, there is nothing left to buy in Metropolis.

MAX WINTHROP

The remains of Lincoln High School at Metropolis.

Wells

THE CALIFORNIA TRAIL joins the headwaters of the Humboldt River near the present site of Wells, and this region saw the westward passage of the covered wagons until the coming of the railroad. It was in September, 1869, that Humboldt Wells was established as a station on the Union Pacific Railroad: a Wells Fargo office, a log shanty saloon, and the station office in a boxcar.

WELLS	
Wendover	59
Elko	50
Jackpot	68
Ely	137

By 1872 stores and hotels had been added to the single business street paralleling the south side of the tracks, and stagecoaches ran south into White Pine County three times a week. Devastating fires in 1877, 1881 and 1900 interrupted development, and lacking any business beyond that provided by the railroad and the ranches, growth was very slow.

Walter E. Scott, later famous as Death Valley Scotty, spent several of his boyhood years in Wells, arriving on his own at age 11 and supporting himself by a variety of entrepreneurial enterprises, selling sandwiches and doughnuts in the saloons and to railroad passengers with the daughter of a local grocer.

"Sometimes when passengers showed no interest in what Scotty and Katie were selling," wrote Wells historian Gene Kaplan, "they'd wait until the train was about to pull out. Then Katie would cut loose with war whoops. As passengers stuck their heads out of car windows to take a look, Scotty ran by with a stick to knock hats off. The train pulled out with surprised bareheaded passengers, and Scotty peddled hats for two bits each when the next train pulled in."

Since the turn of the century, Wells, like many of the old railroad towns, has slowly shifted its center away from the railroad tracks. In the 1940s businesses migrated a block south to US 40, and in the 1980s the little town began an agonizing stretch toward I-80. The last business on Front Street — Quilici's Market, a 60-year institution — closed in 1991. Thirteen saloons once provided entertainment to railroad travelers. But eventually even the Bullshead Bar, the largest and most famous of them, with its big dance floor upstairs, was closed and padlocked.

MAX WINTHROP PHOTOS

Wells' historic Front Street was being restored when the earthquake destroyed it in February 2008.

In the early years of the 21st century restoration of the Bullshead Bar was begun, and facades of the empty structures on Front Street, once the bustling center of activity in the little pioneer city, were cleaned up and painted in an approximation of their bright youth. Informational posters and historic photos were attached to the building fronts, and the 'walking tour' thus created provided visitors with a pleasant and instructive promenade as they read of the San Marin Hotel, the Elite (pronounced in contrarian Nevada fashion as 'E-light') Saloon, Goble Market, the Mint Saloon, the Soya Lung Chinese Merchandise store and more.

In February, 2008, an earthquake registering 6.0 on the Richter scale rolled beneath Wells and devasted the old commercial center. Injuries were few, a broken arm the worst of it, but the structural damage was an enormous calamity. Many of the buildings were so badly damaged that at press time they were scheduled for complete demolition. Ironically, they have become a greater tourist attraction than ever, drawing travelers to drive past the fenced-off row of buildings.

Wells' prosperity today is solidly based in the crossroads created by I-80 and U.S. 93. I-80 is a main east-west transcontinental artery. U.S. 93 extends from Alaska to Panama, and one day you'll be able to gas up at Wells and drive south to Tierra del Fuego. It is a road favored by the Canadian "Snowbirds" — not the aviators, but the folks who like to winter in the south, following the sun. They come down with the geese in the fall, and they head back with them again in the spring, on their way home to British Columbia, Alberta and Saskatchewan. The geese settle down in the Ruby Marshes, but the Canadians prefer Wells.

The 4-Way Casino, at the highway intersection, recently spent a half million dollars to grow bigger. Near the ramp on the west end of town, Chinatown spent more than that but did not survive. The Chamber of Commerce at Sixth and Lake Streets, and the Trail of the 49ers Interpretive Center which it housed, is now closed on account of earthquake damage.

The countryside is considerably wilder than it looks from Sixth Street, Wells' principal boulevard, which is so peaceful that it seems to tame everything within view. But Wells is not far from the bobcat's lair and the eagle's nest; during a recent visit a mating pair of great horned owls was entertaining onlookers on Sixth Street.

Antelope season, which starts in August, provides an outstanding hunt, and an opportunity for a world record animal. There's an upland game season for cottontails, and predator hunting for coyotes. Up at Angel Lake, 8" catchable trout are stocked every year, and the fishing is very good in winter, although you'll have to drill through as much as three feet of ice to wet your hook. Go to Jiggs Creek if you're out for trophy-sized trout, or to Crittenden Reservoir. There you'll catch beautiful big rainbows — as big as 19" in length, and 11-1/4" in girth — with flies and artificial lures. A couple of men who spent 2-1/2 days fishing Crittenden caught and released over 200 fish, only keeping the ones longer than 20".

Go south to the Ruby Marshes and trophy trout go unnoticed because the bass fishing is so good. Try Starr Creek for trophy sized German Browns. And at Dakes' Reservoir north of Montello there are state trophy-sized Northern Pike available. You'll find as much camping, hiking and mountain climbing as you care to indulge in.

The vast lawned City Park across from the high school provides you with picnic tables and barbecue grills and a comfortable romp with the kids. There is also a swimming pool, a children's playground and a "pleasantly undemanding" 9-hole golf course.

The brick City of Wells office on Clover Street was once the dormitory for ranch kids who boarded over the winter in town so they could go to school. These kids ride the bus to school now, but some of them have to ride 50 miles just to meet the bus for its 50 mile run to town. High school attendance still drops during deer season, and whenever livestock is being moved.

Take the paved 12-mile drive to Angel Lake, a small blue jewel tucked up under the summits of the East Humboldts. Fish, swim, or set up in one of the Forest Service campsites. There are more campsites at nearby Angel Creek and from either spot hiking trails lead up to the unusual Hole-In-The-Mountain Peak. Or go northwest the 13 miles to the ruins of Metropolis, the ambitious city abandoned in the sagebrush.

You can travel on the California Trail northeast of Wells by taking Highway 93 north 26 miles to the well-marked Winecup Ranch turnoff to the east, and continuing 15 miles to the sign-marked Mammoth Ruts. This is a section of the California Trail, worn down as much as six feet below the floor of Thousand Springs Valley, one of the few places where the passage of the pioneers can still be seen today. You can continue on about 60 miles to Jackpot, or return to US 93.

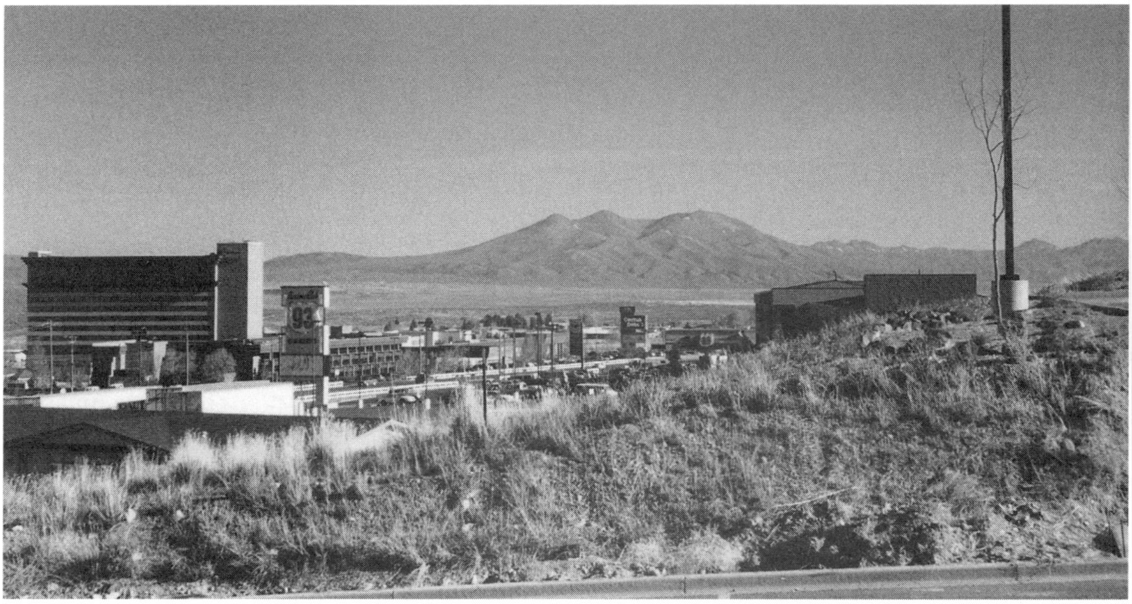

MAX WINTHROP

The cosmopolis in the wilderness.

Jackpot

HERE IN THE HIGH RANCHLANDS of the Bruneau River country, surrounded by vast mountain wilderness, you might be surprised at the bright cluster of casinos where US 93 crosses the Idaho-Nevada line. This phenomenal community about 50 miles south of Twin Falls was the first casino boomtown in Nevada after Las Vegas.

JACKPOT	
Wendover	67
Elko	118
Ely	204
Twin Falls, ID	42

Jackpot owes its existence to the presidential ambitions of Senator Estes Kefauver of Tennessee, who did Nevada a big favor in the early 1950s by crusading against illegal slot machines around the country. When slot machines were turned to the wall and poker games closed down in saloons and club rooms all around Idaho, Jackpot was born as a log cabin full of one-armed bandits just across the Nevada state line.

It was five years before Jackpot had its first blackjack game, but today the casinos here would be right at home in Las Vegas. Cactus Pete's, the first and best-known of them is now a major high-rise, with the Four Jacks Motel, Bartons's Club 93, the West Star Hotel & Casino and the fabulously conceived Horseshu Hotel & Casino, a combination of a Hollywood sound stage and a western mining town.

There are 1,500 permanent residents in Jackpot now, and although the town lacks the supreme symbol of civilized existence, a cemetery, it does have a school, a golf course, a magnificent enclosed swimming pool, tennis courts, over 100 RV spaces and an airport. Despite being on the Nevada side of the line, Jackpot is now one of the largest employers in southern Idaho.

Most of this prosperity derives from the avalanche of visitors who roar south from Idaho every

MAX WINTHROP

This was Jackpot in the pioneer days of '56.

You can't miss the action in Jackpot

MAX WINTHROP

weekend, lured as much by the simple pleasure of a good dinner and the chance to get out of Idaho overnight, as by the gambling games.

For their benefit Jackpot sets its clocks to Idaho time, an hour later than the rest of Nevada. Gambling and entertainment are still the main attractions for the wintertime sunseekers drifting south out of Canada, and for the truckers who highball north and south on US 93 at all times of the year.

Increasingly though, visitors are also attracted to Jackpot for the outdoor recreation available in every direction, from about ten feet out of town to as far as you can see and beyond. The Jarbidge Wilderness Area is in the mountains to the southwest, and the majority of the state's record deer have come from this part of the state. Sage grouse, chukar and pheasant hunting are excellent, and the fishing is even better. The Little Salmon River and its tributaries commonly offer up rainbow and brown trout up to four pounds, with larger fish caught somewhat less frequently. Salmon Falls reservoir across the line in Idaho, boasts of nine varieties of game fish including trout, salmon, bass and walleye. The opportunities for stream, river and lake fishing are unsurpassed.

Jackpot is surely the busiest town in Nevada, maybe the world, with a crowded schedule of golf tournaments, air races, skeet shoots, balloon ascensions and other events both ordinary and exotic. The golf course is open all year (play is with a green ball in winter) and there is an indoor swimming pool that doubles as a visitor information center.

MAX WINTHROP

The Horseshu Inn, Jackpot.

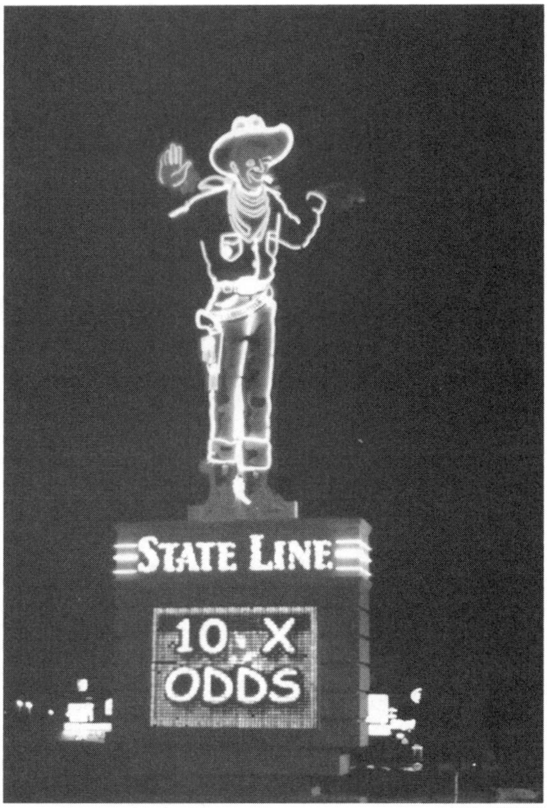

RICH MORENO

Unforgettable Wendover gives a huge welcome.

Wendover

ON THE way into Wendover from the west, the freeway tops a rise and then sweeps down toward the Bonneville Salt Flats below. If you pull over to the side of the road at the crest and park for a few minutes, you can study a view unlike anything else in the world. The Salt Flats extend in a broad white plain, the desert's skin stretched tight, as far as the eye can see — and it curves. The horizon line is a clear arc from side to side, and the two stripes of freeway pavement curve away across the alkali toward the vanishing point. Nowhere else on land can you actually the curvature of the earth.

WENDOVER	
Reno	398
Elko	109
Ely	118
Las Vegas	400

Columbus was right!

Almost as amazing as its shape is the earth's texture and color here, spread out in horrid immensity: surely the cruelest desert your eyes will ever see. And where the bleached and crusty sea of alkali meets a shoreline of dead brown hills, is Wendover.

Feast your eyes on that scene for a while. You'll never forget it.

This remarkable settlement was established in the 1920s when Bill Smith built a gas station beside the road here. The light bulb he erected on a tall pole was only a tiny speck of light in the black desert night, but for years it served westbound motorists as a welcome beacon as they crossed the Bonneville Salt Flats. Thus Wendover developed as an outpost of civilization in the midst of isolation.

Wendover boomed during the war when the Army Air Corps built a bomber training base here. The B-29 crews who dropped the atomic bombs on Nagasaki and Hiroshima trained for their missions here. Some of the base has been converted to civilian use, but most of it has simply been left to warp and tatter in the baking heat and the scouring winds. The roaring engines of the Enola Gay have faded to a distant drone, gone forever from the hot blue sky.

Now a neon cowboy greets the travelers along Interstate 80 and Wendover is booming again. Booming almost beyond description, in fact. Ten years ago Wendover, Utah, looked like a village in Turkey, and Wendover, Nevada, was just the Stateline Club and a lot of substandard employee housing left over from the war. The Rock, they called it.

The Rock has been upholstered since then. Now Wendover has five large casinos and one tiny casino tucked down behind the hill. Bill Smith's old place, the Stateline, is a major casino hotel now, and the Smith family's new Silver Smith, across the street, is twice as big. Between them they offer seven ambitious restaurants, ranging from coffee shop through buffet to gourmet restaurant. The Peppermill, Nevada Crossing and Red Garter down the street provide customers with more choices, and the Hide-A-Way Casino maintains a popular steak house. You can also get Chinese food, pizza and burgers at non-casino restaurants.

Ten years ago is already "the old days" in Wendover. In those days a sign in the desert grit said, "You missed Las Vegas—Don't Miss Wendover." Now you may have missed Wendover too. The population of Wendover, Utah, has been drifting westward across the border as fast as new housing has been developed in Wendover, Nevada. The elementary school that opened in 1985 was immediately enrolled to capacity with kids whose families moved to town to run businesses in the shopping center overlooking the 18-hole golf course. Wendover's population has moved from 2,500 in 1985 (both states) when development slowed on account of the credit crunch, to 5,500 in 1990. Some of Wendover's newcomers, too, are retired people. They like desert life and that eye-popping view, and the glamor and convenience of the great casinos, with Salt Lake City and all its metropolitan touches just two hours' drive across the curve of the salt flats.

Incorporated as a city (officially West Wendover) in 1991, the little gambling center on the Nevada side is about to expand by 800 acres of residential housing, a large water park and a Factory Outlet mall. There's a two-screen movie house, and as if to validate Wendover's new permanence, a large cemetery has been dedicated on a hill above town. Already it contains two graves, one of them marked.

Wendover resembles an old-time mining town in the way it has sprung vigorously to life in the desert wilderness, progressing from next-to-nothing to rambunctious little city in just a few fast years. It is served by a colorful newspaper, the High Desert Advocate, whose office resembles (from the outside) the Goldfield Sun in 1905. The Advocate covers the vast expanses of White Pine and Elko counties with zest and dedication, its front pages blurting out the latest news from Ely, Elko, Wells and Jackpot under headlines that widen the eye. On a recent late summer visit I asked one of the editors whether newspapering in a boom town was as interesting and enjoyable as it has been painted (by Mark Twain among others). "It's actually pretty quiet," he told me. "Oh, there was a shooting at one of the casinos last week, but mostly we're in our silly season now."

Bill Smith's little light bulb would be lost in the glare of Wendover's splashy brilliance now, but the Stateline Club still operates on his original gaming license issued in 1931.

To stretch your legs, take the short climb to Danger Cave: drive east into Utah on I-80 and take the first offramp to the truckstop. Continue past the truck stop and turn left at the dirt road just beyond. As you drive west, you can see Danger Cave on the hillside off to the left ahead of you. You'll find your way with no trouble. Not far away, but more difficult to reach, is Juke Box Cave, which got its name when it was used for dances by the airmen at the base during WWII. The concrete dance floor still remains, as do petroglyphs near the entrance. This was the venue of choice for dances because it was cool even at the height of summer, and because it could be lighted without breaking the wartime black-out.

MAX WINTHROP

Wendover's place in history is secure.

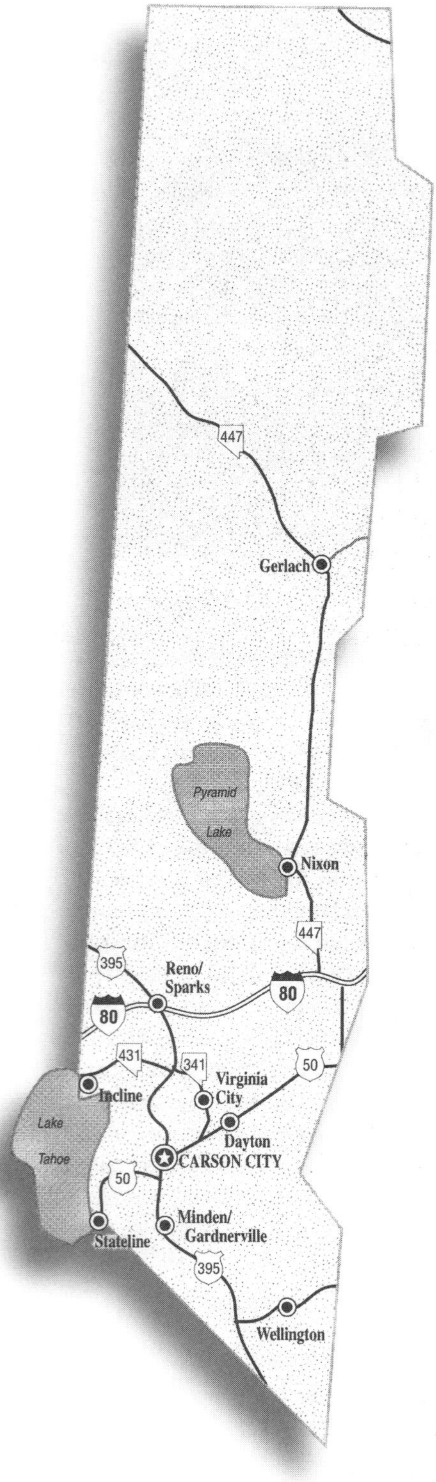

Reno-Tahoe Territory

In its western slopes the Sierra Nevada rises gently in a rumpled succession of foothills to peaks more than two miles above the level of the sea. In the east the mountains drop sharply away from the summits in a sheer, slightly scalloped, granite scarp into the high desert valleys of Nevada. The majestic presence of the Sierra at Nevada's western boundary is responsible for much of the character of this part of the state.

Warm moist air traveling inland from the sea is nudged upward above the inclined foothills as it travels eastward and as it rises the air cools and its moisture condenses. It falls as rain at first, and then as snow. As this chilled sea air scrubs across the summits in winter, its moisture is plundered by the high forest lands. Beyond the crest, where the air swoops down again into the high-floored Nevada valleys, it is relatively dry. As a consequence, the characteristic vegetation of the region east of the Sierra Nevada is low-growing scrub brush, shading upward to pinyon-juniper woodlands on the slopes of the low ranges enclosing the valleys. The broad expanse of grey brush is broken here and there by grassy meadows and alkaline playas, and striped occasionally by meandering lines of cottonwoods and willows that mark rivulets and shallow streams.

Only three rivers plunge down the steep stone face of the Sierra to flow east into Nevada. The Walker and Truckee curl out between the humped and bulged-up desert mountains before damming up in Walker and Pyramid lakes. The Carson, until the construction of Lahontan Dam in 1915, simply spread out across a broad reedy marsh and vanished into the grey desert sand.

Jedediah Smith passed through this country, and so did a few other wide-ranging trapping parties, but the first Americans to enter it in numbers were the California-bound wagon trains pioneering the Humboldt Trail westward from Salt Lake City. After the first of these had come and gone, Fremont came to name and map the rivers, the valleys, the

GOLD HILL NEWS ARCHIVE

Reno street scene, 1910.

mountains, and the passes. On his heels came the gold rushers. Few of them found Nevada (established as Carson County, Utah Territory, in 1854) of any interest except at its far western edge where forage for their animals was relatively abundant.

Recognizing an opportunity, a party of Mormon pioneers in 1851 established a tiny trading post and corral where a small trickle of water splashed down out of the heights to soak a natural meadow at the foot of the mountains. Here they provisioned westward-bound wagon trains with wild hay and supplies hauled the long, dusty way from Salt Lake City. These first merchants prospered, and in the spring of the following year half a dozen more enterprising men established themselves along the route of the wagon trains where there was reliable water and good grass. The original trading post at Mormon Station became the center of population and activity between Salt Lake City and Placerville as more Mormon farmers came out to take up the fertile ground at the foot of the mountains.

At the same time a few Gentiles began prospecting the runty hills to the northeast. By 1853, despite the passage of tens of thousands of California-bound gold rushers and farmers, the non-Indian population of the region — the only permanently settled part of what is now Nevada — was fewer than 300.

In the following year Mormon Station became the seat of Carson County, Utah Territory, and its name was changed to Genoa. With characteristic energy in the face of complete isolation and serious privation, the mostly Mormon farming population created a narrow green strip of attractive and productive croplands between the looming mass of the Sierra and the vast desert distances to the east.

At the same time the small number of prospectors working placer claims on Gold Creek, a tributary stream of the Carson with its mouth near present-day Dayton, was slowly increasing as unsuccessful miners from the California gold fields began drifting back across the spine of the Sierra Nevada. Few of them braved the bleak Utah Territory winters, though. Most returned to California until spring.

Still, by 1857 the population of Johntown, the

tent and shanty camp on Gold Creek, numbered more than 100 during good weather. In that year the steadily disintegrating relations between Brigham Young's Utah theocracy and the national government in Washington threatened to result in violence. Troops were marched toward Salt Lake City to impose the Federal will, and to strengthen his hand in the impending confrontation Young recalled many of the far-flung Mormon colonists home to Zion. Among them were the farmers at the foot of the Sierra. All but one family abandoned what they had built and trailed out into the desert for home.

So when rich gold placers were discovered in January, 1859, near the headsprings of the willowed stream that meanders past Johntown, the society of far western Utah Territory had become secular. Within a few weeks a large part of the population decamped for the new diggings on the flank of Sun Mountain. Several months of furious development followed as the miners realized that this gold-rich rock into which they were digging was the source of the free gold they had been panning for years down canyon.

It was several months more before they discovered that the heavy "blue mud," which fouled their gear and frustrated their efforts to get at the gold, was silver. Both of these discoveries had been made by the summer of 1859, and the ripple of glad news which arrived in California brought a shudder of excitement sending thousands in an eager rush across the Sierra to Washoe. The Johnson

Cutoff Trail past Lake Tahoe became for a while the most heavily traveled highway in the West.

As stimulating as the gold discovery was for the white population, its effect upon the Indians was catastrophic. The white intrusion in such numbers disrupted and destroyed the delicate desert ecological patterns upon which the Indian survival techniques were based. The white man's livestock devoured the desert forage plants far faster and more completely than the Indians could themselves; the white man's rifles decimated the available game and drove away what wasn't shot; the white man's axes felled whole forests to provide timbers for the mines, lumber to build their settlements and firewood for their stoves and campfires. As white preemption of the survival resources accelerated, the Paiute population grew more resentful of the intruders and more dependent on them.

In May of 1860 the thickening stream of traffic over the Sierra brought even more of the gold-hungry from California. As some of the Paiute leaders were meeting at Pyramid Lake to discuss their predicament, nine young men raided Williams' Station on the Carson River, burned down the buildings and corrals, and killed four whites. On the following day, word of the attack (but not of the abduction and repeated rape of two young Indian girls which inspired it) reached the settlements on the Comstock Lode. A panicky defiance suffused the populace. Men mustered themselves awkwardly into military companies and set out toward Pyramid Lake to have "an Indian for breakfast and a pony to ride."

But it was the Indians who had breakfast this time, annihilating about half the expedition in a day-long battle near the Truckee River and sending the rest running for their lives. In June a more businesslike force of regular soldiers drove the Paiutes into the mountains around Pyramid Lake to end the hostilities.

The era of exploitation which had inspired Nevada's brief "Indian War" was just beginning. For more than 20 years the immense wealth of the Comstock Lode drew settlers into the state. Many of them worked in the mines and mills, but there were loggers and sawyers to supply the mines with timbers, teamsters and then railroaders to freight in supplies, farmers and ranchers to provide food. New communities were founded and prospered: Carson City, first as a freight and staging center for the mines and then as capital of Nevada Territory and then of the State; Reno as the transcontinental railhead for the mines. Other small towns huddled along the railroad line east like beads on a string, and other mining strikes were hit, but for the 40 years beginning with its discovery, the Comstock Lode dominated the affairs of the state.

By the turn of the new century, though, the Comstock mines had been 20 years in irreversible decline. Between 1880 and 1890 Nevada's population dwindled by 25 per cent, and from 1890 to 1900 ten per cent more. It was then that the great gold and silver strikes were made at Tonopah and Goldfield, fanning the mining excitements as hot

SOUTHERN PACIFIC

Reno, on its way to becoming the biggest little city in the world.

as ever and inflaming the national imagination the way the Comstock had done. The main benefits of the new strike, though, were realised in the southern part of the state where a little townsite named Las Vegas was subdivided and sold at auction in 1905. Northwestern Nevada continued in depression, and Reno replaced Virginia City as the de facto capital of the region and center of the effort to revive the economy.

Reno then was a dusty, roughneck town dominated by the railroad and thriving on its traffic. Commercial Row, which faced the tracks, was not all business — there were saloons, hurdy-gurdy houses, gambling halls and hotels of varying degrees of elegance. There too were the offices of the State Board of Trade, an organization devoted to promoting the exploitation of the one great untapped resource which the region possessed in abundance: empty land.

Founded in 1889 by Francis G. Newlands to encourage rural settlement, the Board of Trade had the active co-operation of U.S. Senators John P. Jones and William Stewart, both of them leading figures in Nevada politics since the heyday of the Comstock. Jones and Stewart proposed several measures in Congress to bolster the state's agricultural economy. Despite their efforts, and despite interest shown by co-operatives and farm colonists ranging from the Hebrew Agricultural Society to the Dunkards, agricultural development was slow and failure-prone. There was simply too little irrigation water. When Newlands won election to the House of Representatives, it was largely on the basis of his proposal to get federal sponsorship for local irrigation programs.

This proposal was strongly supported by the congressional delegations of other arid western states, but just as firmly opposed by President McKinley. With the succession of Theodore Roosevelt to the presidency, however, the agricultural problems of the western states found a sympathetic ear and the Newlands Reclamation Act was passed by Congress and signed into law.

Thus, in the autumn of 1903, the first federal reclamation project undertaken in the U.S. was begun about a dozen miles east of Reno. There a diversion dam was built to shunt Truckee River water into a 33-mile canal carrying it to the Carson River. Feeder canals were constructed to bring many thousand acres of raw desert soil under irrigation: About 90 percent of the newly arable land lay within the boundaries of Churchill County, and the population there rose from 831 in 1900 to nearly 3,000 ten years later.

The canal project occurred simultaneously with the Southern Pacific's track-doubling program, and Reno became more raffish than ever as scores of footloose men following the construction work roamed the board sidewalks and mud streets on payday, from saloon to bawdy house to gambling hall. Such a Sodom of gambling, liquor and prostitution did Reno become, in fact, that in 1904 the president of the university ordered his students restricted to campus to protect them from the evil influences of the town.

Meanwhile, the great gold and silver discoveries in southern Nevada were stimulating exploration and the re-evaluation of mining properties all over the state. In northwestern Nevada dozens of new claims were staked and old ones reactivated. The Nevada Commercial League issued a brochure praising Reno's prosperous future as "encircled by live mining camps — camps that will make of Reno another Denver." But as this boast was being distributed far and wide, the true sources of future prosperity were stepping gingerly down from the railroad coaches to stand for a hesitant moment on the depot platform: eastern women, bejewelled, beminked and bewildered at the sight of the Commercial Row honky-tonks from which buckaroos, Paiutes, sheepherders, canal diggers, track layers and silver miners gazed out at them like the shy desert creatures they were: wealthy eastern women, come alone to be divorced.

Divorce had always been easy on the frontier. While the states east of the Mississippi had made divorce extremely difficult, in Nevada and other western states it was immediately available on a wide variety of grounds to any citizen. Because western populations were characteristically restless, citizenship was bestowed on any individual who stayed with a state for six consecutive months. No one had taken the matter terribly seriously, even when Sioux Falls, South Dakota, gained a certain notoriety as a divorce capital in the 1890s.

Laura Corey had been a Broadway showgirl, but at the turn of the century her address was Pittsburgh, Pennsylvania, where she was the wife of the president of U.S. Steel. William Corey was the wunderkind of the American steel industry. A protege of Andrew Carnegie, Corey had started work in a steel mill at age 16 and had become president of the world's first billion dollar corporation before he was forty. Fortunately for three generations of Reno lawyers, Corey conceived a great passion for the celebrated actress and singer Mabelle Gilman. Ignoring advice and criticism, the determined Corey sent the despairing Laura to Reno with their teenaged son and instructions to stay there six months and then sue him for divorce.

Sue him she did, but instead of the obscurity Corey had anticipated by bringing the action at remote little Reno, the story was published in installments for six months in newspapers around the nation. Laura Corey was an articulate and attractive person whose plight excited the sympathy of other women across the country. The affair created a continuing scandal which subsided at last when the divorce trial resulted in a two million dollar settlement and custody of their son to Laura. By the time the trial closed, Reno had become indelibly linked with divorce in the national consciousness.

But Reno was a continent away, and many people who had decided that divorce was the inevitable solution to their marital troubles hung back from the long train trip. Reno was distant, small and crude, a tiny outpost on the western frontier.

Enter an enterprising New York lawyer named W.H. Schnitzer. With rare vision, Schnitzer saw the possibilities. He made the long train trip himself, rented a post office box, passed the Nevada bar, and returned as rapidly as possible to New York. There he advertised full divorce services in newspapers, magazines and theatre programs to attract the attention of the unhappily married rich.

Schnitzer's ads and booklets attracted great attention and he was soon shuttling between New York and Reno, shepherding clients into rented Reno homes and apartments for the six months of residency, and then through the Washoe County Court House where uncontested divorces were granted with amiable alacrity. His ads also prompted many people to call their own lawyers to ask about Reno divorces, and eastern law firms began to establish relationships with Reno lawyers.

In 1910 Reno hit the national headlines in still another connection. Tex Rickard and a partner had promoted a heavyweight championship fight in San Francisco between Jim Jeffries and Jack Johnson. Construction of an arena for the match was underway when the California governor bowed to pressure and forbade the fight except as an "exhi-

NEVADA STATE MUSEUM

Gambling at the Louvre, Reno, 1909 .

bition." Rickard, delighted at the storm of controversy, began casting about for an alternative site. When Reno gambler Charley Stout offered $2,500 if the fight moved to Reno by the Fourth of July, Rickard eagerly agreed. On June 20 he announced that Reno would get the big fight.

By the end of June Reno had swollen to about twice its normal population. Special trains brought fight fans from Chicago, Birmingham, St. Louis, Denver, New Orleans and San Francisco. Western Union installed 17 special lines at press headquarters in the Golden Hotel where star reporters like Jack London, Rex Beach and Rube Goldberg were crowded in with journalists of lesser reputation and where late-arriving guests slept in the hallways on 300 cots ordered for the emergency. So heavy were the crowds that one Reno restaurant boasted of serving 3,600 dinners in a single day.

The fight itself, before a crowd of 18,000 (several thousand more than Reno's entire population at the time), was a fiasco. Jeffries was overweight and overcautious. Johnson butchered him on his feet and knocked him out in the 15th round.

As the crowds streamed out of the city Rickard divvied up the gate: $121,000 to the fighters in purses and bonuses and $120,000 to himself and his associates. The biggest profit proved to be Reno's. The front pages of the nation's newspapers had featured Reno for weeks, and articles about the fight appeared in magazines for months afterward. All of them carried references to the natural beauty of Reno's surroundings, to the city's excitements, to its cosmopolitan character and to its role as a marital end-of-the-line. The divorce business boomed in the wake of the fight.

In the following year the Nevada State Bar Association ridded itself of the inventor of its most profitable specialty by censuring Schnitzer for his aggressive marketing tactics and forbidding him to practice law in Nevada for an extended period of time.

Just as they heaved the outsider overboard and prepared to cut up the increasingly lucrative pie among themselves, however, Reno's divorce lawyers encountered a new difficulty. The city's conservative element was increasingly perturbed over the unsavory reputation Reno was acquiring beyond the Rockies. By combining forces with the rural voters around the state (as they had done once before in 1909 to outlaw gambling), the genteel folk influenced the legislature to revise the divorce laws to require a 12-month residency instead of six. Reno's economy flattened at once, and Nevadans claimed for years afterward that no member of the 1913 legislature was ever again elected to public office. In any event the 1915 legislature lost no time in restoring the six-month residency requirement for divorce.

By 1915 Reno had become the beneficiary of the end of the great bonanza period in Goldfield and Tonopah. The mines at Goldfield had bottomed out and at Tonopah the spectacular early boom had quieted into a steady and routine production of silver. Money and opportunity grew tighter in these mining cities, and for more than five years the leading men of the district had been moving north to Reno.

Chief among them was a husky, hard-faced former cowboy, faro dealer and gambling hall operator George Wingfield. So successful had

he been in the mining cities that by 1907 he controlled every producing gold mine in the Goldfield district but one. When he moved to Reno in 1908 he was being called King George Wingfield, the Proprietor of Nevada.

Upon his arrival Reno became the effective capital of the state, with executive offices on the fourth floor of Wingfield's columned marble bank building at Second and Virginia streets. Wingfield himself was the state's national Republican committeeman and one of his lawyers a few doors down the hall held the same position with the Democrats. Thus Wingfield was in a position to dominate the affairs of both political parties in Nevada.

With Wingfield came Tasker Oddie, the Tonopah lawyer who had seen to the original assays for Jim Butler and who was later elected governor. Key Pittman had championed the small miners in Nome (and inspired the famous Rex Beach novel, The Spoilers) before moving to Tonopah and get-

GOLD HILL NEWS ARCHIVE

Reno in the Thirties.

ting elected to the U.S. Senate. George Bartlett, another Tonopah lawyer, served a term in the House of Representatives before moving to Reno to become the city's most prominent single figure in divorce law, as both attorney and judge. Reno native Pat McCarran returned home from Tonopah where he had hung out his law shingle and served as Nye County District Attorney. He became a member of the Nevada Supreme Court and later won election to the U.S. Senate where he served 20 years. Thus Tonopah men simultaneously moved to Reno and took the places of the last of the old Comstockers still in office.

Financiers and politicians weren't Reno's only influential citizens. Perhaps the two most powerful men in the city were Bill Graham and Jim McKay who ran the Bank Club at Center Street and Douglas Alley. The Bank Club was Reno's leading saloon and gambling hall until the passage of Prohibition when it was remodeled slightly and licensed as a cigar store. Prohibition also provided Graham and McKay the opportunity to become the leading bootleggers in northern Nevada. They owned The Willows, a clubby bar, restaurant and gambling parlor, and operated The Stockade, a fenced-in warren of brick cribs on the eastern outskirts of town, each containing a bed, a bureau and a prostitute.

In New York, unless glamorized by Damon Runyon, they'd have been obscure figures. In Reno, still a city of less than 20,000, they may not have been leading citizens, but they were prominent men who commanded the greatest respect. Bill Graham was tough and ruthless, and liked to hold court in the Grand Cafe on Center Street. Jim McKay was warmer, smoother and more social. With George Wingfield running Nevada and Graham and McKay running Reno, the 1920s were golden years.

In 1920 America's Sweetheart Mary Pickford acquired a mansion overlooking the Truckee in which to idle away the six months required to dissolve her marriage to actor Owen Moore. The trial, when it eventually reached court, was marred by suggestions of collusion. These were aggravated by the "coincidental" way that Moore had put himself within the jurisdiction of the court, thus speeding the course of justice. The affair showed some promise of blowing up into a scandal affecting the sanctity of all Nevada divorces had not the entire Reno legal community united to smooth it over and smile it away. America got the message and the divorce trade continued to prosper.

With it continued the publicity on which the city thrived, publicity which drew the line at the unsavory but gloried in glittering and dramatic stories from which people could draw their own conclusions. Leading figures in eastern high society took suites at the Riverside Hotel down the hall from members of European nobility.

To add to the city's legend, the daughter of Reno's mayor married Walter "Big Train" Johnson, the ace pitcher for the Washington Senators, who thereafter made annual visits to Reno and hummed the high fast one past ecstatic Reno youngsters before going on to spring training. On Virginia Street Hispano-Suizas were parked between flivvers and battered ranch trucks, and the chic Reno of the gossip columns interlocked with both the sleazy Reno of speakeasies and backroom gambling dominated by Graham and McKay, and the leather and mahogany Reno of board meetings and conference rooms in which George Wingfield reigned supreme.

In 1927 the Reno Chamber of Commerce drummed up a Transcontinental Highway Exposition to coincide with the paving of Highway 40 over the Sierra summit. The exposition itself was a flop, but it provided Reno with a municipal landmark as compelling as the Golden Gate Bridge or the Empire State Building, both of which it predated: the iron arch across Virginia Street at the railroad tracks proclaiming in neon letters, "RENO -The Biggest Little City In The World."

In the 1930s things began to go wrong for the men who had done so much to create Reno's character.

1929 was a drought year. Steady declines in livestock prices since early in the decade already had the state's cattle and sheep men in trouble. The stock market crash increased their calamity. Wingfield, a major lender already, advanced more cash to tide the helpless ranchers over until prices improved. In effect, he took a second mortgage on the Nevada livestock industry. His investments in every aspect of the state's economy were enormous, and so were his power and influence. But his wealth was not limitless, and a serious loss at any part of the Wingfield empire could topple the entire interlocking structure.

1930 was another drought year. So was 1931. Now the state's stockmen were in desperate trouble, and Wingfield with them. If the ranchers were bankrupted now, the banks would go down with them. Coolly, Wingfield advanced the necessary cash for the ranchers to ship their Nevada herds to out-of-state grazing lands.

Wingfield had called the bet and played his hole card. But to do it he had to siphon funds through his commercial banks from his savings banks, which was not legal. When it came to light, as it shortly did, the governor was forced to declare a 12-day bank holiday. Wingfield's banks never reopened, and of the $4 million he had advanced to the state's stockmen by 1932, the bank receivers recovered only $200,000.

Other banks followed Wingfield's into ruin, and an avalanche of ranching bankruptcies made a shambles of the state's rural economy. Nevada fell again deep into depression. Wingfield himself lost everything except his home, membership in a duck hunting club and a Packard motorcar. According to stories of the time, "King George" was so strapped for cash that he had to go to Graham and McKay for a few thousand dollars walking around money.

In the meantime, faced with a devastated livestock industry, dwindling tax revenues and near universal hard times — as well as the knowledge that Arkansas had passed a 90-day divorce law in 1930 and that several other states, including nearby Arizona, were planning to do the same in 1931 — the legislature acted decisively. It reduced the divorce residence from three months to six weeks and it legalized casino gambling.

Reno became the most celebrated city in the world as a consequence. Divorces increased from about 3,000 to nearly 5,000 in 1931, and an uncontested divorce trial now required only about five minutes of precious court time. Thus, while Nevada's ranchers were watching the remnants of their herds stagger in search of water and the powerful Wingfield political machine was crumbling under the assault of soon-to-be Senator Pat McCarran, Reno prospered.

Surprisingly, perhaps, little of this prosperity derived from the legalization of gambling. It had been intended as a revenue measure, to take the payoff money paid by local gamblers out of the pockets of local politicians and police, and to put them in the public treasury as taxes. But the gambling halls had been operating so long in a pseudo-clandestine way that a move into the full light of day was more than the operators could handle gracefully. Some signs went up, some curtains came down, but few games were moved out front. Reno gambling remained essentially what it had always been, an unglamorous smalltime enterprise catering mainly to low-rolling payday plungers. Graham and McKay bought some new slot machines for the Bank Club (making a total of 91) and footnoted their newspaper ads with the fact that the Bank Club was the biggest gambling casino in the world.

As if to demonstrate that legalization hadn't weakened the fix, when Bill Graham shot 21 dealer Blackie McCracken to death in a Douglas Alley speakeasy, a coroner's jury could scarcely wait for the gavel to rap before declaring it justifiable as self defense.

But "Big Bill" Graham and "Jimmy the Cinch" McKay were not destined to last long in a Reno where gamblers joined the chamber of commerce. On the last day of February, 1934, federal agents swooped down to arrest them on charges of mail fraud, stemming from a "wrong stock" and "wrong horse" sting service they ran on the side. They were taken directly to the railroad station and put aboard the waiting train to New York, at the far end of the continent from the fix.

One of the witnesses subpoenaed by the government was an officer of the Riverside Bank named Roy Frisch. Frisch had seen Graham and McKay receive $117,000 from one of their suckers, and his testimony would prove fatal to the defense. But before the subpoena could be served Roy Frisch vanished. He strolled the few blocks from his home to a movie theater and simply disappeared. The file on his disappearance was never closed and Roy Frisch is still officially a missing person.

Two trials resulted in hung juries, but a determined prosecution finally put Graham and McKay away in 1939. They were fined $11,000 each and sentenced to nine years in prison. After the war, when most of their sentences had been served, Senator McCarran petitioned

President Truman to pardon them, and he did.

The Reno to which they returned was so different from the city that they had left that they slipped at once from the public eye. The Bank Club had not long remained the largest gambling casino in the world. In 1935 an old carny hand named Raymond I. Smith (but called Pappy) took over a 20-foot-wide Virginia Street storefront, christened it Harolds Club, and stood Nevada gambling on its head.

Customers entered the Harolds Club gambling rooms directly from the street rather than through a cigar store or bar. To the old line gamblers to whom legitimacy was an almost unwanted intrusion this seemed a shocking indiscretion. In contrast to their gloomy dens, Smith slapped bright paint on the walls and turned the lights up full. The old timers were again revulsed. Then Smith unveiled an absurd version of roulette, using live mice instead of balls and wheels. This had the old timers gagging. When they saw his 21 dealers they fainted dead away. Women. Not paunchy old guys with yellow eyeballs and spotted ties, but attractive women. After the initial hoo-haw Reno's gamblers sneered at Harolds Club as a gambler's five-and-dime store.

But the customers didn't laugh. People who wouldn't have entered the Bank Club at gunpoint walked into Harolds Club by the dozens, quite giddy and adventurous, and left their nickels with the Smiths. Pappy Smith was the Henry Ford of the casino gambling business, converting it from a handicraft into a volume industry. He made Harolds Club the biggest and best-known gambling casino in the world.

Other changes were in the wind. In 1927 an ex-cab driver, ex-skating instructor, ex-engine room wiper named Norman Biltz had come to Nevada at the head of a Lake Tahoe subdivider's 105-man sales force. He sold thousands of Lake Tahoe lots at $500 each. With the Depression, however, the market for Tahoe property dwindled to nearly nothing and Biltz thereupon concocted a plan which not only revitalized his own lagging career, but also pumped new capital into Nevada's devastated economy.

Biltz compiled a list of the 200 persons in the United States who owned personal fortunes of $10 million or more. He then set about selling these people Nevada domiciles with high-priced real estate thrown in. His sales pitch was based on the fact that many states, floundering to maintain services which Nevada had never provided at all, were tinkering with their tax structures in ways that pinched the wealthy. Nevada did not. By combining an encyclopedic understanding of the tax laws, exhaustive research into the personal foibles and preferences of his millionaire prospects, and an endless willingness to take pains on their behalf, Biltz enticed an estimated 50 to 60 millionaires to Nevada domiciles. He settled them at Lake Tahoe, in exclusive Reno neighborhoods and on the great ranches in Nevada's vast interior.

With the notable exception of Max Fleischmann, however, few of these immigrant millionaires put their money where their mailbox was. Most of them were content to remain as Nevada's star boarders, free to come and go as they pleased, but without kitchen privileges in state politics.

Upon the collapse of the Wingfield empire, Biltz himself came into considerable influence, but he was overshadowed by one of Wingfield's old Tonopah neighbors and bitterest enemies, Pat McCarran. McCarran leapt into the political vac-

SOUTHERN PACIFIC

Jim McKay and Bill Graham with their friend and fellow fight promoter, Jack Dempsey.

uum to win a U.S. Senate seat in 1933. From that moment he became the leading political force in the state and an increasingly influential figure in Washington.

The divorce trade, meanwhile, continued as robust as ever. During the 1930s, the Riverside Hotel, acting like a passenger liner on a perpetual six-week cruise, hired a Social Director. The job was to ensure that no guest needed to endure a single unwanted moment of solitude. The Riverside's Old Corner Bar was crowded every night with couples waiting out their six weeks so they could marry. George Hart, the piano player there, married tractor heiress Marcia Farrell Keresey, but continued working. It was a common occurrence for the telephone resting on the piano to ring with calls from Vienna, New York, Sidney or Philadelphia and the callers to request "their song." Hart would place the receiver on the piano and play for them — as often as not the perennial Reno favorite "I'll Take Care of Your Cares." Thousands of miles away a couple would relive, for a moment at least, their heady romantic days and nights in Reno.

Six weeks in Reno were within the reach of thousands who could not have managed three months. In 1943 nearly 6,000 divorces were granted in the Washoe County Court House and the proceedings had been whittled down to average less than four minutes each. When Judge Thomas Moran died at the age of 70 he had personally granted more than 27,000 divorces.

To the rest of the nation, teased by the media, Reno seemed wider-open than ever, but in fact the Biggest Little City was toning down considerably. In place of Graham and McKay and their gangster clients, Reno's prime movers were a new generation of businessmen gamblers led by Pappy Smith and his sons. They had their flamboyant moments, but they were basically storekeepers. In 1937 another newcomer entered the Bingo business on Virginia street: Bill Harrah, who would eventually become the biggest gambler in the world.

During World War II the Army pressured the city into closing The Stockade, and another symbol of the old Reno was no more.

The war's end accelerated the changes taking place within the city. Reno was no longer isolated. An increasingly affluent and mobile California population discovered the highway up over the Sierra and spent Reno weekends of more or less in-

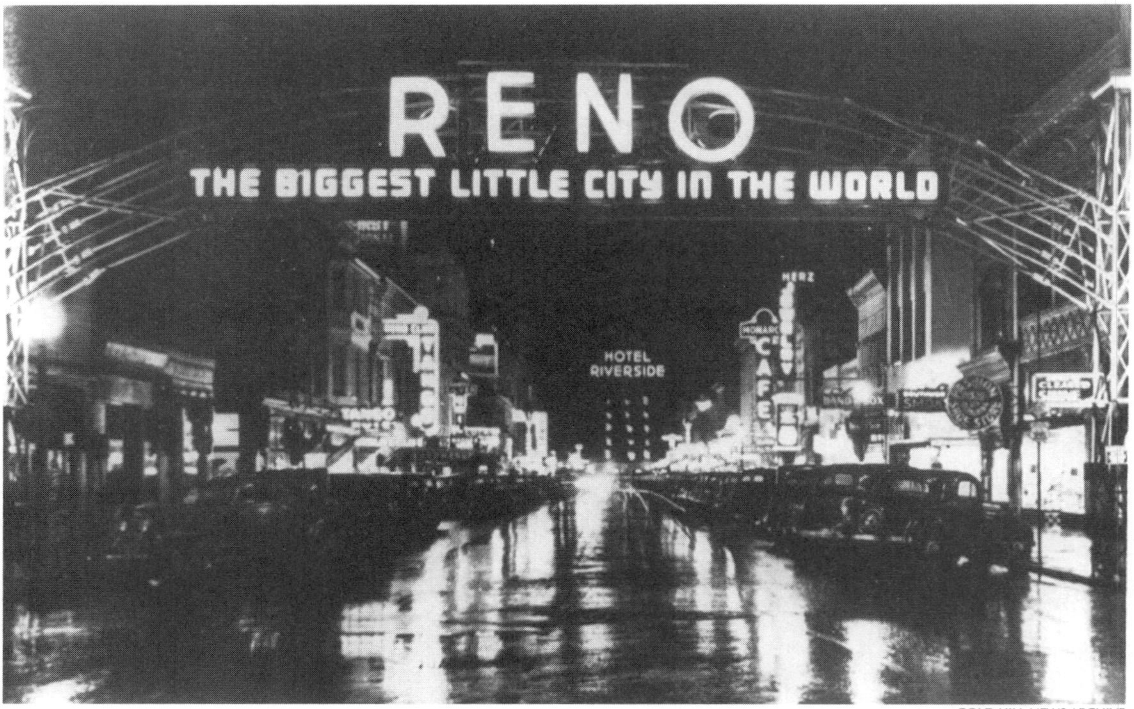

GOLD HILL NEWS ARCHIVE

The Reno Arch, looking down Virginia Street.

nocent hilarity in the busy little casinos on Virginia Street. The city prospered.

Ironically, this surge of prosperity presented the new generation of Reno gamblers with a new problem. Reno's conservative element had been content to look the other way when gambling was confined to the rowdy element. When gambling joined divorce as big business in the community, genteel society began to grumble. The gamblers, not yet big enough to have great influence, took heed. They paid more attention to appearances than the people they were at pains to appease. They policed their operations carefully, not merely to prevent cheating, but to eliminate any hint of the unsavory. Prostitutes were made unwelcome and drunks were quieted quickly or hustled out the back door. Sizeable contributions were made to good causes and in every way possible the gamblers behaved like the solid citizens they were striving to become.

Their efforts have paid off. If none of them were ever admitted into the inner circle of old-line Reno society, neither were they badgered or held back as they might have been.

In 1946 Pappy Smith was flying war surplus barrage balloons from the roof of Harold's Club to attract attention. Two years later the more subdued Harrah's Club was doing so well (190 employees, 1000 pairs of dice a month) that a reporter from the Saturday Evening Post came to admire.

By the middle 1950s, when old John Harrah had retired and young Bill had quit drinking, it was clear that they had perfected the Woolworth techniques of the Smith family into a Sears Roebuck approach of their own: fastidious housekeeping, no hint of roughhouse or vulgarity, and attractive employees to smother customers in services.

As the Smiths had done before him, Harrah shocked the industry, not by hiring women dealers but by employing efficiency experts to study his gambling floor as if it were a factory. By 1965 his smooth, efficient casinos — he had opened a second at Lake Tahoe in 1955 — had made him the greatest gambler in the world. Howard Hughes later bought the title when he went on his historic buying spree in Las Vegas.

In the 1970s the first generation of businessmen gamblers were passing from the scene. Pappy Smith died, and the Smith family sold Harolds Club to Hughes' Summa Corporation. Harrah's went public.

In May, 1978, as the huge new MGM Grand Hotel opened its doors, bulldozers were bashing down the old brick Overland Hotel across from the railroad depot to make room for a major expansion of Harrah's. Barely two months later, as their licenses became effective at midnight June 30, four new casinos opened simultaneously in downtown Reno amid a festive Fiscal New Year's Eve celebration.

Symmetrically enough, Bill Harrah died that night, and Reno entered a new era in which it grows bigger and blander, but does not change much. Perhaps the new age of Reno is best expressed, not by the MGM Grand (which has gone through three owners already and is now the Grand Sierra Resort) but at the corner of Second and Virginia Streets where Harrahs has transformed the old marble and granite First National Bank building into a slot machine arcade. The fourth-floor office from which George Wingfield commanded his empire is now occupied by Harrah's corporate clerks.

Now, with the Riverside converted to artists' live-work studios and the Mapes gone altogether, the massive and magnificent Silver Legacy has risen between the Eldorado and Circus Circus, to make an enormous connected complex of three major casino hotels. It magnifies Reno's attraction as a gambling destination and firmly centers the downtown action north of the railroad tracks for the first time since 1868.

But casinos are playing a diminished role in modern Reno as the region's economic diversification efforts have attracted significant manufacturing and distribution companies to industrial parks to the south and east.

At Lake Tahoe meanwhile, casino development stopped at the south shore with four major properties and two smaller ones. Recently, after nearly 50 years of glaring across Highway 50, Harrah's suddenly swallowed Harvey's. A major project, in which an enormous new roadside hotel anchors a tram lift to the summits above, is just down the boulevard on the California side. At the north shore there are four casinos, smaller than the south shore giants and more relaxed. The upscale communities of Crystal Bay and Incline Village are flourishing, and the lake grows progressively murkier.

Verdi

In 1864 a California lumber company established a logging and sawmill town at Crystal Peak on the eastern flank of the Sierra Nevada a short distance north of O'Neil's Crossing on the Truckee River. By 1868 the town had grown to 1500 people, most of them engaged in cutting and sawing the timbers required by the eastward-snaking Central Pacific Railroad, and in working small gold and silver deposits. The CPRR tracks bypassed the town, however, and by 1869 most of Crystal Peak's vitality had been transplanted to the new railroad townsite at the old crossing on the Truckee half a mile to the southeast. It was christened Verdi to honor the composer, but pronounced in the uniquely Nevada fashion as VUR-dye.

VERDI	
Reno	12
Fernley	72
Carson City	42
Laughlin	555

Verdi's saw, lathe, and shingle mills buzzed incessantly to serve the California market, and by the 1880s the little town had become one of the main collection and storage points for winter ice which found ready markets in California's valley and coastal towns during the summer.

MAX WINTHROP

Fishing along the Truckee River, near Verdi.

Verdi's place in history is secure as the site of the first train robbery in the West. Shortly after midnight on November 5, 1870, five men boarded the east-bound cars at Verdi. When the locomotive left the station, the passenger cars had been uncoupled and left standing on the track. The locomotive, pulling only the mail car and express car, chuffed eastward to a stone culvert, where the engineer was ordered to stop. The robbers opened both cars, putting the train crew in the mail car under guard while they struggled to open the Wells Fargo & Co. treasure boxes. The robbers found $41,600 in the shipment, hurriedly divided it at the edge of the roadbed, and scattered into the night after barricading the track. Within a week every member of the gang had been captured and $39,500 of the stolen money recovered. Two of the men turned state's evidence against the rest and were released; the others drew sentences of from five to 23-1/2 years in the penitentiary.

ANDREW BARBANO

Parts of Verdi remain pastoral despite recent urbanization.

The train robbery was the single exciting week in more than a century-and-a-quarter of calm. Nevertheless, Verdi could boast of a short-line logging railroad of its own before the 20th century was very old. By the 1930s logging had virtually ceased and Verdi was subsisting on the railroad and highway traffic. US 40 uncoiled itself to pass through the town after its sinuous passage over Donner Summit, and by the late 1940s and early 1950s the town was best known for the large Bill & Effie's Truck Stop.

Bill and Effie sold the truck stop, and the new owners moved it out of the center of town to the edge of the freeway and christened it Boomtown, a roadside phenomenon that has far surpassed its origins. The truck driver is still king here, but we ordinary mortals are welcome too. Recently an immense Cabela's sporting goods temple (store is too pale a word) has opened, with enough merchandise to equip the world for the outdoors.

The old logging town shows evidence of its up and downs, but the setting alone is worth the short detour. A dirt road meanders into the Sierra by way of Dog Valley, and at several scenic points along its length the Forest Service has developed campgrounds. The Washoe County Park Department maintains the beautiful Crystal Peak Park at river's edge just south of town.

Gerlach

THIS MODEST OUTPOST 90 miles north of Reno in northern Washoe County is in a region much traveled by the westward-bound covered wagons, and before them groups of Native Americans swept in their turns through this pass between the Smoke Creek and Black Rock deserts. The hot springs here had attracted attention from everyone journeying wearily through. Logically enough, the railroad came this way too, and so the little town was born.

GERLACH	
Fernley	75
Winnemucca	98
Sparks	108
Ruth	418

Modern-day Gerlach is described locally as "a small town filled with small wonders."

The largest of these small wonders are the natural hot springs, which have been recently transformed from muddy bogs into a real pool, tile and all, with changing rooms, showers, even heated floors for your tender feet — quite a magnificent touch in the otherwise heedless wilderness, but closed at press time, with re-opening uncertain.

MAX WINTHROP

Gerlach.

Another local wonder is Bruno's Country Club, famous in three states and eight counties for its homemade ravioli. You can get food and drink to go, if you like, and dine in the shade of the 1909 water tower across the highway, as many a king of the road has done.

There's Planet X, eight miles north of town, the pottery studio that has attracted a worldwide clientele. And there is Doobie Road, a delightful automotive excursion into the artistic vision of Dwayne Williams, about a mile out of town to the north. This treasure was significantly damaged by a gully-washing thundershower a few years back. It is being slowly restored to something like its former magnificence, but it's slow going and Dwayne himself isn't around to supervise the effort.

Gerlach is the gateway to the annual Burning Man Festival held on the playa just north of town, an ecstatic eight-day celebration of life and art that comes to its fiery finish on Labor Day Weekend.

MAX WINTHROP

This sign leads to fine pottery.

Pyramid Lake

NOWADAYS THE 33-mile drive to Pyramid Lake from Sparks via Nevada Route 445 (it's 16 miles via Nevada Route 447 from Wadsworth on I-80) carries you through the slurb spreading north through a succession of shallow depressions between low, brush-stubbled hills. It is a pleasant drive, but long enough to create an awareness of the desert's monotony. After a dozen miles the urban fringe is left behind and when the last rise is topped, the eyesearing expanse of Pyramid Lake stretched out before you is an astonishing sight: a sheet of electric blue cupped between pastel mountains of chalky pinks and greys.

John C. Fremont was the first American to gaze down at Pyramid Lake, and his journal entry of 10 January 1844 records his impressions of the lake: "...we continued our way up the hollow, intending to see what lay beyond the mountain. The hollow was several miles long, forming a good pass; the snow deepening to about a foot as we neared the summit. Beyond, a defile between the mountains descended rapidly about two thousand feet; and, filling up all the lower space, was a sheet of green water, some twenty miles broad. It broke upon our eyes like the ocean."

Despite the enormous changes which have overtaken the world since Fremont's visit in 1844, Pyramid Lake (which he named for a tufa rock formation on the eastern shore) remains as strikingly beautiful and as enchanting as it was before he came.

Pyramid Lake is not like Tahoe. It is shallower, warmer, and substantially more alkaline than Tahoe, lower in elevation, and not so easily accessible. But these differences are not the decisive ones. Tahoe is charmingly beautiful. Pyramid is a shock; in addition to its primitive, challenging beauty, it projects a profound sense of antiquity. Gazing out across its surface is an experience almost four-dimensional.

Pyramid is a favorite hunting ground for the fishermen who wade out deep and cast for trout even in wintry weather. In ancient times this fishery was a magnificent survival resource. For a while, when the first wave of white settlers came, it was big business. Commercial fishermen harvested 100 tons of trout between winter 1888 and spring 1889, for shipment all over the U.S. By 1912 a local entrepreneur was hiring as many as 50 Paiute fishermen to catch and ship from ten to 15 tons of trout a week for sale in the southern Nevada mining camps.

In 1925 a Paiute named Johnny Skimmerhorn caught the world's record cutthroat here; a 41-pounder. Photographs taken in the twenties and thirties show celebrities like Clark Gable struggling manfully to show off a pair of enormous cutthroat, or a group of Nevadans peeking out from behind a curtain of silvery fish that stretches eight feet long: a day's catch. But in the 1940s the cutthroats were gone. Restocking began in the early 1950s, and today five to ten pounders are not uncommon at Pyramid.

There are two fish hatcheries at the lake, one for cui-ui, the other raising and readying cutthroat trout for introduction into the lake. At the larger Numana Hatchery south of Nixon eggs from spawning adults are taken and raised to fingerling size. Tours are offered when staff is available, and your guide will probably be a tribal member (call 775-574-0500 for tour schedules).

The Numana Hatchery is near the site of the first Battle of Pyramid Lake. In May, 1860, some men at Williams Station, a trading post, saloon and stagecoach station on the Carson River, kidnapped and raped two 12-year-old Paiute girls. A force of Paiute men from Pyramid Lake then raided the station and rescued the girls, killing five of their tormentors and burning the buildings. A single survivor escaped to Carson City and passed the alarm: Indian Massacre!

A force of 105 volunteers was hastily assembled from Carson City, Silver City, Gold Hill and Virginia City. Major William Ormsby commanded the volunteers, leading them

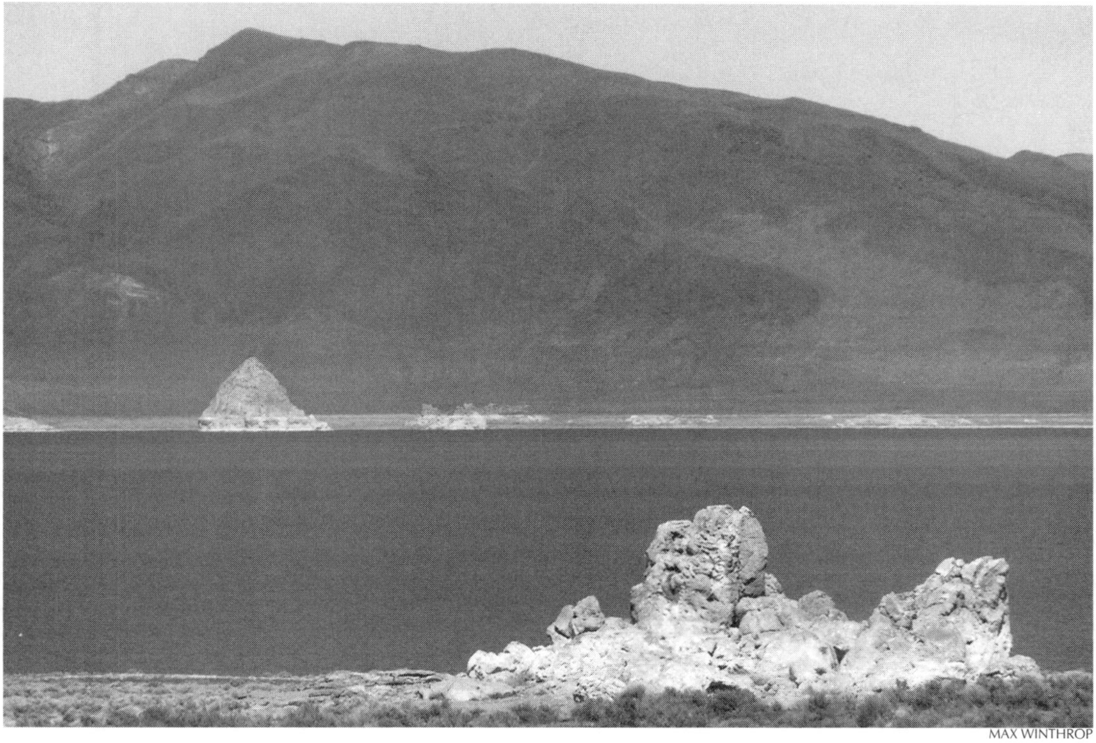

Tufa mounds face the ancient Pyramid across the lake.

into an ambush about five miles south of the lake. Numaga's Paiute fighters killed more than 70 of the white men, including Major Ormsby, and the rest ran for their lives. In June a force of regular soldiers from California, including an artillery piece, attacked the Paiutes and drove them away from the lake until an informal truce was effected in August. These battles prompted the establishment of Fort Churchill on the Carson River.

Everybody enjoys Pyramid Lake in the summertime; serious fishermen are here year around.

Pyramid Lake is not only quite beautiful, largely undeveloped and thus unspoiled, it is also a significant historical locale and well worth a visit. Fishing, camping and day-use permits are available at the Ranger Station just south of Sutcliffe on the lake's southwest shore, at the convenience stores in Nixon and Wadsworth, or at any Long's Store in Reno and Sparks.

A visitor center with a well-stocked store and an impressive photographic exhibit devoted to the life of the lake is located at Sutcliffe on the west shore, as is Crosby's Lodge, a fisherman's clubhouse serving hot food and cold beer.

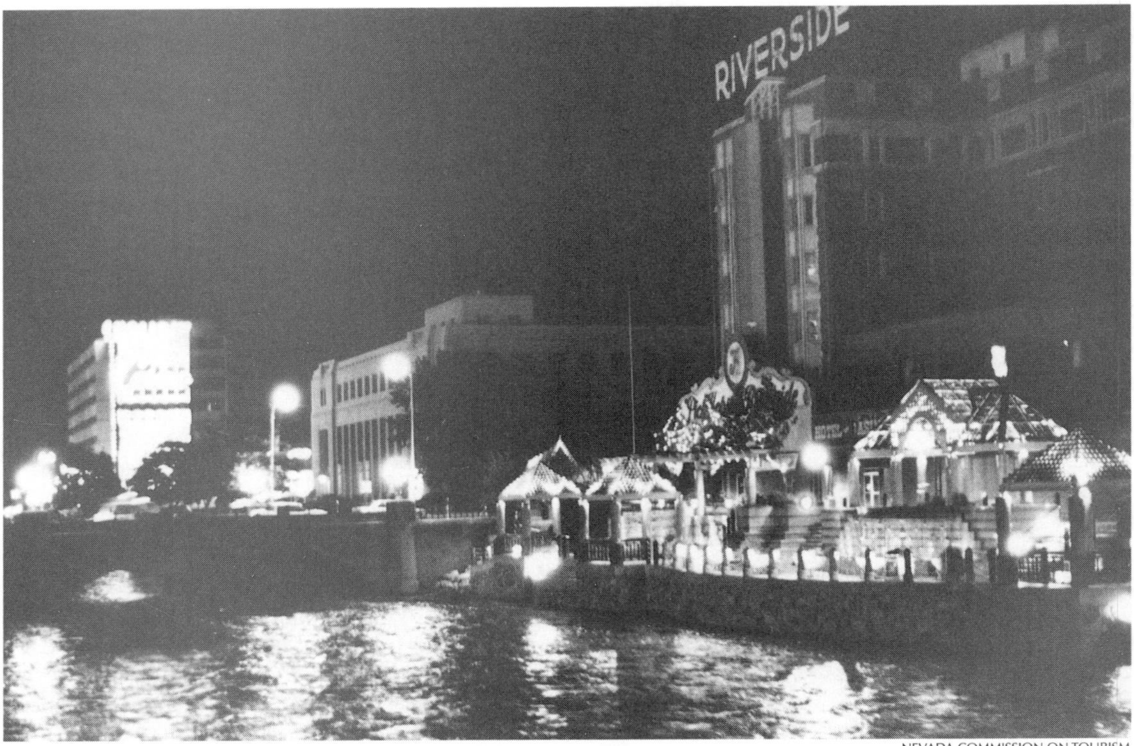

NEVADA COMMISSION ON TOURISM

Reno at dusk.

Reno

ON A FINE SPRING DAY in 1928, Reno held a great municipal celebration at the railroad tracks in honor of paving the two-lane highway over Donner Summit to California. As the band burst into a brassy ragtime, and the bankers, bootleggers and other leading citizens beamed with pride, neon letters on the new iron arch spanning Virginia Street blazed with light for the first time. "RENO," they bragged against a downtown skyline of Edwardian brick, "The Biggest Little City in the World."

RENO	
Virginia City	24
Carson City	30
Elko	289
Ely	317
Las Vegas	446

The iron arch is gone now, replaced by a brighter version, jazzier than the Jazz Age original, and Reno's golden age of society divorcees, bootleg whiskey and basement gambling rooms is gone with it.

Modern Reno dates from another fine spring noontime, almost 50 years to the day after that gaudy little celebration, when an enormous tan tower rose 26 stories from its bright, light-bejewelled base on an enormous asphalt pad near the edge of the airport, far from the city center. The $131,000,000 MGM Grand Hotel greeted every incoming flight to Reno-Cannon International the same way the old arch greeted every train at the railroad depot downtown.

The MGM Grand — it's the freshly painted Grand Sierra Resort now — was the flagship of Nevada's gamblinghouse fleet, the most magnificent pleasure liner ever launched on Nevada's desert sands, and its crew was the pick of the industry. There were glamorous big-name stars and the fabulous Hello, Hollywood review, a magnificent arcade of expensive shops and a gambling floor as big as two football fields. It was the class of the wagering world, and if the title has since been taken by the astonishing new resorts being built in Las Vegas, the huge hotel is still a potent reminder that Reno offers every pleasure a fun-seeking visitor could want, from world class cuisine to pee wee golf.

Twenty years later the Silver Legacy drew the center of attention back downtown. This enormous gambling theme park is elaborately designed and connected organically to its next door neighbor, the El Dorado. It contains, among other attractions, the Brews Brothers restaurant and microbrewery, the first brew pub in a major Nevada hotel casino.

As Reno has continued to grow, development has proceeded in new neighborhoods. Wells Avenue, south and east of the city center, is a lively international — largely hispanic — district with numerous shopping and dining opportunities.

Still, Reno's heart is downtown. The city was was born at Lake's Crossing where Myron Lake's bridge brought the Virginia City road across the Truckee River, and from there the changes wrought since the opening of the MGM Grand are easily visible to the naked eye.

The Riverside, once the grandest hotel in the state, has been half-demolished and converted to artists' studios. The Mapes, built in 1948 as Nevada's tallest building, and the Harolds Club that Pappy Smith built into the biggest and best-known casino in the world, are gone.

A Truckee River Walk extends east and west. Eastward it follows the river all the way through Sparks nearly to the enclosing hills. You'll pass trout fishermen if you walk this way. To the west it takes you past the little amphitheater where the pleasing noon concerts are performed in the summer months, and on across Arlington Street into the "City of Trembling Leaves" (as author Walter Van Tilburg Clark described it) where cottonwoods and elms shade rambling Victorians, left over from a time when divorcees waited out an endless six-week residence for their freedom.

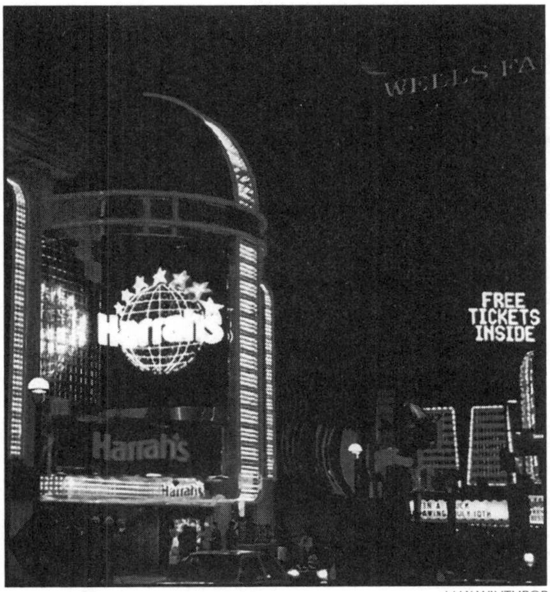

MAX WINTHROP

Virginia Street.

Continue on another pleasant half-mile to Idlewild Park with its rose gardens, broad lawns and ducky ponds. The trail proceeds on, and on, and on, and on about as far as you're prepared to hike, with a small picnic and rest area at its end, many miles from Lake's Crossing.

To the north, Virginia Street between the river and the railroad track is brilliant with casino facades. Newcomers have added to the city's downtown dimensions and moved its center north to Circus Circus. Two of the city's most popular casino hotels, the Peppermill and the Atlantis, are well south on Virginia Street, near the Convention Center.

But enough of geography, let's talk food; here are a some suggestions:

The Eldorado. Here you can choose from one of the state's finest gourmet dining rooms, La Strada, or the city's most highly praised buffet, or six other stylish and distinctive dining choices, including Roxy's. The Carano family has adopted the strategy that brought John Asquaga his fame and success in Sparks: serve the best food. Harrah's offers first class gourmet dining in its classic Steak House. Circus Circus is home to the surprising Kokopeli's, a candidate for the best sushi in town. The Siena offers an interesting bargain in its haute cuisine Lexie's Restaurant from 5 to 5:45 pm nightly: your choice of four entrees, with salad and dessert for $18.95. Oceano in the Peppermill might have the best pan roasts in the Truckee Meadows, but to be certain you'd have to test the Oyster Bars at John Asquaga's in Sparks and the Atlantis on south Virginia Street.

You don't have to find a casino to have something good to eat, of course.

Day on and day out, the best lunch for the price might be at Mimi's at 5090 S. Kietzke. Unless it's The Grill at the corner of McCarran and Talbot, or maybe Francis' Asian Bistro in the Caughlin Ranch Shopping Center at McCarran and Caughlin Parkway. Simon's on Lakeside Drive near Bartley Ranch is an American-fare bistro that caters to seniors with good daily specials and domino tournaments at the bar. India Kabob at Virginia and Vassar offers a popular buffet lunch from 11 to 3 always good. The Spicy Pickle on Longley and The Pita Pit on S. Virginia are both good if you can tolerate the crowds and the precious names. At Thai Chili at 1030 South Virginia Street traditionally attired servers deliver flavorful Thai cooking in a nicely designed setting. If you're feeling adventurous, Inez's Half Way Cafe at 2501 E. Fourth is a local favorites with an ecelectic clientele.

Dinner? Certainly: Try the Stone House Cafe at 1907 S. Arlington; Johnny's Ristorante Italiano way out west 4th St. is very good, and the 4th Street Bistro still farther west is too, LuLou's at 1470 S. Virginia serves good food in small portions; Romano's Macaroni Grill farther south, 5505 S. Virginia at McCarran, features flamboyant chefs in an open kitchen; Zozo's at 3440 Lakeside is good but small and sometimes crowded; Beaujolais downtown on West Street is very French, the Bangkok on Mt. Rose Street just west of Virginia is awesome Thai; you'll have a great Asian/Chinese dinner at Peony in the far northwest at 6340 Mae Ann off Robb Drive. The Santa Fe Hotel on Lake Street is one of Reno's best-known Basque restaurants, having served four generations of local folks their hearty working-man's family style suppers. Louis' Basque Corner, at Fourth and Evans is another traditional Basque favorite.

Art also abounds in downtown Reno, especially during the annual summer Arttown celebration. A unique collection of colorful, carefully sculpted shapes and gleaming surfaces with powerful emotional impact is displayed at The National Automobile Collection at Mill and Lake Streets.

At the E.L. Weigand Museum, 160 W. Liberty, the exhibits are an eclectic mix of traveling shows and local artists. The Stremmel Gallery on south Virginia Street is a busy showplace of leading artists, and there is a row of galleries on Sierra Street between First and Second.

The University of Nevada Reno campus adjoining north Virginia Street is another locus for artists, exhibits and performances of every kind. Campus events are listed at the Jot Travis Student Union (775-784-6589). The Gutzon Borglum statue of Comstock mining tycoon John Mackay has been a landmark for almost a century, and you'll enjoy the minerals collection inside the Mackay School of Mines building behind him. If you're a late-night movie watcher, you may feel a shock or recognition as you cross the great lawn of this classical Jeffersonian quadrangle. Itπs not merely that it's modeled after the University of Virginia, it's — can it be? Yes! This is where Andy Hardy went to College! (in the 1937 movie starring Mickey Rooney, that is.)

The Nevada State Historical Society is located at the farwestern edge of the campus. Here you'll find handsomely mounted and informative exhibits depicting the physical and social environments established in the ebb and flow of Nevada history, as well as research collections and facilities.

The queerly shaped building across the way is the Fleischmann Planetarium. Inside is a specially constructed domed theater where a unique cinematic process provides visitors with the "experience" of space flights, an eagle's eye view of the growth and development of a fluffy wisp of cloud into a ferocious thunderstorm, the birth and death of a star, and other cosmic wonders of the universe.

NEVADA COMMISSION ON TOURISM

The Thomas Flyer, winner of the New York to Paris Race, in 1908.

Mountain View Cemetery, Reno

MAX WINTHROP

Rancho San Rafael a few blocks west of the University, is an enormous county park, with open green space, playgrounds and a gallery devoted to the interests of Wilbur May, the May Co. Department Store heir whose charmed life ended peacefully a few years ago. The exhibits center on the animals whose lives he ended on hunting trips, and on the art which he collected as avidly as he collected heads. The autumn Great Reno Balloon Race ascensions are made from here in a scene of magical frenzy.

Speaking of green space, no law says you have to confine your graveyard strolling to old mining towns. You might enjoy a half hour at Mountain View Cemetery, accessible from Stoker Avenue via west Fourth Street. Only a few of the old-fashioned angels, lambs or obelisks survive the trend to gang-mowing, but this burying ground contains the earthly remains of some of Nevada's greatest figures from the past. Pay your respects to Senator Pat McCarran, Mayor Ed Roberts, the Pittman Brothers, Bill Stead, Alf Doten and thousands of others more or less prominent in their lifetimes. Their present serenity belies the passions that once stirred them, and the neat rows and simple plaques bear no relation to the complex and sometimes tangled lives they lived. Mausoleums of the rich and famous (now mostly forgotten) still stand in great gloomy rows, and a dirt-surfaced Potter's Field on the downslope behind the maintenance sheds provides additional food for thought.

For miniature golf, and who doesn't love that?, there are three fantastic courses at Magic Carpet Golf, four miles south of downtown on Virginia Street, and it's open every day, weather permitting.

Welcome to Reno

Museums

NEVADA HISTORICAL SOCIETY
1650 N. Virginia Street. 775-688-1190
Nevada's oldest cultural institution collects and preserves the records and mementos of Nevadans and provides public access through exhibitions, tours, educational programs and publications. Whether a display of Nevada art, a traveling show, or a special exhibit, there's always something new at the Historical Society. Walking distance from downtown Reno.

Shopping

THE NEVADA STORE
3362 Lakeside Court. 775-825-3318
The Nevada Store proudly represents ALL THINGS NEVADA in the Moana West Shopping Center. Member of the Made In Nevada program sponsored by the State of Nevada Commission on Economic Development. Wolf Pack, Battle Born, Silver State logo items, local honey, art, candy, soaps, flags, jewelry, Nevada shaped gift baskets.

SUNDANCE BOOK STORE
1155 W 4th Street #106. 775-786-1188
Sundance Bookstore and Music was founded in 1985, and is locally owned and operated. Our store hours are 9am to 9pm Monday through Friday, and 10am to 6pm Saturday and Sunday. We have an extensive selection of Nevada books, maps, and gifts and welcome special orders.

RENO NEWS BUREAU

Wild Waters, a summertime oasis in Sparks.

Sparks

ADJACENT TO RENO on the east, Sparks was an afterthought of the railroad's, created in 1904 to replace Wadsworth as the big switching yard on this section of the Southern Pacific Railroad. Sparks is Nevada's fourth-largest city and offers abundant services to travelers. The Chamber of Commerce provides area information at the little railroad station on Victorian Avenue just west of Pyramid Way.

SPARKS	
Reno	1
Pyramid Lake	33
Haawthorne	129
Henderson	453

Originally named Harriman after the railroad tycoon, Sparks was rechristened to honor Governor John T. Sparks, whose ranch was nearby. This gesture of respect and admiration was made just as an anti-railroad rebellion boiled up in the legislature, eventually resulting in the creation of the Public Service Commission to regulate tariffs.

Family oriented and hard-working, Sparks was so solid and dull that it sometimes became the butt of local jokes. Early example: "Reno is so close to Hell you can see Sparks."

In 1907 a reform-minded city council outlawed the popular local pastime of driving up to a saloon in a buggy and having drinks at the curb. Other than the endless banging of the boxcars in the switching yard and the clanging and hissing and whistling and squealing of the through trains in and out of the station, everything was quiet in Sparks for nearly 50 years as the little city grew slowly with the railroad. Sparks eventually achieved a place in history by having the longest single-sided street (B Street, now Victorian Avenue) in America.

In the 1950s Sparks changed. Acre upon acre of brown composition roofs blossomed up out of the brown dirt as one curbed-and-guttered subdivision after another appeared in the grazing lands of the northeast. For more than a dozen years the growth continued, and Sparks became even quieter as a residential community in which the railroad played a much diminished role. In the 1970s Sparks began to grow in a new and unexpected direction. Family farms and pasturelands south of the city were transmogrified into lowrise warehousing, small manufacturing plants and light industry connected by an asphalt grid of new streets. In recent years new residential neighborhoods have taken over the sagebrush far to the north of the old downtown.

Now Sparks has changed again. John Ascuaga

gave Sparks its first skyscraper, and now the homely old business structures of Harriman are being replaced or restored to a confectionary Victorian dream of luxury and romance they never aspired to a century ago. B Street — oops, Victorian Avenue — is bright with lights and lively with public events the year around now.

GARY ELAM

Victorian Square is Sparks' downtown activity center.

Some of the architecture may be more Walt Disney than Queen Victoria, but there's no doubt that the vivacious scene downtown reflects a brighter, more inviting character for Sparks than ever before.

In Sparks any discussion of food starts (and sometimes ends) with John Ascuaga's Nugget, where huge hotel towers and an immense parking garage were built on the enormous success of the eight restaurants — the Rotisserie Room, the Oyster Bar, Trader Dick's, and others — in this otherwise unremarkable gambling hall. Some of Nevada's best food is served at the Nugget, but there are other enjoyable options in Sparks as well.

The Silver Club across the Avenue has a grand buffet and restaurant, and Jack's Coffee Shop down the street serves a classic breakfast and lunch menu. Farther east at 846 Victorian Avenue is the Great Basin Brewing Co., a brewpub established in 1993 caters to a mostly local clientele with a hearty food menu in addition to the prize-winning beers, ales and porter. You can pull your rig in at a truck stop and join the truck drivers in feeding at platters of hearty fare: Sierra Sid's is on McCarran just north of the freeway; the Alamo is just south of the freeway between the Sparks and Vista Avenue exits at the far eastern side of the city. At the southeast corner of McCarran and Prater you can choose between great Vietnamese food at Saigon 88 and the loong-established BJ's Barbecue. Ofelia's Mexican Food & Bakery at 1125 Rock Boulevard next to Butcher boy is authentically Mexican.

Enlightening the atmosphere on Sparks' east side is Wild Island, a water park devoted to providing enjoyment exhilarating or soothing as you please. The mountain peaks against the western sky seem especially lovely and far away from the splashing sprays of water and the eager voices of the children, and the summer sky is never brassier than when observed from an innertube meandering around on the long, slow sissy ride around the perimeter of the park. To experience the thrill of victory or the agony of defeat in the mildest possible way, you can also stop in at Adventure Golf next door and go a round or two.

MAX WINTHROP

The Sparks Chamber of Commerce.

GART ELAM

Washoe Lake in winter.

Washoe Valley

Bowers Mansion

20 MILES south of Reno, 10 miles north of Carson City via U.S. 395 and marked, paved access road on the west side of the valley. Built in the middle 1860s by Sandy and Eilley Bowers, the structure represented an attempt by the illiterate Scots prospector and his boarding house-keeper bride to live as grandly as their newfound Comstock wealth allowed. Furniture and appointments were shipped around Cape Horn from Europe after Sandy had sold his Gold Hill claim for enough money, as he said, "to throw at the birds." Throw it they did, much of it coming to rest in their two-story stone mansion.

Sandy died within a few years, but Eilley lived on long after the money had all been spent. She closed off progressively more of the immense stone house, ultimately selling the monument to grandeur and moving back to Virginia City where she lived out her years telling fortunes. "The Washoe Seeress," as she was known as an old woman, eked out a slender living by whispering of fortunes coming to her gullible clientele. She died broke.

The mansion passed through a number of hands before being acquired by Washoe County;

for a time during Prohibition it was operated as a road house and earned a faintly notorious reputation. The county has restored the old home to a condition approximating its original grandeur.

Tours of the mansion are conducted, there are picnic areas for groups and for families, broad lawns, a swimming pool, and a snack bar is open during seasons of good weather. Campsites are available at nearby Davis Creek Campground.

Franktown, a water stop on the V&T Railroad farther south, is where Will James (a convicted cattle rustler drom White Pine County who served his sentence in the State Prison at Carson City) wrote his best-selling "Smoky".

Washoe City

The small commercial cluster on the highway isn't exactly a true descendant of the old milling settlement, but it's at about the same locale. Much of what's here is geared to provide visitors with a cheery stop. There is a pioneer cemetery here, but the little log cabin beside the Cattlemen's restaurant isn't really a remnant of the frontier, it was built for a movie.

East side of Washoe Lake

New Washoe City spreads across the landscape to the east of Washoe Lake, an eclectic collection of homes, some brought here from elsewhere, some conventional tract-style houses (but horsier) and some profoundly individualistic efforts. There is a small commercial center with a convenience store and a few shops and services, but the main attraction here is Washoe Lake State Park.

The park is a comprehensive recreation area developed along the southeast shore of the broad, shallow lake. A succession of dry winters had left the lake completely dry in 1993, an enormous dry flat beginning to sprout brush. Now its waters sparkle again, and visitors are strolling the dunes, swimming and boating (no motors).

Carson City

THIS CALM AND PLEASANT CITY has been the Nevada capital since the Nevada Territory was established in 1861, and government has provided the dominant influence on the municipal character for a century and a half. While it doesn't have the size or reputation of Reno or Las Vegas, Carson City provides interest and enjoyment to visitors by virtue of its frontier architecture, historical attractions and its wide range of hospitalities. Children are easy to entertain here, and Carson City is no longer just a one-martini town.

CARSON CITY	
Minden	15
Stateline	26
Reno	30
Fallon	49

In 1851, Eagle Valley had been settled by ranchers, many of them Mormon families sent out from Salt Lake City. A few years later an energetic and enthusiastic booster named Abe Curry bought the richest part of the valley for $500 and a remuda of horses. In 1858 Curry plotted a townsite on his land and named it for the river that had itself been named in honor of John C. Fremont's most celebrated scout. In the spring of the next year, to his everlasting delight, the discovery of the Comstock Lode brought his townsite to life as a freight and transportation center. He then built the crude Warm Springs Hotel a mile to the east, and when Carson City was selected as the territorial capital in 1861, he leased it to the Legislature as a meeting hall.

The Territorial legislature established Carson City as the seat of Ormsby County (named for one of those killed at the Battle of Pyramid Lake). It then leased the Warm Springs Hotel to serve as the Territorial Prison, and hired their genial host and landlord, Abe Curry, to be its first warden. The property was eventually purchased by the state and is still a part of the state prison system — drive east on Fifth Street to see the gloomy sandstone walls across from the sewage treatment plant, or see it from the inside as the setting for the Tom Selleck movie "An Innocent Man."

Carson City was confirmed as Nevada's permanent capital upon statehood in 1864, and after that development was no longer completely dependent on the health of the Comstock mines. Until they began to decline in the 1880s, these mines provided Carson City with most of its economic importance as a freight and staging center, and as a marshalling point for much of the timber harvest in the Lake Tahoe basin.

GOLD HILL NEWS ARCHIVE

Governor's Mansion.

Long wooden flumes, capable of carrying enormous pine logs in a shallow spill of fast water, swooped down the steep eastern slope of the Sierra from Spooner Summit to Carson City. Scorched and smoldering where they had rubbed against the flume's sides in their dashing descent, the logs were fed into sawmills where they became timbers for the underground mines, and planed boards for the surface cities. The finished lumber was then loaded onto flatcars and rolled off to Silver City, Gold Hill and Virginia City via the Virginia & Truckee Railroad.

The V&T was completed between Carson City and Virginia City in 1869, with the railroad's shops and main offices in Carson City. Three years later, the V&T rails were extended north through Washoe Valley to the transcontinental railroad at Reno. By 1874, when the Comstock mines were reaching their peak production, 36 trains a day passed through Carson City. The huge sandstone V&T engine house and roundtable dominated the northeast corner of the city for well over a century. Neglected and falling into ruin ater the track was torn up in 1950, they have now been torn down, the stones sent to create winery facades in California's Napa Valley.

Like many another Nevada town in its youth, Carson City was made lively and occasionally dangerous by the presence of rootless, restless men. Shootings, stabbings and street brawls were commonplace around Nevada, but Carson City was unique in contending with outbreaks from the State Prison.

The strangest episode at the prison involved a renegade warden. In the spring of 1863 a change of administration resulted in the request for Warden

Mark Twain's First Day in Carson City

SAM AND ORION Clemens arrived in Carson City by stage coach in 1861. Orion had been appointed Secretary of the newly-formed Nevada Territory, and his younger brother was running away from the Civil War, hoping to be the secretary to the Secretary. Instead he became Mark Twain, and described 1860 Carson City this way when he wrote "Roughing It" a few years later:

"It was a 'wooden' town; its population two thousand souls. The main street consisted of four or five blocks of little white frame stores that were too high to sit down on but not too high for various other purposes. They were packed close together, side by side, as if room were scarce in that mighty plain. The sidewalk was of boards that were more or less loose and inclined to rattle when walked upon. In the middle of town, opposite the stores, was the 'plaza' which is native to all towns beyond the Rocky Mountains — a large, unfenced, level vacancy, with a liberty pole in it, and very useful for a place of public auctions, horse trades, and mass meetings, and likewise for teamsters to camp in. Two other sides of the Plaza were faced by stores, offices, and stables. The rest of Carson City was pretty scattering.

"We were introduced to several citizens, at the stage office and on the way up to the governor's from the hotel — among others to a R. Harris, who was on horseback; he began to say something, but interrupted himself with the remark"

"'I'll have to get you to excuse me a minute; yonder is the witness that swore I helped to rob the California coach — a piece of impertinent intermeddling, sir, for I am not even acquainted with the man.

Then he went over and began to rebuke the stranger with a six-shooter, and the stranger began to explain with another. When the pistols were emptied, the stranger resumed his work (mending a whiplash), and Mr. Harris rode by with a polite nod, homeward bound, with a bullet through one of his lungs, and several in his hips; and from them issued little rivulets of blood that coursed down the horse's sides and made the animal look quite picturesque. I never saw Harris shoot a man after that but it recalled that first day in Carson."

Dickerson's resignation so that a political supporter of the new governor could be rewarded. Dickerson refused to resign. The new warden was appointed anyhow, and in due course presented himself at the prison to take up his duties. Warden Dickerson refused to open the gate. The Governor, the Attorney General and the Secretary of State each drove east out Fifth Street to clear up the trouble, and each one in turn clattered back to town in frustration. A force of 60 riflemen and a howitzer had been drawn up before the prison gate before Dickerson surrendered and permitted himself to be superceded.

After the turn of the century Carson City participated vicariously in the Tonopah and Goldfield booms far to the south. Much of the freight and passenger traffic bound for those two celebrated cities was routed to Reno and then through Carson City to Mound House on the V&T railroad. From there the narrow gauge Carson & Colorado carried it to Sodaville where freight wagons and stage coaches — after 1903 they were automobiles — were waiting for the last leg of the journey.

This traffic through Carson City came to a sudden halt when the Southern Pacific built a branch line that bypassed the V&T altogether, connecting with the C&C from the east. The capital then resumed the quiet lifestyle that evolved after the decline of the Comstock, and which has only recently given way to modern times.

In an effort to replace the Tonopah-Goldfield traffic, the V&T extended its line south into the Carson Valley, but agriculture didn't generate anything like the revenues of mining boomtowns, and the railroad — and Carson City — slipped back into quiescense. In 1930 the population had dwindled to 1,800, about a quarter of what it had been at the peak of the mining boom 50 years earlier. "Life was peaceful and leisurely with time to enjoy friends and extended hospitality," a long-time resident recalled. "Money was no status symbol. No one was very rich, nor was anyone very poor. While life was quiet, it was never dull."

In 1933 the highway was paved through town, but for a long time afterward kids could roller skate on it without worrying too much about traffic. In those innocent days Carson City advertised itself as America's smallest state capital.

In 1960 Carson City regained its 1880 population level, and in the 1970s Ormsby County was merged into Carson City to consolidate government services in the 145.6 sq mi area. There are now 11 state capitals with smaller populations than Carson City, and only seven that are physically larger.

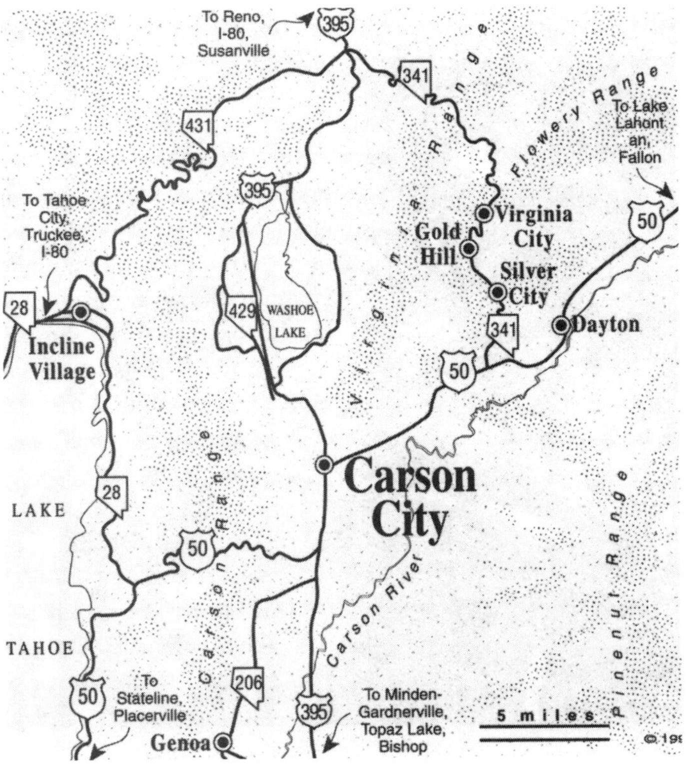

For all its 19th century appeal, the bright lights along Carson Street and the overwhelming presence of state government, Carson City really shines as a manufacturing center. Dozens of medium and small sized manufacturing firms have located in Carson City over the past 15 years. About 20% of Carson City's employment is now in manufacturing (compared to 5% for the state as a whole), a surprisingly high figure for a community 35 miles from the Interstate, with no railroad or regular air service. Some of the attraction may lie in the ski resorts in and around Lake Tahoe, but the large labor pool and relatively low wage scales and property prices are big attractions too. To see Carson City's industrial side, go east on Arrowhead Drive from north Carson Street to Goni.

Attractions for Visitors

Carson City Visitor Center

From Fairview and South Carson Street turn west and enter the Nevada State Railroad Museum grounds. You'll see the Visitor Center agead on the right. Stop in for an information packet (or go to www.visitcarsoncity.com and download a few things in advance), particularly the map of the Historic District. As you'll see, it contains a suggested walk. I will suggest another so you'll have two to choose from, but first, just walk next door

Nevada State Railroad Museum

The 19th century locomotives, tenders and cars on display are so enormous, so painstakingly restored and so immaculate that they loom like huge sculptures, idealized forms rather than working machines.

Don't consider that a criticism, quite the opposite, the effect is powerful and it will stay with you. And besides, the museum maintains a busy 2007 Operating Schedule for motorcar and steam trains on the Museum grounds.

And to put things into a smaller perspective, migrate to the far corner of the exhibit building to find a model railroad, still under construction at press time. The purpose of these miniature choo-choos in the same barn with the iron giants is to demonstrate other eras of railroading beyond the Victorian, and maybe to have something that moves and makes sounds in the stillness. The model layout is being assembled by volunteers, and other volunteers do the many hands-on jobs required to repair, restore, maintain and operate the gleaming beauties on display here. The building also houses one of the best take-a-present-home for the kids (or grand-kids) gift shops in Nevada. It's railroad oriented, which means there's something here for everyone (does anyone have too many striped engineer's caps?).

Nevada State Museum

The immense production of gold and silver from the Comstock mines prompted the establishment of a branch U.S. Mint in Carson City in 1866. The handsome structure on the northeast corner of Carson and Robinson Streets was built of prison-quarried sandstone and produced nearly $50 million in coin of the realm until it closed in 1933. The old coin stamps are still inside (and still put to use to make commemorative coins for special occasions). Exhibits range from stuffed animals in glass cases through walls bristling with guns to the unique facsimile of a silver mine down in the basement. Dat-So-La-Lee's woven baskets are a national treasure, and the mineral exhibits are exceptional. 600 N. Carson street.

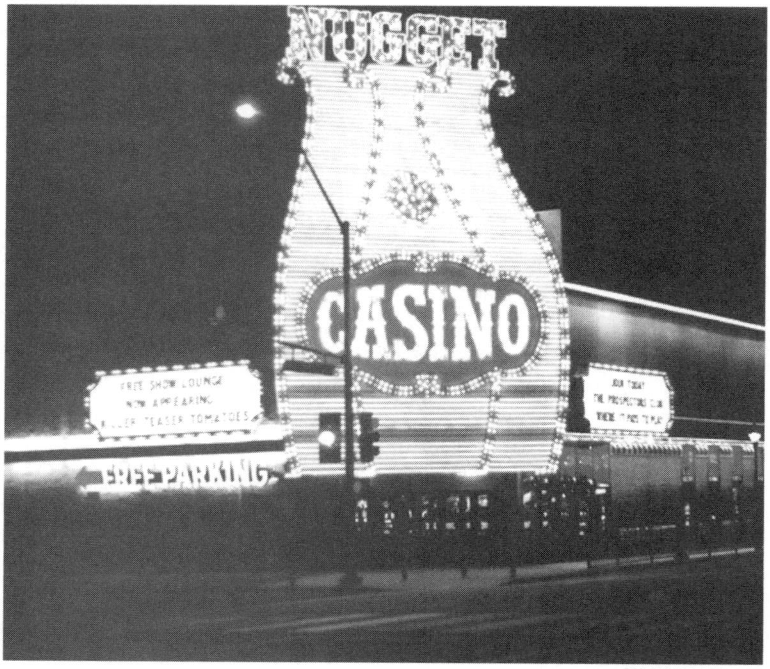

GREAT BASIN GALLERY

Carson City's brightest corner

The Great Basin Art Gallery

This former stagecoach station behind the old Supreme Court Building at the corner of 2nd and Curry streets displays fabulous, exquisite, wonder-

MAX WINTHROP

The Great Basin Art Gallery in Carson City.

ful Nevada art. Besides the brilliant Nevada landscapes of co-proprietor Jeff Nicholson, the gallery exhibits the work of many fine contemporary Nevada painters, sculptors and photographers. Enter at your own risk.

Historic District Walking Tour

While you're in the neighborhood, spend an hour wandering the streets of the historic district, map in hand. These houses reflect the early city of the 1860s and '70s, and the walk is almost enough to take you back there. To help with the time travel the Visitor Center will outfit you with a CD with dramatized tales of these houses and their inhabitants. You can listen to these on the web (www.visitcarsoncity.com), but the impact is undeniably stronger when you're standing (or parked) right at the gate at 502 North Division Street as Sam Clemens, aka Mark Twain (portrayed by McAvoy Layne), tells us about his elder brother Orion and this fine house he built in 1863. I used to recommend a certain path to follow through the streets of old Carson City, but I get to writing novels about the original residents (Orion's daughter Jenny died at the age of 10 and is buried here) and get all turned around in my directions. Thanks to me, visitors were wandering around for days looking for the Ferris Mansion — yes, the ferris wheel Ferris lived here for a while as a boy — and other marvelous residences in all the wrong places.

Nevada State Capitol

Carson Street, at the center of town. Open during office hours; no admission charge. This solemn old sandstone monument to the 19th century has been earthquake-proofed and renovated throughout, but its Alaskan marbled halls are still decorated with elaborate friezes, and hung with the portraits of former governors, back to "Broadhorns" Bradley and James Nye, the Virginian whose loyalty to the Union Abraham Lincoln rewarded with the governorship of the Nevada Territory in 1861. The present governor and other top state officials continue to do the state's business here, but the original Senate, Assembly and Supreme Court Chambers upstairs are most often used for exhibit space and usually open to visitors. The octagonal afterthought out the back door was added in 1908 when the burst of economic and political activity at Tonopah prompted an expansion of state government.

That oddity was the last benign addition in

the neighborhood of the capitol; now a gallery of architectural compromises presses in closer and closer around the old silver-domed building of the pioneers.

The promenade between the Capitol and the Legislature Building has become populated with sculpture. Kit Carson, lifesized and personal, is studying the trail from horseback, his rifle ready in his hand. Adolph Sutro, larger than life-size, is poised to drive his pick into the famous four-mile tunnel he dug to drain the Comstock mines. And Abe Curry, pioneer real estate developer and city builder, stands earnestly in a badly cut coat, clutching a bronze wad of blueprints like a club.

GOLD HILL NEWS ARCHIVE

The 1870 Nevada State Capitol.

Carson Hot Springs

1500 Hot Springs Road. Open daily 8 am-9 pm (11 in summer). Admission: kids $8, Adults $10. This natural hot water pool complex has been a favored relaxation spot since long before the white man came. The large mineral pool and the hot baths are the main attraction, but food, drink and entertainment are also available depending on the time of day. The water is also bottled for drinking (75¢ a gallon).

Lone Mountain Cemetery

Corner N. Roop Street and Beverley Drive. Open daily. No admission charge for brief visits. Stagecoach driver Hank Monk is probably better remembered than the pillars of local society (including five governors) who are buried around him here. It was Hank Monk who bounced Horace Greeley up the mountainside to California, lashing the horses over the rocky road and yelling down into the coach, "Keep your seat, Horace, I'll get you there on time!" As one of his contemporaries remarked, "He drank so much hard spirits that he often forgot what he was doing when it came to the incidental tasks connected with staging, and fed whiskey to his horses and watered himself on numerous occasions, thus becoming accidentally sober enough to handle the inebriated team."

Many pioneer families are represented here, some beneath or within elaborate burial monuments, others quite modest. A cast-iron civil war soldier keeps endless vigil.

The Childrens Museum

813 N. Carson Street. Open Tuesday through Thursday, 11-4. Admission: Adults, $4; under 12, $2; under 2 free. This venerable building was once Carson City's library, but there's no shushing inside these days, as toddlers through pre-teens find their way through this agreeable environment. A friendly hands-on entertainment for kids.

Two of the five best Nevada gift shops are in Carson City. One is at the State Railroad Museum on the south side of the city; most of the books and merchandise on sale here is choo-choo stuff of course, but it's good choo-choo stuff, some of it quite exalted, with a broad enough selection to find something good for every grandchild on your list and half the adults.

For the rest of them you will find something exceptional at the gift shop in the Legislature Building just south of the Capitol. Walk in through the front door just like an influence-peddler, get an affable nod from the pistol-packing concierge, and continue eastward into the building. About half way toward the back entrance you'll see the shop ahead on the left, a surprising range of Nevada goods, from books to parkas to cocktail glasses, nicely displayed and all bearing the Nevada state seal or that of the Legislature. For selection, quality and prices, this is a real hidden treasure.

Just over the Douglas County line to the south are a pair of large mercantile campuses with national name stores. The most-appreciated: In-N-Out Burger and Trader Joe's. I'll bet the traffic between Carson City and Reno is down by 10% since

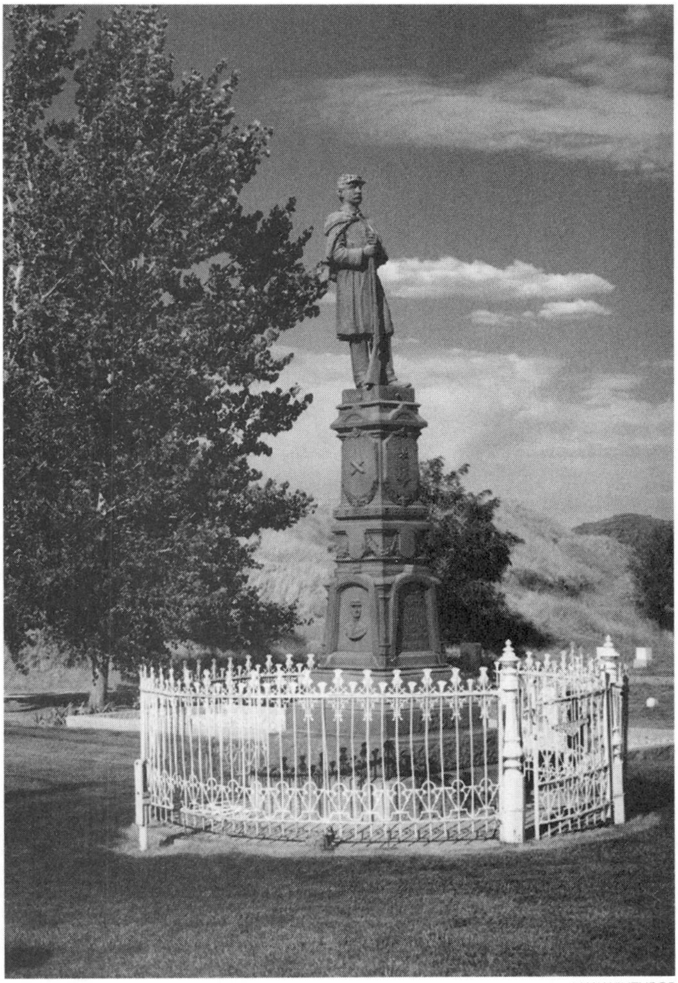

MAX WINTHROP

This cast iron sentinel stands eternal guard at the cemetery.

Carson got its own Trader Joe's.

All but a few of Carson City's hotels and motels lie along Carson Street (U.S. 395), and most of the rest are within a block or two. As elsewhere, the gambling houses shine the brightest: the Ormsby House is (still) closed for renovation but the nearby Carson Station and the Nugget a few blocks north have now been joined by the Gold Dust West and Slot World on the east side of town and the Fandango on the south as the city's biggest gambling houses. Bodine's, still farther south at the corner of US 395 and Clear Creek Road, is nearly ready to open at press time.

Dining options are numerous in Carson City nowadays.

Some breakfast favorites: Heidi's Dutch Mill, on Carson Street where US 50 turns east is an institution along US 395, serving omelettes and stylish lunch specialties until 2 pm. Or try the Cracker Box a few blocks east at Stewart Street for hearty breakfasts designed for duck hunters and truck drivers. The Villa Basque Deli 3113 North Roop, serves breakfast and lunch and you can take some tasty chorizo home with you.

More lunch possibilities: Z Bistro across the parking lot from the Basque Deli is an eclectic French-flavored temple of casual cuisine. Basil Thai at 311 N. Carson Street is a big local favorite. Mo & Sluggo's at 110 W. Telegraph Street serves a largely professional clientele, and the Fox & Firkin, in the St. Charles Hotel at Third and Carson Street is an inviting re-creation of Edwardian dash. Ghenghis Khan, in the Crossroads Shopping Center just east of Winnie Lane, serves a varied buffet with Mongolian barbecue. Red's Old 395 Grill serves lunch and dinner at 1055 S. Carson Street

More dinner selections: the elegant Glen Eagles at 3700 N. Carson Street; Bollywood, at 2329 N. Carson Street; Adele's, serving French cuisine in its doll house Victorian near the center of town at 1112 North Carson Street; Mings Chinese & Japanese fare at 2330 S. Carson Street and El Charro Avitia at 4389 S. Carson Street

For more Mexican food try Mi Casa Too on far north Carson Street, Tito's at the center of town or Taqueria Las Salsa, in the Warehouse Market shopping center on US 50 east. All are authentic and informal.

Of course there are many more choices for good food, and at least two places you can enjoy a refreshment at any time of day: Comma Coffee, on Carson Street across from the Legislature provides an eggzuberant menu of espresso drinks, fruit smoothies and sandwiches in a comfortable environment that becomes a venue for music at the snap of a finger; and the D'Vine Wine & Tapas Bistro at 200 N. Stewart Street, an determinedly modernist source of refreshments.

GOLD HILL NEWS ARCHIVE

The Corbett-Fitzsimmons championship fight, 1897.

Carson City has a busy schedule of events throughout the year, but perhaps the most interesting ones for visitors are the Indian Pow-Wows at Stewart, and the annual Kit Carson Rendezvous, a wildly imaginative evocation of frontier life before the coming of the iron horse. A weekend event in early June, it offers an abundance of sights, sounds, flavors and scents that can combine to produce sensory overload. Nevada Day is the annual celebration of statehood on the Saturday closest to October 31, highlighted by a fabulous parade on Carson Street.

Welcome to Carson City

Area Information

CARSON CITY VISITORS BUREAU
1900 S. Carson St.. Suite 100. 775-687-7410
Stop by our newly remodeled visitors center for all the information you will need to enjoy Nevada's Historic Capital. We have walking tour maps and CD's, visitors guides, Nevada Books and a huge selection of authentic Native American jewelry. 9-4, M-F, 10-3 weekends. We can help make your visit memorable! 800 NEVADA-1

Art Galleries

GREAT BASIN GALLERY
Second & Curry Streets. 775-882-8505
A must-see one of a kind art gallery in Carson City's formidable historic district. Devoted to bringing the finest of Nevada art and artists, past and present, to the Reno-Carson-Tahoe area. Custom framing: challenge us!

Museums

NEVADA STATE MUSEUM
600 N. Carson Street. 775-687-4810
The Nevada State Museum showcases the state's natural and cultural heritage. See the historic Carson City Mint, featuring Coin Press No. 1. Walk through a mine and ghost town. View exhibits on history, geology, fossils, Datsolalee baskets, and Native Americans. Visit the museum store. Open daily 8:30 to 4:30.

NEVADA STATE RAILROAD MUSEUM
2180 S. Carson Street. 775-687-6953
Experience Nevada's rich railroading heritage. See extraordinary collections of vintage railroad equipment, artifacts and exhibits. Browse the museum store while the children watch our operating model railroad or play in the Kid's Station. Enjoy a train ride aboard restored railcars on weekends May through September. Daily: 8:30 - 4:30.

NEVADA INDIAN COMMISSION

The annual Stewart Powwow is held each June, everyone is welcome.

Stewart Indian School

5366 Snyder Avenue, east of South Carson Street. Open Mon-Sat 9-5:30; Sun 9-4. Free Admission.

The Stewart Indian School once occupied these beautiful grounds, and the attractive stone structures were built by Indian craftsmen. Established in 1897, it was an effort to deal with the captive children of the western reservations. Over 83 years of operation it accommodated children from 20 tribes, instructing them in a new set of survival skills which required trading labor for pay rather than relying on handcrafts and hunting and fishing skills.

The buildings, constructed of native stone by Native American artisans, now house state offices (including the State Indian Commission in the former Superintendent's residence) and a branch campus of Western Nevada College. A self-guided walking tour of the old Indian School is being prepared. Visitors will use cell phones to access dramatic recordings at each of the school's buildings, which will also be designated with signs and an informational kiosk.

Annual Pow-Wows in March and June attract Native Americans from around the west, many of them alumni and the descendants of alumni of the old Stewart School, others are on hand to socialize with friends from all around Indian country. It is a festive family gathering, with dancing, good food and craftspeople at their traditional work. For information about schedules and events, call 775-687-8333.

GARY ELAM

Native America celebrates its roots.

GREAT BASIN GALLERY

C Street, Virginia City's busiest commercial thoroughfare in the 1870s

The Comstock Lode

In February 1859, a raggedy band of prospectors in Gold Canyon had made a raggedy camp they called Johntown. They were panning flecks from the stream to eke out a bare living, and looking for the source of the gold to strike it rich. During a sunny midwinter thaw, when the snow melted from the sagebrush and the ice from the little stream, eight men set out upcanyon to see what they could find.

They tested the streambed here and there as they toiled uphill toward the little knob that came to be called Gold Hill, and when they had all puffed their way to the top, one of them stuck a shovel into it, bringing up a small gob of mud that he scraped off into a pan with his boot. He added some slush and swirled the mud into a slurry. And in the grit lining the pan, here and there, were flecks of gold. Tiny flecks worth about 15¢! "We're rich!" they exulted behind their wide eyes. Fifteen cents from a little gob of mud meant big money in 1859, and soon Gold Hill, with its famous Red Ledge, was a crosspatch of small claims with men digging deep holes with the help of windlasses, both hand- and horse-powered.

The rest of the population of Johntown, and everyone else who heard the news, hurried up the canyon to find their own little gobs of rich mud, but without success. In June, two prospectors were working further north, around the hip of the mountain in the higher elevations of Six-Mile Canyon. Peter O'Riley and Patrick McLaughlin had abandoned the increasingly company-dominated Mother Lode to prospect across the Sierra Nevada where a man could still wash wages out of a stream bed. They were excavating a small reservoir to store water for their placering. As they dug their pond, they discovered gold-rich gravel that rivaled the discoveries at the Red Ledge a mile to the south.

Henry Comstock (Old Pancake, they called him) one of the original locators at Gold Hill, cut himself in on the claim by insisting the men were digging on his "ranch."

As a settlement began to form at the site, still another prospector, James Finney from Virginia, was making his way to his brush-roofed dugout one evening with a bottle of whisky in his coat pocket. He had transferred some of the whisky from the bottle to his belly, and as he staggered over the rough ground in the dark he stumbled and fell, breaking the bottle. Staring woefully down at the

ALF DOTEN

Gold Hill News Staff, 1870s.

whisky soaking into the yellow dirt, he made the best of a bad situation by raising a hand to the sky and "christening" the new camp Virginny, after his home state.

Thus was founded the west's most extravagantly rich mining camp.

As the wealth and the extent of the lode (to which Comstock's name early became attached) was recognized, Virginia became less a camp and more a city. The helter-skelter of discovery had given way to a more formal rhythm of production by 1862. Many of the mines were tangled together in litigation and starved for the ready cash required to sink shafts, extend tunnels, and ship ore to the mills.

By bringing order to the monetary chaos, William Sharon and the Bank of California came into control of many of the lode's leading properties. More quickly than in California a decade earlier, the Comstock passed from the era of the individual prospector into the era of syndicates and corporations. The economic cycles smoothed after an extended period of readjustment, and in 1869 an enormous body of high-grade ore discovered at the nine hundred-foot level of the Crown Point brought that mine's stock up from a low of $2 a share to more than $1,800. Other stocks rose in sympathy, and almost at once other new discoveries were made.

The $5 million extracted from the Crown Point was matched by the Belcher, and in 1873 the "Big Bonanza" was struck deep in the Consolidated Virginia, a concentration of ore that eventually yielded $105 million in gold and silver. By the middle 1870s there were 25,000 permanent residents in Virginia City, another nine or ten thousand in Gold Canyon, and thousands more in smaller communities in Six-Mile, Seven-Mile, Flowery, and other nearby canyons. In Virginia City alone there were over a hundred saloons, six churches, four banks, and a railroad with as many as fifty trains a day during the busiest peaks. When a great fire destroyed three-quarters of the city in 1875, rebuilding began immediately.

But the new Virginia City never matched the old one. Mining continued unabated, but the ore was getting thinner in its values and no large new discoveries were made. In 1878, after nineteen years of production in which nearly $300 million in gold and silver had been bucketed up from the shafts, the lode entered decline.

The Sutro Tunnel was completed the following year, too late to have an appreciable effect on the fortunes of the lode. Pumping water from the

GOLD HILL NEWS ARCHIVE

The Crown Point trestle of the V&T Railroad, Gold Hill.

mines was made easier, but without the high grade ore to send to the mills, production continued to slide. Only $400,000 was produced in 1899.

Still, after the turn of the century, the Comstock continued to produce more than a million dollars a year until the mines were closed at the outbreak of World War II.

In 1974 exploration geologists began a systematic exploration of the Comstock. In 1976 a medium-sized Texas oil company joined the venture, and in 1978 mining began again on the Comstock, when bulldozers began scraping the dirt from the site of the Consolidated Imperial Mine in Gold Hill.

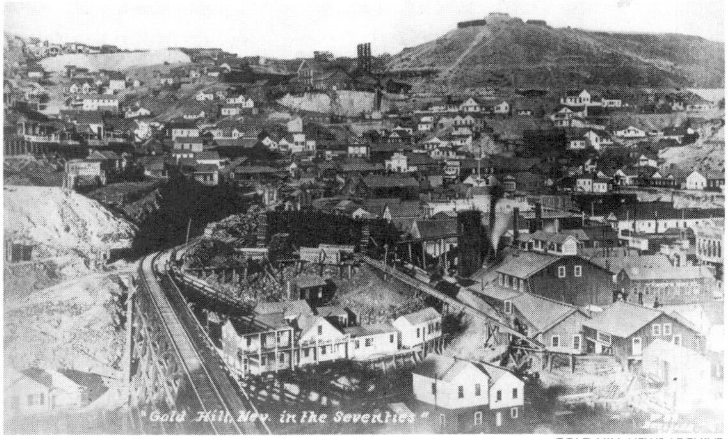

GOLD HILL NEWS ARCHIVE

Gold Hill in the 1870s.

The Con Imperial was one of the most famous of the great mines of the lode, a combination of several of the discovery claims, including the one that made Sandy Bowers a celebrated millionaire. In the early days it was known as one of the hottest mines on the lode, and became one of the deepest, with shafts descending more than 3000 feet into the mountain. The Con Imperial turned out to be barren below 1200 feet, but the upper workings were driven into highly mineralized rock with large quantities of low grade gold. This ore had not been worth mining in the bonanza days, and huge amounts of it had been left behind. But in the late 1970s this ore had value, and to get at it, the company began enlarging a shallow pit worked briefly in the I950s. The result was a catastrophe for all concerned.

Blasting, roaring engines and the constant traffic of 35-ton ore trucks through the little town of Gold Hill brought local residents to a slow boil. When the company condemned a parcel belonging to one of them — as Nevada mining law still permits a company to do — and buried it under thousands of tons of overburden, a furor erupted. A death occurred at an unfenced mine shaft, and two people barely escaped with their lives when the company's waste dump damming the Crown Point Ravine gave way during a thundershower and flooded their home with mud. Cracks appeared in the highway, and as a grand finale the steeply dug pit fell in on itself.

To clean up the mess the company bought property at the top of the canyon, spending stupendous sums to acquire eight residences, including those of some of their most outspoken opponents. The company then offered Storey County a million dollars to permit relocating the historic houses and digging up the old roadway. The offer created enormous controversy locally and around the country, and public meetings on the subject were heavily attended. Eventually the county commissioners voted 2-1 to accept the company's offer, but by then opposition had become so intense, and the price of hillside property so high, that the company eventually threw in the sponge. In February 1981 the company announced it would no longer seek to enlarge its pit, but would shore up the roadway and the houses at the edge of its pit wall and be content to mine what it could without disturbing any more of the old town.

Ironically, while controversy raged around the activities in Gold Hill, another mining company was quietly burrowing beneath Virginia City almost unnoticed. This company, United Mining Corporation, ultimately took over from the departed Texans, and for the first time in history, all the bonanza mines of the Comstock Lode were under a single management. United has since suspended operations, and Marshall Earth Resources which also carried on some underground exploration, has done likewise. Exploration is being carried out sporadically still, but there is no production currently underway.

GOLD HILL NEWS ARCHIVE

Virginia City.

Virginia City

FOR 25 GLORIOUS YEARS Virginia City was the leading city in Nevada and the brightest and most important settlement between Denver and San Francisco. Then came 75 bad years during which mining production slowed and finally stopped. The city shriveled, but it never quite died, and in 1950 Lucius Beebe was one of a handful of literary folk from the East who rediscovered the ancient metropolis. Beebe, a former New York City society columnist, railroad buff, and heir to many productive acres of Washington apple orchards, brought the old Territorial Enterprise back to life.

VIRGINIA CITY	
Gold Hill	1
Silver City	4
Carson City	16
Reno	24
Pioche	427

The revival of the Enterprise brought something of the original spirit of the Comstock back to life with it. The tourist boomlet of the 1950s accelerated beyond all expectation in the 1960s with the debut and continuing popularity of the "Bonanza" program on television. Suddenly Virginia City had an economy again.

Since then, mining has started up and closed down again several times, but the tourists keep right on coming in droves. They come to see one of the most exciting cities in the west, authentic beyond any doubt, where Mark Twain made a name for himself, and where John Mackay and a few others made great fortunes.

Some of them are disappointed, repelled by the commercial exploitation rampant in the historic old city. The advertising signs that bristle above the old board sidewalks and line the road into town are given credit for creating a Coney Island atmosphere in Virginia City.

But here's what J. Ross Browne wrote in 1863: "One of the most characteristic features about Virginia City is the inordinate passion of the inhabitants for advertising. Not only are the columns of the papers filled with every species of advertisement, but the streets and hillsides are pasted all

GARY ELAM

Justice is not blind in Storey County.

over with flaming bills." So maybe the Coney Island effect is authentic. And perhaps it's not the commercialism itself that bothers people, but that this inauthentic commercialism doesn't satisfy. They've come for — what, oysters and champagne? — and found hot dogs and Budweiser instead. Maybe the real problem is that most local businesses and their customers are a step removed from the extraordinary history the Comstock Lode represents. It's all a little unfamiliar now, and degraded by fleeting images vaguely remembered from television.

Now that Margaret Marks is gone, there is no longer anyone still in business on C Street who can remember Virginia City when the mines were working. The Crystal Bar, owned and operated by the Marks family since the 1880s, is now the Virginia City Visitors Center. Its staff is enthusiastic and helpful, but they only know what they've read. They've never seen the miners up from their labors below ground, crowded into the downstairs bar at the Frederick House for an after-shifter made by the Chinese bartender. A Chun Kee liner, it was called in his honor, and it cost a dime. Now ten dollars won't buy a Chun Kee liner in Virginia City because nobody knows how to make one and nobody knows enough to order it: one miniscule example of how authenticity gets lost.

Still, Virginia City does hold a special place in the heart and the history of the American West, and despite the increasing distance from the glory years, Virginia City's antic history can come to life in your imagination when you visit.

"Entering the main street," Browne wrote, "the saloons along the board sidewalks are glittering with their gaudy bars and fancy glasses, and many-colored liquors, and thirsty men are swilling burning poison: organ grinders are grinding their organs and torturing their consumptive monkeys; hurdy-gurdy girls are singing bacchanalian songs in bacchanalian dens. All is life, excitement, avarice, lust, devilry, and enterprise."

Or just like a modern day Sunday in August (except for the hurdy-gurdy girls and the monkeys).

Today's C Street is still lined with thriving saloons — The Delta, which first opened its doors in 1863, and the lively Bucket of Blood across the street are the biggest of them. The celebrated Union Brewery is going strong, and the Washoe Club, a survivor of theGreat Fire, is approaching its sesquicentennial.

Because of aggressive DUI policing, the bar business isn't what it used to be in Virginia City, but you are never more than ten steps from a t-shirt. Souvenirs aside, Virginia City's shops do reflect the old city's variety. Jewelry, Indian goods, rock and mineral shops, clothing-it's an eclectic collection of shops and stores, and a long way from Rodeo Drive. One exceptional enterprise is the Pioneer Emporium a few steps south from the Post Ofice on C Street, where Pascal Baboulin not only reflects something of the international character of the bonanza years, he has restored a lost craft as well. At a table near the ront of his store, Pascal makes hats, by hand, just as hats were made a century ago. You can watch him do it for a customer, or step up and be fitted for that dove grey Tom Mix model you've always wanted. There are other treasures among the t-shirts, and you'll enjoy browsing and windowshopping as you clomp along the wooden sidewalks.

Museums abound, and even though they are of uneven quality, there is something of interest in each of them. The Gambling Museum displays an eclectic collection of dicey artifacts; the Fourth Ward School at Virginia City's south end is a wonderful Victorian schoolhouse turned museum. The signatures of the Class of 1936 — the last to graduate — still decorate the blackboard upstairs. The Way It Was Museum on the north side of town is devoted to the underground workings and the men and machinery that dug them.

You can tour the mines underground at the Chollar Mine, on South F Street near its junction with the Truck Route and at the Best & Belcher, accessible through a back room at the Ponderosa Saloon at the corner of C & Taylor Streets. And you can satisfy your curiosity about Virginia City and Nevada at Mark Twain Books and at the bookstore in the Gold Hill Hotel.

You can't walk ten steps without finding another snack to try. For something more substantial look for the Sawdust Corner with its extensive lunch menu next door to the Delta Saloon, the Mandarin Garden across the street with its million dollar view, and the Palace, long a local favorite. Bob's barbecue, on south C Street next to the Methodist Church, offers hearty fare and the Cafe Del Rio, a little farther to the south, draws customers from surrounding communities as well as locals. The Gold Hill Hotel, a mile downcanyon toward Carson City is the Comstock's premiere dinner house, and serves bar food too.

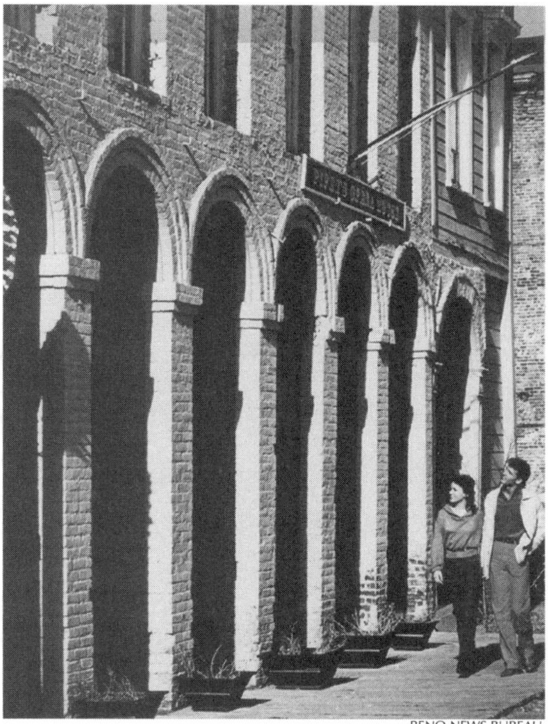
RENO NEWS BUREAU

Piper's Opera House, Virginia City.

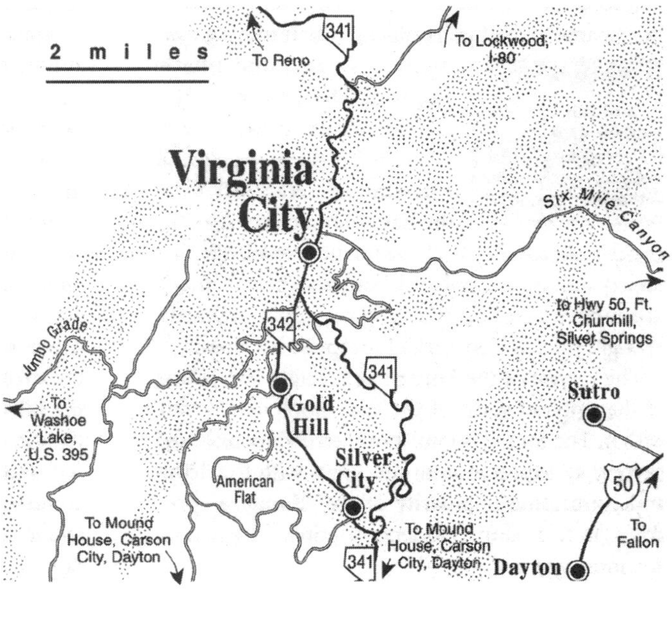

It's too bad so much is centered on C Street, though, if only because the steepness of the mountainside streets discourages people from exploring further, and much of Virginia City's character does not emerge from a single view. Many of the Victorian homes on the hill above town, dating back to the 1870s and 1880s, have been restored and stand in splendid fashion once again. B Street, next above C, is certainly worth a stroll. The Storey County Court House is a distinguished example of western Victorian public-building architecture, and visitors are encouraged to view the building which still houses some of the creaky machinery of county government. This building, like most of those now standing in Virginia City, was constructed after the great fire of 1875. It is distinguished not only by its impressive dimensions and spacious elegance, but by the statue of Justice above the main entrance gazing with unblindfolded intensity at her scales.

Chief among the attractions along this promenade is Piper's Opera House, once the leading

GARY ELAM

The famous V&t RR has been restored for found trip service between Virginia City and Gold Hill.

ible below the town is the former St. Mary's Hospital. Operated by an order of nuns until shortly before the turn of the century, it became the Storey County Hospital until it finally closed in the middle 1930s. Now, as St. Mary's Art Center, it houses an active summer arts program.

One of Virginia City's greatest attractions is the Virginia & Truckee Railroad, once the richest (and crookedest) short line in the world, now in the process of restoration and already operating a regular passenger schedule between Virginia City and Gold Hill from Memorial Day through October. Locomotives pull excursion cars between the depot car on F Street, and the Gold Hill depot, about two miles around the hill and through the tunnel as construction proceeds to extend the tracks to Carson City once again.

Below town to the north are Virginia City's nine cemeteries. The burying grounds — and please don't call them Boot Hill, that's in Pioche, or Tombstone, Arizona — were once like gardens, a showplace of tree-shaded walks and carriageways between the elaborate enclosures, monuments and headstones. With the decline of the mines, the cemeteries fell into delapidation and disrepair along with the rest of the city.

They were rescued from abandonment by a team of convicts from the State Prison working under the direction of the priest at St. Mary In The Mountains. The overwhelming majority of visitors to Virginia City pay a visit to the dead — how can they resist? —and they put about $75 a week in the collection jars to support restoration.

Virginia City's playful spirit erupts in a number of civic celebrations over the course of the year. Some of these are town parties where local folks celebrate their great good luck in living on the Comstock, and the public is invited. You'll find chili cook-offs, mountain oyster fries, parades, cakewalks and frolics of every description, some scheduled and some spontaneous in this magnificent old city.

theater on the lode. The opulent International Hotel stood across the street from it (until it burned in 1914), making B and Union the toniest corner on the Comstock during the glory years. World famous actors, singers, musicians, and troupes played Piper's, and one of its impressarios was the young David Belasco. Entertainers such as Michael Martin Murphey, the Comstock Cowboys and the incomparable Will Strickland now attract audiences to the restored Opera House once again.

Next to Piper's stands a row of often-photographed buildings, including the Knights of Pythias Hall (still used by an active aerie of Eagles) and the Miner's Union Hall (occasionally serving as a theater for melodrama or as a dance hall).

Below C Street are attractions just as compelling. St. Mary's in the Mountains on E Street, and St. Paul's Episcopal Church on F are both open to worshippers and casual visitors alike, and services are still conducted on Sundays, as they are in the old Presbyterian Church on south C Street. St. Mary's, rebuilt by Father (later Bishop) Patrick Manogue after the Great Fire, was restored a century later by the late Father Paul Mienecke. It is a structure of grace and eloquence, recognized as one of the finest remaining examples of western Victorian church architecture, and its basement now houses a museum and gift shop selling Mad Monk wines and other items to support the restoration effort.

The large, rather forbidding brick building vis-

Welcome to Virginia City

Area Information

VIRGINIA CITY VISITOR CENTER
86 South C Street. 775-847-4386
"Step Back In Time - Virginia City, Nevada" Just one admission fee for a full day of family fun and adventures! Ticket package includes a value packed discount at participating stores, saloons and restaurants. Come to the Visitor Center at 86 South C Street for your Silver Line Express ticket.

Attractions

VIRGINIA & TRUCKEE RAILROAD
F and Washington Streets. 775-847-0380
Ride over the historic Virginia & Truckee Railroad from Virginia City, through tunnel 4 to Gold Hill, Nevada. Sit back, relax and enjoy the spectacular mountain scenery. Hear the conductor narrate the amazing Comstock bonanza story while the train, steam or diesel, chuffs past many famous Western mine ruins. May through October.

Lodgings

EDITH PALMER'S COUNTRY INN
416 South B Street. 775-847-7070
Our comfortable Country Inn is an authentic 1863 historic Victorian building. Eight rooms and two family suites are available for your stay in the largest National Historic Landmark. Weddings and Celebrations can be enjoyed in the stone Cider Factory complete with banquet and bar service.

Museums

COMSTOCK WILD HORSE MUSEUM & GIFT SHOP
C Street across from the Post Office. 775-847-9453
We care for over 1,000 federally unprotected wild horses on the Virginia Range. Visit our tax-free gift shop and museum in the yellow railroad car. We have t-shirts, books, music, mugs, jewelry, gems, salsa, photos of our horses, and more! Your support keeps them free and wild!

FOURTH WARD SCHOOL MUSEUM
537 South C Street. 775-847-0975
Beautiful on the outside and fascinating on the inside. Explore the authentic Fourth Ward School. Sit in the original 1876 desks used for 60 years by the students living in what was known as the richest place on earth. Interpretive exhibits on mining, Comstock history, Mark Twain, letterpress printing.

THE WAY IT WAS MUSEUM
East side North C Street.
See the most complete collection of Comstock artifacts anywhere in the world, scale model of the hundreds of miles of underground workings, working models of stamp mill and Cornish pump, historic mining equipment including original Sutro Tunnel mule-train mine cars, priceless Comstock mineral collection, rare photos, lithos, prints and more.

Shopping

THE SILVER STOPE
58 North C Street. 775-847-7900
Unique shop offering outstanding Native American silver jewelry, assorted silver and gold jewelry, quality motorcycle leather for children, women, & men. We have a large selection of Black Hills gold as well as gift and souvenir items. The 1870s building has its charm and is worth visiting.

MARK TWAIN BOOKS ...and other records of history
111 South C Street. 775-847-0454
Virginia City's only bookstore, purveying the history of Virginia City, Nevada, and the old West. All Nevada titles plus rare & out of print Nevada books. Buy and sell historic artifacts, documents, photographs, mining and rail documents. Summers 10 - 5, 7 days; Winter 11 - 4, closed Mondays.

VIRGINIA CITY HATMAKER
144 South C Street. 775-847-7717
Welcome to Virginia City Hat Makers! We offer quality custom handcrafted beaver felt hats made in the style of your choice. Watch us work. We employ only the old traditional hatmaking techniques. Two characteristics our customers always look for in a handmade hat are authenticity and quality. And we deliver!

GARY ELAM

Virginia City's Camel Races are one of Nevada's strangest events, and one of its most popular.

Pogonip, the New York Mine, Gold Hill.

MAX WINTHROP

Gold Hill

GOLD HILL GREW UP AROUND the site of the original discovery of the Comstock Lode, just where the great raw pit mine has been dug beside the S-curve in the highway slightly south of Virginia City. Nine thousand people once lived in this canyon, though by 1960 the population had fallen below 50.

GOLD HILL	
Silver City	3
Virginia City	1
Carson City	15
Reno	24
Nelson	487

More than 100 people live in Gold Hill now, and the historic community's business district, although much diminished from the glory years, is showing unmistakeable signs of life. In the spring, summer and fall you can hear the whistle of the V & T locomotives floating in the air, and the Gold Hill Depot is active again after a hiatus of nearly 50 years. Restoration of the railroad is proceeding, eventually to extend all the way to Carson City. The California Bank building, once a great center of influence up and down the Lode, is an archaeological office now. The only saloon stands across the street, on the site of the town's principal business blocks in the early days, and a few of the rock-and-mud walls still poke up from the brush.

Recently the residence of John P. Jones, hero of the Yellow Jacket Fire in 1869 and US Senator from Nevada for 30 years from 1873 - 1903, has been rebuilt to something like its orginal glory, while the last of the city's early wooden structures sag and melt into the hillsides.

The Gold Hill Hotel is the state's oldest, and since a recent restoration and enlargement, one of its finest. A favorite for weddings and receptions, the hotel offers both modern and old rooms upstairs above the Great Room. The restaurant is one of the most estimable in the state, drawing its regular clientele from Carson City, Lake Tahoe and Reno.

These and other historic structures shrink in contrast with the great open pit that occupies the original discovery site of the Comstock Lode and the claim that made Sandy Bowers rich. Now just a huge hole in the ground, it exemplifies the disparity between the techniques of modern mining and the economy built on historic remains of the underground mines and the cities they built in a previous era. A mining company effort to eliminate the northern part of town and expand the pit fizzled out a few years ago, and Gold Hill has so far been spared further devastation.

Right: Silver City cemetery.

Below: During a recent Armistice Day Parade, soldiers of fhe Silver City Guard executed Bartles and James for crimes against humanity.

BILL GERMINO (2)

Silver City

SILVER CITY IS THE THIRD of the three great communities of the Comstock Lode, (four if you count Dayton) but it never achieved the prominence of Virginia City or Gold Hill, although some of its mines were exceedingly rich.

SILVER CITY	
Virginia City	4
Dayton	6
Yerington	63
Searchlight	512

A toll gate once stood at the head of town in the eroded lava formation called Devil's Gate. There was a hotel, a brewery, and extra teams stabled here to help haul loaded freight wagons up the steep grade to Virginia City.

For today's travelers there is a post-office and a historic cemetery behind the hill to the east. No commercial enterprise remains — even the pay phone has been unplugged and hauled away.

The Silver City Guard is Nevada's oldest military unit still under arms, and is Nevada's last line of defense. Designated as Armed Rabble, its original members were annihilated by Paiutes at the Battle of Pyramid Lake in 1860. Twice a year, on Memorial Day and Veterans' Day, modern-day members of the Guard form up into a mob bristling with weapons and amble to the cemetery. There they fire a ragged volley over the grave of Asa Phelps, in the mistaken belief that he died of wounds received at the Battle of Pyramid Lake, and devolve into a gossipy band of neighbors.

Also buried here is Hosea Grosch, who with his brother Alan recognized the enormous silver values in the native rock. Both brothers died before they could establish their claim to it.

Dan DeQuille, Mark Twain's fellow reporter on the Territorial Enterprise, was a Silver City resident in 1860, and Dave Moore, editor of Nevada Magazine, maintained Silver City's literary reputation before retiring to a pleasure dome in Dayton.

Orson Hyde

WHEN THE MORMON FAITHFUL returned to Zion in 1858 at the call of Brigham Young, many were required to abandon the fruits of their labors in the shadow of the Sierra Nevada. One such was Orson Hyde, the magistrate sent west to arrange the affairs of Carson County. He had constructed a sawmill in Washoe Valley between the present sites of Reno and Carson City and had sold the mill before returning to Utah. But he had managed to get only "one span of small oxen, and an old wagon," as part payment on the $10,000 sale price. The rest was never forthcoming, despite Hyde's best efforts to collect.

After five years Hyde despaired of ever collecting, and planted his suit "in the Chancery of Heaven" by reading, in the Utah legislature of which he was a member, an open letter to the people of Carson and Washoe valleys. The letter read in part:

"The Lord has signified to me, his unworthy servant, that as we have been under circumstances that compelled us to submit to your terms, that He will place you under circumstances that will compel you to submit to ours, or do worse.

"That mill and those land claims were worth $10,000 when we left them; the use of that property, or its increased value since, is $10,000 more, making our present demand $20,000.

"Now if the above sum be sent to me in Great Salt Lake City, in cash, you shall have a clean receipt therefor, in the shape of honorable quitclaim deeds to all the property that Orson Hyde, William Price, and Richard Bentley owned in Washoe Valley. The mill, I understand, is now in the hands of R.D. Sides, and has been for a long time. But if you shall think best to repudiate our demand or any part of it, all right. We shall not take it up again in this world in any shape of any of you; but the said R.D. Sides and Jacob Rose shall be living and dying advertisements of God's displeasure, in their persons, in their families, and in their substances; and this demand of ours, remaining uncancelled, shall be to the people of Carson and Washoe valleys as was the ark of God among the Philistines. (See 1st Sam. fifth chapter) You shall be visited of the Lord of Hosts with thunder and with earthquake and with floods, with pestilence and with famine until your names are not known amongst men, for you have rejected the authority of God, trampled upon his laws and his ordinances, and given yourselves up to serve the god of this world; to rioting in debauchery, in abominations drunkenness and corruption....

"I have no sordid desire for gold, and have manifested by my long silence and manifest indifference; and should not say anything now had not the visions of the Almighty stirred up my mind...

"I care not what our mill and land claims are, or were considered worth — whether five hundred thousand dollars or five cents — twenty thousand dollars is our demand; and you can pay it to us, as I have said, and find mercy, if you will thenceforth do right, or despise the demand and perish...."

Carson Valley

The Carson Valley is one of the earliest-settled, richest, and most productive of the state's agricultural regions. In spring, summer and autumn, when the valley is bursting with life, the vast irrigated tracts are a green velvet patchwork quilt upon which the stacks of baled hay stand like giant cheeses, and cottonwoods and poplars rise up like flashing green flames. The meadows are sopped with water from the Sierra, fat and languid cattle browse placidly everywhere.

MINDEN/ GARDNERVILLE	
Topaz Lake	23
Reno	45
Yerington	56
Austin	186

Gardnerville

Gardnerville is a farm town established in 1879 to serve the valley's agricultural population in a more conveniently central location than Genoa. Minden is the railroad's child, born in 1905 as a planned and platted subdivision with a brick depot, a central park and a grid of quiet streets.

The pioneer town of Gardnerville had its share of rough characters in its youth, but the farmfolk were generally less frivolous and more peaceful than their mining town counterparts. So genteel were the residents of Sheridan, a nearby hamlet, in the years around the turn of the century, that when a U.S. Senator came to campaign for reelection, the townspeople nailed the town drunk inside a piano crate for the afternoon to ensure tranquility. The old farm town of the 19th century has been elongated by the presence of US 395 now, and most of the business enterprises, many of them catering to visitors, face the highway.

Only a few years ago the picturesque Basque restaurants clustered toward the south end of town provided Gardnerville with such fame as it enjoyed beyond the confines of the valley. These family-style eating places were originally established to serve the large population of sheepherders from the Pyrenees who wandered with the bands of sheep. In Gardnerville, as in many of northern Nevada's towns, Basques established boarding-house hotels where the sheepherders could stay between jobs or for their two-week vacations. For the non-English-speaking sheepherders the hotels were a special convenience, as well as being inexpensive and hearty feeders.

In time, other townfolk came to appreciate the modestly priced suppers served at these workingmen's hotels, and today dining out at one of them is considered a treat. Most of them are still family operations, with mom and dad supervising a work force of sons, daughters, aunts, and nephews. There are no longer Basque boarders with rooms upstairs; all of them have bars, and except in the peak summer months, the clientele is largely local. The J-T and the Overland have deserved reputations for excellent food. Skip the Rob Roys and the Coors Lites and have a Picon Punch. It's an Old World cocktail which leaves the mind clear as the knees turn to jelly and the feet turn to lead.

The venerable Sharkey's has been sold, and the venerable Sharkey himself has passed on, his wonderful memorabilia collections auctioned away. Boxing, rodeo, Indians and the circus — all gone though the new owners vow they're maintaining the prime rib tradition. The Adaven Hotel across the street has been refurbished as the comfortable Historian Inn with suites and large rooms. Lampe Park, south of town, has tennis courts, ball fields and playgrounds. The golf course at the Carson Valley Country Club two miles south was seriously

MAX WINTHROP

The old brick buildings in downtown Gardnerville are being restored and revived.

damaged by the floods of '97, as was the popular Basque restaurant there. Both are now restored to health.

There are three supermarkets and a Starbucks at the south end of town, and almost all the businesses catering to travelers are located on the highway that runs from the south end of Gardnerville to the north end of Minden.

Minden

Minden adjoins Gardnerville to the north. These once-separate communities have fused together the way Reno and Sparks have, and to visitors the demarcation line is of little importance. Nevertheless, Minden is quite distinctive, a tidy turn-of-the-century picture postcard. It was established when the V&T's profitable Tonopah and Goldfield traffic was snatched away by the more direct S.P. spur through Hazen. The V&T then extended a line south to harvest the Carson Valley trade.

By this time, however, the only feasible right of way had long been the property of the Dangberg family. The Dangbergs were agreeable to the railroad laying tracks across their ground — as long as the railroad built its depot on the Dangberg land at the north edge of Gardnerville.

This the railroad did, and when the small brick depot was built a two-block business street had been staked and named Esmeralda, with a large park separating it from a neat grid of residential streets.

This tiny enclave of Americana retains much of its original appeal. Downtown workers who eat their lunches in the park sometimes get up noontime softball games that anyone can join in. Except for mild excitements like this, Minden is magnificently quiet; on a spring day you can hear the buzzing of the bees in the gardens and the shouts of children in the schoolyard three blocks over. You can pick up a Walking Tour brochure at the Town Office on Esmeralda Street and inform yourself about what you see along the way. Despite the occasional celebrity (Mary Pickford, Clark Gable, Baby Face Nelson), most of Minden's past has been as comfortably pleasant and serene as its present.

In 1964, Bently Nevada was the first high-profile, high-tech company to relocate from California to Nevada. A slow migration of high-tech companies continues, many of them clustered around the airport farther north in the valley. At the same time Tahoe casino workers, unable to afford life at the Lake, have migrated down the Kingsbury Grade to buy houses in the Gardnerville Ranchos. These new populations of well-paid, highly educated people have remade the character of the Carson Valley. This transformation is typified by the Carson Valley Inn just north of the old Minden Creamery, a modern hotel with highly manicured grounds, casino, meeting rooms and restaurants.

And on Minden's north side a new development on the east side of Main Street (US 395) at Lucerne is home to a cluster of surprisingly cosmopolitan restaurants (including sushi!) and the Sierra Nevada Trading Company, a grocery store that only stocks the good stuff.

Minden is at the intersection of three of the most scenic highways in the west and is the closest Nevada community to a fourth. Nevada 88 takes off from the north end of Minden for the California state line, where it becomes California 88 and climbs into the high summits of the Sierra. It squeezes through Carson Pass and drops down the other side into the Mother Lode foothills. Nevada 207 is the Kingsbury Grade, which climbs the sheer eastern face of the Sierra Nevada to drop into the Tahoe Basin at Stateline. This is the route of the Pony Express and of the Overland Stage ("Keep your seat, Horace, I'll get you there on time!") although much smoothed, leveled and straightened from the steep, narrow and curly original. You'll get the airliner's view of the great valley as you soar upward above the cloud level, really quite thrilling.

Welcome to Minden

Lodgings

CARSON VALLEY INN
1627 US Hwy 395 N. 775-782-9711
The Carson Valley Inn features 152 hotel rooms, a 75-room motor lodge, 59 RV sites, a casino, three dining facilities, two lounges, free nightly Cabaret Lounge entertainment, 6,000+ sq. ft. of convention and banquet space, the Chapel at the Inn, an indoor pool/spa/fitness facility, and a Shell convenience store.

Genoa

GENOA (pronounced Juh-NO-uh) 12 miles south of Carson City via US 395 and Jack's Valley Road is the oldest permanent settlement within the present state of Nevada, and one of the most attractive little villages anywhere in the American West. Established as a trading post in 1851 to serve the wagon trains as a resting place between the open desert and the granite barricade of the Sierra Nevada, Mormon Station (as it was called then) became a small farming center. It is now a gentrified enclave of the wealthy, but still retains much of its pioneer aspect.

GENOA	
Minden	5
Stateline	11
Carson City	17
Overton	461

In 1854 this tiny burg was proclaimed the seat of Carson County, Utah Territory, and in 1861 of Douglas County, Nevada Territory. Genoa's utility as a center of government had been reduced with the discovery of the Comstock mines in 1859, and Genoa's importance was largely local by the time statehood was granted in 1864. Even that importance was largely eclipsed by Minden and Gardnerville after 1910 when a resident of the county poor farm, tormented by bedbugs, tried to fumigate his mattress by lighting a pan full of sulfur underneath it. The resulting fire wiped out half the business district, the County Courthouse, and the original Mormon Fort. This ancient structure had never managed to acquire a patina of historical reverence; by the time it burned it had been a cafe, a chicken coop and a pig barn. The present structure is a replica, housing a small museum.

In 1916 Genoa lost the county seat to Minden and the town dwindled further in size and importance. There are only about 50 original relatively humble dwellings in the place now, along with dozens of big new mansionettes snugged together on small lots, and a dozen or more businesses centered on the intersection at the center of town.

Small as it is, Genoa can provide a pleasant afternoon and as deep into the evening as you're prepared to go. The Country Store on the corner is a good place to have a mid-stroll snack, and your stroll should take you across the street to Mormon Station State Park, and across the other street to the old brick Genoa Courthouse Museum, where murderers, stagecoach drivers and Pony Express riders share exhibit space with butter churns, plow harnesses and other less spectacular aspects of pioneer life. Walk north and then west to the cemetery to spend a pleasant half hour wandering the monuments and enjoying the heavenly view: snow-capped mountains floating in the bright blue sky above the broad valley, and at your feet the evidence of mortality.

The Genoa Bar, oldest in the state, is now serving whiskey in its third century. A few years ago its claim to antiquity was challenged by the Delta Saloon in Virginia City, but the Delta had moved once since it opened its doors in 1860, and the Genoa Bar is secure in its championship. The tree at the center of town was used to hang an offender in the early days. La Ferme (in the former Pink House) offers elegant French country dining, and if you've had the foresight to book ahead, you can

MAX WINTHROP

Genoa was the first permanent settlement in the Carson Valley.

MAX WINTHROP

Genoa's quietude is perfect for strolling.

proceed to your room at one of the comfortable bed & breakfasts, preferably with a bottle of the local wine under your arm.

The wonderful David Walley's Hot Springs resort is a few minutes south, near the foot of Kingsbury Grade. You can swim and soak in the natural hot spring fed pools the way the Indians did before their world crumbled, and the way the Comstock wealthy did afterward, with food and drink close at hand. There are overnight accommodations and luxurious amenities.

Some people come for the golf. Three magnificent 18-hole golf courses (with restaurants attached) are open to the public.

Welcome to Genoa

Resorts

DAVID WALLEY'S HOT SPRINGS RESORT
2001 Foothill Road. 775-782-8155
What Mother Nature spent centuries creating, David Walley's perfected into a world-class resort and spa. Come for a day of pampering or a week's vacation. Enjoy deli service for breakfast and lunch. For dinner dine at DW's restaurant. Beautiful rooms and suites. Perfect for weddings, specials occasions, and business events.

Shopping

TAHOE RIDGE WINERY & MARKETPLACE
2285 Main Street. 775-783-1566
Tahoe Ridge Winery — Nevada's Winery is nestled on the eastern slope of the great Sierra Nevada mountain range. Home to Genoa — Nevada's Oldest Settlement (1851). Tahoe Ridge Winery sources grapes from our own vineyards along with quality-focused growers who farm grapes throughout Nevada and California.

Wellington

WAS IT A DREAM, or was it Wellington? That's a question I'm still asking after my most recent visit to this enchanted village.

WELLINGTON	
Smith	4
Topaz Lake	12
Yerington	18
Aurora	32

Wellington is a scatter of mostly old, some quite antique structures along a mile or two of Nevada Route 208 at the southern end of Smith Valley. Reach it from Gardnerville or Topaz Lake on the west via Holbrook Junction, or it's not quite an hour's drive south from Yerington.

This comfortable little settlement dates back to the 1860s when its main street was the main artery of commerce between Carson City and Aurora. Stagecoaches and freight wagons creaked through in an endless parade. By the late 19th century, though, Aurora we dead, Smith Valley had become highly productive farmland, and Wellington had transformed itself into an agricultural community rather than a way station for highway travelers.

The beautiful green valley is stippled here and there with cottonwood trees, barns and farmhouses, there are chalky brown hills beyond, and the brilliant sky dappled with bright, silver-white clouds overhead.

The CG Cafe across the street from the Mercantile offers refreshment after your stroll.

The Heyday Inn, down the road about a mile, occupies what was originally Pierce Station, a competitor to Wellington Station. It was also operated with a dance hall upstairs, and served temporarily as both a schoolhouse and a post office. In 1945 it was transformed into the Heyday Ranch Inn, serving dinners with cocktails available from the bar.

Wellington offers two B&Bs. One, the 1875 Hoye Mansion, with five magnificently furnished upstairs rooms is being restored to its original 19th century grandeur by new owners who have also acquired the next-door property where the Wellington Mercantile stood. The Mercantile was famous for the variety of its goods: you could walk through the front doors and find whatever you needed, from a galvanized tub to a fresh-baked pie. They plan to rebuild it.

There are also two RV parks, the Wellington Station Resort at the west edge of town, and the wonderful Walker River Resort on the way to Smith.

Topaz Lake

THIS IS THE OTHER lake shared by Nevada and California. It has a cluster of bright lights overlooking the sun-spangled waters below, and the steep crags of the Sierra Nevada tower photogenically above, but for some reason it's Tahoe that gets all the attention.

Maybe it's the trees. Nevertheless even without trees Topaz is an exceedingly pleasant place to visit. Deer browse down the mountainside, birds decorate the sky, and rainbow trout lure anglers down to the lake in season. At roadside, a mini-casino — more like a fishing lodge with a gambling motif — caters to travelers on US 395. Facilities at Topaz include boat launch ramps, boats for rent, campsites with trailer hookups as well as more formal lodging. On a sunny day in springtime, when the snow is still clinging to the Sierra and the rainbow are hitting the hook, it's hard to avoid having a good time.

MAX WINTHROP

Haying season at Wellington.

GOLD HILL NEWS ARCHIVE

Lake Tahoe

Lake Tahoe

Tahoe lies at the back of California's neck, just where Nevada's elbow juts into it. At an elevation of 6,229 feet it is an alpine sea ranking with the most spectacular mountain lakes in the world. The lake encompasses nearly two hundred square miles in this mountain grandeur well over a mile above the level of the ocean. To the west of Tahoe the peaks of the Sierra Nevada rise up to 4,000 feet above the lake, and to the east the craggy summits of the Carson Range soar even higher. Tahoe is cupped between them, nearly forty cubic miles of water, in a pine-blanketed setting of such compelling majesty that within twenty years of its discovery in the virgin wilderness (by John C. Fremont in 1844) the lake had become one of the West's leading vacation spots.

Today, after more than a century of development, Tahoe and its basin rank as one of the finest all-season recreation areas in the world, but the matchless scenic beauty of the region has been exploited at such a pace that the sight of the lake through the pines is as likely to inspire depression as exhilaration.

Lake Tahoe's modern history began in 1844 when Fremont spied it from a pinnacle in the Carson Range to the east. It accelerated four years later when John Calhoun "Cock-Eye" Johnson connected Placerville, California, with the Carson Valley by a looping trail across the Sierra that skirted Tahoe's south shore. Mart Smith arrived in 1851 to open a small trading post at the present site of Meyers, California, and became Tahoe's first permanent settler — other than the peaceful Washo Indians whose claim to the region was considered no better than that of the other forms of wildlife.

When the first trans-Sierra stagecoach run was made in 1857, it followed the Johnson Cutoff trail with a stop at Smith's Station. Two years later, with the discovery of the Comstock Lode drastically swelling traffic over the road, two competing stagecoach lines maintained regular schedules with Tahoe stops, and when the Pony Express was inaugurated in 1860, it took the old Johnson Cutoff route as well.

By 1861 the Comstock Lode's voracious need for timbers and fuel had prompted the beginning of a logging industry in the Tahoe Basin. One of the early prospectors for productive timberland at Tahoe was young Sam Clemens, who hiked the twelve miles up to the east shore of the lake from Carson City in 1861. After locating what seemed to be a goodly stand of trees, Clemens and his companions spent several memorable days vacationing.

"So singularly clear was the water," he wrote years later in Roughing It, "that where it was only twenty or thirty feet deep the bottom was so perfectly distinct that the boat seemed floating in the air! Yes, where it was even eighty feet deep. Every little pebble was distinct, every speckled trout, every hand's-breadth of sand. Often, as we lay on our faces, a granite boulder, as large as a village church, would start out of the bottom apparently, and seem climbing up rapidly to the surface, till presently it threatened to touch our faces, and we could not resist the impulse to seize an oar and avert the danger. But the boat would float on, and the boulder descend again, and then we could see that when we had been exactly above it, it must still have been twenty or thirty feet below the surface. Down through the transparency of these great depths, the water was not merely transparent, but dazzling, brilliantly so. All objects seen through it had bright, strong vividness, not only of outline, but of every minute detail, which they would not have had when seen simply through the same depth of atmosphere. So empty and airy did all spaces seem below us, and so strong was the sense of floating high aloft in mid-nothingness that we called these boat excursions 'balloon-voyages.'" Clemens left Tahoe to more business-like developers after inadvertently starting a raging forest fire in his camp, and rowing out into the lake for dear life.

By the middle 1860s, few Tahoe visitors took much time to admire the scenery. Comstock-bound traffic past the lake from the central valley of California had become incessant, and a string of hotels, corrals, stores, and businesses had been established along the lake's south shore to cater to the travelers. In a single three-month period in 1864, 6,667 men afoot, 883 more on horseback, and another 3,164

GOLD HILL NEWS ARCHIVE

Emerald Bay, on the California side of the lake.

GREAT BASIN GALLERY

Logging at Spooner Summit.

in stagecoaches paraded past the lakeshore. Plodding along with them were 5,000 pack animals and nearly that many cattle. A daily average of 320 tons of freight was drayed past by 2,564 teams. One entrepreneur even drove a flock of turkeys from California to Virginia City by way of Lake Tahoe. Hay to feed this endless stream of beasts was grown, harvested, and hand-baled at the west shore of the lake for delivery by two-masted schooner to the docks on the south shore where it sold for as much as $250 a ton.

Tahoe's first resort was built in 1863, at Glenbrook, to provide the leisured aristocracy of the booming Comstock with a vacation spot conveniently located at the head of the new turnpike to Carson City. It was a spa which could compare with the celebrated Saratoga in New York for elegance, gaiety, and the beauty of its surroundings. The first privately owned vacation "cottage" was built at the lake that same year at Emerald Bay, for stagecoach magnate Ben Holladay.

The phenomenal lakeshore traffic slowed to a trickle with the completion of the transcontinental railroad in 1869, and the lake settled down to a dreamy existence of summer frolics and winter hibernation. There was a prodigious logging industry, centered at Glenbrook, but with crews working everywhere in the basin. Commercial fishermen shipped trout by rail from Truckee to the coast and to the Comstock at fifteen cents a pound. Otherwise all was idyllic calm.

These activities went largely unreported in San Francisco and Sacramento, and as far as the outside world was concerned, Tahoe was for play. The elegant new Grand Central Hotel, erected at Tahoe City in 1871, with walnut furniture, Brussels carpets, and an ornate cast iron kitchen range that cost $800, eclipsed Glenbrook House as Tahoe's toniest resort the day it opened. The Grand Central was superceded in its turn by Elias J. "Lucky" Baldwin's Tallac House farther down the beach.

As early as 1879, when Baldwin purchased "Yank" Clement's hotel, the property was one of the few which had not been logged by timber cruisers, and by the early 1880s, Tahoe folk were remarking on the obvious decline in native trout. They were affected both by the efficiency of the market fishermen (commercial fishing was not outlawed until 1917) and by the effect of the logging and sawmill operations on the spawning creeks, which became choked with sawdust, slash, and other debris.

The first tangible demonstration of what the

future held in store for Tahoe did not arrive until 1900, but when it came it was right on schedule, shrieking and clicking and belching smoke: a narrow-gauge railroad that connected Tahoe City with the transcontinental railroad at Truckee. The arrival of the railroad prompted construction of the marvelously gabled four-story Tahoe Tavern a little south of town to set a new standard of elegance at the lake, and increasingly more people enjoyed Tahoe excursions and vacations. The lake steamers glided across the smooth summer surface of the lake as before, trailing languid plumes of black smoke. Logging at the east shore had largely ended with the decline of the Comstock mines, and conversion of the railroads to coal.

Just then, enterprising eyes began to focus on Tahoe's water. In 1900 A. W. Von Schmidt, president of the Lake Tahoe and San Francisco Water Works, proposed to furnish the city of San Franicisco with a water system capable of delivering thirty million gallons of Lake Tahoe water a day in return for $17,690,000. As a matter of fact, he was agreeable to building a system which could deliver up to a hundred million gallons a day, at a proportional increase in price. The San Francisco County Board of Supervisors went so far as to visit the proposed site of his diversion dam on the Truckee before allowing the idea to lapse. Three years later a San Francisco attorney named Waymire proposed a tunnel through the side of the Tahoe basin to drain the lake into the Rubicon branch of the American River and thus supply limitless power and water to San Francisco. The Waymire project made even less headway than Von Schmidt's.

A third attempt to drain Tahoe was backed by the Department of the Interior, and it nearly succeeded. The U.S. Reclamation Service, discovering it had made massive miscalculations in estimating the amount of water required to make the Truckee-Carson Irrigation District in Nevada a success, moved to acquire the outlet dam and control gates in 1903. With control of the outlet, Reclamation Service engineers could release whatever amounts of water were needed downriver, and thereby wash the egg from their chins.

The Truckee Electric Company refused $40,000 for the property on which the dam was located but made a counter-proposal. The company would present the Reclamation Service with the dam and gates gratis, in return for rights to a guaranteed flow of four hundred cubic feet of Tahoe water a second. The anxious Reclamation Service engineers agreed at once.

Negotiations dragged, however, and it was not until after Taft's election to the presidency in 1908 that an amended contract was agreed upon. In it, further concessions were granted to the utility company. The company could locate pipes and reservoirs anywhere it might choose on public land.

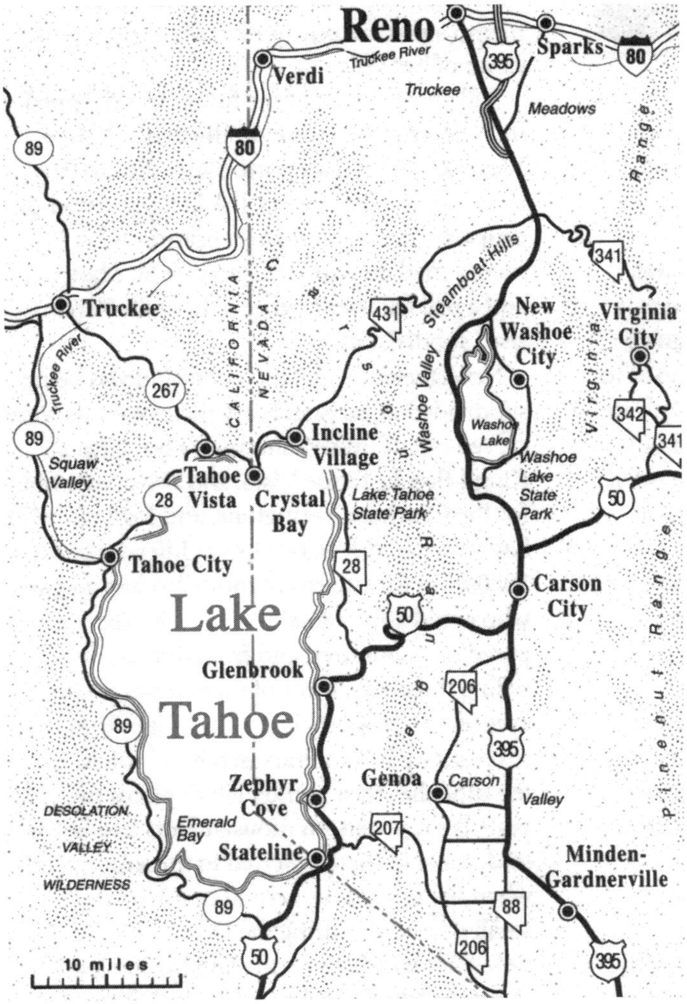

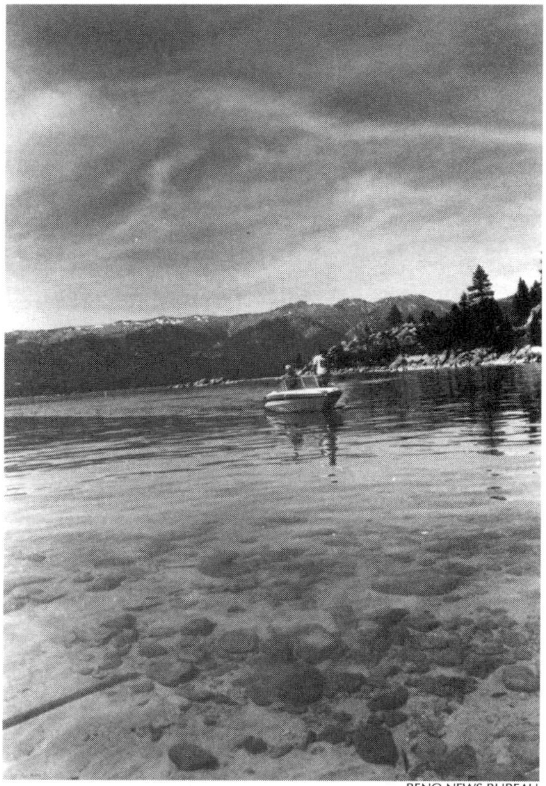
RENO NEWS BUREAU

Fishing in the crystal clear waters of Lake Tahoe.

Most important, it was granted the right to locate another outlet diversion at any depth below the lake's surface. This concession amounted to blanket permission from the federal government to drain Lake Tahoe into the Nevada desert for the purpose of generating electricity for sale.

The chief forester for the Department of Agriculture got wind of the contract before it could be signed, however, and he waged a vigorous delaying battle against it. In 1912, property owners at the lake succeeded in getting an injunction against the power company to prevent it from cutting into the rim of the lake.

One side effect of the affair was to raise again the question of ownership of Tahoe's water. Not until 1935 was an agreement finally reached which provided that the level of the lake was to be maintained at a minimum elevation of 6,223 feet above sea level and allowed to fluctuate upward to as high as 6,229.1 feet. Thus the top six feet of Tahoe are in essence reserved for the downriver farmers in Nevada — less the million and a half tons a day that are lost to evaporation.

An even more portentous herald of the future arrived at Tallac House in 1905 in the person of Mrs. Joseph Chanslor, a merry woman of almost oppressive determination who had clattered and churned up over the summits from Sacramento, all alone, in her chain-driven Simplex. She made the trip in the remarkably fast time of eight hours. The automobile had come to Lake Tahoe. When Mrs. Chanslor sputtered off toward Sacramento again, no one quite realized the significance of her visit.

Still another hint of the future was dropped in 1911 when lots were subdivided at Tahoe Vista on California's north shore. But to the horror of the developers, the first purchaser of property turned out to be a notorious Sacramento madam named Cherry de St. Maurice, and a pall fell over further sales in the "exclusive" subdivision.

Nevertheless, by 1927 Tahoe land was being subdivided in earnest. Forty thousand lots were carved out of Robert Sherman's holdings at King's Beach, Tahoe Vista, and Brockway, not for the Crockers, Yeringtons, and Birdsalls who had purchased spacious lots at Idlewild in the 1880s, but for citizens of more modest means who could afford $500 for a smaller slice of paradise. A hundred and five salesmen were selling those lots, most of them never laying eyes on the property itself but selling from maps set up in San Francisco hotel suites. By the time the stock market fell to pieces two years later, seventeen thousand lots had been sold. Most of them reverted to the subdivider when the new owners could not meet their small payments during the Depression. In an awkward, painful way, the Depression had saved the lake from wholesale exploitation, at least temporarily.

As early as 1900, bills had been introduced in Congress to create a national park at the lake in order to preserve it forever, but not until the middle 1930s did the proposal reach even the investigative stage. In 1935 an inspector for the national park system reported his conclusions in Washington: ". . . in its pristine state, the proposed Lake Tahoe National Park area was worthy of recognition as a national park; however, under the present conditions, I do not feel justified in recommending this area for future considerations as a national park." The inspector cited as reasons the facts that: 1) more than 90 percent of the proposed park area, slightly

GREAT BASIN GALLERY

Stateline, Lake Tahoe, 1930s.

less than two hundred square miles along the lakeshore, was already in the private hands of about two thousand individual owners; 2) the speculative prices on lake frontage made acquisition costs prohibitive; 3) "ruthless commercial enterprises...have destroyed to a great extent the natural character and charm of the most valuable portion of the proposed national park site — the land immediately adjacent to the lake." Despite the urgings of other Park Service personnel, notably wildlife technician Robert T. Orr, who saw in the Tahoe basin a unique and relatively pristine alpine habitat "which might well be considered as of National Park merit," the recommendations of the inspector were accepted and the proposal for a Lake Tahoe National Park was shelved for good.

Still, at the end of World War II Tahoe still had only about a thousand permanent residents in the villages and hamlets rimming the lake. After the War the 20th century began to arrive at Tahoe with such rapidity and with such impact that conditions at the lake went rapidly out of control.

By the late 1940s Tahoe vacation resorts were turning away customers, and new ones were being built to accommodate the overflow. Skiing, never popular on the West Coast except as a countrified pastime in isolated mountain communities, became the fashionable wintertime equivalent of tennis. In the early 1950s Tahoe's recreation potential had caught the attention of everyone on the Pacific Coast — including that of the Nevada gamblers. In 1956 Harvey Gross tore down the little cafe-cum-slot machines he had been operating at the state line on the South Shore and erected a gambling hall and hotel. The next year, Bill Harrah built a big casino across the street, with its gambling rooms in Nevada and its parking lot in California. At once the character of the adjoining California shore began to change. With new weekend visitors driving to the lake from California's coastal and valley towns to gamble, hundreds of Tahoe property owners began a scramble to provide them with the other services they required for a comfortable visit: motels, stores, restaurants, and auto garages.

Logged-over land at Bijou, on California's south shore, had sold for less than two dollars an acre in the late nineteenth century. By the end of World War II it brought as much as $150 per front foot, and by the early and middle 1950s tht figure had leapt to $500. A vacant lot which sold for $3,800 in 1954 increased in value to $18,000 by 1957, inspiring a San Francisco newspaperman to write, "If you

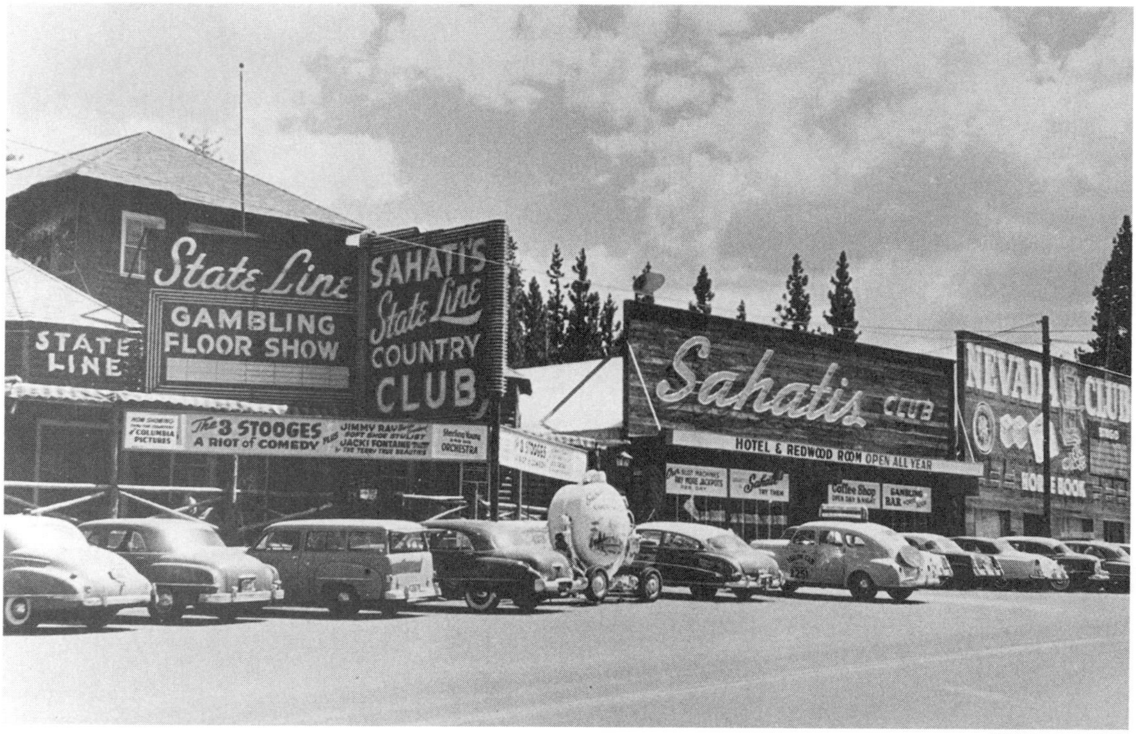

GREAT BASIN GALLERY

Tahoe's South Shore as it looked in the pre-Harrah era.

have some money in the bank, run — don't walk — to the south end of Lake Tahoe. More is waiting if you know what you are doing."

At about the same time, ski developments began to multiply, gradually transforming Tahoe's "season" from a busy four-month summer to a brawling year-round affair. When the 1960 Winter Olympics were held at nearby Squaw Valley, Tahoe's commercial exploitation accelerated in quantum jumps.

One consequence of this profitable activity has been the continuing degradation of the lake's famous clarity.

But despite the development, despite the traffic, despite the drought, despite the algae, despite everything, Lake Tahoe is still one of the most pleasant and beautiful places on earth.

GOLD HILL NEWS ARCHIVE

The setting for skiing at Tahoe is unsurpassed.

MS DIXIE COLLECTION

The MS Dixie II takes Tahoe visitors on escursion cruises from Zephyr Cove.

Touring at Lake Tahoe

A visit to Lake Tahoe can be anything you want it to be. You can ski, hike, fish, swim or sunbathe, depending on the season. You can spend $500 a day for a penthouse suite at Harrah's or you can roll up in a sleeping bag and gaze at the stars for nothing. You can snack on goose liver pate or dine out on a Big Mac and fries, sip champagne or gulp a slurpee. You can rent anything to get around on from a helicopter to roller skates, including boats of every description — fast ones to pull you around on waterskis or slow ones for trolling. And speaking of boats, at night you can dance to a jazz band aboard the paddlewheeler cruise boat in the moonlight, or draw a "full boat" at the poker table at one of the gambling houses.

South Shore

The present community of Stateline sprawls across the area occupied in Tahoe's quiet past by a pair of settlements called Lakeside and Edgewood. Lakeside was centered on Carney's (formerly Lapham's) Stateline House, an inn built in the early 1860s to serve the flood of Comstock traffic and bisected by the California-Nevada boundary survey of 1873. The inn burned in 1876 and was not rebuilt until 1892, by which time a small settlement had grown up on the site. By 1901 Lakeside had flourished to the extent of having a post office and a boat landing with regular steamer service. A new survey in 1899 placed the heart of the community a half mile deeper into California, and as the years passed in tranquility, Lakeside became an attractive little enclave of summer cottages. With the scrambling dash toward exploitation which began in the early 1950s, Lakeside property values soared enormously because of the proximity of the Nevada casino developments. It became a clutter of motels, gift stores, cafes, and other enterprises auxiliary to the gambling trade next door in Nevada. Some of that clutter was swept away recently when a number of aging motels were taken by right of eminent domain, paid for, demolished, swept away and replaced by the modern new hotel you see next door to Harrah's and the base station for the mountainside trams.

Edgewood originated in yet another of the strategically located stations on the Johnson Pass Road, the renowned Friday's Station established by Friday Burke and Big Jim Small in 1860. As soon as a log barn and a shed could be thrown together to accommodate, respectively, horses and men, Friday's served as Nevada's westernmost relay station for the Pony Express. Friday's was home station for Pony Bob Haslem, the messenger whose famous ride — 380 miles on horseback through hostile Indian territory — ranks as the outstanding feat of that spectacular organization. Burke and Small also controlled the toll road franchise past their expanded station, and collected as much as $1,500 a day in the peak months of the Comstock traffic before the railroad. The Pioneer Stage Line used the station as a horse change and dinner station as well.

When the railroad destroyed the lake's roadside prosperity, the partners split their holdings. Small kept the old station and Burke the lakefront land to the east as far as Round Hill. By the 1880s Small was publicizing his "Buttermilk Bonanza Ranch" by reporting tongue-in-cheek sightings of a mermaid "with a fine chest development, beautiful white mustache one and one-half inches long, and a most amenable nature" frolicking just offshore.

Remarkably enough considering the rush to build everywhere along the lakefront, the old Friday's Station still stands opposite the golf course, a small white building in the trees. Its original hand-hewn interior walls and floors are intact. It goes unnoticed by the iron tide of traffic that floods past it each day, bound for the blaze of lights just down the road.

Stateline today is politically part of Nevada, but economically a part of California. Most of the millions who visit the Tahoe basin have driven up from northern and central California, and most of the thousands who serve them drinks, deal them cards and carry their luggage on the Nevada side of the Lake go home across the California line after work.

The casinos attract their crowds not only with their Tahoe surroundings, but with fine food in great variety, entertainment, service and luxury. Harrah's, and the Montbleu (formerly Caesar's) rank with the finest hotels in the world. Add the pioneering and ever-popular Harvey's and the Tahoe Horizon (originally built as Del Webb's Sahara Tahoe) rising hugely up across the boulevard, and an astonishing stage is set — every imaginable enjoyment within easy reach and served in a setting of incomparable natural majesty.

The 18-hole Edgewood Tahoe Golf Course, a beautiful par 74 championship course, is open May through November. A little farther on, Nevada 207, the Kingsbury Grade, intersects on the east, leading over the summit to the breathtaking descent into the Carson Valley.

East Shore

Round Hill Village is an enclosed shopping center housing a variety of shops, cafes, bars and restaurants. A paved road leading to the lakeshore provides access to Nevada Beach for swimming, boating and picnicking. The network of roads serving the residential developments on the mountainside above provides any number of magnificent views.

Zephyr Cove is a couple of miles farther north, the lodge a familiar Tahoe favorite, and the Marina serving as home port for the stern wheeler MS Dixie II, the graceful trimaran Woodwind and a fleet of lesser vessels for rent. The Dixie makes several daily lake cruises. The itinerary varies according to the weather but usually includes Emerald Bay and the scenic north and west shores. The Zephyr Cove Riding Stable rents horses for a scenic ride that affords a view of all four shores of the Lake.

The State Park system provides some parking for shore fishermen with restrooms and boat launching ramp. Beyond Glenbrook, US 50 turns west and climbs toward Spooner's Summit and Carson City. At the junction with Highway 28, Lake Tahoe traffic takes a left turn and continues north. A short distance beyond the junction is Spooner Lake, a developed recreation area in the Lake Tahoe State Park. The trail around the lake is slightly longer than a mile-and-a-half and represents an easy and pleasant hour's stroll, with herons, squirrels and dragonflies for companionship. A tougher challenge is the five miles of uphill trail to Marlette Lake, and while overnight camping is permitted, campers must register at Sand Harbor park headquarters beforehand. In winter the Spooner Lake trails are used for crosscountry skiing.

The two lane highway continues to meander north along the Lake's eastern shore, passing the entrance to Thunderbird Lodge, one of the greatest residential estates on Lake Tahoe from the period in which prominent San Francisco society built homes on the lake. Access is limited and tours given only by prior arrangement. George Whittel, the wealthy builder of the lakeside mansion also owned the legendary 55' speedboat Thunderbird, which still cruises the lake.

Most of the east lake shore is undeveloped and much of it is included in Nevada's Lake Tahoe State Park. Park headquarters are at Sand Harbor, about eight miles beyond Spooner Lake. Sand Harbor was created as a swimming beach and boat launching facility at one of the loveliest sites on the lake. There is car and boat parking available. Bathrooms and water are available, but no overnight camping is permitted. A mile and a half walk to Hidden Beach provides a secluded spot for swimming and sunbathing. Hidden Beach is also the trailhead for

GREAT BASIN GALLERY

Crystal Bay at Tahoe's north shore in the '50s.

routes to Hobart Creek and Marlette Lake. Sand Harbor park personnel can provide all information about recreation opportunities at Lake Tahoe State Park, including the Shakespeare performances at Sand Harbor, special events for kids, guided nature hikes and other activities through the year. Fees are charged for use of the facilities and the park is open year round.

North Shore

A short distance north of Sand Harbor stands the former site of the Ponderosa Ranch, the setting for one of television's most popular programs.

The community of Incline Village spreads along the Tahoe shore and the pine-forested slopes above it. Here begins the urbanized section of the north end of the Lake, a more relaxed and less crowded form of city life than the L.A.-in-the Pines at the south shore. There are no traffic jams here, anyhow. Yet.

There are excellent restaurants here, though, among them the American eclectic Bobby's Uptown (barbecued ribs, Louisiana gumbo, roast turkey), the China Chef (lemon chicken, wor bar), and Marie France (filet mignon of pork with pears and red wine sauce, roasted duck with rhubarb sauce).

The Hyatt Regency is a capsule of cosmopolitan luxury in the forest, and its Lone Eagle Grille on the lake shore is an inviting haven for food and drink.

Crystal Bay

Crystal Bay begins where Incline Village leaves off and extends to the California state line where a concentration of small gambling houses has been doing a seasonal business since before World War II. During Prohibition the bar at the Cal-Neva Lodge was an uproarious rendezvous, one of the most famous and fashionable speakeasies in the American West, with gambling games presided over by genial Jim McKay, whose career came to an end with a term in Leavenworth. More recently it was owned in part by Frank Sinatra until the state gaming authorities yanked his license (later restored) for having unsuitable playmates.

The Cal-Neva today is as respectable as any gambling house in the state, and the largest at Crystal Bay with 200 rooms in a ten-story tower overlooking the Lake. The state line slices through the swimming pool and the lobby, but the gambling rooms are firmly on the Nevada side.

The Crystal Bay Club and the new Borderhouse Brewing Company add to the interest at the California line. "The season" has finally become a 12-month affair here, although some businesses here still close for the winter.

California begins at the west edge of Crystal Bay, and California 267, an all-weather highway north from King's Beach, puts Truckee and Interstate 80 only a dozen miles away.

Pony Express Territory

WHILE THE WAGON TRAINS plodded along the twisting course of the Humboldt River to the north, Russell, Majors & Waddell chose a shorter, rougher route to the south for their adventurous transcontinental message delivery system, the Pony Express.

Despite its brief existence nearly a century-and-a-half ago, their incredible enterprise is still a potent symbol of the American West, and the flavor it added to the character of Nevada is still a part of the feast.

In the spring of 1860 riders for the western division of the Pony Express were recruited in Carson City. About 60 men were sent out, with their ponies, revolvers, blankets and Bibles, to the new stations being built in a westward chain from Salt Lake City. Their heroics set a standard for the frontier, yet the names of only 27 of the Nevada riders are known today. Two of them lie buried not far from Austin, both killed by Indians. Billy Tate was 14 when he slapped his horse on the rump and turned to face the Bannocks and Utes who were chasing him toward Fort Ruby.

As described in the BLM's excellent book, The Pony Express in Nevada, the demanding duties of the division superintendents give a sense of the dimension of the challenge faced by the men of the Pony Express.

"These men were on the trail most of the time, meeting and disposing of emergencies as they arose. It was up to the division superintendent to see that the livestock was kept in good condition; to apprehend horse thieves; to keep stations supplied when no supplies were in sight; to see that substitutes were available when riders were sick, or injured or had suddenly quit the service, and to build on the ruins of stations that had been destroyed by Indians. From Kearny to Carson City, each superintendent on his allotted part of the Express Trail was general, judge and jury."

In 1860, Sir Richard Burton, a famous British explorer and writer of the day, traveled to Salt Lake City, drawn by his curiosity about Mormon polygamy. From Salt Lake City he proceeded to California, traveling with a mule train along the Pony Express Trail. His diary provides us with some of

Sand Mountain.

BILL GERMINO

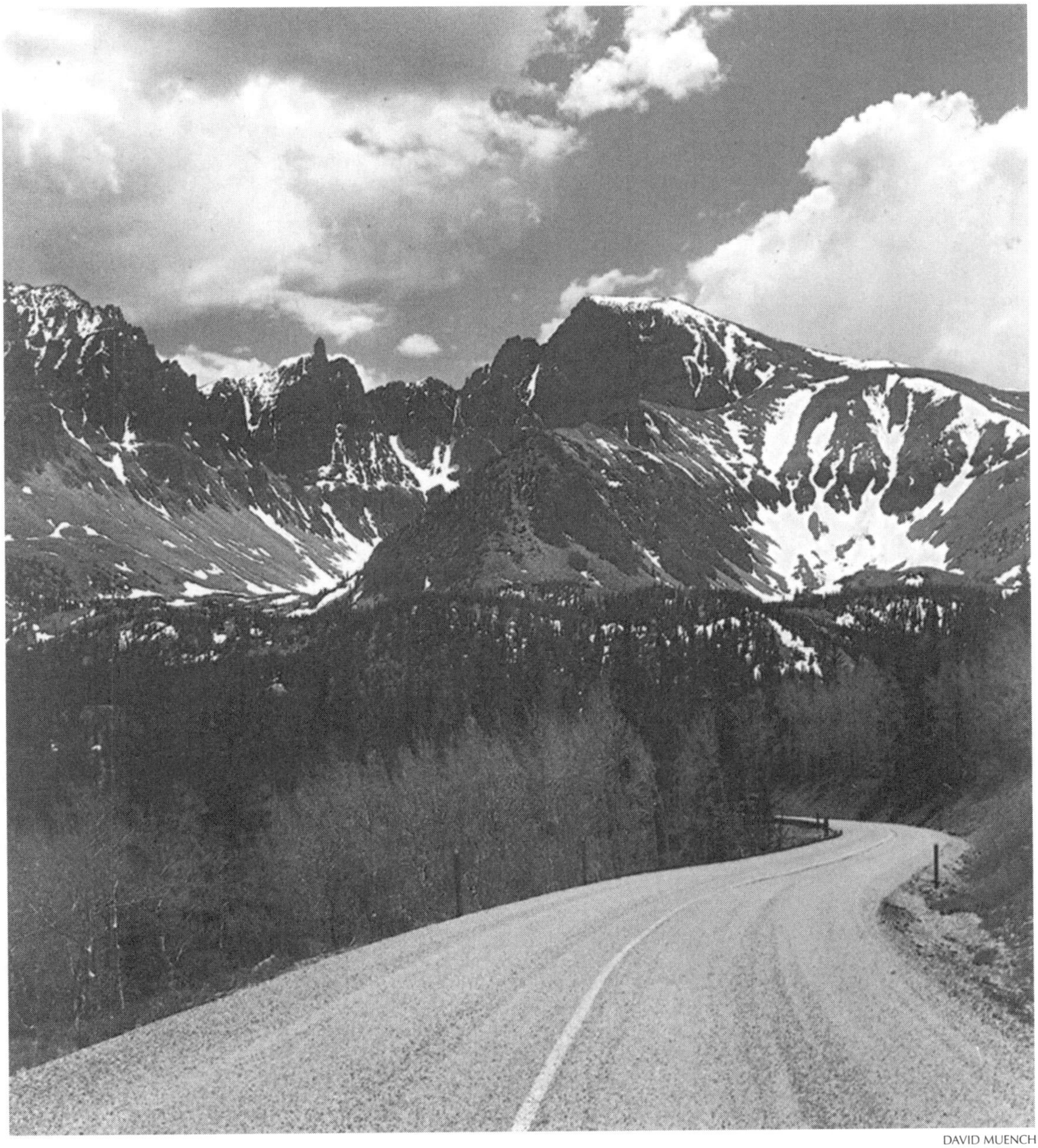

DAVID MUENCH

Mount Wheeler

the clearest glimpses we have of central Nevada in that period.

Sand Springs Station, October 17, 1860:

"At last at 2:30 a.m. thoroughly 'knocked up', we sighted a roofless shed, found a haystack, and reckless of supper or of stamping horses, fell asleep upon the sand. . . .

"Sand Springs deserved its name. Like the Brazas de San Diego and other mauraises near the Rio Grande, the land is cumbered here and there with drifted ridges of the finest sand, sometimes 200 feet high and shifting before every gale. Behind the house stood a mound shaped like the contents of an hour glass, drifted up by the stormy S.E. gale in esplanade shape and falling steep to northward or against the wind. The water near the vile hole was thick and stale with

NELL MURBARGER

Ruby Valley Pony Express Station.

sulfury salts: it blistered even the hands. The station house was no unfit object on such a scene, roofless and chairless, filthy and squalid, with a smoky fire in one corner, impure floor, the walls open to every wind, and the interior full of dust. Hibernia, herself, never produced aught more characteristic. Of the employees, all loitered and sauntered about desoeuvre's as cretins except one, who lay on the ground crippled and apparently dying by the fall of a horse upon his breastbone."

So much for the romance of the frontier.

The Pony Express died with the completion of the telegraph. But before it quite gave out, the Overland Mail Company bought it for the stations, and began stagecoach service between Salt Lake City and San Francisco across Nevada. For a few months in 1861 the Overland Stage shared the route and facilities with the Pony Express, and it was during this time that Sam Clemens of Hannibal, Missouri, came west on the Overland Stage to make a name for himself.

Clemens had resigned his position with the Confederate Army one night in 1861 to come west by stage and join his brother in Carson City. In Roughing It eleven years later, he recalled one of the most stirring experiences of his journey:

"We had a consuming desire, from the beginning, to see a pony-rider, but somehow or other all that passed us and all that met us managed to streak by into the night, and so we heard only a whiz and a hail, and the swift phantom of the desert was gone before we could get our heads out of the windows. But now we were expecting one along every moment, and would see him in broad daylight. Presently the driver exclaims:

"'HERE HE COMES!'

"Every neck is stretched further, and every eye strained wider. Away across the endless dead level of the prairie a black speck appeared

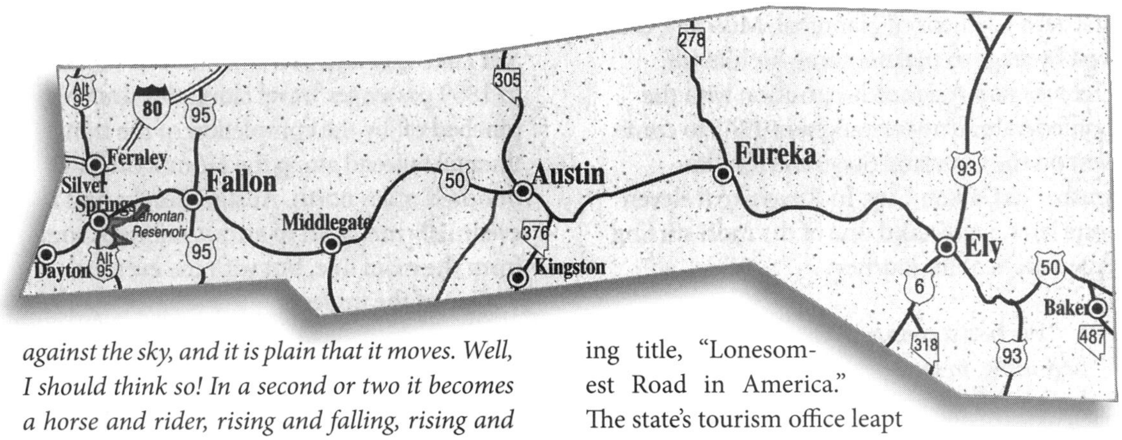

against the sky, and it is plain that it moves. Well, I should think so! In a second or two it becomes a horse and rider, rising and falling, rising and falling - sweeping toward us nearer and nearer- growing more and more distinct, more and more sharply defined - nearer and still nearer, and the flutter of the hoofs come faintly to the ear- another instant and a whoop and a hurrah from our upper deck, a wave of the rider's hand but no reply, and man and horse burst past our excited faces, and go winging away like a belated fragment of a storm!

"So sudden is it all, and so like a flash of unreal fancy, that but for the flake of white foam left quivering and perishing on a mail-sack after the vision had flashed past and disappeared, we might have doubted whether we had seen any actual horse and man at all, maybe."

The stagecoach put some of Nevada's earliest settlements on the main line of travel between Salt Lake City and Sacramento. But suddenly in 1869 passenger travel along this route was pinched off by the completion of the transcontinental railroad along the Humboldt Trail a hundred miles north. Austin, Eureka and Ely eventually managed to attract railroads south from the main line, but with the eventual decline of the mines, these railroads reduced their schedules and eventually stopped running altogether.

In our own time, completion of Interstate 80 as the major east-west bridge across the state has further reduced the traffic along the old Pony Express Trail, and US 50 traverses a region that has been left pretty much to itself — until a mining excitement boils up, or the military has a plan that needs some unprotected landscape to carry out.

About ten years ago a Life Magazine photographer drove this highway and was so impressed by its solitude that his photo appeared under the daunting title, "Lonesomest Road in America." The state's tourism office leapt at this opportunity, and now you can get everything from t-shirts to bumper stickers proclaiming you as a survivor of this lonesome highway.

It wasn't always lonesome. There were dozens of booming towns out here once, mining towns that shared a certain sameness to their stories. Each of them began with a man alone, or a few men at most, high up in some nameless canyon, chipping chunks of likely looking rock away, stuffing it into pockets and knapsacks, and piling up cairns to mark corners of claims and then plodding across the desert miles to record the claim with the mining district and assay the ore.

If the strike didn't die away to nothing with the assay report, and many did, the men returned to their find to await the rush following close behind them. Every threadbare adventurer, every loosely-tethered mining man for a hundred miles around who heard the news hurried to put together a pack and hot-foot it to "the mines" — nothing more than gopher holes scratched into the hillside.

They scrambled to find promising ground as yet unclaimed. Failing that, they claimed barren ground as near as possible to the richest holes. They pitched tents, roofed dugouts with brush, propped up lean-tos, then broke out their picks, shovels, singlejacks and drills and set to work.

If the camp didn't dry up and die after a few weeks of feverish effort — and many did — if some promise of treasure remained, no matter how false or fleeting, the first small-time entrepreneurs began to find their way to the camp. A man unloads used lumber from a rump-sprung wagon, tacks a plank floor together on the ground with some bent and rusty nails, slaps up a flimsy framework above it, and hangs a patched and mildewed canvas tent on that. He carries bags, barrels and boxes through the door flap, and puts up a hand-painted sign over it: GROCERIES.

Another tent encloses a cast-iron cookstove: BAKERY Fresh Bread Pies. A third tent carries the shaky legend LODGINGS and a fourth calls itself a CAFE with its tin chimney launching an occasional spark out over the canvas rooftops of the sudden little town. And every second tent sold whisky.

If the village didn't die of economic paralysis, and many of them did, if enough ore was getting, somehow, to a mill, somewhere, to maintain a trickle of cash and an atmosphere of optimism, a somewhat better-upholstered class of entrepreneurs began to appear. Gamblers and prostitutes caught the scent of ready money across the miles of desolation, and came to earn their share. Real estate promoters and mining stock speculators materialized, measuring the prospects with their eyes a-glitter. They platted townsites and bought up claims from paper millionaires.

Two or three of the whisky tents had gambling tables now, and sleeping quarters were available by day or by the shift to men who worked for wages. Teamsters whipped their struggling animals into camp and began unloading a printing press and racks of type: the place was a city now, with a newspaper to trumpet its miraculous richness far and wide. A stage line established a regular schedule to connect the camp with established communities nearby. Main Street extended a hundred yards from end to end and several hundred people were settled in and running nearly 30 businesses. More were arriving every day, each with something to sell, if only his labor.

If the settlement didn't die then, if the mines continued to show promise, bull-whackers appeared in the low desert distances, inching along the valley floor with immense loads of machinery. Hoists and stamps, pumps and crushers came slowly up the mountainside. Wagons carried planed boards from faraway sawmills, and a brickyard in a nearby canyon was selling every crudely-shaped, rock-riddled brick baked in wood and brush-fueled kilns. Permanent buildings began to rise along the business street, and if there were mines actually producing in the district, some of the buildings towered as tall as three stories.

Already the character of the place was very much changed from its beginnings just a few months before. It was still a rough place, with very few women and children — who were careful to avoid certain sections of town — but it was no longer a free-for-all. The will-o'-the wisp prospectors who had first rushed to the place had sold their claims and moved on to prowl some other lonesome canyon. Those who had no claims to sell moved on anyhow, or transformed themselves reluctantly, usually unsuccessfully, into wage-earning miners working a regular shift for a boss in somebody else's mine. Churches were built, a board of trade formed, fraternal lodges chartered, schools established and teachers hired. Civilizing influences of every kind proliferated.

If the town didn't die then, if the miners deep underground continued to drift into rich rock, the combination of self-conscious municipal pride and the desolate social and physical environment prompted the importation of culture. Lecturers, musicians and repertory troupes added the new burg to their back-country itineraries. A baseball team was formed. If a railroad could be lured by the prospect of a profitable long-term freight busi-

GOLD HILL NEWS ARCHIVE

Wild horses still roam free.

WALT MULCAHY

Smith Creek Station, oriinal adobe structure with more recent rock additions.

ness, townspeople contributed to its construction.

A telegraph line was stapled to the few remaining runty trees and extended over the hilltops to join the main line. Streets were illuminated. A movement was drafted among the influential citizens to snatch the county seat away from an enfeebled rival, a hotel was built with Belgian carpets and fireplaces in every room —

And then it died.

Just died.

The veins pinched out six, eight, twelve hundred feet underground and the city died the way a tree dies when its roots no longer provide sustenance.

Miners and mill workers were laid off their jobs, and after a few uneasy days or weeks waiting for the work to begin again, they moved away, leaving calendars on the wall and lace window curtains fluttering in the dry desert breezes. With their departure the business district shriveled, and the newspaper, deprived of readership and advertisers, but wheezing optimism to the last, coughed up one small, final edition and was loaded unceremoniously into a wagon to reappear in a new scatter of tents. The whores went, and the gamblers. The mills were dismantled and their machinery hauled back down the mountainside. The railroad pried up its rails and abandoned the roadbed.

A few stayed; a few always did. Men who had burned all their bridges, hurried too often to the next elusive bonanza, lost their taste for the chase. They rummaged in leased mines to scrape out a living, and tore down abandoned houses for winter firewood. Despite the presence of these old men, sagebrush grew back in the streets, and the buildings along Main Street began to sag.

And burn. A careless fire, a creosote-caked stovepipe, a gust of wind, a spark on a roof of sun-warped shingles, and what was once a lively neighborhood of mining families became a black patch on the canyon floor with only a handful of swooning structures left intact.

You'll find the roofless ruin of New Pass Station in the mountains east of Sand Spring. Pull in. A chain link fence now protects the remains of this rugged structure better than repeating rifles did when it was new. Only your car and the fence intrude on a landscape that is the same as when the stagecoach rattled in to change horses.

This slender thread of pavement runs east-west across the north-south grain of the mountains, through what remains of the authentic frontier. As you travel here you'll find that nothing has been glamorized, fancified or falsified. This is the real West, what little remains of it.

MAX WINTHROP

Downtown Baker on a sunny winter's day.

Baker

THIS TINY SETTLEMENT in the Snake Valley a few miles from the Utah line is the capital of an enchanted realm in the high summits of Great Basin National Park, the subterranean mysteries of the Lehman Caves and the sleepy village itself, where peace competes with quiet to be the main attraction.

BAKER	
Ely	70
Wells	207
Tonopah	237
Las Vegas	354

Baker is another of 'Nevada's Hidden Treasures'. When David Letterman sent his producer Biff Henderson here, Biff reported on the show: "It's quiet, peaceful, beautiful and the people are friendly."

In the 1870s the Osceola-to-Frisco stage came this way, and the wide spot in the road through the Baker Ranch eventually got a post office. It is nearly metropolitan now, with T&D's store offering all provisions as well as hunting and fishing licenses in Nevada and Utah, food, drink and gasoline. And you'll find a choice of lodgings. When a new owner took over the Silver Jack Motel (now The Silver Jack Inn), I wondered if its ineffible charm would survive, but he has laid any qualms to rest. The former gift shop — originally the town's General Store — has been transformed into a bright and friendly dining room, serving espresso, french toast and omelettes in the morning and an eclectic menu throughout the day: "Like Life, Our Menu Changes Daily". The bar is stocked with the finest American-made wine and beer — yes, he has Ruby Mountain Amber Ale — and fine spirits from around the world. Or you can sleep where it's quiet on the Utah side of the state line at The Border Inn on US 6/50 at the Utah line (the slot machines are on the Nevada side, of course). Any way you do it, Baker is an enjoyable base camp for exploring the Park.

The Border Inn is the site of the Old Sheepherders' Party each January. There's a traditional sheep camp buffet dinner on Friday night followed by Open Mike entertainment. Saturday begins with a sourdough pancake breakfast followed by a day of lollygagging and socializing, and a Saturday night dinner in the traditional Basque family style: beef tongue, bean and cabbage soup, lamb roast and sorbet. Oh, and wine. A lot of wine, and a Sheepherders' Ball that continues late into the night.

The popularity of the event has drawn more participants each year, and the Inn is expanding itsr main building in large part to accommodate it. But as enjoyable as the party is, there are fewer and fewer sheepherders to enjoy it. "The last of the Basque sheepherders working around here left the range in 1977," owner Denys Koyle explains. "After that it was Scotsmen and then Navajos; they're all Peruvians these days. And where I used to have 30 or 40 of them in here on a Saturday night, I might get 8 or 9 now.

"So when people say to me, 'Your party will be as big as the Cowboy Poetry Gathering before long,' I say, 'No it won't.' But I'm not doing this to build a big event. I'm doing this to make some old men happy."

Wildlife abounds: a herd of 20 antelope eluded my camera on my most recent visit, mule deer and mountain lion are hunted here. There are five streams teeming with the native Bonneville Cutthroat at elevations above 7,000 feet, and rainbow, German brown and brook trout (as well as hybrids) at Baker and Johnson Lakes. The Spring Creek Rearing Station, about 10 miles south of Baker via Nevada 487 and graded dirt road, rears trout for planting all over the state (including the nearby Silver Creek Reservoir) is open to visitors — fishermen and their kids will enjoy it.

Other enjoyments include hiking to Wheeler Peak on the afternoon of a full moon to watch the sun set and the moon rise from 13,000 feet. Or you can resolve to take your time as you drive from the town to the Park, driving and pa using, driving and pausing so as to admire the art: A few years ago Baker's Permanent Wave art movement (like New York's Ashcan School, but more cheerful) began decorating the fence posts and bobwar between Baker and the Park. Now the fences are alive with whimsical images. And you can always sip a cool drink on the porch while watching the clouds drift by.

Welcome to Baker

Lodgings

THE BORDER INN

US 6/50 at the Utah Line. 775-234-7300

Your comfortable base camp for exploring Great Basin National Park. Complete 24-hour service: gasoline, diesel, Motel, Cafe with home-made breads and pastries, slots, bar, laundromat and showers. New dining room and space for private parties. Owner Denys Koyle likes satisfied customers. Her goal is to have you come back again!

The Permanent Wave Society

"It was the magic of the moment," as Doc Sherman explained it. Doc was the founding father of the Permanent Wave Society, and he was recounting the day that art broke out into full public view in Baker.

"There was the fence post … there was the glove … and one thing led to another," he explained, in words worthy of a historical marker. The first glove giving a permanent wave inspired a variety of other foam-filled gloves, fingers lifted in a permanent wave, and then more sophisticated constructions, and soon the entravbce road to the National Park was

lined for most of its length with light-hearted art of considerable verve and diversity. In this majestic landscape of sky, mountain, sagebrush and clarity, the Permanent Wave Society became a powerful rtistic movement (like the Ashcan School, but more cheerful) involving many people in the community.

"I work at it off and on, but there have been lots of other local contributions," Doc said. "And they're always getting stolen. But if you could put them all over the country you'd eliminate road rage. Everyone would be smiling, even on the LA freeways."

Doc Sherman has passed away, and the art has thinned out and weathered somewhat. But the road is still alive with his wit and good cheer, a perfect prologue to your visit to the Park.

Great Basin National Park

THIS 77,100-ACRE preserve is one of America's newest National Parks, and the only such federal enclave in Nevada, except for the corner of Death Valley National Park that overlaps far western Nye County. Centered on 13,063 ft Wheeler Peak, the park embraces western landscapes characteristic of great tracts of Nevada, Utah, California, Oregon, Idaho — even a little nibble off the southwestern tip of Wyoming.

The Visitor Center, open 8-5, 362 days a year, lies about an hour's drive east of Ely via US 6/50, five miles west of the town of Baker and about 13 miles west of the Utah border (by road). The Lehman Cave Gift Shop & Cafe is open April through November.

Call 702-234-7331 for information about Park programs, activities and schedules.

The Park provides unlimited opportunity to experience the Great Basin landscape, with developed facilities such as the visitor center and scenic drive, campgrounds and hiking trails. It also contains the Lehman Caves (centerpiece of the former 640-acre Lehman Caves National Monument), one of Nevada's crown jewels.

The cavern itself, which extends much deeper into the mountain than casual tour parties can safely proceed, began formation two to five million years ago. The Snake Range was higher then, and the climate far more humid. Carbon dioxide-charged water, filtering down through cracks and fissures in the limestone of the mountain, dissolved the stone, widening the cracks. Over time the more soluble rock was dissolved, leaving large vaulted rooms. Fault and joint planes were widened into connecting passageways, eventually forming a labyrinth of corridors and smaller winding tunnels.

As lower channels drained water from the upper levels, the calcium-bearing water gathered as drops or spread out as thin films on the ceilings and walls of the caverns, depositing some of the calcium as dripstone. The resulting forms, colors and textures are so spectacular and so exquisitely delicate that a book can't do them justice. See them.

Entering Lehman Caves is so unexpected an experience after the inevitably long, occasionless sagebrush drive to get there, it is like meeting a staunch plain ranch wife and then, unaccountably, entering her unconscious, otherworldly and most wonderfully lovely interior dreams. During the summer the 60- and 90-minute Ranger-guided tours are of-

DAVID MUENCH

Mt. Wheeler, Great Basin National Park

Lehman Caves, Great Basin National Park.

fered seven days a week, 8:30 am-4:30 pm. Tours are limited to 20, and tickets ($8 age 16 and over; $4 age 5-15) can only be purchased at the park on the day of the tour or by telephone (775-234-7331 x 242) up to 30 days in advance. Hint: On some busy days the tours sell out early; buy yours early to be sure of a place. A Candlelight Tour is offered daily at 5 pm to a maximum of 15 persons.

There are also introductory Patio Talks throughout the day during the summer, providing an introduction to the resources within the Park. Evening Campfire programs are offered at Wheeler Peak and Upper Lehman Creek campgrounds. Check at the Visitor Center for details on these and other special activities and events.

A handful of hiking trails provide the best way to see the Park: on foot, and far away from your car (although the scenic drive is also recommended for the views). There's an easy half-mile Self-Guided Loop Trail near the Visitor Center providing a sense of the variety of geologic and life forms represented here. One of the most interesting of these, the Bristlecone Pine Trail, includes trees that are among the oldest living things on earth. The most accessible stand of bristlecones is a 1-3/4-mile hike from the end of the Scenic Drive. It is the trail to the left.

The Baker Creek Trail extends six ruggedly beautiful miles from the Baker Creek Campground to the little cup of cold water called Baker Lake.

The 4-mile Lehman Creek Trail connects Upper Lehman Creek Campground and Wheeler Peak Campground at the end of the Scenic Drive, climbing 2,000 feet in the process.

The Johnson Lake, Big Wash and Lexington Arch Trails are relatively difficult and remote; current details about them should be obtained at the Visitor Center.

RICH MORENO

Bristlecone pine are the oldest living things on earth.

Great Basin National Park also offers some of the most scenic and inspiring areas for backpacking trips. Permits are not now required, but for safety's sake you are encouraged to fill out a voluntary back-country permit and obtain the latest information on trail conditions at the Visitor Center.

Developed Campgrounds

Lower Lehman Creek Campground, 11 sites accessible via the Scenic Drive is at 7,500 feet. Water and pit toilets are provided. $5/day fee; open all year.

Upper Lehman Creek Campground, half a mile farther along the Scenic Drive and 300 feet farther from sea level, provides 24 sites with water and pit toilets provided; $5/day fee; open mid-May to Mid-October.

Wheeler Peak Campground is at the end of the Scenic Drive and at nearly 10,000 feet above sea level. There are 37 sites, water and pit toilets; $5/day fee; open mid-June to Mid-October.

Baker Creek Campground, at 8,000 feet offers 32 streamside sites and pit toilets, no water other than what runs in the stream (and which should be boiled for at least 5 minutes before drinking).

Ward Charcoal Ovens

SEVENTEEN MILES SOUTHEAST of Ely via US 6-93 (for 7 miles) then south on a marked and graded gravel road leading to six huge beehive-shaped charcoal kilns. Built in 1876 of native rock to provide fuel for the Martin White smelter at Ward, they are about 30 feet high. Each oven enclosed about thirty-five cords of pinon-pine wood, stacked in layers. The wood was kindled and the fire controlled by opening and closing small vents around the base of the ovens.

After the smelter closed in the 1880s, the ovens were used for a variety of purposes; as stables, as campsites for sheepherders and buckaroos, and even, according to the story anyhow, as the bridal suite for Addie Hacker and her gambler fiance, who whitewashed one of the kilns in anticipation of the event. They quarreled, alas, and the marriage was not consummated in the oven after all.

Six undeveloped campsites are available here, and little has been done to "improve" the site for visitors: there is no water; no privies, even. But the ovens provide not only unequalled atmosphere for the afternoon meal, but a welcome cool haven during the summer months. A fence has been erected around the ovens to keep the livestock from interfering with the tourists, but the turnstile remains unlocked. A side trip most worthwhile. A Nevada State park (NSP). No fee.

Osceola

39 MILES SOUTHEAST of Ely via US 6-50 and graded dirt road. Organized as a placer mining district in 1872, Osceola staggered along for nearly a decade before canals brought water to the claims in volume enough to permit large scale operations. In the middle 1880s hydraulic mining began and proved profitable for about fifteen years. In 1886 a $6,000 nugget caused considerable admiration and excitement when it was washed free from the hillside. After the turn of the century individual placer miners continued active in such numbers that the town survived, but by 1920 the pickings were too slim to support a post office any longer. Still, Osceola never died completely, and a few residents remain today, though the few remaining business buildings are in ruins.

GOLD HILL NEWS ARCHIVE

Ward Charcoal Ovens.

GOLD HILL NEWS ARCHIVE

Osceola in its heyday.

MAX WINTHROP

Nevada Northern Railway Depot, Eleventh Street, East Ely.

Ely

ELY IS THE GREAT CITY of eastern Nevada, closer to Salt Lake City than to Reno or Las Vegas. It is located where the southern end of the magnificent Steptoe Valley meets foothills of the Egan Range, at the conjunction of Highways 6, 50 and 93. Ely offers many excellent lodging, dining and recreation options in magnificent natural surroundings.

ELY	
Reno	317
Wells	137
Tonopah	163
Las Vegas	284

Ely's greatest attraction to visitors is the Ghost Train, the restored Nevada Northern Railway that takes passengers from the old depot in East Ely (take 11th Street north from Highway 93/ Avenue F/Aultman Street) on excursions west to Ruth and northeast to McGill from Memorial Day through Labor Day. Additional trains are scheduled during the winter months, the Polar Express has Santa aboard, and the Photo Shoot specials in February attract photographers from around the world.

Built in 1906, the Nevada Northern connected the enormous pit mines at Ruth with the smelter on the old McGill Ranch, and then with the main line at Cobre for an overall run of not quite 150 miles. After considerable repair and restoration, the Nevada Northern began carrying passengers again in 1986.

Railroad buffs now converge on Ely from all over the world. They light up with pleasure as the antique locomotives squeal and hiss up to the passenger depot. They exult at the conductor's "All Aboard!" They thrill at the thought of an Ely-McGill-Cherry Creek excursion train, and they faint away with joy at the prospect of going all the way to Cobre.

No wonder: Magic happens as the antique steamers chuff solemnly away from the station. Wheels clickety-clacking, cars swaying, the world gliding slowly by, kids waving from their bikes, cows looking up in dim curiosity, sky spread big and bright overhead — it's a unique and delightful experience for its own sake, and even more for being the real thing — this is not a reconstruction or a restoration. Fares hover around $10 for adults, $4 for kids (call 702-289-2085 for details).

In addition to the scheduled runs, trains can be rented for special excursions, and tours are taken through the enormous shops, offices, depot, engine house and other facilities from Memorial Day weekend through Labor Day weekend.

The White Pine Public Museum at 2000 Aultman Street is the showplace for a mineral collection of considerable variety, and for unique items like the home-made cannon which once guarded the Court House in Hamilton. The museum is open seven days during June, July and August, and Monday through Friday the rest of the year. Admission is free.

Ely was established in the 1870s as a stagecoach station and post office. Only after it was designated the White Pine County seat in 1887 did the population climb to 200. Most of the activity in the region was at the surrounding mining camps of Ward, Cherry Creek, Osceola and Taylor.

After the turn of the century, immense copper deposits near Ely began to attract attention away from the failing gold mines, and by 1906 a boom had developed in copper. The Nevada Northern Railway was completed in the fall of that year to connect the mines with the Southern Pacific Railroad at Cobre. In 1908, when the smelter at McGill went on the line, mineral production leapt from barely more than $2000 the year before to more than $2 million.

RICH MORENO

Street scene, Ely.

By 1917 annual production climbed to nearly $26.5 million. The Kennecott Copper Company began acquiring Ely copper mining companies in 1915. By 1958 these acquisitions resulted in control of the region's copper mines and dominated the local economy.

The mines are at Ruth, six miles west via US 50. Originally underground mines, they came to be worked from the surface: five great open pits in a line measuring six miles east and west. Each working day about 80,000 tons of waste dirt and 22,000 tons of copper ore were hauled up out of the immense holes. The waste was dumped on the hillside terraces, and the ore went by train past the depot and shops in East Ely to the smelter at McGill, where it was processed into "blister copper." This was poured in 60-lb. cakes and hauled north to the main line of the S.P. When the cars returned, they brought coal to fire the enormous power generation plant. All that is in the past tense, however. In 1978 the copper mines closed, the smelter closed, the railroad closed, and most of Kennecott's 1500 local employees were laid off.

The departure of Kennecott was a watershed event in White Pine County history, and for nearly 20 years nothing quite took up the economic slack. The economic downturn precluded widespread renovation, and the early 20th century small-town architecture

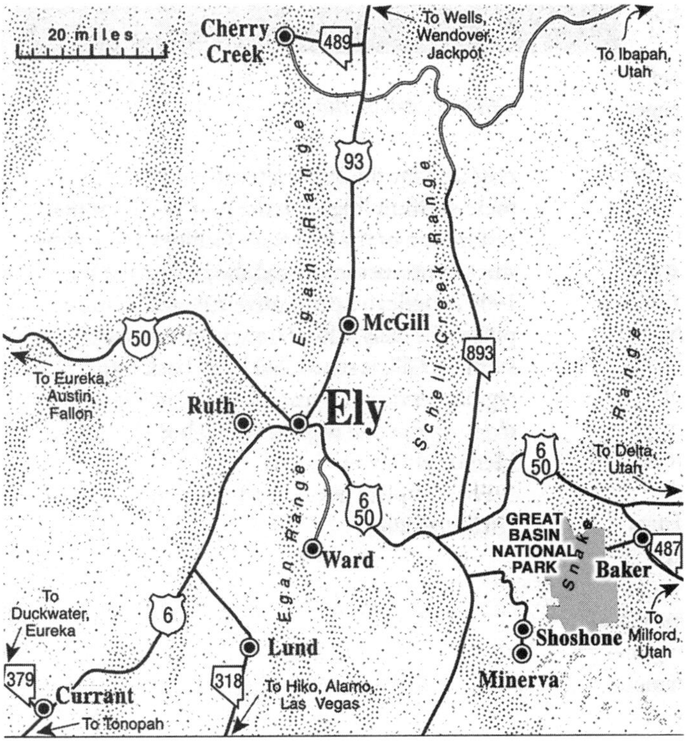

The Nevada Northern Railway

FROM THE CENTER of Ely drive east on Aultman Street through the stop light at 7th Street, which is the boundary line of East Ely, created as the railroad's terminal town to avoid the difficulties and expense of taking the railroad into Ely proper. Turn left on 11th Street, and the depot is directly ahead. This was a major commercial boulevard in the early years of the century.

Established in 1906 to haul copper ore from the mine to the smelters and copper cake from the smelters to the main line, the Nevada Northern maintained regular Pullman service until 1920, and delivered Ely-McGill commuters to jobs and school until 1938. Freight operations continued until the mines at Ruth shut down for good in the early 1980s.

In 1983 the departing Kennecott Copper Company gave the people of Ely a priceless gift: the last operating short line railroad in Nevada, and the best preserved short line in all of North America. The railroad comprises some 30 structures clustered around the depot in East Ely — including a fully-equipped, if wonderfully archaic machine shop — three steam, five diesel and two electric locomotives, six passenger cars (one with easy chairs and a bar), 70 freight cars, a few cabooses and a snowplow, among other odds and ends.

The White Pine Historical Railroad Foundation was created to manage the gift, and in 1987 restored the "Ghost Train" to service from mid-May to mid-September. Pulled by 1910 Baldwin 10-wheeled steam locomotive #40, the Ghost Train maintains an almost year-around schedule of steam- and diesel-powered excursions on the 26-mile Hi-line and 14-mile Keystone routes. There are also numerous special runs: winter photo shoots, wine trains, barbeque trains, Oktoberfest beer trains, the Chocolate Express, the July 4th BBQ & Fireworks Train, the Polar Express (with Santa on board) and more. By special arrangement you can rent a caboose and drive the locomotive. Fares vary according to the event, with regular excursions hovering around $24 for adults, $15 for kids age 3-12.

NEVADA COMMISSION ON TOURISM

Old #40, still on duty.

There are also guided walkthrough tours of the shops and facilities at the East Ely depot Wed-Sun from May into September ($4 ages 11 and up). Even if you're too young to remember them, you can be overwhelmed by nostalgia for the 1930s after five minutes in these surroundings. On the tour you'll see that restoration of the railroad's facilities and rolling stock continues in the old shops, and the huge 1909 American Locomotive #93, which once pulled the daily school train back and forth from McGill, is back into regular service. Both steam locomotives will operate together on Labor Day and Memorial Day weekends.

For complete fare and schedule information: or www.nevadanorthernrailway.net; 775-289-2085.

MAX WINTHROP

Ely.

that dominates its center give Ely a familiar look. Norman Rockwell would have liked it, and you will like it too.

For a while in the early 1990s it seemed the tide had turned when the old Kennecott property at Ruth was acquired by Magma Copper Co. in 1991. At the time, Magma's president predicted "this could be the last big copper project in this country."

The company spent $314 million to establish a state of the art mill capable of processing 46,000 tons of ore per day. Mineable reserves of 252 million tons were blocked out, and in January 1995 enormous electric shovels ($6 million each) began scooping 40 tons at a bite from the old Liberty Pit. A fleet of 240-ton haul trucks ($1.6 million each) hauled overburden and stockpiled ore for processing. Original estimates called for mining through 2010, and in 1996 425 employees produced 146,000 pounds of copper, 366,000 ounces of silver and 16,000 ounces of gold, prompting talk of expanding the operation. In 1997 it closed down. It has since been reopened by a new company.

Excellent lodgings are plentiful in Ely. The jewelbox Steptoe Valley Inn B&B is a block from the railroad station. The Copper Queen Ramada Inn is a block south on US 93 — its rooms open directly into a great central room containing the casino, bar and swimming pool. The Prospector Hotel, formerly a Holiday Inn, welcomes guests on US 93 at the north edge of town, and more motels welcome travelers on Aultman Street. Downtown the modern new Jailhouse Casino and Motel is a phenomenon in its own right, occupying the site of the original city jail and offering the unusual opportunity of cellblock dining without being arrested, charged or convicted.

Across the street the historic 6-story Hotel Nevada & Gambling Hall presides over downtown as it has done since 1928. For three generations it has been the city's principal hostelry, and for 20 years — until 1948 — it was Nevada's tallest building. Along with much of the downtown, it had become shabby, but new owners have restored it far beyond its original eminence. Murals by Nevada's favorite artist Larry Bute decorate the hoitel inside and out. Deluxe rooms are named for the celebrities who have stayed there over the years — Hoot Gibson, Ingrid Bergman and Tennessee Ernie Ford among

MAX WINTHROP

Murals decorate many prominent Ely buildings.

them — and the 6th floor suite, once reserved for visiting Kennecott executives, has been made lavish and luxurious (Did Elvis sleep in that bed?).

Many of Ely's downtown buildings are distinguished by murals, most of them sponsored by the Ely Renaissance Society, a group formed after the closure of the big copper mine eliminated more than 400 local jobs. The murals were intended to help spruce up the 11-block central core of the city, and to create a new attraction that would help bring visitors. Depicting a variety of local subjects in a variety of styles, the murals and other outside art provide a pleasant and interesting stroll.

Another great attraction for visitors may be the magnificent surroundings. The new Great Basin National Park provides an obvious and rewarding destination, but there is no limit to the outdoor recreation here. Hunting, fishing, camping, hiking, exploring, cross-country skiing and anything else you enjoy doing outdoors is available in the countryside around Ely. Chamber of Commerce information is available on Aultman Street.

You can make a quick — perhaps two hours if you can do it without stopping along the way, or bring your fishing gear and take all day — tour of the high country by taking the Success Summit Loop Road through the Schell Creek Range to the east. Access is via U.S. 6/50/93 east out of town. The road winds north past several campgrounds in the forested heights and takes 33 beautiful miles to find its way back to US 93 north of McGill.

If you enjoy the great outdoors, Ely and its neighbors along US 93 may become your favorite Nevada destinations.

Welcome to Ely

Area Information

WHITE PINE CHAMBER OF COMMERCE
636 Aultman Street 775-289-8877
Ely is the most comfortable city in Nevada, surrounded by the most beautiful country in America. We have it all, and if you'll visit our downtown office we'll help you find everything you're looking for. If you like it here as much as we do, we'll help you relocate too.

Attractions

ELY RENAISSANCE VILLAGE
400 Ely Street. 775-289-8769
Renaissance Village and Historic Murals Step back in time to early day Ely, circa 1900, as miners and railroad workers recruited from abroad, poured into this community creating "Where the World Met and Became One." Visit world-class murals and a village interpreting early Ely. Art Trail brochure available. Information: www.elyrenaissance.com.

NEVADA NORTHERN RAILWAY
11th Street at Avenue A. 775-289-2085
Visit a century old National Historic Landmark the Nevada Northern Railway, consisting of a railyard with 63 buildings, shops and structures; including three steam (two operating) locomotives, six (three operating) diesel locomotives and over sixty pieces of historic railroad equipment. Excursion trips available, the grounds are open year round.

Lodgings

HOTEL NEVADA & GAMBLING HALL.
5th and Aultman Streets downtown. 775-289-6665
We have renovated a dozen rooms on our upper floors to reflect the luxury and gracious appointments of another time. We offer Casino Rates to everyone all year 'round, starting from: $19.95 Single - $24.95 Double* Deluxe Rooms from $38* to $85* You'll enjoy breathtaking Western views, free cable television. All major credit cards. (* plus tax) www.hotelnevada.com. 888-406-3055.

Museums

EAST ELY RAILROAD DEPOT MUSEUM
1100 Avenue A. 775-289-1663
The East Ely Railroad Depot Museum features two fully restored historic buildings on the Nevada Northern Railway complex. The Depot and Freight Building are open to the public. Walk through waiting rooms, baggage storage and offices used by one of the nationís most important railroads.

NEVADA HISTORICAL SOCIETY

Cherry Creek, 1898.

Cherry Creek

54 MILES north of Ely via US 93 and Nevada 489. Established at the mouth of Cherry Creek Canyon in the winter of 1872, the town drew a Wells Fargo office, a post office, the first public school in Nevada and about a thousand hopeful residents.

Two years later a decline in ore production dimmed their hopes and caused a slow dwindling of the town's population, but in 1880 new ore bodies were located and by the following year Cherry Creek's population had increased to nearly 1,800 people.

MAX WINTHROP

Cherry Creek cemetery.

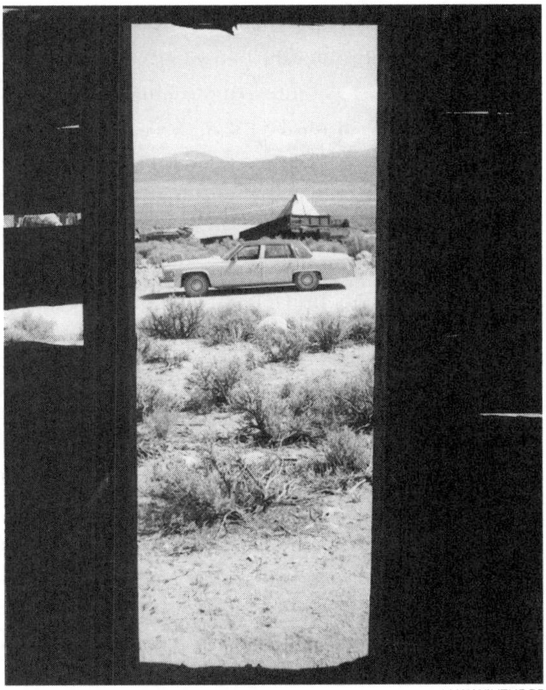

MAX WINTHROP

Miss Daisy through the jailhouse door.

Two years later still, the mines went into decline again, and the alternation between excitement and the doldrums continued until 1940. Since then it has been pure doldrums, with only the prospect of the railroad's restoration offering faint hope for revival.

Less than a dozen permanent residents remain, and the town's children, when there are any, go to school in Ely now. Many structures still survive from the early days, including saloons (out of 27 that flourished here, only one is still open for business), stores, an assay office and the now doorless town jail. A fire in 1901 accounted for most of the rest, but the cemetery remains as a memorial to better times.

EUREKA OPERA HOUSE

Eureka!

Eureka

NEAT, CLEAN AND prosperous, Eureka is one of the best-preserved mining cities in the American West.

Silver strikes made here in 1864 by prospectors from Austin proved uneconomical to work at first because of the high lead content of the ores. Ore was shipped to England and Wales for reduction until 1869, when the first of 16 successful smelters was constructed. Within a decade three mines alone had paid out in dividends more money than had ever been invested in all Eureka County enterprises combined, and Eureka was famous as the "Pittsburgh of the West" because of the black smoke squeezing out of smelter smokestacks to smear the sky and poison the hardy desert vegetation (and the residents too). Eureka produced more than four times the wealth that Austin did, yet its history is rather prim and staid compared to adventurous Austin. Perhaps it was because the principal product of the mines was lead, rather than silver or gold, and drew a less romantic breed of citizen; perhaps it was because, being richer, Eureka was simply less hysterical.

EUREKA	
Ely	77
Austin	70
Carlin	93
Gardnerville	256

In any case, Eureka overtook Austin in size and mining productivity during the middle 1870s when the Eureka & Palisade Railroad was extended south from the Central Pacific without the necessity of bulging the city limits to meet it. By 1878, when Austin had already begun its decline, Eureka had a population of about 9,000 and had taken second place among Nevada cities. There were dozens of saloons, gambling houses and bawdy houses, three opera houses, two breweries, five volunteer firefighting companies, and two companies of militia as well as the usual complement of doctors, lawyers, merchants, bankers, hotels, newspapers, and other businesses. Fifty mines produced lead, silver, gold, and zinc for the smelters, which could process more than 700 tons of ore a day.

In 1879 though, flooding became more of a problem and economy measures were taken. One of these was to reduce the price paid for charcoal at the smelters. The Carbonari ˜ members of the predominantly-Italian Charcoal Burner's Association ˜ answered with a boycott. The smelters shut down for lack of fuel and passions flamed up. Threats and counter-threats raged between all the parties to the dispute. When the Carbonari threatened to make charcoal of all of Eureka, a sheriff's posse ambushed a number of them, killing five and wounding more.

Mining production peaked in 1882 and tailed off rapidly after 1885; by 1891 the major mines had been shut down, and production lapsed into the long snooze that had claimed Austin a decade earlier. Eureka's mining fortunes may be rising again as the Homestake company has reopened the historic Ruby Hill property.

Many of Eureka's buildings are impressive, but the city's architectural jewel is the recently refurbished Eureka Opera House. Built in the fall of 1880 on the smoldering site of the burned-down Odd Fellows' Hall, its grand opening was celebrated with a New Year's Eve gala masquerade ball. The Opera House now welcomes small conventions from around the state, performances by nationally recognized artists, even dinner theater, a cosmopolitan touch long unavailable in Eureka. The

RICH MORENO

Interior of Raine's market, Eureka.

Opera House also serves as a Cultural Arts Center with a permanent fine arts collection, open for visitors during normal business hours.

RICH MORENO

Eureka Sentinel Museum.

The 1877 Jackson House next door has been restored to its original elegance, with nine Victorian bedrooms upstairs and a bar and gourmet restaurant downstairs. The bar and restaurant have been closed for several years, but the rooms may be rented at the Best Western. The splendid Eureka County Court House across the street has been restored to original 1879 condition (but with 1995 foundations); visitors are welcome.

The Eureka Sentinel Building a block south has been converted to a wonderful museum, with the old newspaper back-shop as it was left when the last tramp printer finally called it quits. It is fully equipped with type cases and working presses await an experienced hand, and the walls are papered with posters and handbills dating back to the 1880s. Local area information is available here as well, including a self-guided tour leaflet with information about many of the interesting buildings around town.

Some structures are less remarkable to look at than to know about. The Farmers and Merchants Bank building, for example, was original-

MAX WINTHROP

Street scene, Eureka.

ly a brewery, connected with the hotel across the street by an underground tunnel. The boom days were long over when the bank was organized by former District Attorney Edna Plummer, but it was solid enough to remain open through the National Bank Holiday of 1933. Banks were ordered to remain closed after the conclusion of business on the stated date, but the Eureka Bank avoided the closing by not concluding business, instead staying open day and night until the "holiday" ended.

About those tunnels: the story is that because Eureka's breweries were located on opposite ends of town, the heavy winters (and the availability of skilled miners) prompted the business people to drive tunnels underground from one end of town to the other in order to ensure the prompt delivery of beer to the saloons along Main Street. But that's only one story; according to family recollection, Nevada governor Reinhold Sadler, whose two story brick home is half a block north of the Colonnade House, used a tunnel to get to his Main Street store in the winter so that he wouldn't have to meet his neighbors on the street. Much of the old tunneling has collapsed or is unsafe, but in its heyday it was quite comfortable to use, fancy,

MAX WINTHROP

The Colonnade Hotel, one block south of Main St., in Eureka.

even, with bricked walls, and arched brick chambers reminiscent of medieval dungeons.

As the city's economy shrank with the closing of the mines, businesses and residences were acquired and maintained by the families (many of whom had come out of poverty in Europe) that stayed. Al's Hardware, to take one example out of many, still looks and functions as it did in 1880 when it was the Eureka General Mercantile store.

The Sundown Lodge and the Best Western Eureka Inn on Main Street offer overnight accommodations. The Colonnade Hotel, a block to the south, is being restored and refurbished but is not now open. The Eureka Gallery occupies a former bank building on Main Street with gleaming safe intact. Main Street Gift & Garden is a reliable source of good wine in the wilderness, and next door is the locally-famous Outlaw Outhouse (the story is posted inside) which was once located on the Bartine Ranch west of town and is surely the only 5-hole outhouse in Nevada.

The Owl Club is famous for steaks, but the menu includes some interesting variations, and the wine list is first class. The Pony Espresso Deli at the south end of town was operated by a family of Mennonites, but they have moved to Costa Rica, and at press time it was closed.

Raine's Market provides for the needs of a few hundred people in this isolated community with precision and flair. In its 19th century building ˜ pressed tin ceiling, oiled wood floor ˜ Raine's stocks everything under the sun, or rather under the hunting trophies: moose, deer, mountain lion, antelope, elk, bear ˜ all gaze serenely down on the humankind grazing through the aisles.

There are several cemeteries in Eureka, including one that was set aside for smallpox victims.

Tax money derived from the Carlin gold mine at the far northern end of the county has built a new high school and other modern community facilities in Eureka, including the enclosed pool open six days a week year-around.

The country around Eureka will probably always provide excellent hunting, and simply breathing in the cedar-scented air of the wide open spaces is an act of pure pleasure, utterly unimaginable to the people who lived here breathing its poisonous smoke in the 19th century.

Welcome to Eureka

Attractions

EUREKA OPERA HOUSE
Main Street. 775-237-6006
Enjoy the historic elegance, relaxed small town atmosphere and full convention and meeting services that the Eureka Opera House offers. Call us today to reserve your event. Call to get a schedule of our cultural events and enjoy a performance in the award-winning Grand Hall. Stop in and visit.

Museums

EUREKA SENTINEL MUSEUM
One block south of Main Street. 775-237-5010
Located in the old EurekaSentinel Building, site of the town's longest running newspaper, the museum displays artifacts from Eureka's 1870s lead/silver mining era. Complete press room from the 19th century, with posters printed here and then plastered on the press room walls. 10 am - 6 pm (May - October: daily; November - April: Tuesday - Saturday).

Shopping

EUREKA GALLERY
41 N. Main Street. 775-237-5303
The Eureka Gallery features unique art created by Nevadan artists. Whether you are shopping for paintings, photography, ceramics, turquoise jewelry or momentos of your visit, you will find it at the Eureka Gallery. Open seasonally and by appointment.

MAIN STREET GIFT & GARDEN
21 North Main Street. 775-237-5522
Western gifts and jewelry, Nevada and Highway 50 souvenirs and postcards. For the thirsty traveler we carry soda, beer and have the largest selection of fine wines in the area. We have greeting cards, houseplants and are a full service florist. Stop by and tour the Outlaw Outhouse.

RAINE'S MARKET
81 North Main Street. 775-237-5296
We're the "friendliest store on the Loneliest Road in America," and our 1886 buildings feature pressed-tin ceilings and solid oak floors. You can buy everything from whiskey to horseshoe nails at our supply and information center for travelers, hunters and locals. A must-see even if you don't need groceries.

Austin

FEWER THAN 300 residents remain in Austin from a peak-year population of more than 10,000. The mile-long main street has withered to half its length and gaps appear in the crowded rows of ramshackle buildings ascending the steep sides of Pony Canyon. Yet Austin has a dowager's presence: she may be reduced in circumstances, even raggedy at the elbows, but she is still somebody.

AUSTIN	
Eureka	70
Fallon	110
Reno	170
Las Vegas	324

And recently a new wave of energetic residents has begun to transform the old city again. The Trading Post, stocked with a wide selection of jewelry, Indian goods and historical artifacts, occupies a former service station, and the Main Street Shops are now a thriving presence across the street. The modern Silver State Bar & Grill has opened and closed again, plans are indefinite at press time. There are turquoise shops and other small enterprises up and down Main Street.

You'll find local people friendly and willing to help you find your way around. Chamber of Commerce information is available upstairs at the old Court House, and a Historical Museum occupies the former ForestService building just uphill on Main Street. Food, drink and automotive services are available, and overnight accommodations are available in three modest Main street motels.

Night life proclaims itself in the Main Street saloons that serve as Austin's social centers: Mary & Dessie's and the Owl Club. The International serves a full menu from early morning until late at night, and the Toiyabe Cafe is quite good (hint: taco salad).

Austin's architectural tour de force is Stokes Castle. A marked dirt (sometimes mud) road proceeds south beside the gas station at the lower end of Main Street a quarter-mile to this architectural curiosity. You can see it as you approach Austin from the west, a stone sentry standing on a rocky foothill of the Toiyabes. It is a copy of a Roman villa, built in 1897 as the residence of a prominent mine owner. It is 50 feet square at its base and built three stories high of hand-hewn native granite. The first floor housed the kitchen and dining room, the second floor an immense living room and bath, with bedrooms and another bath on the top floor, and a sun deck on the roof. The nearby overlook offers a view only a half a degree less magnificent than from the Castle's roof.

Another local treasure, the stone and brick St. Augustine's Roman Catholic Church which looms above Main Street, is being restored for use as

NEVADA STATE MUSEUM

International Hotel, Austin.

a community center. The little house just to the north was the home of Dr. Wixom, whose daughter Emma ("Little Wixie") became the world-renowned opera singer Emma Nevada. Her square grand piano has just been returned to the community center in the former Methodist Church.

The cemetery is at the mouth of Pony Canyon west of town is an inviting spot for a historical stroll and a philosophical picnic.

Founded in 1862 as a consequence of the discovery of silver-bearing quartz ledges showing values as high as $7,000 to the ton, Austin had attracted 2,000 residents by the summer of 1863. In its early months, Austin was so isolated and primitive a camp that J. Ross Browne wrote in Harper's: "lodgings in a sheep corral had to be paid for at the rate of fifty cents per night in advance," and that "it was a luxury to sit all night by a stove, or to stand against a post behind a six-foot tent. I have heard of men who contrived to get through the coldest part of the season by sleeping when the sun was warm, and running up and down Lander Hill at night; and another man who staved off the pangs of hunger by lying on his back for an hour or so at mealtimes with a quartz-boulder on his stomach."

This view of Austin is taken from a pioneer diary of 1864:

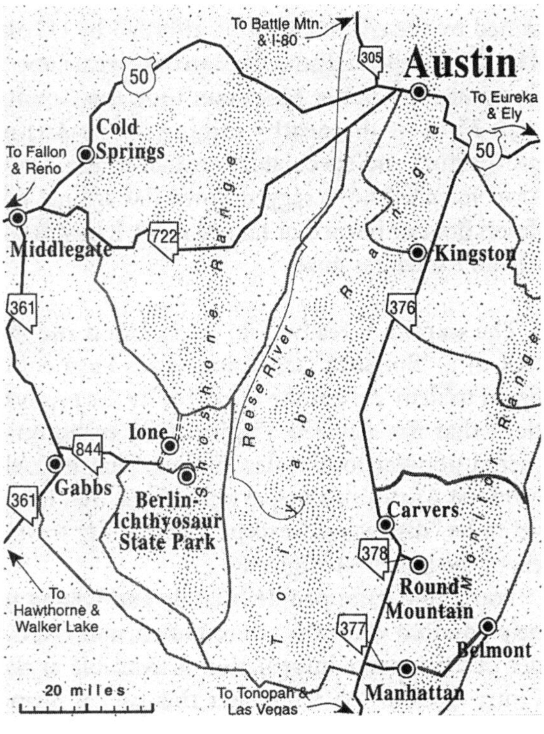

MAX WINTHROP

In the Austin cemetery.

The country is new and the population heterogeneousãyou see every grade of every nationality represented — Americans from everywhere that have been everywhere — elderly portly capitalists that are here to invest — keen elegant speculators that have been successful — hairy, hungry, "hard" looking miners, some that have "struck it" & some that haven't. Mill owners & mill hands — merchants, doctors, lawyers, sailors, saddlers, "butcher & baker" every thing and everybody — riches & rags — broadcloths & fustians — "greasers" with their black faces and slouched hats, "Castilians" with their fierce moustachios & jingling spurs — Frenchmen, Englishmen, Prussians Russians Poles Swiss Dutch Jews Irishmen & Scots — Indians with their blankets & half naked squaws with their papooses bound to a board, hanging down their back from a band that passes around their head. You can live as you please, dress as you please, eat as you please, make money as you please or lose it as you please, go where & as you please & die & be buried or not as you please. One man hurrahs for Abe, his neighbor for Jeff one man drinks to the health of the Repubs or "Blks" as they call them here & another gives as his toast "Davis & his cabinet!" or "Lee & his Gents." In the street you hear every tongue and language from the grunt of the Shoshones to the soft music of the Italian — see every costume coats cloaks shawls wraps poncho serapes and blankets — great long droves of pack mules, driven usually by Mexicans with their little ponies & queer whips, passing some great towering wood or lumber wagon holding two or three cords of wood & hauled by their overworked oxen which require the most peculiar & extensive profanity that you ever heard to get them along — along will come the coach with its thoroughly groomed & well fed horses dashing through the narrow street — perhaps running into a drove of camels with their long beards and ugly necks at which sight the horses most decidedly "shy" & no wonder. You see great big freight wagons from California or Salt Lake, bigger than the old National Road wagon drawn by 10 & sometimes 20 mules all driven by a single line. Everybody, women as well as men ride at full galop up hill and down — almost everybody gambles, play faro, monte rondeaux or billiards checkers chess & dominoes — women usually Spanish or French hire tables in the different saloons & play all night. The Chinamen with their loose shirts, long queues & wooden shoes do nearly all the washing.

By 1865 Austin was Nevada's second largest city, headquarters for the prospectors who trekked out in every direction in search of new mineral discoveries, and for the camps which sprang up around the strikes they made.

More than 60 mining districts were chartered by Austin-based prospectors in the 1860s and '70s, and more than 40 mining camps were settled. In Austin and its immediate environs, more than 2,000 mining and milling companies had been incorporated by 1865, many more than there were actual mines or mills. "Of the vast number of mining properties offered for sale in New York," Browne reported, "it is scarcely necessary to say that the great majority are valueless. Every adventurer who possesses the shadow of a claim takes it or sends it east in order that he may realize a fortune."

Many of the Austin mining shares were honest offerings, but some were extraordinarily fanciful. Among them was the mine advertised as being within half a mile of a railway, which stretched the truth nearly a hundred miles, and "within the

NEVADA STATE MUSEUM

Stokes Castle.

immediate vicinity" of the rich mines of the Comstock, a 200 mile exaggeration. The most preposterous fraud in Austin's extensive collection had only indirectly to do with mining, though. The Reese River, which flows north out of the Toiyabe Range to pass the entrance of Pony Canyon on its journey to the Humboldt — and the railroad — near Battle Mountain, was one of the few landmarks on the empty map of central Nevada in the 1860s. Shares in the Reese River Navigation Company, formed to freight ore in barges to the railroad, sold briskly to investors who recalled the strategic importance of the Sacramento River traffic to the Mother Lode mines of California fifteen years earlier. Unfortunately for them, the Reese at floodtide has barely the breadth of a man's hand and the depth of his fingers. Stagecoaches forded it at a full gallop, and in the dry season the Reese is even less spectacular.

The Methodist church at Austin, receiving so many mining shares as donations to its building fund, incorporated as the Methodist Mining Company and sold its own shares in other parts of the country. The church building erected with the proceeds was the most opulent in the state.

Austin was the birthplace of what may have been the first national fund-raising campaign in 1864 when Charles Holbrook, the Union candidate, defeated Democrat Dave Buel for Mayor. Grocer Reuel Gridley (coincidentally an old school-mate of Sam Clemens' from Hannibal, Missouri) had backed Buel, his fellow Southerner, so enthusiastically that he lost numerous election bets. The most extravagant one called for him to take 50-lb sack of self-rising flour from the shelf at his store in Upper Austin, decorate it with rosettes and small Union flags, and to march down Main Street through town with it on his shoulder, the municipal band parading along behind him playing the Battle Hymn of the Republic and other Union tunes. The procession continued all the way to Clifton, a mile down the canyon.

There, perhaps because of an outpouring of national spirit, perhaps simply to keep a lovely party alive, someone brought a table out of the saloon at which the parade had stopped, someone else volunteered as auctioneer, and someone else started the bidding that went up, up, up to $350. Sold! The money went to the Sanitary Fund (civil war forerunner of the Red Cross) and the sack of flour was donated back to go on the auction block again. The celebrants bought the flour sack over and over again, each time donating it back to be sold again. By the end of the day the citizens of Austin had contributed $4,549.80 in gold and silver coin, $24 in county scrip, 32 city lots and two dozen calf-bound ledger books.

Gridley then took his sack of flour to the Comstock, where auctions at Dayton, Silver City, Gold Hill and Virginia City raised $25,000 more. He continued on to Sacramento and San Francisco, stopping at every town and village along the way, and then took ship for the East with his remarkable sack of flour and his accumulation of wealth. By the time he returned home to Austin — almost a year after he had carried the sack of flour down the hill from his little stone store — he had sold the flour more than a thousand times and had raised nearly $250,000 for the Union hospitals.

If you stand on Main Street on a sunny afternoon you can easily picture Gridley grinning sheepishly as he hiked downhill with the sack of flour, its little flags fluttering, and the band playing behind him. Wouldn't you have fallen in with the impromptu parade, the way the Austin people did all those years ago?

Despite Austin's fabulous silver production and relative isolation, the town did not attract a railroad until 1879 when construction of the Nevada Central line began at Battle Mountain. A bill had passed the legislature granting Lander County authority to issue bonds in the amount of $200,000 to subsidize

Reuel Gridley with his magical sack of self-rising flour.

the project, but by the time rails were finally spiked to ties, the deadline for completion was only five winter months away. If the railroad failed to reach the city limits within the stipulated time, the operating subsidy would lapse and the railroad would fall immediately into bankruptcy.

Through blizzards and freezing weather the construction gangs made good progress, but despite every effort they were still a couple of miles short of the entrance to Pony Canyon when the midnight deadline drew near. Unwilling to see the project doomed, the Austin City Council met in emergency session as the work crews labored. A unanimous vote of the council resulted in a hasty dash out into the cruel weather and a gallop through the swirling snow to the railhead, where a sign reading Austin City Limits was planted in the ice with minutes to spare.

But the railroad did not save Austin from the ultimate decline of the mines, and by 1887 Austin had hit bottom. There have been attempts at reviving the mines in subsequent years, and some operations have continued spasmodically on a small scale, but for most of the past century Austin has been withering quietly away, barely sustained by

GOLD HILL NEWS ARCHIVE

The Gridley Store at upper Austin.

the trickle of traffic afforded by US 50. The city has been disincorporated for years, and Battle Mountain has taken the county seat. Most of the nearby mining towns Austin prospectors and speculators created in the 1860s have vanished now too, sagged down flat against the desert floor, burned or been hauled away.

The scarcity of ready cash, the isolation, and the lack of a "Bonanza" television series have combined to deny Austin the opportunity for promotion that has allowed Virginia City to become such a popular tourist destination. That in itself is one of Austin's principal attractions: that it has yet to be "discovered" except by the appreciative travelers on the Loneliest Highway.

MAX WINTHROP

Uptown Austin.

Austin Area Camping

FOREST SERVICE campgrounds south of Austin in the Toiyabe Mountains...

Bob Scott Campground

8 miles east of Austin, this 10-unit campground adjacent to and slightly elevatedbabove US 50 (convenient, but hardly secluded) accommodates family groups and trailers up to 22 feet. There are rest rooms, hot and cold running water and a $2/day fee.

Kingston Campground

33 miles from Austin via US 50 (east for 11 miles), Nevada 376 (south for 14 miles) and then by marked and graded dirt road west through Kingston Village and into the Toiyabes. 12 campsites and outhouses are provided, and the stream running through provides both drinking water and excellent trout fishing, as does the recently man-made Groves Lake a little higher up the canyon; $2 overnight fee.

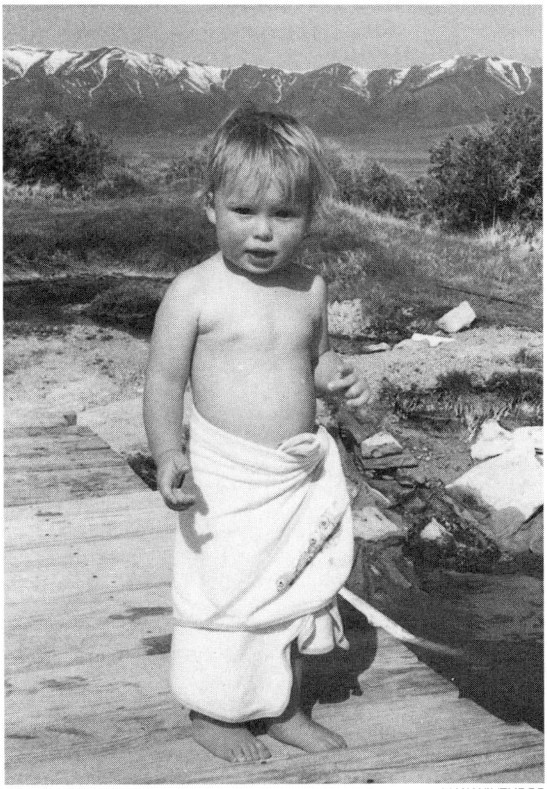

MAX WINTHROP

Bathing beauty at Spencer's Hot Spring near Austin.

Big Creek

Continue up Kingston Canyon, over the summit (tight, steep switchbacks make the uppermost portion of this road impassible to trailers) and down the other side 5 miles from Kingston Campground (or west from Austin via US 50 for 2 miles, south on Nevada 21 for 8 miles and southeast via marked and graded dirt road for 3 miles). 5 single units and a large group area are available with outhouses; no water other than the fishing stream running behind the campsites.

ROBIN COBBEY

Over Ione Summit into Reese River Valley.

Hickison Summit Petroglyph Site

This BLM campground 28 miles east of Austin offers luxurious accommodations with 21 camp-sites, picnic tables, cabanas and outhouses. No running water, but lots of shade and the fascination of numerous petroglyphs in this old Shoshone hunting ground.

GOLD HILL NEWS ARCHIVE

Diamond Springs Pony Express Station.

The Pony Express

COLD SPRING Station was established in March 1860 and put into use with the first galloping riders in April. Long afterward, J.G. Kelly, an assistant stationmaster at Cold Spring recalled his experience there:

The war against the Paiute Indians was then at its height, and as we were in the middle of their country, it became necessary for us to keep a standing guard night and day. The Indians were often skulking around, but none of them ever came near enough for us to get a shot at him, till one dark night when I was on guard, I noticed one of our horses prick up his ears and stare. I looked in the direction indicated and saw an Indian's head projecting above the wall. My instructions were to shoot if I saw an Indian within rifle range, as that would wake the boys quicker than anything else. So I fired and missed my man.

Later on we saw the Indian campfires on the mountain, and in the morning many tracks. They evidently intended to stampede our horses, and if necessary kill us. The next day one of our riders, a Mexican, rode into camp with a bullet hole through him from left to the right side, having been shot by Indians while coming down Edwards Creek, in the Quaking Aspen Bottom. He was tenderly cared for, but died before surgical aid could reach him.

As I was the lightest man at the station, I was ordered to take the Mexican's place on the route. My weight was then 100 pounds, while I now weigh 130.

Two days after taking the route, on my return trip, I had to ride through the forest of quaking aspen where the Mexican had been shot. A trail had been cut through these little trees, just wide enough to allow horse and rider to pass. As the road was crooked and the branches came together from either side, just above my head when mounted it was impossible for me to see ahead for more than ten or 15 yards, and it was two miles

GOLD HILL NEWS ARCHIVE

Cold Springs Station.

through the forest. I expected to have trouble, and prepared for it by dropping my bridal reins on the neck of the horse, putting my Sharp's rifle at full cock, and keeping both my spurs into the pony's flanks, and he went through that forest like a streak of greased lightning.

At the top of the hill I dismounted to rest my horse, and looking back saw the bushes moving in several places. As there were no cattle or game in that vicinity, I knew the movements to be caused by Indians, and was more positive of it when, after firing several shots at the spot where I saw the bushes in motion, all agitation ceased.

Several days after that two United States soldiers, who were on their way to their command, were shot and killed from the ambush of those bushes, and stripped of their clothing by the red devils.

GOLD HILL NEWS ARCHIVE

Excavating Sand Springs Station.

LAHONTAN VALLEY NEWS

Fallon celebrates the bounty of its havest each year at the Canteloupe Festival.

Fallon

WHEN MIKE FALLON BUILT a crossroads store on his ranch property in 1896, the sparsely settled region of the Carson Sink had a nucleus for the first time since Kenyon's trading post at Ragtown, to the west, served the wagon trains. In the same year the county renovated the old Virginia City-to-Fairview telegraph line (for which it had paid $975 in 1889) to serve as a single-line telephone system linking the farms and ranches in the area. The telephone system is still owned and operated by the Churchill County, the only one in the USA still run as a public utility.

FALLON	
Reno	60
Carson City	61
Ely	257
Las Vegas	383
Mesquite	449

Creation of the Truckee-Carson Irrigation District by the U.S. Reclamation Service shortly after the turn of the century prompted a tremendous spurt of settlement in the region to be provided with irrigation water, and the tiny settlement at Fallon took the county seat from Stillwater in 1902. A bank was established in 1908, and Fallon was incorporated. By this time the intensive agricultural development had begun to pay satisfying dividends. Fallon's Hearts O' Gold cantaloupes graced the menus of fine hotels and restaurants in the biggest cities of the nation, and Fallon turkeys brought premium prices. The Cantaloupe Festival in October is still the community's premiere annual event, but the Spring Wings Bird Festival in May attracts birders from across the USA.

For the Fourth of July celebration of 1911 the town fathers imported a wrestler who challenged all comers after lying down in the dirt and gravel of Maine Street (Fallon is the only Nevada town to add the stately E to its big street's name, after founder Warren Williams' native state) and permitting his trainer to drive an automobile over his rigid body. In 1915 the Nevada State Fair was held in Fallon, and the townspeople built an enormous "palace" of hay bales at the intersection of Maine and Center. The roofless structure measured sixty feet square and its walls rose eighteen feet high. At night dances were held within it while the king and queen of the fair presided on thrones of Fallon hay.

Construction of Lahontan Dam was also completed that year.

Prices turned down after World War I, and Fallon fell into 20 years of dull times. Even the mining excitements in the nearby hills did not entirely lift the depression. In June, 1942, however, the Navy began construction of a small air station southeast of town, and Fallon's economy jumped up again. The station was closed in 1946, but reopened during the Korean War. In 1958 it was dedicated to Lt. Cdr. Bruce Van Voorhis, a Navy pilot from Fallon awarded the Medal of Honor. The 14,000-ft. runway is the Navy's longest.

It is also one of the busiest just now. The Navy's use of the air space over a big part of the country to the east, to train pilots in combat techniques has filled the air with dogfights and sonic booms. Bomb drops, oil and fuel spills have accumulated enormous environmental damage. At the same time, the base has expanded its activities to become the national Top Gun training school. Its payroll has also expanded, and Fallon is enjoying the prosperity.

For all the uproar, Fallon goes about its business with an air of quiet satisfaction, an easy, amiable, tree-shaded town except for the acres of asphalt on the west side of town. Meals and lodging are easy to find, and all automotive services are available. The Overland Hotel on Center Street serves lunches and dinners in the Basque style. There are Mexican, Italian and Chinese restaurants, as well as more common fare.

On a warm summer's evening, after a scurrying rain squall has wet down the fresh-cut alfalfa and dusk has set the frogs and crickets to singing, Fallon is at its comfortable best. Take the kids swimming at the pool, or watch a Little League game at the City Park. One of the most pleasant images in my memory is from this park, of a little leaguer, the tail of his number 7 tucked halfway down his pants, and waving a glove the size of a satellite dish at the baseballs flying over his head.

The Churchill County Museum is on south Maine and admission to the 14,000 square feet of engaging and vivacious exhibits is free. You'll see a new exhibit on Native Americans, an antique fire

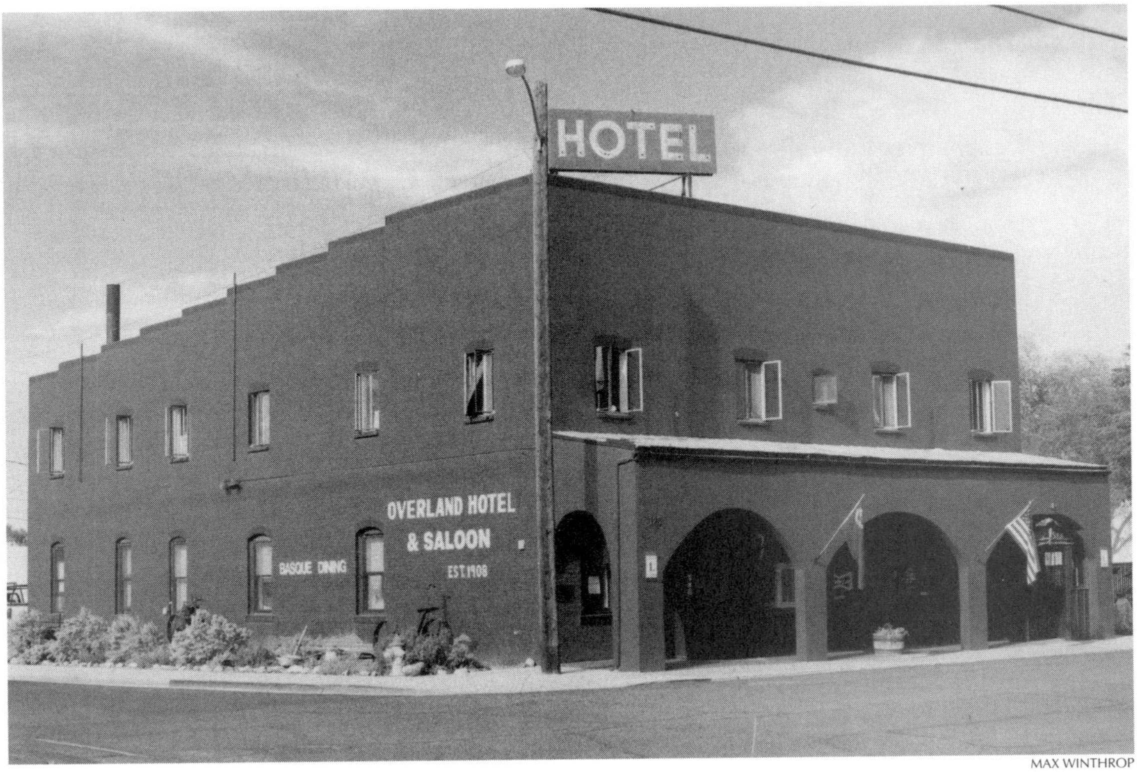

MAX WINTHROP

The Overland Hotel, Fallon.

truck and a thousand items in between, from lithic tools to a hand-pumped vacuum cleaner. If you're in town on a Tuesday or Wednesday, take in a livestock auction. Sales starts at 10 am Tuesday mornings at the Fallon Livestock Auction west of town on Highway 50.

Stillwater, briefly and long ago the Churchill County seat, is headquarters for the Fallon Paiute-Shoshone Reservation. Some years ago, Stillwater resident Fortunate Eagle flew to Rome, dressed in traditional style. Upon arrival he descended to the runway and planted his lance in the asphalt, claiming Italy on behalf of the American Indians by right of discovery.

The celebrated storyteller "Squaw Tom" Sanders lived near Fallon for many years, and many of his tales were of the local Indian life. He is buried in the reservation cemetery at Stillwater.

In the early 1950s, Fallon's literary tradition was further enriched when a "poor, skinny, dreamy kid" of 21 from Portland, Oregon, showed up at the door of the Eagle Standard on Williams Street — the poet Richard Brautigan, who stayed only briefly. Here are poems he wrote there which appeared in the weekly "Gab & Gossip" column on July 25, 1956 and which may be his first published work:

MAX WINTHROP

Oasis Bowl, Arcade and Casino, Fallon.

"The Breeze"

In the time
of the evening
all things
grow cool again
in Fallon
when God
starts caressing
this city
with
His great hands.

"Storm over Fallon"

Thunder roared
across the sky
like the voice
of an angry man.

Rain started falling,
slowly at first,
the faster and faster,
and louder and louder.

The man became silent.

The voices of the rain
chattered like
little children
at a birthday party.

FERNLEY CHAMBER OF COMMERCE

Fernley Veterans' Cemetery on Memorial Day.

Fernley

UNTIL A FEW YEARS AGO this pleasant community has been the hardest one in the book to describe and define for the benefit of a visitor. There are a couple of small casinos, a variety of restaurants including at least two good ones, a supermarket, all automotive services, an in-town park and an out-of-town park (to the east). The town has been thriving in a small way since the freeway redefined things around here. There are new schools and an indoor swimming pool, and people are friendly. All Fernley lacked was an identity, and that is taking shape at last. Fernley is now the fastest-growing community in the fastest-growing county in the fastest-growing state in America. Pahrump is bigger, better-known, and has been on the fast-growing list longer, but Fernley is now growing twice as fast (18.7% vs 9.1%), with population passing 17,000 on its way to the moon.

FERNLEY	
Reno	33
Fallon	27
Carson City	49
Yerington	46
Caliente	393

This recent growth has been stimulated by the growth and rising home prices in Reno, 30 miles west, and by industrial development which has attracted major companies: amazon.com and Wal-Mart both have major distribution centers here, and Trex, the company which transforms recycled and reclaimed plastic grocery bags, pallet wrap and waste wood into composite decking, has a plant here.

The source of the name remains a mystery. A few unconvincing theories have been tried, but no living soul truly knows who or what a Fernley was. That reveals something about the transitory nature of fame, but it is irritating to people who like their history neat and tidy.

Fernley's life began in 1906 with the railroad, but it was relatively eventless until the Newlands Reclamation Project resulted in the construction of Derby Dam and the establishment of irrigated farms. These small family homesteads supported a scattered population, but many of them were foreclosed during the Depression.

The community's main attraction, other than the Semi-On-A-Stick you see from the autobahn, is visible to the north: the Veterans' Cemetery, where rest the remains of hundreds of former service men and women. There is an extensive collection of Native American stone-, bone- and beadwork displayed on the walls of The Wigwam Cafe. The artifacts are arranged in their frames with creative flair, which is interesting, but without information, which is frustrating. The old Fernley & Lassen railroad depot is being restored on Main Street and will become a museum.

Fort Churchill

GARY ELAM

FORT CHURCHILL IS eight miles south of Silver Springs and 24 miles north of Yerington via US 95A, a short distance west of the highway. The best way to get there, though, is by the historic wagon road that extends south from Virginia City (Six Mile Canyon Road) across US 50 and along the meandering and sometimes washboard road that follows the Carson River east past ranches and livestock to the old Fort. This was a major highway in the 19th century.

Established in the aftermath of the short-lived Paiute War of 1860, Fort Churchill garrisoned about 600 officers and troops by the end of 1861. As the Civil War demanded increasing numbers of seasoned troops in the eastern battlefields, elements of the California Volunteers replaced the regulars at garrison duty. The federal government refused the offer of a group of Nevada patriots to arm and equip a unit for service against the rebels, and most Nevadans serving the Union during the war enlisted in companies at Fort Churchill. Company F of the 2nd California Volunteer Infantry was an all-Nevada company.

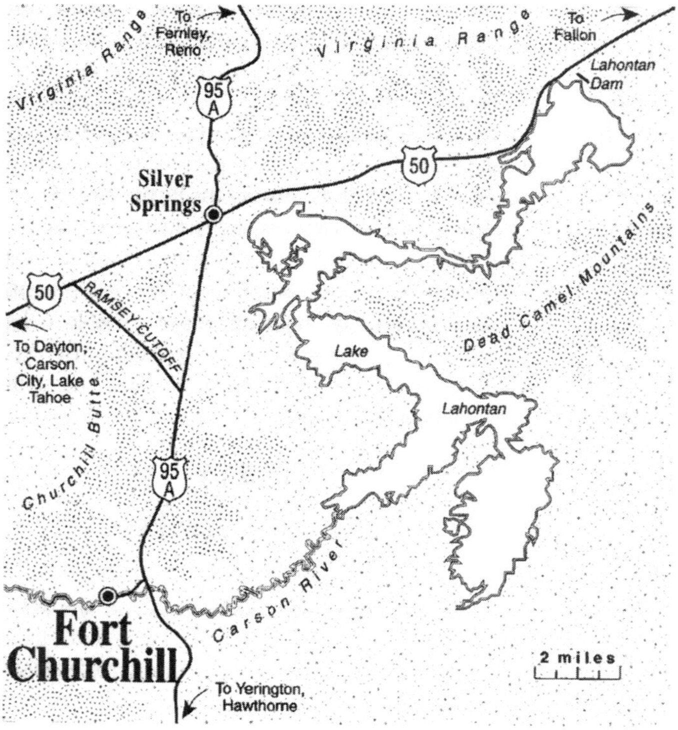

By 1863 Nevada volunteers, most of whom had enlisted at Fort Churchill, comprised two companies of infantry and two of cavalry. Nevada troopers received their first brass hat inspection in September of that year, During the course of the ceremonies, an aide-de-camp with the rank of major staggered through a second story doorway at a Carson City inn, apparently under the impression that there was a balcony. There wasn't. R.I.P.

Most of the military activity at Fort

Churchill consisted of patrolling the Overland Stage route, the only transcontinental stagecoach route since the more southerly Butterfield route was closed by the war. Sometimes they chased after small bands of Indians who made occasional forays against isolated settlers. It was inglorious, unglamorous, boring, and largely unproductive duty, and of the 1,200 Nevadans in federal service during the Civil War, nearly 400 deserted. One of them was apprehended as he was negotiating the sale of his troop's horses to the stagecoach line. Nine Nevadans were killed or died in service, and virtually all of the survivors had been mustered out of service by Christmas 1865.

By 1867 the adobe buildings of the fort housed only a single company and in 1869, when the railroad superseded the stage line, the fort was abandoned. It was ultimately purchased for $750 by the proprietor of Buckland's Station, a half mile to the south. Acquired in the recent past as a state park, the fort was declared a national historic landmark in 1964.

Despite the fact that the roofs and many of the timbers were removed after its abandonment, thus leaving the thick adobe walls unprotected and exposed to the elements, enough of the old fort remains in gaunt and melted ruin to be impressive. CCC crews rebuilt some of the structures with adobes manufactured on the spot, but their mix was too rich in clay and their work has melted away. What remains is the original. Further restoration is now in progress with a new recipe. The park rangers have identified the remaining structures and the sites of those buildings which have not survived, and a model in the visitor's center reconstructs the old outpost in small scale to aid visitors in their explorations.

MAX WINTHROP

Buckland's Station

The 20 cottonwood-shaded camp sites near the river are provided with piped drinking water, as are the group and individual picnic areas. 14 day limit. A use fee is charged.

Fort Churchill was the first military post in the state, and until World War II Nevada never had a larger or more important one, with the possible exception of the Army encampment during the labor troubles at Goldfield early in the 20th century. Today Fort Churchill is one of the state's most interesting parks, open the year around, with military re-enactments throughout the year.

Buckland's

ABOUT 1/2-MILE east of Fort Churchill on US 95-A. Established on the Carson River as a trading post in 1859, Buckland's had grown by the following year to include a tavern and a hotel as well as the proprietor's ranching headquarters. By the time a blacksmith shop and wagon repair facilities were added, Buckland's had been selected as the seat of Churchill County. This exalted status lapsed when a change in county boundaries put Buckland's in Lyon County. The station continued to prosper, largely because of the nearby presence of the Fort Churchill garrison.

In 1870 the two-story frame building which dominates the tiny settlement was erected as a hotel serving stagecoach travelers with its bar and dining room, and the local ranching population with the large dance hall. With a decline in stagecoach traffic, Buckland's faded, losing its status as a community and surviving as a ranching headquarters. Buildings are occupied, and tourists are not invited to prowl the grounds. Nevertheless, because the old place sits just at the side of the highway, a few minutes parked at the edge of the road will provide a glimpse into the way things looked at an isolated 19th-century stage station. Several more recent buildings interfere somewhat with the reverie, but restoration by the State was recently completed and you may be able to explore the place more intimately when you visit.

ADRIAN ATWATER

On the Carson River near Dayton.

Dayton

HERE IS EARLY 21ST century Nevada in microcosm, with new curbs and gutters running past tumble-down shanties and swaybacked cottages, and a four-lane highway slicing around the old stone and brick downtown, now populated with upscale restaurants. There is a traffic light in Dayton now, and companies escaping the costs and confinements of California have built modern factories out past the new schools and new burbs on Dayton Valley Road. There's even an airport and golf course, and on the far eastern side of town a supermarket surrounded by fastfood cafes — and a Starbucks!

DAYTON	
Virginia City	11
Carson City	14
Fallon	47
Yerington	53
Lamoille	311

Only a few years ago the golf course and subdivisions were ranch land, and Dayton's primary attraction to visitors was the glimpse it gave of the old Nevada. Now it is worth a visit because it gives a clear view of the old Nevada giving way to the new.

Dayton was originally a trading post at the junction of Gold Creek with the Carson River, where west-bound wagon trains rested, foraged and watered in preparation for the struggle over the mountains.

Dayton is one of a very few Nevada communities that can mount a credible challenge to Genoa's status as Nevada's first permanently settled community. But even if the claim were disallowed, Dayton's place in Nevada history is secure as the site of the Territory's first marriage, first divorce and first public entertainment, all of which occurred in 1853.

The wedding took place when a prospector injudiciously left his 14-year-old daughter with friends while he searched nearby streams for the elusive glint of gold. When he returned to town he found his daughter had married another prospector. He immediately took her off to California, pursued by the outraged bridegroom and by friends who wanted to avert bloodshed. When they all met on the trail a heated discussion ensued. Eventually it was agreed that the girl be given her choice of continuing west with her father or returning to camp with her new husband. She elected to go on, thus becoming Nevada's first bride and first divorcee within the space of a few days.

Later in the year a New Year's party was held, probably at Spofford Hall's Trading post (now the site of an immense gravel pit). Some 150 prospectors swapped lies about their claims, traded news from the states, and danced with the females (four women and five little girls) who were present.

After so exciting a beginning it has been mostly downhill for Dayton.

Dayton had a Pony Express station and prospered as a milling center during the early years of development of the Comstock Lode. Its most celebrated citizen in the early days was a former San Francisco storekeeper, Adolph Sutro, who operated a small stamp mill here in 1860, and who conceived the plan for draining the water from the deep Comstock mines. Dayton achieved its present configuration by the middle 1860s, after which Comstock milling was done at more convenient places. Two municipal events stand out in the years since the mills closed, both of them taking place at the Odeon Hall on Pike Street. The first was in 1879 when ex-President Grant addressed a crowd of local citizens from the balcony. The second was in 1960 when John Huston, Clark Gable, Marilyn Monroe, Arthur Miller, Montgomery Clift, Thelma Ritter and Eli Wallach came to town to film "The Misfits." Marilyn Monroe's exceptional paddle-ball performance at the Odeon bar marks the high point of the 20th century in Dayton.

The drowsy charm of Dayton's downtown is enhanced by its attractive setting. The Odeon Hall, one of Dayton's most impressive landmarks, is the location for Chuck's Steak House, an excellent restaurant with a historic bar. Across the street, J's Bistro occupies another historic stone building, originally a mercantile store, which served for many years as Wheels' garage. A block up the street, the excellent Gold Canyon Restaurant at the back of the ancient Wild Horse Saloon serves lunches and dinners. The Roadrunner Cafe serves traditional diner fare of considerable variety and is a local Sunday morning favorite. Terrible's Casino on the east side offers coffee shop cuisine.

Cemetery Road takes you past the old Bluestone Building, originally a mining office, and after that for many years a general store. Now it houses the Lyon County offices. The interior remodeling is worth a look to see how the old structure has been restored to modern uses. Continue on the half mile past painter Steven Saylor's Evergreen Studio to the cemetery, which is the earliest-established burying ground in Nevada (take that, Genoa). It contains the mortal remains of Governor Charles Russell and Judge Clark Guild, founder of the state museum, among its tenants. James Finney, who christened Virginia City after his home state, was brought to rest here after a balky jackass kicked him in the head, and the carefully tended grounds provide a pleasant diversion for those who enjoy wandering in pioneer cemeteries. The overview of the town and rich river bottom country it occupies provides a most satisfying panorama.

MAX WINTHROP

The Fox Hotel in old downtown Dayton.

Pioneer Territory

The mountains of Nevada are like sleeping women, sprawled languorously across every horizon. They are not pretty mountains. They have been scuffed and worn too long by desert winds, and their skirts are stained with the dried mud of long-vanished seas. Even the primitive elegance of a forested crest is denied to all but a few of them, and they make do with threadbare patchworks of juniper and piñon pines draped across their summits. And yet the serene, infinitely feminine presence of these rumpled ranges is mysteriously compelling: their smooth, slumberous forms shade to blue, to purple, to windowglass gray as they recede, rank upon rank, into the distances. In this great central heartland of Nevada, more than twenty thousand square miles, there are only two communities with as a many as a thousand citizens each, and the mountains sleep around them undisturbed.

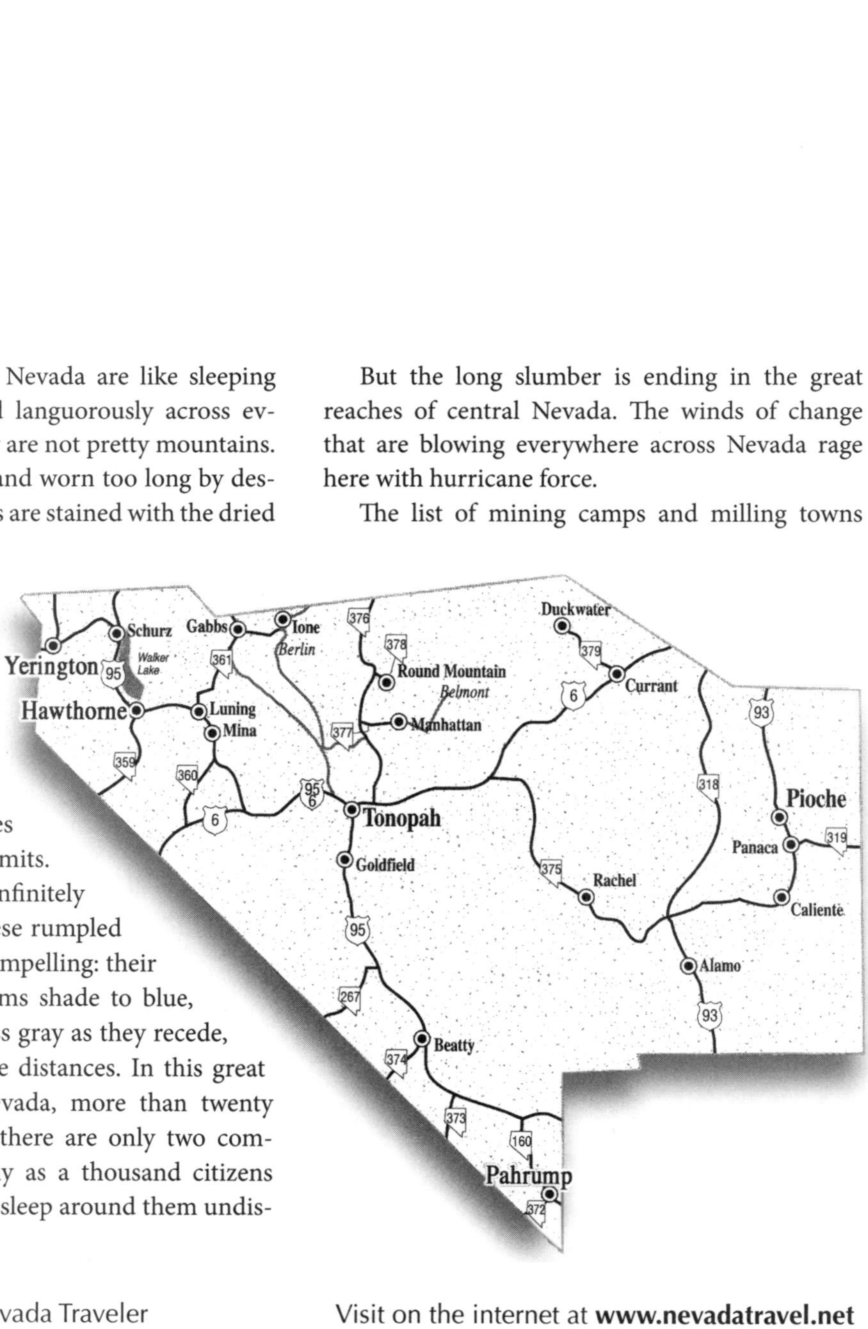

But the long slumber is ending in the great reaches of central Nevada. The winds of change that are blowing everywhere across Nevada rage here with hurricane force.

The list of mining camps and milling towns

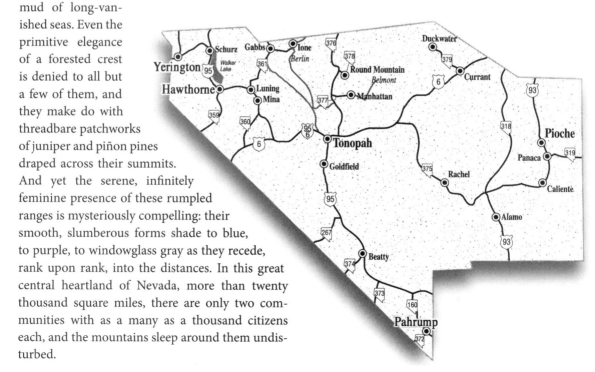

NEVADA HISTORICAL SOCIETY

Car trouble, 1911.

bursting into feverish, fitful existence in the 1860s contains hundreds of names, few of them even dimly remembered today by any except scholars and near neighbors.

Exploration and discovery continued into the seventies-but the seventies were more remarkable as years of consolidation and improvement. Small claims were combined, huge investments made in machinery and technique. Tiny anthill workings plagued by violence and lawlessness grew into respectable towns, scrub towns swelled to become substantial cities. Shafts and tunnels stabbed deep into the guts of the mountains and new foothills were built of the ore dragged out.

Mining ebbed in the 1880s. A few new strikes were made, and a few new towns began their doomed lives, but for the most part the eighties in Nevada were a time of petering out. Even the inexhaustible mines of the Comstock Lode, which had produced bonanza after bonanza, were clearly giving out. The nineties were worse. By 1900 only forty thousand people remained in the state. and then by God if it didn't start all over again. Jim Butler was shanking it across the desert from the county seat at Belmont toward the dwindling camp of Klondyke in May, 1900, when he found some interesting rock. The rock assayed at $50 to $600 a ton, mostly silver, and a rush brought a population of a thousand, including photographers and reporters for the national press. Their colorful representations of mining camp life-and the continuing discovery of rich deposits in the district-brought thousands more adventurers. The Tonopah strike fanned the enthusiasm of prospectors once again, and soon rich finds were made at Goldfield, Kawich, Rawhide, Pioneer, Rhyolite, Transvaal, Bullfrog, Seven Troughs, Mazuma, Midas, Wonder, and a hundred other remote locations on the Nevada landscape.

At Royston, $20,000 in silver was dragged up from a shaft only twenty-four feet deep. At Weepah, ore was uncovered worth a reported $70,000 to the ton. At Wahmonie, prospectors came jouncing across the desert in a fleet of automobiles and fifteen hundred of them built a town in two months. At Monarch, the Reverend Benjamin Blanchard promoted a valise-full of dubious assay reports into a community of 2,400 lots surrounded by "ranch sites" and "mining claims" before departing with $50,000 of sucker money and leaving $73,000 in unpaid bills behind him. None of these particular communities survived a single season.

Still, a number of these twentieth-century min-

NEVADA HISTORICAL SOCIETY

Prospectors from Round Mountain prowled the countryside in search of paydirt.

ing camps were founded on solid ground. Tonopah and Goldfield became two of the nation's great gold and silver producers and grew to be the principal cities of the state. Rhyolite attracted three railroads to itself before it faltered and failed. Mining continued on a small scale throughout the state through the dismal Depression years; even the Comstock Lode was still producing gold and silver on the eve of World War II.

During the war Nevada's gold and silver mines were ordered closed by the War Production Board. Copper assumed extreme importance, and more exotic minerals such as tungsten, barium, and mercury were profitably produced.

Few gold or silver mines could afford to reopen after the war. The years of disuse had made many of them unsafe without extensive (and expensive) retimbering. Labor costs had risen, but the price of gold had not. Mine owners did their annual assessment work and waited.

They waited twenty years before seeing any significant new mining activity, and thirty years before mining resumed on a wide scale, but they are waiting no longer.

Dramatic rises in the price of gold, as well as indications that overseas sources of scarce minerals might become uneconomical or unavailable, prompted an enormous intensification of interest in domestic minerals production in the mid-1970s. Established mining companies began casting around for mining opportunities, and several of the nation's large and middle-sized oil companies formed minerals divisions or subsidiaries to join in the hunt for ore.

These days independent prospectors still strike it rich on occasion, but most discoveries are made by geologists who work out of Denver or Houston or Reno. They may direct core drilling rigs for years to test their findings. The Anaconda company had been drilling at the site of their mine outside Tonopah since 1955. The core samples are assayed and a three-dimensional map compiled of the hidden ore deposits showing width, breadth depth and value of the ore beneath great sections of ground. Only after they assure themselves that a mineral deposit is large enough, rich enough, accessible enough and workable enough do executives of a modern major mining company commit themselves to development.

The cost of prolonged exploration is high and

NEVADA HISTORICAL SOCIETY

Tonopah, April, 1901.

can mount into hundreds of millions of dollars. With stakes so high there can be no mistake, especially since the ore is of low grade. At the Carlin Gold Mine, which went into production when the price of gold was controlled at $35 an ounce, there was no visible gold in the ore at all. It occurs in particles so small that they are only detectable in the assay. A modern mill must be built with equipment

GOLD HILL NEWS ARCHIVE

Hornsilver blossomed brightly and briefly in the southern Nevada desert.

NEVADA HISTORICAL SOCIETY

Tex Rickard and prospectors at the boomtown of Bovard in 1908.

husky enough to process thousands of tons of ore daily, yet delicate enough to recover gold particles as small as 0.01 microns, about the equivalent of 75 atoms.

No longer does a reduction mill thunder with the beat of giant stamps pulverizing hard rock with smashing hammer blows. No longer does the earth quiver beneath and a pall of dust hang in the air above. These modern mills are humming factories. From the loading of the ore trucks in the ever deepening pits through the cleanup at the presses, the mills are automated, transistorized and self-regulating.

The mining boom of 1979-81 produced mineral wealth equal to any big bonanza in Nevada's earlier, more glamorous years. Yet no tent cities sprang up at these modern mines, and none will. Occasionally, as at the Anaconda project outside Tonopah, temporary trailer and RV parks are established at or near the work site during construction, but almost without exception company buses hauled permanent employees to the outlying mines, and established communities grow larger and richer. The single exception is Hadley, a brand-new company town in the Smoky Valley created because the ramshackle old town of Round Mountain had the bad luck to be built on an enormously rich ore body.

This in itself is a revolutionary change in a state where the leading industry — gambling — has built cities. The resurgence in mining is felt in these cities, especially in Reno, where many companies active in the state have established offices, but its greatest impact is on the small towns in the vast rural reaches of Nevada. Here gambling has never grown into the mainstay of the economy.

Yet for all its vitality, Pioneer Territory is still a profoundly vacant region. It is one of the ironies about central Nevada that back before the turn of the century, and again during the Depression, people tried everything they could think of to promote that land, get businesses started, fill it up — anything to bring in a little cash. But they failed. All that vast country stayed as empty as ever: some sheep and some cows, some men to tend them, and a few shabby towns along the lonesome highways.

More than half this region is off limits to everyday activities: wilderness areas, wildlife ranges and the huge tracts contained within the Nellis Air Force Range, including the NevadaTest Site, the Tonopah Test Range and Area 51.

And now that California is so overcrowded that a person can't get solitude there without signing up for it in advance and standing in line for it, the remaining great emptinesses of Nevada's Pioneer Territory are drawing more visitors than even before, precisely because they are so empty.

Just how long they will stay that way remains to be seen.

MAX WINTHROP

Yerington potatoes.

YERINGTON

COMING TO YERINGTON is like taking a day off. It's a half hour away from the nearest east-west and north-south highways, and getting here is like taking a Sunday drive to a home town you never had. Drive in from the north through Wabuska, down the cottonwood-bowered two-lane highway, with family farms spread out across the valley on both sides (including the magnificent Masini ranch house on the west side of the road). Or come in through Wellington and Smith from the south and traverse the rich pasturelands of the Smith and Mason Valleys.

YERINGTON	
Carson City	67
Hawthorne	57
Silver Springs	32
Smith	14

Situated in Mason Valley on the Walker River, Yerington began its existence as a small trading post and whiskey store called Pizen Switch, a reflection on the poor quality of the whiskey. When the tiny settlement had grown to hamlet size, municipal pride demanded a more genteel

MAX WINTHROP

Downtown Yerington.

MAX WINTHROP

Casino West in Yerington.

handle and the citizens agreed on Greenfield.

A few years later, in the 1870s, townspeople gambled that renaming their modest burg in his honor would be the decisive enticement for H.M. Yerington to extend a branch line of the Virginia & Truckee Railroad their way. Greenfield became Yerington, but H.M. did not bring the railroad. A railroad finally did materialize in Yerington, but not until the second decade of the 20th century when copper deposits worked briefly in the 1860s were brought back into production. Smelters were built and the Nevada Copper Belt Railroad extended from the mines west of town around the Singatse Range to connect with the Southern Pacific at Wabuska. In the 1920s the district produced copper valued at several millions, but production dwindled after the end of the decade.

After the outbreak of World War II the Anaconda Mining Co. bought control of the major mines, but decided against bringing them into large-scale production because of the long lag time required. When the Korean War broke out in 1950, however, Anaconda began producing copper under government contract.

The company built 255 houses in a rather prim company town called Weed Heights in honor of the superintendent, Mr. Weed. Digging began in 1952 and two years later the big shovels uncovered the ore. The mining revival came too late to save the N.C.R.R., however, which had torn up its tracks and expired in 1947. In 1978 copper mining ceased again, and Weed Heights became a sudden ghost town. Bright turquoise-colored water began seeping into the great pit, slowly rising to provide a home for bass and trout.

Now the mine has been developed as an industrial site and an RV park, with campsites around the lip of the spectacular pit and on the benches down deep inside it. Tricycles have appeared on the patchy lawns in front of some of the Weed Heights houses again and the community is coming back to life.

In the Indian Colony there is a monument to Yerington's only famous native, the Paiute prophet Wovoka. He was a major figure during the final downfall of the Indian nations; his Ghost Dance movement led to the slaughter at Wounded Knee. His vision of the return of the buffalo, and of the Native American lifeways, was an attractive prophecy to a people whose culture was melting inexorably away, and it was fervently believed and spread through the Indian world. The granite monument that sketches his life stands within sight of the fields where his wickiup was a common sight before his death in 1932.

Most of Wovoka's memorabilia is at the Badlands Museum in North Dakota, but the Lyon County Museum at 215 S. Main displays an interesting variety of frontier relics, from dolls to shooting irons, and a case devoted to Chinese antiqui-

Wovoka

NEVADA MAGAZINE

Wovoka and cowboy actor Tim McCoy.

IN DECEMBER, 1887, a husky 31-year-old Paiute woodcutter was hard at the white man's work, cutting firewood in the Pine Nut Mountains, when he was visited by God and lifted up to Heaven. "It was the most beautiful country you can imagine, nice and level and green all the time." All the dead in this bountiful heaven were enjoying themselves immensely.

God told Wovoka he was to carry a message of love and peace to the people of the world. And he was to tell the people they must dance for five consecutive nights but then not again for three months. The dance was called The Ghost Dance, and by the time a year had passed the Lyon County Times reported "big dances every night now."

When he made it rain, made a block of ice fall from the sky, fell into deep trances to visit with God, and sat unscathed in the path of a shotgun blast, Wovoka gained in stature. When he awoke from a trance just as a solar eclipse was ending, people said he saved the world. He told them if they would dance the Ghost Dance, love one another and live in peace, they would be reunited with their friends and loved ones in another world.

With wild enthusiasm the people who visited Wovoka spread the Ghost Dance all across the west. The Sioux in particular became obsessed with it. More than 3,000 people were dancing on the reservation at Wounded Knee when a fight broke out with soldiers of the Seventh Cavalry. Three hundred of the Sioux were killed in the ensuing massacre, and 25 soldiers. Wovoka was held in high regard as an elder and as a prophet (and as a mail-order eagle feather salesman) until his death in 1932.

The Great Yerington Sack Race

Yerington intermittently hosts what must be the most grueling single competition staged anywhere in the west. It doesn't appear in the list of annual events because it isn't held every year — contestants can't be found that often. It's the World Championship Sack Race, and it dates back nearly a century when a young farm hand named Harry Warren made local history.

Harry was working as a ranch hand near Wabuska. He and some other men were loading a wagon with 120-lb. grain sacks, and in the process they got to talking about how far a man could carry one of the sacks without having to put it down and rest. Harry made the outrageous claim that he could carry one all the way to Yerington, about ten miles away.

When his fellow workers challenged his wild statement, Harry said, "Oh, I can do it all right. But you'll have to make it worth my while."

So some of the biggest and strongest men in the valley experimented with carrying the heavy sacks, and none of them made it more than a quarter mile. Harry's challenge spread around the valleys, and a fund of $1,500 was accumulated to call Harry's bluff.

On the day of the great event Harry heaved the sack up onto his shoulders and started off toward Yerington at a rapid walk.

To the utter astonishment of every witness, Harry made the ten miles to Yerington in about two hours, stopping to rest only once, and never slowing his relentless pace.

One of the amazed backers of the bet was a local bee keeper. "The bees never stung me," he said ruefully, "but Harry Warren sure did."

ties found in the area. The museum also includes some standing structures: a one-room eight-grade school house where generations of ranch children were educated, and a 19th century grocery store, fully stocked with cash register at the ready. The museum is open week-ends, but on weekdays you can ask at the Visitor Center next door and they'll call a volunteer to come over and give your party the tour.

Yerington boasts the largest trap shooting range in central Nevada, the golf course is open all year, and a week-long summer softball tournament attracts teams from all around Nevada and the West. But one of Yerington's principal attractions is subtler: the unhurried, friendly way people here go about their business. I have watched a man spend ten minutes getting down a single block, amiably passing the time of day with four different neighbors.

For the best view of Yerington and its green valley setting, find a friendly native and ask the way to the dump. Pass the cemetery (after a visit, perhaps) and climb the lumpy hill that rises behind it. No need to go all the way to the dump, unless you've accumulated some travel debris; you'll see a convenient pull-off near the top of the hill where you can park and enjoy a picnic lunch overlooking the little paradise spread below.

Despite its small-town lifestyle, Yerington's Casino West offers the traditional combination of craps, cards and video slot machines, with food and lodging available. Dini's Lucky Club is another Yerington tradition, with Giuseppe's dinner house a local favorite on weekends. El Superior, on Bridge Street, lives up to its name, and the China Chef is popular for lunch. But Yerington's hidden culinary treasure is at the back of the Supermercado Chapala, where you will find a spectacular meat counter and a tiny 3-table deli where burritos are as big as footballs and truly magnifico.

Welcome the the Fallon Cantaloupe Festival…

…and to all the other small-town celebrations Nevadans will be enjoying over the coming year. They're part of the pleasure of living where simple pleasures prevail, and life follows the traditional pattern of small tyown America.

A complete calendar of Special Events arlund the statte is available online at the Nevada Commission on Tourism website: **www.travelnevada.com**

Is this heaven?

Cold beer, hot sun, warm mud — it's not for the weak.

PHOTOS BY MAX WINTHROP

NEVADA STATE MUSEUM

Governor Colcord riding through Aurora, 1890.

Aurora

27 MILES SOUTHWEST of Hawthorne via Nevada 359, Lucky Boy Pass Road, and marked dirt road. A party of prospectors who had missed their chance at rich ground in Virginia City found exposed quartz ledges bearing heavy deposits of gold while searching for water and game. Their claims attracted many from eastern California as well as more of Virginia City's disappointed, and Aurora began to take shape. Brick from the Pacific Coast was more readily accessible to the town's early entrepreneurs than finished lumber, so Aurora's business district was largely made up of substantial brick buildings.

So rapidly did the town grow that when the California legislature created Mono County in the spring of 1861, Aurora was named its seat. A few months later, the territorial government of Nevada also proclaimed Aurora the seat of Esmeralda County. Thus two county governments, each duly authorized and fully staffed, held sway at opposite ends of town.

In the meantime Aurora continued to grow, and one of the hopefuls attracted by the stores of gold and silver was a young Missourian named Sam Clemens. He arrived in the spring of 1862 and worked briefly as a miner, and even more briefly as a mill laborer, before abandoning mining and Aurora altogether for a newspaper job in Virginia City. When he departed, he disposed of his mining claims in a quitclaim recorded in "Aurora, Mono County, California."

All the while, Aurora grew larger and more substantial. By the summer of 1863, its population was counted in the thousands, and the brick and stone business district encompassed ten or twelve blocks. There were a dozen hotels and as many boarding houses, 20 stores and 21 saloons, two newspapers, and a proportionate number of professional offices.

In its flowering, Aurora had ranked with Virginia City and Austin, a solid and substantial city built over a rich patch of rock on the western slope of the Wassuk Mountains.

The brick in its principal buildings came from kilns in England, laid down as ballast in the bilges of sailing ships bound for America. From the Atlantic coast the brick continued around the continent of South America to San Francisco. There it went aboard river steamers as deck freight to Stockton, where it was off-loaded onto wagons pulled by mule teams. The wagons hauled the brick as high up into the Sierra as roads would allow, and when they couldn't go any farther, the bricks were carried the last leg of the way by mule train.

The freight charge from Stockton to Aurora was a dollar a brick. No wonder brickyards were among the earliest local enterprises.

In September of 1863 county elections were held, and Aurora citizens could vote both for their California candidates at the police station and for their Nevada candidates at the Armory. Three weeks later the special border survey working south reached the district and drew the state line about four miles west of Aurora, putting it firmly within Nevada. The Mono County officials were forced to make the reluctant move west to the small camp of Bodie.

Perhaps because of the sudden reduction in the number of sheriffs from two to one, the rough element in Aurora became increasingly bold and troublesome. Thievery was common, and homicide was ordinary, but when, in February, 1864, a stationkeeper named Johnson was shot down in the street, his throat cut, and his clothes set on fire, the townspeople had had enough. After the sheriff arrested three of the murderers and set out in pursuit of the fourth, a special vigilante committee was formed, armed, and deployed through the town. Roughnecks and rowdy characters were escorted to the edge of town or put in jail, and the regular law officers were held in their homes under guard. When the sheriff's posse returned with their quarry, the prisoner was locked up in jail and the sheriff was locked up in his office.

Governor James Nye, receiving word of the usurpation of government, sent a wire to one of Esmeralda County's commissioners at Aurora urging against violence. He received in reply a telegram reading: "All quiet and orderly. Four men will be hung in half an hour." It was and they were.

But by the end of the year even the most peace-loving citizen might have considered letting the scruffnecks back into Aurora if they would bring prosperity back with them. For Aurora's mines and mills, exuberantly over-promoted, began to fail in the summer of 1864. By the summer of 1865 half the town's population had vanished, and by the end of the decade the richest surface deposits had been worked out, after producing nearly $30 million in bullion.

A locally famous newspaper exchange began when the Aurora paper noticed the departure of a local family for the more prosperous, but notoriously rough camp of Bodie. The report quoted a pretty little girl, riding on the load of her family's possessions as the wagon clattered out of town: "Goodbye, God. We're going to Bodie."

The Bodie paper bristled in reply that the words were right but the punctuation was wrong. What the dear little cherub had actually said was, "Good, by God! We're going to Bodie!"

Operations resumed for a few years in the late 1870s, but by the early 1880s the Esmeralda county seat had been lost to Hawthorne, and by the late 1890s the post office was closed.

On a sunny summer day in 1946 I walked with my great-grandfather in Pine Street, looking as you see it there, and wandered in the empty city. He was 88, and I was 10. We had traveled to Virginia City, Gold Hill, Bodie, Lundy and to a half-dozen other places he'd worked as a young man. Now he was showing me Aurora, a city he and his partners had bought in 1904. They had then revived the mines, with the participation of George Wingfield, the great mining millionaire of Goldfield.

The partners laboriously traced property owners who had long since abandoned the old city, he told me, generally offering $10 for a parcel of ground, maybe $20 if it had a building on it. Much of the property had already gone over to the county for non-payment of taxes, and the partners bought some of it at auction.

Altogether, he told me, they paid about $400 for all of the city there was to buy. By that time Aurora's original boom had been over for 30 years, and only a handful of old men still lived there.

He showed me where their company's offices had been. He showed me the stage depot where the

Franklin and Reo touring cars had pulled in, full of passengers hauled over Lucky Boy Pass from Hawthorne.

He showed me the enormous brick hardware store. They had opened it by sawing off the padlock and swinging the iron fire doors apart, and had found it still fully stocked. In the bins and on the shelves were all the tools, tubs, nuts, bolts, nails, chain, and other items necessary to brace sagging stairways, patch leaky roofs, replace broken windowpanes and otherwise bring an abandoned city into semi-repair. When they brought Aurora back to life for another dozen years, the hardware store was a mainstay of the community.

So was the saloon. They had popped its front doors open to find whisky on the shelves and barrels of wine and brandy in the basement. The wine had turned to vinegar, he said, but the brandy was still good and they had called an impromptu party to celebrate the discovery.

Now, 40 years afterward, we peered through the window into the gloomy old barroom, empty again — but with no brandy in the basement this time. He told me of the mines beginning to produce again, and how they had reopened the saloon. He had often stood there at the bar, he said, pointing through the grimy window. I could dimly see chairs shoved back from the dusty poker table in the back. A gambling man had leased that table from the house and dealt poker there. One night when Harry Gorham was standing there, at the bar near the door, the card game was being dealt as usual, with some of the young fellows from the mine sitting in.

Suddenly one of the young miners jumped up from the table. "Double dealing!" he shouted. The gambler sat quietly with his hands on the sawed-off shotgun in his lap.

"I heard the commotion and looked over at the card table," my great-grandfather told me as we squinted through the window.

"I saw the shotgun come up. All I could think to do was drop to the floor and crawl around behind the bar. I was still on my way down when it went off. Most of the pellets hit him in the chest, but some of them missed the man and went the length of the room and right out this front door, which was standing open. One of them hit a burro walking by outside, and sent it screaming and kicking down the street. Some others," he said, extending his hand and pointing at the top of the door frame, "made these marks."

I can still see his age-mottled hand pointing at the weathered wood, and the little dents made by the shot clearly visible.

The young miner was killed. The gambler jumped up and ran out the back door, leaving the saloon filled with smoke, shock and confusion.

"And when the undertaker's hearse clattered out to the burying ground the next morning," my great-grandfather said, "it passed beneath the gambler's body, which was dangling by a rope from the cemetery gate, left there by the young miner's friends, who had tracked him down and killed him."

I remember the awe I felt, listening to the old man's voice in the empty brick city on that bright summer afternoon.

The revival held until 1919. Then the old city began emptying out again. By the time we came to see it together in May, 1946, it was guarded by an old Italian man with a Model A Ford and a shotgun who got a little grubstake in return for running off vandals and thieves.

Three months later, in August, all of Aurora's brick buildings were demolished by a materials-hungry building contractor from Southern California, and hauled away on trucks. The ancient buildings are now factory chimneys in San Pedro and Wilmington — if they haven't been knocked down and carried off again. The remaining wooden structures, unprotected now, have been pulled down by vandals — even the gravestones have been stolen from the cemetery — now only a few scraps and sticks remain of this fine bold city in the wilderness.

Except for what's left of the cemetery, a few photographs, and the memories of the few hundred people still living who actually laid eyes on it, Aurora is gone. Except for the fascinating chapter it recorded in Nevada history, it might never have existed at all. Its only remains are some shallow depressions, a few broken bricks here and there, and a few scattered sticks of weathered wood, one of them perhaps bearing the indistinct impressions of shotgun pellets that missed their target a century ago.

MAX WINTHROP

Hawthorne's identity has been closely linked to the Ammunition Depot for most of a century.

Hawthorne

HAWTHORNE	
Tonopah	104
Yosemite	65
Yerington	57
Ichthyosaur Park	66
Boulder City	335

LIKE A HARDY LILAC persisting through drought and indifference, Hawthorne continues to blossom to the south of Walker Lake. It is a large town with numerous restaurants and motels offering provisions, diversions and accommodations for tourists and travelers.

Hawthorne's crown jewel is the long-established El Capitan, where the chicken-fried steak (the Nevada state bird, according to one of our critics) is a tradition. Joe's Tavern across the street is another major landmark, a classic Nevada saloon, decorated with an eager desire to reveal all. There are rusty implements from mine, farm and kitchen, guns of all shapes and sizes, helmets and other accourements of war — the memorabilia of three generations — including the headlight from one of the narrow-guage locomotives that rattled through town in the early days.

Hawthorne's most wonderful landmark is rarely seen by visitors, though. It's a five minute drive out of town to the north, but instead of continuing to Walker Lake — Hawthorne's fourth and grandest wonder — turn west into "the Depot." This was once the headquarters for the US Navy Ammunition Depot, and is now a minor paradise enjoyed by its residents and by visitors alike. After a long period of neighborly waves to arriving visitors, there are now guards on duty at all times. Still, even though entry calls for more than a breezy wave nowadays, you can still take a ten minute driving tour of this astonishing remnant from another age and play golf on one of the prettiest courses anywhere.

Your tour ends at the Walker Lake Country Club, where a beautiful 9-hole golf course (open to the public) was the best-kept military secret in America for 50 years. It was built by base employees, four holes at first, and then two at a time until the ninth hole was completed. A visiting golfer wrote in Nevada Magazine:

"A canopy of spring rainclouds was held aloft by rows of towering trees. At their feet spread fairways. The greens were of an exotic weave, floating in elevated pools at each fairway's end like green satin pillows on a velvet bed.

"Where is everybody?" we asked the manager.

"'I don't know,' he said. "It's always like this out

here.' I thought he was going to add, 'in heaven.'"

The club house is a favorite meeting place for local decision-makers.

The Mineral County Museum on the north end of town is an enjoyable collection of local area artifacts and discoveries dating back as far as the Miocene Era fossils from nearby Stewart Valley and as recent as the collection of hand-made knives taken from prisoners at the state prison. Among the mounted butterflies, the buggies and the sun-purpled inkwells is a display case devoted to a collection of mysterious brass bells. They were discovered between Luning and Hawthorne a few years ago, by a plinker shooting at cans. When one of his shots made an odd sound, he investigated and found one of these small bells poking up out of the grit. He dug around and eventually uncovered 18 groups of them — weighing about 200 pounds — as if they had been buried or otherwise left behind by a traveler along an ancient "Spanish Trail" there. It is obvious from their design that the bells had a common origin, and some of them carry the inscription "Mejico" and dates ranging from 1810 to 1818. Who might have left them, and why and when, remains unknown, although the suspicion is growing that they are modern replicas made for the tourist trade in Mejico. A lesser mystery is also on display: a blue military uniform dating to the 19th century with unique brass buttons that seem to depict the State or Territorial seal. The museum staff would be grateful if you can identify the unit of the soldier who wore it.

MAX WINTHROP

Mineral County Museum, Hawthorne.

Hawthorne's many lunch and dinner choices range from the family-style Maggie's Restaurant to the Chinese food at Henry Wong's Chinese Fast Food down the sreet from the El Cap to the ubiquitous McDonald's on the north side of town. They are all on the highway route through town. There is a Safeway supermarket on the north end of town.

For the most part Hawthorne's quiet streets are better suited to freckle-faced kids on bikes than to fun-hungry visitors. Hawthorne's tourists are mostly the outdoorsmen who camp, hike, hunt and rockhound in the nearby mountains and fish for bass and cutthroat trout in Walker Lake at the foot of mighty Mt. Grant. The Cliff House provides a grace note of elegance in this unique setting, overlooking the west side of the lake a few minutes' drive north of town, but it has been closed for a few years.

Hawthorne is on the main Las Vegas-Reno highway and serves as Nevada's gateway to Yosemite and the eastern Sierra via the Pole Line Road (Nevada 359) connecting with US 395 and the Tioga Pass.

Founded in 1881 as a division point on the Carson & Colorado Railroad, Hawthorne's site was selected by the mules used by the work crews to grade the right-of-way. Turned loose to forage for

MAX WINTHROP

Walker Lake, a few minutes north of Hawthorne.

MAX WINTHROP

Hawthorne street scene.

themselves in the winter, they found the most sheltered spot on the valley to protect themselves from the freezing wind. The humans had the wisdom to accept their critters' advice, and Hawthorne was established in this favored location in the valley.

Hawthorne became the Esmeralda County seat in 1883, replacing Aurora where the mines were in deep decline. Hawthorne's growth was hardly meteoric; the 1890 census taker counted 337 residents in town. By 1900, when the Southern Pacific acquired the C & C, there were only 99 more. In 1905 the SP changed over to standard gauge and bypassed Hawthorne completely by going around the east side of Walker Lake. The railroad built a new terminal at Mina and in 1907 the booming mining city of Goldfield took the Esmeralda County seat away. But mining discoveries in the vicinity helped maintain Hawthorne's prosperity through the hard times, and by 1910 the population had actually increased by 35 people.

In 1911, State Senator Fred Balzar of Hawthorne was able to persuade his fellow legislators that Esmeralda County was too large. Mineral County was created from its northern part with Hawthorne as its seat, and the old Court House was put back into service. But mining fell off again after World War I, and in 1920 only 226 residents were hanging on. Mina, meanwhile, with its mining and busy railroad, had grown to 680.

In 1926 half of Hawthorne's business district burned down, but even this was not enough to kill the tough little town.

And finally Hawthorne had some luck. Lake Denmark, New Jersey, was blown off the face of the earth by a huge explosion at the naval ammunition depot there, and Congress wanted to find some less valuable real estate for the new one. After a nationwide search, Hawthorne was the choice, the Yucca Mountain of its time. The following progression illustrates the result through World War II:

1930 pop.: 680
1940 pop.: 1,009
1944 pop.: 13,000
1950 pop.: 1,861

With more than 7,000 armed forces and civilian workers at the arsenal during the war, Hawthorne was the busiest Nevada boomtown in a generation. By 1950 nearly 2,500 people still lived in government housing at nearby Babbitt, but even as the Korean War broke out, the boom was over. Growth since has been slow, and today the ammunition depot plays a diminishing role in Hawthorne's economy, although its bunkers still pimple the desert as they have for more than 75 years. The Gulf War brought more good times to Hawthorne, and the depot — now under civilian management — is bulging more than ever with munitions.

In 1984, after nearly 50 years without a major mishap, one of the storage bunkers exploded. The blast was contained as intended, blowing up instead of out, and the deeply feared chain-reaction causing immense damage and loss of life did not occur.

Hawthorne Area Ghost Towns

Candelaria

22 miles south of Mina via US 95 (for 15 miles) and southwest along a graded dirt road. Founded at the site of a silver strike made by Spanish prospectors in 1863, Candelaria sprang into prominence a decade later when the Northern Belle went into production. In 1876 Candelaria had a two block business district, but development was limited by the high cost of shipping materials, and water — drinking water cost four and a half cents a gallon delivered, and a bath was two dollars, retail. Despite its remote and desolate location, the prosperity of the mines prompted further growth in Candelaria. By 1880 the town had a population of 900, and nearly twice that number three years later.

The arrival of the Carson & Colorado Railroad in 1882 seemed to assure eternal prosperity for Candelaria, which by this time had also developed a municipal water system as well as 27 saloons (and no churches). But fire, mining litigation, and labor disputes combined to end the town's forward motion. By the early 1890s Candelaria had entered a deep and lasting coma, broken only by a few hiccups of activity in the long years until 1979 when mining resumed. The cemetery is in relatively good repair, and provides a pleasant browse for those who take their pleasure this way; of the town itself there are rock ruins and wooden cabins in various stages of decay. Little shade and less water.

Marietta

About 9 miles beyond Belleville to the west. Founded in 1877 to serve the borax works at Teel's Marsh to the south and west, Marietta was built largely of adobe and native stone. Even bleaker in its surroundings than Candelaria, Marietta was also visited by gale winds across the dry marsh, carrying suspended within them immense quantities of grit. Adding an extra ingredient of excitement to the life of the community was the fact that the stagecoach from Aurora was robbed thirty times in a single year, and four times in one week.

Aboandoned with the richer and more accessible orax discoveries near Death Valley in the 1890s, Marietta's business structures and residences have survived with only marginal success. One of the best-preserved is the store once operated by "Borax" Smith when his borax empire was still young and building. The unspectacular remnants here are of a little-known town, and are accessible only by a 10-mile drive across some fairly rough country, and located at the edge of a barren dry lake. There are no distractions once the car's engine is turned off, and the transistor radio, to cushion the impact of the implacable Nevada desert. An hour's meditation at Marietta in mid-day should provide as much understanding about pioneer life in Nevada as a whole library of books on the subject.

Belleville

14 miles southwest of Mina via US 95, Nevada 360 and graded dirt road (marked "Marietta"). Located around the mills built in the middle 1870s to serve the mines at Candelaria, Belleville was a wide open humdinger of a town that went on a prolonged binge beginning the day it was founded, and ending when the mills shut down ten years later. Relics here are mostly related to the old mill workings, but a small cemetery remains also.

Hawthorne Area Campgrounds

Walker Lake

Two developed sites along U.S. 95 in Nevada's mining country are on the west shore of Walker Lake about 15 miles north of Hawthorne. Tamarack Point and Sportsmen's Beach are both camping and picnic sites with water, toilets, showers and tables, some of them shaded. Tamarack Point also offers a free boat-launching ramp heavily used by waterskiers and fishermen. Fishing is excellent during the fall and winter months. Both areas are open all year. 14 day limit. BLM.

Alum Creek

10 miles south of Hawthorne on Nevada 359 then west 3 miles on graded dirt road. Toilets, no water. 14 day limit. No fee.

MAX WINTHROP

Ione City Park — bring your own picnic.

Ione

23 MILES NORTHEAST of Gabbs via Nevada Route 844, 52 miles southwest of Austin via US 50 and the graded dirt road south through the Reese River Valley or just 7 miles north of Berlin.

IONE	
Gabbs	22
Austin	56
Middlegate	50

Attractively located in a beautiful canyon setting in the autumn of 1863, Ione grew rapidly to a population of about 500 and upon statehood became the first seat of Nye County. It maintained this distinction for three declining years until Belmont took the prize away. Ione's mines never achieved their early promise of richness, but neither did they altogether give out, and the town has never been completely abandoned.

Today, populated by a handful of humans, a few horses, and 13 buffalo, Ione is the faintly-beating heart of all that remains of the old Nevada. If you have seen the movie Tremors (a great Nevada movie!), you are prepared for Ione. In the movie the only business was a store. Here it's a saloon, with a tiny kitchen, pool table and long, long bar populated by an interesting assortment of customers.

An inviting "City Park" across the dirt street offers picnic tables and a pleasing place to relax. Cattle sometimes wander through the old town's streets, and a handful of weathered wooden buildings, including the original Nye County Court House (an airy structure built of weathered-silver pine logs), still stand. Dugouts and ancient rock cabins decorate the residential neighborhoods, although the modern single-wide homes of present-day mine workers predominate. Three of these trailers have been refurbished as rentals, furnaces and swamp coolers repaired, the bullet holes filled and painted over. There are also some RV hookups and campsites. That's it for Ione accommodations, so plan ahead and phone ahead (775-964-2003) if you want one.

Berlin-Ichthyosaur State Park

This unusual and agreeable combination of historic ghost town and prehistoric antiquity on the west slope of the Shoshone Mountains offers an intriguing overnight excursion. The park includes the weatherbeaten remains of Berlin, a small 19th century mining ghost town, and the fossil remains of 19 Ichthyosaurs, huge swimming reptiles of the Upper Triassic period.

Sixty miles southwest of Austin via US 50 (2 miles), Nevada 722 (8 miles), and 50 miles of graded gravel road via Ione. Or: 93 miles northwest of Tonopah via US 6-95 (3 miles), north on 67 miles of graded gravel and dirt road, then Nevada 361 to Gabbs and east 20 miles on Nevada 844. Or: 52 miles northeast of Luning via Nevada Route 361 to Gabbs (32 miles) and Nevada Route 844 (20 miles). As you see, this is not the trip for a spur of the moment jaunt. You should plan carefully and pack everything you will need in case of car trouble.

GOLD HILL NEWS ARCHIVE

Berlin in the good old days.

Park Headquarters are at Berlin. Originally developed in the late 1890s, Berlin's record of silver production was less than spectacular. The mine and mill attracted perhaps 250 people to this remote location seven miles south of Ione, of whom 200 were miners. By 1909 the mine had ceased operations and the town did not survive the winter. Its remains were largely ignored for sixty years. Park rangers now maintain Berlin in the picturesque state of "arrested decay" achieved over the years of emptiness and abandonment, and lead tours through the remnants of the old community. Underground tours of the Diana Mine were suspended at press time because of safety concerns.

The ichthyosaur display is east of Berlin, in beautiful Union Canyon. The rock from which the fossil bones protrude was once the bed of a vast inland sea. For a period of about 110 million years, beginning about 180 million years ago when much of Nevada lay beneath this sea, the sixty-foot long ichthyosaurs ("fish lizards") were abundant. They were the largest animals of their day, with bodies eight feet around and ribs nine feet long. Only some dinosaurs of a later period and some modern day whale species are larger.

One by one, over the course of time, a number of individual ichthyosaurs became beached along the shoreline of the sea, and were trapped there by the receding tides to die. Their bodies, washed parallel with the shoreline by the gentle shoving of the wavelets, decayed to skeletons, and were buried in the soft alluvial ooze at the shore.

Eventually, 3,000 feet of mud and slime overlaid the bones of the fish lizards and hardened to shale. Eons later, this shale stratum was capped with lava and then uplifted, and for tens of millions of years eroded, at last exposing the fossil bones again in this high desert canyon.

Thirty-four fossil ichthyosaur skeletons have been excavated in part, and a display quarry containing the fossil remains of three of the huge creatures is maintained as an in-place exhibit. Restrooms, tables and barbecue grills are provided and water is piped in. Fourteen campsites are connected with the fossil shelter by an easy and enjoyable nature trail, and another leads from Berlin to the cemetery in which the bones of several dozen human beings are presently decaying beneath a few feet of dirt.

An entrance fee is charged and 14 campsites are scattered through the park, with fire ring, BBQ grill, covered table, drinking water (mid-April to October), and restrooms nearby. An RV dump station is available. There is a picnic area with tables, grills, drinking water, and restrooms near the fossil shelter. Forty-minute tours of the fossil shelter are offered twice a day from March 15th to November 15th at 10 am and 2 pm; (three daily on weekends from Memorial Day to Labor Day); From November 15th to March 15th tours are available by advance arrangement only.

GOLD HILL NEWS ARCHIVE

At Round Mountain the trucks are as big as the mine where they're used.

Round Mountain

ROUND MOUNTAIN	
Carvers	10
Manhattan	21
Tonopah	56
Oasis	276

NAMED FOR the prominence that provided the initial gold discovery in 1906 — and which has been slowly whittled down to ground level — Round Mountain rapidly grew to about 400 people within its first six months. Gasoline engines powered the hoists, and Round Mountain mines produced more than a million dollars in their first five years of development. Placer deposits were also worked, first with dry wash machines, then by piping water from springs five miles distant to permit large scale hydraulic mining. Underground mining dwindled in the 1920s and had ended by the middle 1930s. Placer mining continued intermittently for twenty years more, but by the 1960s there were only about 20 families hanging on here.

With the resumption of mining by the Smoky Valley Mining Co. the town began to bustle again. Several hundred truck drivers, shovel operators, mill and office workers moved to town with their families, and soon the school and other community facilities of the ramshackle old place had burst their seams. The huge mine dumps piled up closer to the old town, and rich ore was discovered beneath it.

So the mining company built a new town down in the valley, with paved streets, curbs and gutters, a gas station and store with outside lights, and new houses for their employees. It is termed a "subdivision" of Round Mountain, perhaps in anticipation of the day when the last 200-ton load of the mountain is hauled to the crusher to be pulverized, and what little is left of the little old city can be scraped away to extend the mine.

Moving the store down into the valley created a void in the life of the old town, and the last remaining bar has inevitably fallen into it. In an unfortunate lapse, the Nye County Clerk failed to patent the townsite years ago, and now title to the jumble of houses, shacks, sheds, house trailers, rusting mining equipment, mining claims and public lands is in such a snarl it will take an act of Congress to straighten it out. A new Round Mountain is probably a good idea all around.

And if, as is rumored, the enormous rich ore

body here extends beneath it, the old town's end is certainly in sight, so by all means visit the place before it disappears. A tour of Original Round Mountain (actually the third townsite created during the 1906 boom — Brooklyn and Shoshone preceded it by a few months but did not survive) requires only five minutes, but you will remember it for the rest of your life, especially if the light is good and you look off to the northwest at the rugged summits of the Toiyabes rearing up in white-capped majesty, with the communities of Hadley and Carver's lost in the vastness of the broad valley floor beneath. A small cemetery dates back to the earliest days of the camp, and the old stone jail is falling down around its rusting iron cells.

Big Smoky Valley

THIS LONG, BROAD valley, enclosed by the majestic Toiyabe and Toquima mountains, is one of the most historically interesting and naturally beguiling regions of the state. The valley is enormous, a broad sweep of flat brushy bottomland extending 140 miles in a generally north-northeast by south-southwest direction. The enclosing mountain ranges burst up abruptly to enclose the valley along its east and west sides, with deep canyons and steep ravines extending high into the craggy summits.

The Big Smoky Valley (the valley was named from the north while undergoing a windstorm in the south) was originally inhabited by Shoshone and Paiute Indians who followed a hunting and gathering lifestyle with seasonal habitations at various places around the valley floor and in the surrounding foothills. The hot springs were particularly attractive places to live, and there is evidence of human activities in the valley deep in prehistory.

The first non-Indians to establish themselves in the Smoky Valley may have been Mexican silver prospectors who trekked north into the valley and discovered ore in the mountain canyons, which they mined expertly with hand tools. Who they were, and where they went — and why they never returned — is not known. Did they lose a boxful of bells at Walker Lake? John

MAX WINTHROP

This pioneer structure with the sod roof and million dollar view has been both a ranch hoouse and goat barn.

Frémont came through here in 1845.

Beginning in 1857 the U.S. Mail crossed the northern part of the valley on its Salt Lake City-Sacramento route, later used by the Pony Express and the Overland Stage.

In 1862 the discovery of silver ore in Pony Canyon brought hundreds of gold seekers into this remote region, and from the teeming camp of Austin, prospectors prowled out into the wilderness to explore. Promising discoveries were made in several of the canyons in the mountain ranges rimming the Smoky Valley.

Ranches were established in the valley in the 1860s, and stations on the Belmont-Austin Stage line provided horse changes and feed for both horses and passengers, and local connections for nearby mining camps. Over the century since, mining has had ups and downs, the scattered ranches have changed hands over the generations, and the Big Smoky Valley has continued to be remote and sparsely settled. The great granite mountains and the vast valley between them have seemed nearly changeless, as much alike in 1878 and 2008 as pavement and automobiles will allow. But today, suddenly, there are two "new" communities in the Smoky Valley.

Hadley

First, and most astonishing to people who have not visited the valley lately, is this bright new town, built on the valley floor at the foot of the talus slope below Round Mountain. Curbs and gutters! Paved streets! Lawns! It's worth a little side trip from the

MAX WINTHROP

Smoky Valley Granite, stone corns on the toes of the Toiyabe foothills.

highway just to see these exotic accoutrements in a central Nevada town. If you're an old-timer, you'll want to go slow — the sight of a 9-hole championship golf course out here might cause you to black out behind the wheel. This is a stunning example of the unexpected, almost surrealistic change that is overtaking Nevada — if there can be a golf course in the Big Smoky Valley why not a Cathedral on the Las Vegas Strip? Wondering, "What next?" is one of the pleasures of living here. There is also a grocery store and an all-year heated swimming pool in Hadley.

Actually, this "new" town of Hadley is an extension of the venerable community of Round Mountain about 4 miles to the east. As large scale mining continues there, the original 1906 townsite is increasingly old and in the way. Thus the new community has been developed by the mining company primarily to provide new housing and facilities for their employees. The name Hadley is now being relegated to history as eventually the old town will be scraped off the rocky slope to allow expansion of the mine, and the Hadley of memory will become Round Mountain, completely removed to the valley floor.

Carver's

Food and drink has been served to travelers at Carver's for generations, and a significant amount of the valley's social life has been centered here. The restaurant at Carver's is closed as we go to press, but there's an active community including a small grocery and a new-fashioned general store selling everything from fresh flowers to car parts, with a strong emphasis on recreation in the out-of-doors. You can outfit yourself for camping, hunting and fishing with gear of every description from a folding picnic table to a hunting bow and arrows to a weatherproof canvas jacket.

This wealth of merchandise in what was very recently an empty patch of ground, is another example of the way Nevada is changing and developing. The opportunity to buy a rosebud in the Big Smoky Valley is just as revolutionary as the opportunity to sink a putt on a manicured green. At this rate, the state is still evolving out of the 19th century just about the time the 21st century gets fully underway. Some old timers are skeptical of the change, but others figure as long as Nevada can stay about a hundred years behind the rest of the country we'll be all right.

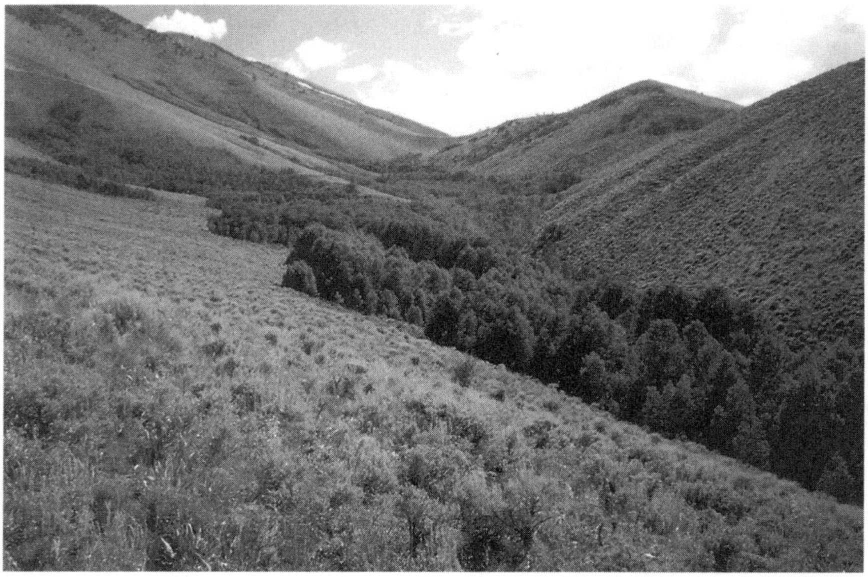
MIKE GREENAN

Birch Creek in the high country of the Toiyabe Range.

Central Nevada's Wilderness Areas

Arc Dome Wilderness

This 115,000-acre wilderness area was created in December, 1989, and comprises the southern one-third of the Toiyabe Mountains, 45-70 miles north of Tonopah. **Arc Dome,** the dominant peak in the southern part of the range, rises to 11,788 feet and is Nevada's 7th highest mountain. The Toiyabe Crest Trail follows the spine of this rugged range of mountains from north to south, and is intersected by hiking trails up Cow Canyon from the west, Peavine Canyon from the south, North and South Twin Rivers from the east, and Stewart Creek from the Northwest.

Alta Toquima Wilderness

About 60 miles north of Tonopah, this 38,000-acre wilderness area is within 10 miles of Nevada Route 376 and accessible by hiking trails from Monitor and Big Smoky valleys. Pine Creek Trail and Pasco Canyon Trail give access from the east, Moore's Creek from the north, and Summit Trail via Meadow Canyon on the south. **Mount Jefferson,** standing in solitary splendor at 11,949 feet, is the highest peak in the Toquima Range and the fourth highest in the state. These Wilderness Areas are administered by the Tonopah Ranger District, 775-482-6286

Table Mountain Wilderness

Table Mountain, located in the central part of the Monitor Mountains, this 98,000-acre wilderness area is about 60 miles northeast of Tonopah and provides habitat for large herds of mule deer and elk. From the south side the principal entry is by way of the Barley Creek trail; Willow Creek, Green Monster Canyon and Clear Creek from the east; Morgan Basin from the north; and Mosquito Creek from the west.

MAX WINTHROP

The Manhattan STANDARD *Building, Manhattan.*

Manhattan

TO THE GREAT DISGUST of its residents, Manhattan was listed as a ghost town in a previous edition of this book. If the old camp has ever been a ghost, it is now alive again. In 1980 and '81 sleek-sided doublewides were set in place between the frail old structures remaining from the boom years, the population doubled to nearly 75, and the pace of the old town speeded up to a walk. This mining renaissance is over for now, but some of its benefits remain, including a population large enough to support one, sometimes two saloons, and a community television cable system. TV you can see anywhere, but the saloon life in Manhattan is as unique, and possibly as endangered as the desert pupfish. Stop in and have a cold one.

MANHATTAN	
Tonopah	41
Round Mtn.	14
Belmont	14
Denio	309

Until his holdings were disposed of after his death, the gold and silver properties here were a part of the mining empire assembled by Howard Hughes, and they were the only ones he actually mined. Small quantities of ore were trucked to the batch plant in Tonopah for processing. The miners here had perhaps the best summertime view in Nevada, out over the vast reaches of the Big Smoky Valley. But the winter wind blows hard, and at 9,000 feet it cuts to the bone.

Manhattan Gulch was originally settled when a silver discovery was made in 1866, but abandoned three years later. It burst into permanence and prominence in 1905 when a cowboy named Frank Humphrey discovered rich gold ore and staked some claims. By the end of the year several hundred prospectors and miners were in camp, and by January, 1906, the boom was on in earnest. By spring a business district had taken shape along the length of the Gulch, telephone service and electric lights installed, and 4,000 people had flocked here. More rich discoveries were made in 1906 and 1907, but the San Francisco earthquake of the former year, and financial panic of the latter, made capital scarce and slowed development. Nevertheless, by 1909 Manhattan mines were operating at high capacity, producing gold, silver and copper. Production fell off during the 1920s but continued through the Depression and World War II, and totalled more than $10 million before it ended in 1947.

You'll enjoy an hour or two exploring Manhattan, and in good weather the loop trip east over the Toquima Range through Belmont and south to Tonopah makes a full day of early 20th century mining cities.

MAX WINTHROP

Belmont, an almost actual ghost town.

Belmont

14 miles northeast of Manhattan via graded dirt road over the Toquima Mountains, or 47 miles northeast of Tonopah via US 6, Nevada 376 and the mostly-paved Monitor Valley road.

Another of many occasions in Nevada's early history when a mining discovery was made by an Indian who was then sent on his way while white prospectors made their fortunes, this one resulted in the founding of a major Nevada city and, ultimately, its decay into one of the most interesting of the state's remaining ghost towns.

Discovered in 1865 and developed in 1866 into the most important community south of Austin, Belmont took the Nye County seat from Ione in 1867. In 1868 mining slowed, but it picked up momentum again in the early 1870s, attracting a population of about 2,000 until the late 1880s when the mines shut down. In 1905 Tonopah took the county seat and Belmont went into a coma from which it is only now awakening.

The original brick Nye County Court House still stands, as do many of the buildings along the town's principal business blocks. One lamented exception is the often-photographed Cosmopolitan saloon, destroyed by vandals. The cemetery is extensive and still in a relatively undisturbed condition, and the ruins of the large stamp mills are most impressive.

The Court House is now a State Historical Monument, and part of the Nevada State Park System, but until recently only the vigilance of its residents has prevented the vandalism and thievery which has resulted in the destruction and disappearance of other Nevada ghosts.

Belmont was never entirely abandoned, and some Tonopah folks have been part-time residents, but until recently Dick's Saloon was the only business in town, when it was open. Now the highly regarded Belmont Inn B&B is operating in elegantly refurbished old structures, and is attracting an enthusiastic clientele. At last report two small shops were open at least some days of the week as well. For old Belmont this is renaissance.

My last visit was in early winter. There was a crust of snow on the town that rendered it beautiful beyond description, and just for the fun of it I made the drive over the summit to Manhattan. It was plowed clear, but snow-melt made the clay roadbed greasy here and there toward the summit. Miss Daisy slid and wallowed daintily through it, eventually reaching firm ground without any real difficulty. This is a pleasant drive in any season, invitingly remote and yet easy enough for a big, soft sedan. But if you go in winter, be sure you have the gear to dig yourself out in case you're unlucky, and enough food to sustain you until the movie people can get there to bid on your story.

MAX WINTHROP

Belmont, street scene.

MAX WINTHROP

Tonopah always did love a parade

Tonopah

A HUNDRED YEARS AGO Tonopah was a sprawling city of 3,000 people served by stagecoaches, five newspapers, more than 30 saloons, and a pair of churches. Now, for the second time in a century, a sudden mining boom has ended in a mighty crash and extended depression. In a way this makes Tonopah an even more attractive stop for visitors — the sense of "Ghost Town" is very strong. There are plenty of lodgings and several dining choices for visitors (even a McDonald's at the top of town) and the Tonopah Mining Park and Central Nevada Museum are inviting attractions, but times are tough for residents.

TONOPAH	
Austin	110
Hawthorne	135
Las Vegas	207
Reno	256

Tonopah sprang to life in 1900, just as the mining excitement at Nome, Alaska, was tailing off, and drew a large number of sourdoughs, among them Tex Rickard, Wyatt Earp, and Key Pittman. The Tonopah boom also coincided with the last waning of the Comstock as the center of political and economic influence in Nevada, and Tonopah

TONOPAH CONVENTION CENTER

Jim Butler lives again, Tonopah.

men managed much of the state's affairs for more than a generation afterward. Key Pittman went to the U.S. Senate where he was known as "The Senator from Tonopah" because of his vigorous support the silver mining industry. Tasker Oddie, Jim Butler's attorney, was both a U.S. senator and a Nevada governor. Earp made himself useful as a gambling dealer and "persuader" in local politics; even in his fifties he was not a man to fool with, though the dent he made in Tonopah history is nothing like his previous impact on Tombstone, Arizona. Rickard's flamboyant Nevada career led him eventually to Madison Square Garden with a young fighter named Jack Dempsey.

Butler was an energetic and efficient miner, but he has been described as the laziest mining tycoon of all time because of his practice of giving leases to others to develop his properties. The leasers, working against deadlines, established Tonopah as a major mining bonanza by taking $4 million in ore from Butler's mines and building a substantial city. By 1905 it had captured the county seat from failing Belmont; by 1907 Tonopah was thriving with five banks, several theaters, numerous hotels, and many of the most impressive residences in Nevada, and the Big Casino, a dance-hall-and-brothel occupying a square city block.

Like Austin forty years previously, Tonopah was the headquarters and fitting-out place for hundreds of prospectors prowling the brushy wilderness of central Nevada, and whose discoveries helped raise Nevada from the economic coma it had been suffering for 20 years. They also restored the state to its accustomed place on the front pages of the nation's newspapers. Tonopah peaked in the years leading up to World War I, when the mines averaged 38.5 million a year in production.

From there it was a long, slow downhill slide. As the '20s gave way to the '30s, and the '30s to the '40s, mining slowed and finally stopped. Ranching and the highway trade became the main economic resources. Population dwindled and for 50 years of hard times the increasingly shabby city clung to the barren swale between Mounts Oddie and Brougher, half awake and distracted. It was silver the old city wanted, with three shifts a day in the shafts and half a hundred hammering mills crushing rock day and night.

In 1979, after nearly 60 years of decline, Tonopah erupted in its second mining boom of the 20th century. Suddenly the Mizpah Annex Cafe was a crush of men in Air Force fatigues or the flannel shirts and blue jeans of construction workers and miners. Waitresses raced from table to table with pots of coffee and platters of flapjacks.

Fleets of buses hauled the men out of town to work. Nine hundred of them were building the great new Anaconda molybdenum mine and mill, and hundreds more worked in a dozen gold and silver mines producing bullion at a furious rate. The Air Force was so busy at its missile test range beyond the mountains to the southeast that it had

Jim Butler Strikes It Rich

Jim Butler gave this account of the great discovery in the spring of 1903, three years after it took place.

"Tonopah is an Indian name, which, I learned when a boy, signifies a small spring. The Indians, on their periodic trips from the Cowitch Mountains and other places to Rhodes' Salt Marsh, camped at this sprinbg. Rich mines had been discovered in the San Antonio Range, and the country being highly mineralized, I long considered the mountains in the vicinity of the springs a good field for the prospector.

"Attention to other matters kept me away from the range until May, 1900, when I left Belmont, the seat of Nye County, on a prospecting expedition to the south. I passed over the Manhattan Mountains, left Rye Patch, and traveled all day to the spring known by the Indians as Tonopah, near which I found quartz. I followed up the float and found leads. There were bold black croppings of fine-grained quartz, showing a great quantity of mineral, so much in fact that I considered it of very little or no value. However I took several samples, passed over a great number of ledges, went on about four miles, and camped on May 19th on what is now known as the Gold Mountain Mines, and saw those leads also, but, as they were small compared with the large ledges I had discobred early in the day I did not think much of them, though I took samples with me which I afterward had assayed.

NEVADA HISTORICAL SOCIETY

Jim Butler.

"The first sample from Tonopah which I had assayed contained 395 ounces of silver and 15-1/2 ounces of gold to the ton. I spent some time in waiting for an assay to be made at Southern Klondikwe by B.F. Higgs, and on May 26 returned to Tonopah, made a dry camp, and the next day took about 75 pounds of ore from several ledges which I subsequently has assayed by W.C. Gayhart of Austin, the result being 640 ounces of silver and $206 in gold to the ton. I was absent from Belmont when the returns from the assay reached there and when I did return to Belmont I had office duties to attend to and also to harvest the hay on my ranch, so did not return to Tonopah to locate the mines until ugust 25, 1900. Mrs. Butler accompanied me and assisted materially in locating the claims. My first locqation was the Desert Queen,next to the Burro, and then I told my wife to name one, which she did, naming it Mizpah, which at that time did not look any better than the others, but since has proved to be the richest on record. I also located the Valley View, Silver Top and Buckboard, and the group as a whole proved to be the richest opened up to date in any country."

Jim and Belle Butler had an interesting relationship. Belle was married and running a miner's boarding house in Belmont. Jim was the Nye County District Attorney and he happened by as Belle's husband had flown into a rage and was hitting her.

"Don't raise your hand to her!" Jim said.

"who the hell are you?" the man replied. "I'll hit her when I want to hit her!"

He stepped back to take another swing and Jim pulled out his pistol and shot him down dead.

Jim and Belle were married a short time afterward, requiring him to leave his Indian wife and children behind. He gave Belle full credit for helping stake the claims that made their fortune, but when he said he had to harvest the hay he forgot to mention he had to do it because Belle insisted he do it before she'd let him do his tomfool mining.

to lease whole motels in Tonopah to accommodate the troops.

The population went from fewer than 2,500 to more than 4,000 in about a year. When school was out in June, 1980, there were 475 kids enrolled in school. When school opened again in September, there were more than 700 students for whom to find classrooms and teachers. At the only grocery store in town the clerks worked steadily to restock the shelves with almost 6 tons of groceries every day, and customers idled their cars in the street, waiting for spaces to open up in the parking lot.

Every structure with a roof over it was rented. A temporary 300-space campground was built at the Anaconda worksite. Every vacant lot that could accommodate a trailer was put to use, giving the tangle of old streets an incongruous look: a flamingo-pink aluminum cube stuck between a swaybacked old cottage on one side and a fitted stone mansion on the other. There was an armed robbery, the first

MAX WINTHROP

The Mizpah, the "Finest Stone Hotel in the Desert."

in more than 60 years, and Tonopah congratulated itself on its return to full municipal vigor.

On the northeast side of town Anaconda built a 500-acre subdivision of new homes, with a new school and a park so their permanent employees wouldn't have to live in their cars. The rattle of hammers and the snarl of saws was heard everywhere in town, and workers from Reno, Las Vegas, Salt Lake City and Sacramento stood in line at the pay phones after work every night to call home. Plans of every optimistic kind were announced one after another. One Friday afternoon over coffee at the Silver Queen Restaurant on Main Street I watched a man float from booth to booth around the room, keeping five separate deals going at once.

And then one day the boom was over. The price of gold and silver slid and the mines closed down. The market for moly went so bad that even mighty Anaconda had to close down its operation and sit on its $240 million investment. The Air Force got enough of its base built to move the men inside, and then encouraged them to stay there. Tonopah slowed down again.

The most prominent symbol of this boom-and-bust history is the Mizpah Hotel at the center of the city. Built in 1907 and '08 on the site of one of Jim Butler's old camp sites, the five-story hotel was immediately the center of glamour and elegance in dusty, hard-working Tonopah. It had steam heat, electric lights and elevator service, and advertised itself earnestly as "The Finest Stone Hotel on the Desert." When a husky young roustabout named Jack Dempsey strode into the flourishing Mizpah six years later, Tonopah was at its peak.

The Mizpah slipped into poverty during the long decline along with the rest of the city. It livened up briefly during World War II when the Air Base was busy training bomber crews, but this flicker of prosperity ended with the war. In 1950 new owners erected the now familiar lights on the roof. The lobby was remodeled to accommodate a small casino and cocktail bar, but the economic tide was still running the wrong way. By the late '60s an inside room (in which the window opened onto the corridor, rather than to the outside) rented for $2.50. With a bare bulb dangling from a frayed cord, and a swaybacked metal bed hugging the wall for support, these rooms were great favorites with cowboys sleeping off a payday Saturday night.

But in 1937 a kid from Las Vegas fell in love with the historic brick and stone structure while traveling to a high school track meet in Yerington. Nearly 40 years later, as the president of a multi-million dollar construction company and builder of the Union

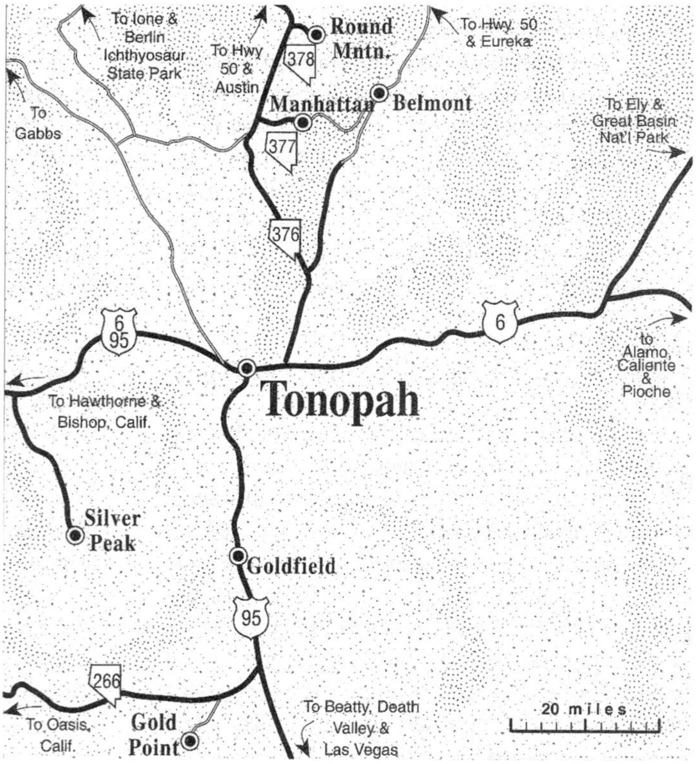

MAX WINTHROP

The Tonopah Mining Park and the old Nye County Courthouse (background) go back to the early 20th Century.

Plaza Hotel in downtown Las Vegas, he bought it. In 1979, after three years and $4 million, Frank Scott opened the glamorous old hotel, its rooms and suites furnished with antiques. It was a glittering jewel box designed for high-rolling gamblers. But Scott's dream of his remote "ghost town hotel" was trampled under the feet of commercial travelers hurrying to sell goods and services to the mines and military in Tonopah, and the fine furnishings and appointments were superfluous to these practical visitors. The later collapse of the boom left the Mizpah with only the highway clientele, and a few years ago it was stripped of the furniture Scott had so fondly installed, and closed in bankruptcy. It was still closed as this edition goes to press.

Another symbol of the mining boom is the Scolari's supermarket at the south end of town, which brought old Tonopah all the way into the 20th century about 30 years ago. As Tonopah struggles into the 21st century local folks are worried that it might close. Next door, the modern Station House Hotel-Casino did close for a while, but a new owner reopened it in fine style.

The best symbol of all is probably the new community sports complex a short distance out Radar Road on Tonopah's north side, with swimming pool, exercise rooms, handball courts and other work-out facilities. It was a farewell gift to Tonopah from the Anaconda company, and it's open to the public.

The mining and military boom left Tonopah with a large number of new motels — the Jim Butler Motel across the street from the Mizpah was designed and factory-built in modules, trucked to town and erected in two days. The modern Hi-Desert Inn, Silver Queen and Sundowner motels are all on Main Street. The Clown, on the north end, is the newest.

You can spend half a day exploring Tonopah's old neighborhoods and you can spend a lifetime exploring the beautiful country nearby. The Central Nevada Historical Society Museum — you'll see it on Logan Field Road on the south (uphill) side of town — displays relics and memorabilia of central Nevada, meticulously and lovingly preserved. Slide shows on local history are available, and antique mining machinery decorates the parking lot.

The 70-acre Historic Mining Park is at the original discovery site at the end of McCulloch Street on the east side of town. The remaining structures and underground works of four old mines are being restored to working condition, with exhibits, displays and a Visitor Center in the 1905 Tonopah Mining Company power house. You can take the self-guided tour of the magnificent ruins and acquire souvenirs in the small gift shop. Access is easy; you'll see the road heading uphill from the Mizpah parking lot on Main Street.

You'll also see numerous sculptures and murals here and there around the old city. They've been placed there in the hope they will lure you to park and get out of your car for a few minutes. Do it, you'll enjoy it.

Tonopah has a swimming pool and a lawned park with playground and picnic tables. Barsanti Park, named for the "Fighting General from Tonopah," is at Bryan and Booker Streets. A couple of smaller parks can be easily found in the Anaconda subdivision off Radar Road, and Jim Butler Park overlooks the town from the east.

Welcome to Tonopah

Area Information

TONOPAH CHAMBER OF COMMERCE
301 Brougher Street. 775-482-3859
Tour the Historic Mining Park, visit the Central Nevada Museum, mine for turquoise, shop our unique stores, discover local artists and much, much more! At night, enjoy the skies voted the Best Star Gazing Destination in North America! See you in Tonopah. Stop in, we'll help you find the fun.

Attractions

TONOPAH HISTORIC MINING PARK
520 McCulloch Street. 775-482-9274
Wonderful outdoor museum, the Tonopah Historic Mining Park is over 100 acres of mining spanning the last 100 years. The park preserves the rich history through exhibits of equipment, minerals and self-guided tours. The park collects, restores and interprets mining artifacts on site and in the original buildings.

Lodgings

BEST WESTERN HI-DESERT INN
320 Main Street. 775-482-3511
Best Western Hi-Desert Inn is nestled in the center of Tonopah right on Highways 6 & 95. All rooms are equipped with a micro/fridge, and high speed internet access. Enjoy our Fresh Baked cookies at night and our hot complimentary breakfast in the morning. Ask about Business and Family Suites.

CLOWN MOTEL
521 N. Main Street. 775-482-5920
Tonopah's newest motel offers large, clean, affordable rooms next to the pioneer cemetery on the north side of town. Knowledgeable staff will ensure you get the most from your visit to Tonopah, and we put the coffee on early each morning. Stay with us!

JIM BUTLER INN & SUITES
100 South Main Street. 775-482-3577
Visiting the Jim Butler Inn is like visiting a favorite friend's home. We make you feel welcome, give you a wonderful room, and help you find your way to all the sights in the area. Our guests from around the world return to visit us again and again. Reservations: 800-635-9455

SILVER QUEEN MOTEL
319 Cross Avenue. 775-482-6291
The Silver Queen Motel is quietly located one block off Highways 6 & 95. Our large rooms have convenient exterior entries, refrigerators, coffee pots, and 27 inch televisions. We offer reasonable rates to our guests staying nightly or weekly. Kitchenette and Family rooms rent quickly so make reservations early!

Museums

CENTRAL NEVADA MUSEUM
1900 Logan Field Road. 775-482-9676
Our museum describes the history of the area from prehistoric to present, including a variety of indoor and outdoor displays, an extensive research library, and a small gift shop. Open year-round, Wednesday through Sunday, 10 am - 5 pm, closed 1 - 2 pm for lunch. Free admission, donations welcome.

Tonopah Area Campgrounds and Hiking Trails

THERE ARE few developed campsites in this huge territory. Of the nearly two dozen canyons that notch the eastern face of the Toiyabe Mountains, only two, Kingston and Peavine, offer prepared facilities of any kind. Roads of varying quality give access to the other canyons, and many of them receive relatively heavy use. Most contain streams offering fair to good trout fishing, and most support a population of deer, making them at least slightly hazardous during hunting season.

Recently established Wilderness Areas in the Toiyabe, Toquima, and Monitor Ranges contain many hiking trails, including the spectacular Toiyabe Crest Trail that runs along the spine of this mighty range of mountains, and can be reached from a number of canyons. Our maps don't permit the necessary detail to depict these trails accurately; get up-to-date information and seasonal advice at the Tonopah Ranger District, Toiyabe National Forest, PO Box 3940, Tonopah 89049; 775-482-6286.

Columbine Campground

7 aspen-shaded campsites at 8,500 feet, accessible by marked and graded dirt road 9 miles east into the Toiyabes from Nevada 21 at the Reese River Ranger Station (35 miles south from US 50, or 9 miles northeast of Ione). Water is available in Stewart Creek, a popular fishing stream, and you can hike the trail into the Arc Dome Wilderness Area, the Arc Dome summit itself, and the Toiyabe Crest Trail which runs the length of the range.

Peavine Campground

50 miles north of Tonopah via Nevada 376 and marked, graded dirt road leading west into the southern end of the Toiyabe Mountains at 5,500 feet. 6 campsites and a group use area. No drinking water is provided, but a stream runs through the campground. A trail from the campground provides access to the Arc Dome Wilderness Area and joins the Toiyabe Crest Trail.

Pine Creek Campground

70 miles north of Tonopah via Nevada 376 (13 miles), the Monitor Valley Road (40 miles) and Forest Service Road 009 (17 miles) west into the Toquima Mountains, climbing to 6,500 feet. 24 single sites and 2 group sites, maintained by the Forest Service; there is no piped water, but Pine Creek runs through the pine-forested campground, with brown, brook and rainbow trout stocked in the spring. The campground is at the eastern edge of the Alta Toquima Wilderness Area.

Saulsbury Wash

At the side of US 6 25 miles east of Tonopah, this 6-unit campground is provided with water, toilets and a group use area, but no shade.

Ghost Towns

TYBO 65 miles northeast of Tonopah via US 6 and a graded dirt road. Tybo grew slowly from the initial discovery of lead and silver in 1870 until 1874, when capital was used in quantity to develop the mines. By 1875 about 1,000 residents were supporting an active business district and fighting among themselves along ethnic lines — Irishmen against Cornishmen and everyone against the Chinese. The town withered away after the failure of the Tybo Consolidated and was for all practical purposes dead from 1891 until 1929 when new smelters went into operation. Production ceased for the last time in 1937. The brick and wood remnants of the old town date from its glory days and from later attempts at revival, in addition to the successful one in 1929.

JEFFERSON 7 miles east of Round Mountain via dirt road. Jefferson was founded in the middle 1860s and was thriving by the early 1870s. A Jefferson mine supplied a 40-lb. ore sample buttered with nuggets for the Philadelphia Centennial Exposition in 1876, but by 1878 Jefferson's buildings were empty. Revival attempts, including one in 1917 financed by Charles Stoneham, owner of the New York Giants baseball club, were unprofitable and short-lived. There is an abundance of frame and stone ruins.

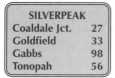

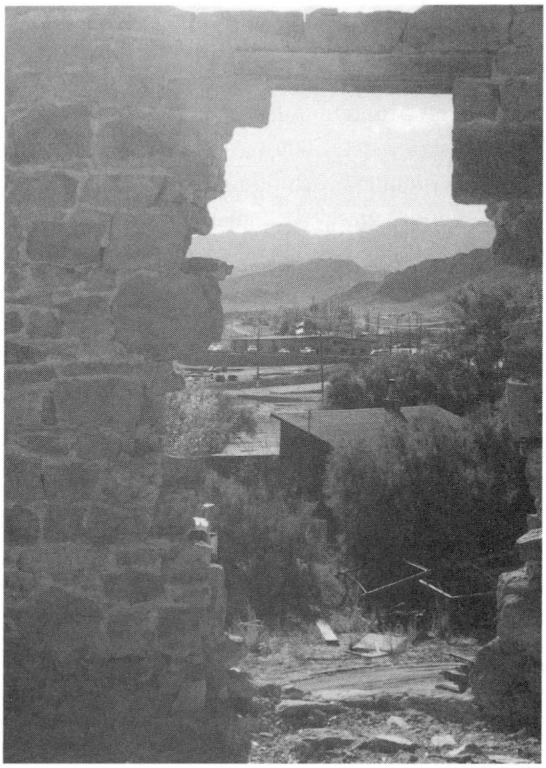

MAX WINTHROP

This is the last piece of 19th Century Silverpeak; the rest was burned up, torn down or blown away.

Silverpeak

AUSTIN-BASED PROSPECTORS happened on rich ore here in 1864 and the next year established a small mill around which a mud and adobe village took form, all operations coming to an end in 1870. In 1906 the mines revived briefly, but the resulting failure was conclusive. Silver Peak's local heroes were the mining promoters Fred Vollmer Sr. and Jr., whose faith in Silverpeak led eventually to its long-term revival.

SILVERPEAK	
Coaldale Jct.	27
Goldfield	33
Gabbs	98
Tonopah	56

But in those eary 20th century days of borrasca Fred Sr. lived quietly with his family in a small cottage, eking out a precarious living by the most careful economies, and Fred Jr. was only a boy. Somehow coming into possession of $80, Fred Sr. hitched a team to the buckboard and headed to Mina, 50 miles across the desert, for groceries. To his wife's increasing concern he was late getting back, and when he finally arrived two days overdue, the wagon was empty. Her children huddling around her skirts and the unrelieved desert vastness spreading away in every direction, she speared him with a questioning look.

"Three queens," he explained.

The Vollmer-inspired revival in the 1930s brought Silver Peak into production and prominence once again, and on Labor Day, 1939, former World Heavyweight Champion Max Baer came to town for a prize fight. Admission to the bout was $2.50 for three preliminaries and the main event: Max Baer vs. "Big Ed" Murphy, a local miner. Referee for the event was the famous Tom Sharkey. Murphy threw the first punch of the fight. Baer missed a right cross and caught the Irish miner in a clinch. Murphy pushed free and landed another punch, crowding Baer into a corner. Baer clipped the young hero with a left jab, and Murphy countered with a hard right that jerked Maxie's head back. That persuaded the Champ to call it a night, and he responded with two left hooks to the breadbasket and a right cross to the head, sending Big Ed to the canvas for the 10-count.

"You're all right, pardner," said Baer as he dragged the groggy Murphy to his feet.

"He can punch hard and he's a good kid," Baer assured the crowd with a wave while he, his manager and Tom Sharkey bundled themselves back into their La Salle sedan and sped away toward Las Vegas with their winnings.

Gold mining recently revived, sputtered and closed down again. A steady production of lithium has kept Silverpeak alive, with an elementary school, a post office, a 5-unit motel and a saloon.

Fires have destroyed virtually every historical trace of the tough old town of the 1860s, and what does remain has been transformed by time. The old schoolhouse, for example, became the Vinegaroon Saloon, itself now closed. On a visit I made a few years back, the teacher who presided over the classroom when it closed 25 years before was playing the quarter slot machines where her desk used to be.

Silverpeak is small, gritty and isolated, yet a part of the modern world: while billowing a rooster-tail of dust past the lithium ponds on the way to Goldfield several years ago I was listening to a public radio interview with Boy George from London.

GOLD HILL NEWS ARCHIVES

Goldfield street scene, 1906.

Goldfield

THIS ESMERALDA County seat was exuberantly (and briefly) named Grandpah by its enthusiastic founders in 1902. Goldfield was producing $10,000 a day by 1904, and by 1906 was a bigger city than Tonopah. On Labor Day in that year saloonkeeper Tex Rickard promoted a prize fight for the Lightweight Championship of the World between Battling Nelson and Joe Gans. He offered the biggest purses in the history of prize fighting: $20,000 to the champion Nelson and $10,000 to Gans, the black challenger.

GOLDFIELD	
Tonopah	**26**
Pahrump	**140**
Las Vegas	**182**
Reno	**261**

It was hailed as "The Fight of the Century" in the national press, and reporters from the east coast papers joined writers from the Pacific coast at ringside. The fighters battered each other for 42 punishing rounds before Nelson, bloodied and sagging, fouled Gans in a clinch. It was "as dirty a foul," the Goldfield Sun reported, "as was ever witnessed by spectators at ringside." Gans was awarded the victory and the championship, but the big winner was Tex Rickard. The $72,000 gate was a record, and the fight was the first in a long career of prize fight promotions that took him eventually from his Northern Saloon in Goldfield to Madison Square Garden in New York City.

So rich was the ore at Goldfield that miners employed hidden overall pockets, hollow pick handles and false heels on their boots to high-grade the best pieces of it. That practice, combined with the growth in influence and activity of the International Workers of the World, prompted the mine operators to persuade Governor John Sparks to call on President Roosevelt for Army troops to maintain order. The presence of the soldiers accomplished the mine owners' objective, which was to crush the union without open violence.

By 1910 the Goldfield mines were in decline, but at its peak of prosperity Goldfield was an eccentric combination of wild western boomtown, and decorous, respectable city. There were miners and prospectors and saloon roughs, plenty of them, but there were also stenographers and telephone operators, bankers and stock brokers. Goldfield was the largest city in Nevada and the Goldfield Hotel was the most opulent stopping place between Kansas City and the Pacific Coast.

George Wingfield was Goldfield's most prominent citizen. Wingfield had been a buckaroo on ranches around Burns, Oregon, and Winnemucca, Nevada, in the years before the turn of the century. He rode south when word of the Tonopah excitement radiated north, stopping in Winnemucca just long enough to borrow $150 from a banker there named George Nixon. Wingfield arrived in Tonopah with most of his stake intact, but instead of investing in a prospector's outfit, he put it down on the faro table at the Tonopah Club and ran it up to $2,200. He eventually acquired an interest in the gambling concession at the club and began dabbling in wildcat mining shares on the side.

When Goldfield's bonanza was struck, Wingfield called for more backing from banker Nixon, and eventually from eastern financiers like Bernard Baruch. With their help he all but cornered the market in Goldfield mining stocks. By the time of the labor troubles with the IWW "Wobblies", Nixon and Wingfield were the bonanza kings of Goldfield. With the decline, Wingfield moved to Reno, where he dominated the state's financial and political activities. His influence on Nevada's development for the first 30 years of the 20th century was incalculable. Fortune Magazine called him "King George" Wingfield, "proprietor of Nevada."

In September, 1913, a flash flood wrenched houses from their foundations and laid waste whole neighborhoods. In 1918 Goldfield was the stone husk of a city left in the desert to die, and it died badly. In 1923 a fire blazed up to make ashes of 53 square blocks. Abandonment and decay have accounted for much of the rest. Today only a small village remains alive in the heart of this once-great city.

But there are landmarks of considerable interest in Goldfield still, and if you have a taste for Nevada antiquities, you can spend a full day exploring the old city and still not see all there is to see. Principal among them are the mines and dumps at the foot of Columbia Mountain on the north side of town. Until a generation ago the Florence Mine was still worked by a man and his wife; he blasted and mucked the ore, she ran the hoist: They are gone now, but the old workings draw continued interest from mining companies. Gone too is Hymie Miller, the blind miner who walked four miles each way from his home to his mine and back again after work, locating the seams of ore by taste.

Flesh and blood relics of the old times are few in Goldfield now, but brick and stone survives in profusion here. The most wonderful relic of the city's past is the great Goldfield Hotel, at the corner of Columbia and Crook streets. It dominates the city today just as it did in its prime. Built in 1908 at a cost of just under a half million dollars, the hotel contained 154 guest rooms, furnished with Brussels carpets and brass beds. The lobby was appointed in mahogany and furnished with overstuffed leather settees. The lobby ceilings gleamed with 22-karat gilt, although it has been somewhat stained and dimmed by water and by time. The dining room menu included delicacies such as squab and lobster, a thrilling item so far from the sea, and in a city where the staples were flapjacks, beefsteaks and beans.

George Wingfield owned the hotel, and it is said that when Goldfield's glory days were over he had a portfolio of photographs taken to show the building's luxurious touches to their best advantage. They were sent east, where they persuaded New York bankers to mortgage the property for a considerable sum — $100,000 by one report. He imme-

MAX WINTHROP

One of Goldfield's cemeteries.

MAX WINTHROP

Tex Rickard's Northern Saloon *reflected the rush from the frozen Klondike to the deserts of southern Nevada.*

diately abandoned the place to them, and it passed through several hands, each time at a considerable loss. By the 1930s, as the story goes, the hotel's newest owner tried to sell it back to him at the bargain price of $50,000, using the same set of photographs. Wingfield turned it down.

Spared by flood and fire, the hotel could not survive the decline of the mines, and it closed in 1936. But it was reopened in 1942 to provide housing for Army Air Corps personnel sent to the Tonopah Air Base. It closed again for the last time in 1949 and has never reopened. A new owner repaired the roof and began a major restoration, but expenses far exceeded the original estimates, and work has been stopped for so long that pigeons have reinhabited the huge old place, leaving mounds of guano beneath favored roosts, and feathered corpses in the upstairs hallways.

The massive old high school now stands forlorn and empty, but the castle-crenelated Esmeralda County Court House, an architectural curiosity of the Edwardian variety, is open to visitors. You will notice the original Tiffany lamps still used inside.

The intersection of Main and Crook streets was once one of the busiest in the city, with a saloon on each of the four corners. The one where the E-Z Serve gas station now stands was Tex Rickard's famous Northern Saloon. So much beer did these dispensaries sell that they had to build stone warehouses nearby to store their kegs. Two of them still stand. So does Tex Rickard's house, which is the brick residence with the decorated ridges at the corner of Crook and Franklin and which boasted the only lawn in Esmeralda County — the whole town turned out to watch when he mowed it. The second house to the north of it, otherwise perfectly ordinary looking, is built of beer and whisky bottles.

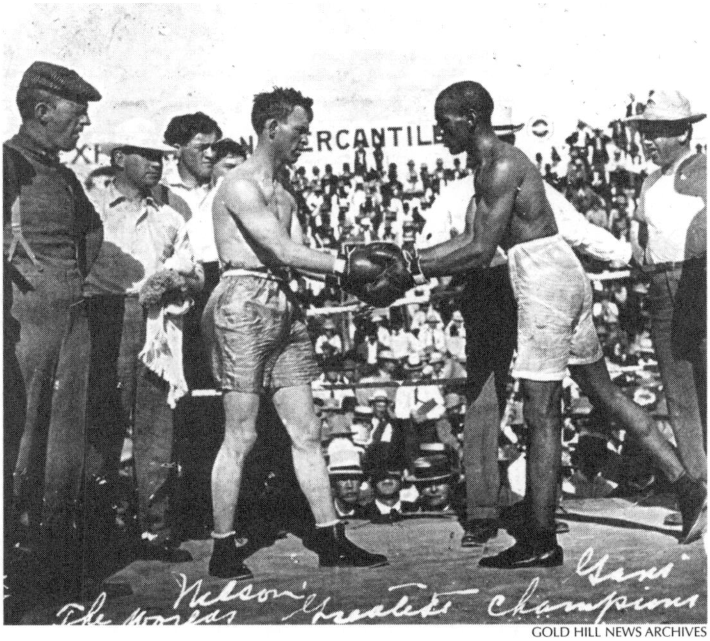
GOLD HILL NEWS ARCHIVES

Gans-Nelson 1906 Lightweight Championship, Goldfield.

There's a new Northern Saloon now, next door to the Mozart Club, with a hand carved Italian bar and a restaurant serving lunch and dinner. The menu is based in traditional favorites, but with a gourmet flair.

The Santa Fe Saloon is one of

RICH MORENO

Tex Rickard's residence.

Goldfield's longest-lived and most famous relics. Once it served the miners more than drinks, as the small cribs out back attest. Still a popular oasis today, the Santa Fe is almost as busy on a peak summer weekend as it was during the mining bonanzas, and the cribs have been replaced by a 4-unit motel. Another special glimpse of time gone by is provided at the Brown-Parker Garage where a 1920s-era machine shop is preserved intact. The elaborate system of archaic belt-driven machinery still works perfectly, and is a magnificent sight in full operation.

Joshua trees lend their weird presence at the Goldfield Cemetery where Virgil Earp — Wyatt's brother and fellow gunfighter — was laid to rest. His eternal repose was only temporary, however, as his body was dug up and hauled away to Southern California many years ago.

There are so many wonderful remnants to be found — the weed-infested pool of the former Turkish Baths, for example — that your first stop in Goldfield should be the Chamber of Commerce, where you can get detailed information about otherwise difficult-to-locate ruins, and the fascinating truth about the huge, empty (and is it really haunted?) Goldfield Hotel across the street.

Goldfield was once the biggest and busiest city in Nevada.

RICH MORENO

Visitors are welcome at the Esmeralda County Courthouse during office hours.

MAX WINTHROP

The interior of the bar at Gold Point.

Gold Point

30 MILES SOUTHWEST of Goldfield via US 95 and Nevada Routes 266 and 774.

Founded in 1869 as Lime Point, a small settlement struggled for life here as mining proceeded in fits and starts until 1905 when high-grade silver deposits were found. A rush lifted the town out of depression and changed its name to Hornsilver. The boom peaked in 1908 when more than two hundred tents and buildings lined the streets of the town; in 1910 lawsuits ended production in many of the most profitable properties and the town began to decline. This lasted until 1915 when operations resumed. In 1922 Charles Stoneham of the New York Giants baseball club headed a syndicate which purchased the Great Western Mine, and production continued until 1942. The town took its present name in the 1930s. Production resumed on a small scale after WWII and continued sporadically into the 1960s when it finally stopped altogether.

State Senator Harry Wiley and his postmistress wife, Ora Mae were Gold Point's best-known modern residents. They operated a little general store and a Standard gas station, and Ora Mae was Gold Point's Postmistress from 1940 to 1964. The 4th class Post Office closed three years later. Harry died in 1955, Ora May in 1980. There are six permanent residents at Gold Point now.

Herb Robbins, who is a major property owner, grew up in Sacramento and developed an appreciation for Nevada ghost towns as a young man. That interest led him out into the desert when he moved to Las Vegas, and he discovered Gold Point almost 30 years ago. With partners Walt and Chuck Kremin he has been buying property here since 1978. He bought the old Post Office in 1981 and now owns 24 of the town's 55 buildings.

Herb has upgraded four of the old cabins (clean and comfy on the inside, still swaybacked and weatherbeaten on the outside), which are available as rentals. Television & shower facilities are up the street in the Main House. The Radkie House is the deluxe accommodation, with running water, bathroom and kitchenette (with refrigerator, coffee maker & microwave). All overnight guests enjoy an all-you-can-eat breakfast, and dinners are served family-style. There are also seven RV spaces available.

The ebullient Mayor Robbins also hosts at least two annual events, the Firemen's Benefit Chili Cook-Off & Dutch Oven Stew Contest over Memorial Day Weekend and the "Day After Thanksgiving Turkey Dinner" in November. You can get more information from the Gold Point website, or by calling Sheriff Stone (Herb's alter ego) at 775-482-4653.

Lida

34 MILES SOUTHWEST of Goldfield via US 95 and Nevada 266. Founded as Lida Valley in 1872 by miners who thought they were in California. Operations slowed drastically at the end of the decade when the richest of the ore was exhausted, but boomed again in sympathy with the discoveries at Goldfield and Tonopah. Production dwindled in 1907, picked up again, fell off, increased — and finally stopped altogether. The town, what is left of it, now serves as the headquarters for what was once Art Linkletter's Nevada ranching operation. Cowpunchers bunk in the old schoolhouse, and horses are corralled in the gaps between buildings on the single street remaining. No services.

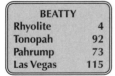

MAX WINTHROP

A local favorite since 1905.

Beatty

FOUR YEARS AFTER the discovery of silver ore at Tonopah, and two years after the fabulous discoveries at Goldfield, prospectors organized the Bullfrog Mining District and established a number of small communities, Beatty among them. Because of its favored location astride the Amargosa River (which makes most of its long winding way to Death Valley underground), Beatty survives while the livelier mining towns of Bullfrog and Rhyolite are dead.

BEATTY	
Rhyolite	4
Tonopah	92
Pahrump	73
Las Vegas	115

Beatty today is important as a gateway to Death Valley, as the first community of size north of Las Vegas, and as a headquarters for exploring and rockhounding. An information station for Death Valley National Monument Park is located just west of the stop sign at the center of town, and the Chamber of Commerce is a short distance to the east of the sign.

The Exchange Club at the center of town is a hardware store now, and the Burro Inn, on the south side of town is now the new Death Valley Inn. The Stagecoach Casino Hotel on the north side is augmented by a big gas station and candy shop. A couple of restaurants, a small grocery store, and services for motorists are available.

The enclosed hot spring pool at Bailey's on the north side of town is open to visitors for a small fee, or stay in an RV space and your soak is included.

Beatty's environs — including Death Valley National Park — are among the most spectacular in the world, and Beatty is a good base for exploring the southwestern Nevada countryside.

Nevada Route 374 leads to the historic ghost town of Rhyolite and over Daylight Pass — or better, take the unique and thrilling digression through Titus Canyon when it's open — into Death Valley. Rhyolite is covered separately on a following page and most of Death Valley is mostly in California, placing it, alas, beyond the embrace of this book.

South of Beatty there are two areas of particular interest. One is the Beatty Dunes, west of US 95 and accessible by graded dirt road. This romantic feature was the setting for much of the movie Cherry 2000, starring Melanie Griffith as its future-shocked and violence-prone heroine. Most

MAX WINTHROP

The Death Valley Nut & Candy Company on Beatty's north side; below, the Stagecoach Hotel Casino.

days you'll have this curious geographical feature to yourself.

The ruins of Carrara, a marble quarry named for the famous source of Michelangelo's raw materials, are easily visible to the east about nine miles south of Beatty. There are a few concrete ruins along a bumpy track that proceeds from the highway into the colorfully uplifted and folded strata of the hills. The striped hillsides attracted the stone workers who established the quarry in 1904, shipping their cut and dressed stones to Las Vegas by rail from the Tonopah & Tidewater depot here. A hotel with a large bathing pool made stopping here a special pleasure in the old days.

Rhyolite

THIS SPECTACULAR COMMUNITY has been one of the most colorful cities on the Nevada map since the day it sprang to life around some claim markers in the Bullfrog District in 1905.

Rhyolite was quickly settled by speculators from Tonopah and Goldfield to the north, and Las Vegas to the south. Many of the district's mines were rich producers, notably the Montgomery-Shoshone, Original Bullfrog, National Bank, and Tramp. At its peak in 1908 their prosperity had brought Rhyolite into the first rank of Nevada cities, with 6,000 people, three railroads, four local newspapers, four banks, an opera house, a board of trade and a telephone exchange. Residential neighborhoods spread out for blocks from the electric-lighted streets of downtown.

The harsh light of noon is unkind to Rhyolite's bleached bones. The front of the Porter Brothers' store stares blankly out at the concrete ruins of the Overbury Block across the empty boulevard. The vault in the rubble-strewn interior of the John S.

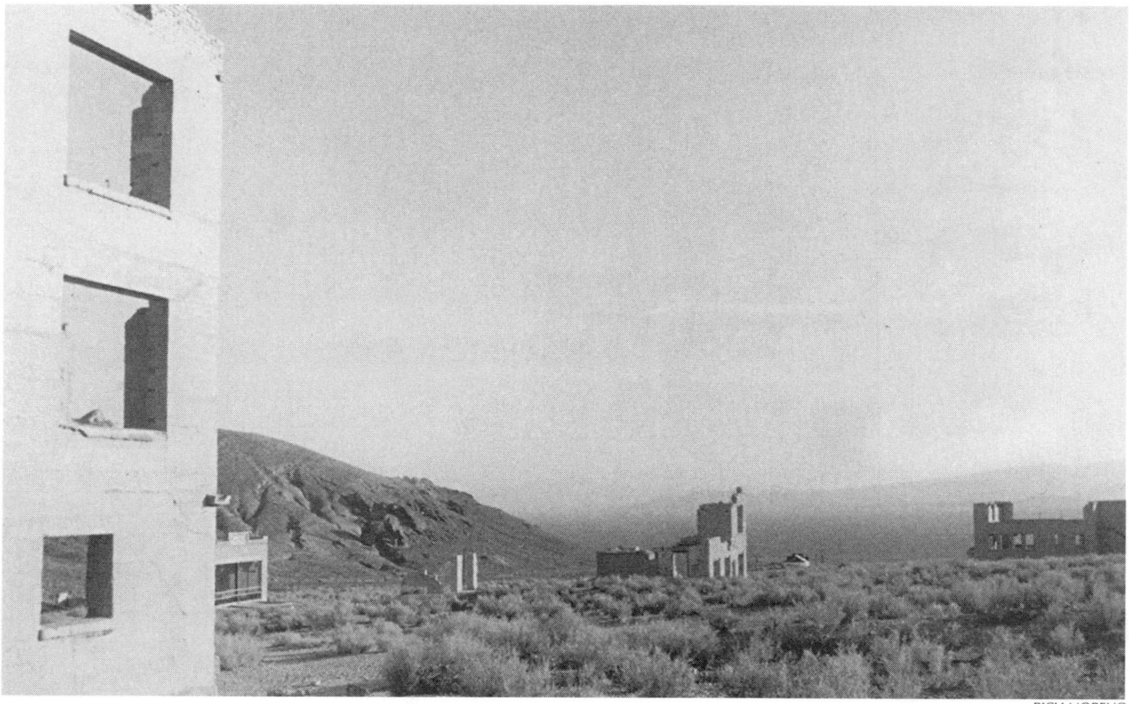
RICH MORENO

Rhyolite.

Cook Bank is empty. The old town is better visited by moonlight, or near dusk when the late light of afternoon gilds the desert floor. Then the silky pinks and blues of the overhanging sky soften the desolation of Golden Street and the old Las Vegas & Tonopah RR Depot at the top of town.

On a long summer's evening the clarity of the air and the sweetness of the colors make it possible to imagine Rhyolite as it was when the railroads huffed and hissed into town, when the mills crashed continuously and the streets were full of flivvers. Just as the mines were toppling into bankruptcy after the Panic of 1907, in other words. Barely 700 people stuck it out in 1910. By 1920 the city was empty.

Almost empty. Several of the remaining residences have been occupied through the years, including the famous Bottle House. Many Nevada towns have houses made of bottles, but this is the famous one. Originally constructed during the meager 1920s, it was for many years occupied as a residence, occasionally operated commercially. It is now looked after by a BLM watchman who will open the gate to let you inside if you ask.

Once a year the old city comes briefly to life when the Friends of Rhyolite produce the nostalgic costumed dream called the Resurrection Festival. A handful of other historic sites such as Gold Center, Leadfield and Bullfrog are within a few miles of Rhyolite, though little or nothing remains of them.

The Goldwell Open Air Museum occupies a few acres of brushy ground and a big red barn below town. The museum began in 1984 with a white fiberglas sculpture depicting the Last Supper, by Belgian artist Albert Szukalski, a life-size representation of Christ and his disciples. That was joined by a 25-foot high pink woman made of cinder blocks, a glittering tangle of chrome car parts; and a ceramic sofa, among other flights of fancy. The red barn is a 2,250 square foot desert studio used by painters, sculptors, printmakers and theater groups.

Welcome to Rhyolite

Museums

GOLDWELL OPEN AIR MUSEUM
Lower end of town. 702-870-9946
Goldwell Open Air Museum features nine large scale contemporary sculptures including the famous Rhyolite "ghosts" by Belgian artist Albert Szukalski. Open 24/7 and always free. The Red Barn Art Center, just down the hill in nearby Bullfrog, offers art exhibits, workshops and studio space, plus a gift shop, weekends 12-4.

MAX WINTHROP

The Pahrump Winery produces award-winning varietals.

Pahrump

MODERN PAHRUMP is a rambunctious little city, one of the fastest-growing communities in the west. It attracts refugees from Las Vegas, Los Angeles and other urbs, and much of it is still the modest pioneer amalgam of mobile home, cinder block and crackerbox. Lately, though, modern features are increasingly conspicuous — there's a two-story bank building, three bright casinos now compete for attention along the highway (Nevada 160), and the tasting room at the Pahrump Valley Vineyards on Winery Road is bigger and busier than ever. There are traffic lights, city-sized supermarkets and shopping centers, and asphalt is covering more of the gritty downtown acreage than ever before. Critical mass is being achieved.

PAHRUMP	
Las Vegas	70
Beatty	73
Laughlin	165
Panaca	234
Wendover	470

"Pahrump is like Las Vegas when it was small," a local booster told me, while outside the pavers were laying asphalt across the desert grit.

In the 1880s, Aaron and Rosie Winters, discoverers of the vast borax deposits in Death Valley, retired to a ranch in this oddly named valley (it means Big Spring in the Southern Paiute language) an hour's drive west of Las Vegas. The valley had been a familiar stopping place for travelers long before the Winters came. Twenty years earlier in fact, the valley attracted great attention when prospector George Breyfogle appeared in Austin, far to the north, and showed amazingly rich samples from a huge deposit of gold he said he'd found here.

Assured of the great value of his samples, the excited Breyfogle hurried south again at the head

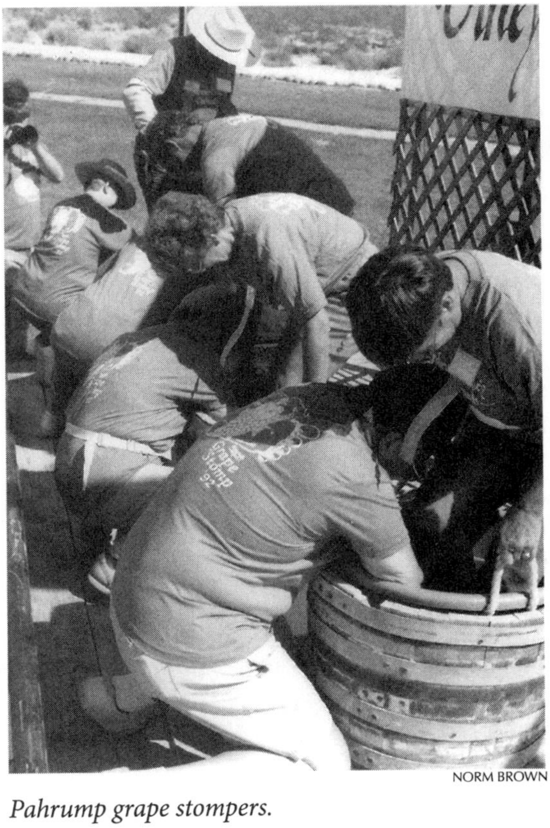

NORM BROWN

Pahrump grape stompers.

MAX WINTHROP

Terrible's Lakeside Casino & RV Park brings water to the desert.

of an eager mob of gold seekers. But storms or the vagaries of memory had played over the landscape to such an extent that the confused prospector could not find the spot where the gold was waiting.

The disappointed crowd returned to Austin in disgust, but Breyfogle and other determined prospectors prowled the Pahrump Valley and other likely locations for years in search of the gold. You may be the one to find it — no-one else has.

By the time the ranchers in the valley managed to attract a Post Office in 1891, most of them were growing cotton, and for the past several decades lettuce, golf and retirement real estate have been the main cash crops. More than a century later winemaking returned with the establishment of the Pahrump Valley Vineyards.

The distinctive Mission-style structure — but with a bright blue roof! — occupies a prominent place on the slope below Mount Charleston, which provides an impressive, almost-Swiss backdrop when it is capped with snow. The winery grounds are nicely landscaped, lawned and watered, but as the two-year-old grape vines were about to deliver their first crop a few years ago, they were eaten by wild horses.

A cautious replanting was made, but up until the 2005 zinfandel harvest California growers supplied the grapes for the eight varietals produced and bottled on the premises, including prize winning reds (exceptional cabernet sauvignon and merlot) and whites made with the Symphony grape. The tasting room, gift shop and restaurant have all been enlarged and upgraded, and reflect the highest traditions of the contemporary wine culture, including free tours. The winery itself has been outfitted with new equipment from Germany.

There are now sturdy fences protecting the vineyard from the horses and zinfandel grapes are now flourishing A 2005 zin is being bottled at press time, the first estate-bottled red to be produced in Nevada in more than a century. There are concerts and other public events held on the tree-shaded grounds in good weather but the biggest event of the year is the annual Grape Stomp, held the same weekend as the Pahrump Fall Festival, Pahrump's annual celebration of itself. There are two 18-hole golf courses, an inviting park with picnic tables and a swimming pool are enjoyable the year around.

Pahrump is on the major Las Vegas-Death Valley route, and you can make an enjoyable loop trip by taking Nevada 372 west from Pahrump to Shoshone and then north on California 127 to Death Valley Junction and back to the Nevada line at Amargosa with another 16 miles to Lathrop Wells and US 95. Turn south and return to Pahrump at the Highway 160 turnoff and contiunue to Las Vegas or take Nevada Highway back to Pahrump.

Rachel & Area 51

JUST A FEW YEARS ago this little collection of double-wides, shacks and shanties on the south side of Nevada 375 between Tonopah and Ash Springs, was called Sandy, for obvious reasons. But when Rachel Jones was born — the first child born to a Sandy resident — the town renamed itself in her honor.

RACHEL	
Alamo	48
Caliente	78
Pioche	104
Tonopah	96
Las Vegas	142

Then she moved to Alaska.

More recently, since the Air Force closed off the faraway precincts of the Tonopah Test Site to test the Stealth bomber and who knows what else, the little settlement has gathered an international reputation as a favored vantage point for observing the mysterious doings in Area 51.

Locally-fanned legend has it that these include the reverse engineering of alien spacecraft, and by extension the activities of the slender, grey, big-eyed little beings who travel by flying saucer.

So enjoyable and compelling have these tales become that media stars ranging from Larry King to "Current Affair" have made the long, lonely drive from Las Vegas to scan the night skies, peruse the locally-maintained archives, and interview the locals about UFO sightings.

Newspapers around the country have reported on the activities of the Air Force, the extra-terrestrials and the curiosity-seekers who have found their way to Rachel. Even the sober-sided editors at Business Week and the Wall Street Journal have fallen under the spell of the space aliens and published reports with the Rachel dateline. The Little A'le'Inn and the Area 51 Information Center welcome visitors daily from all over the solar system.

In January, 1996, hoping to stimulate even more traffic to this sparsely traveled region the state officially designated Nevada 375 as "the Extraterrestrial Highway." New signs, designed to be difficult to steal (we'll see), are going up to christen the road. According to the Nevada Commission on Tourism, the signs will be mounted both vertically and horizontally so the extraterrestrials can see them as they land.

What they can also see is an 87,500 square foot image of Colonel Sanders, staring back up at them! It turns out that 65,000 one-foot square tile pieces (6,000 red, 14,000 white, 12,000 eggshell, 5,000 beige and 28,000 black) were assembled like a giant jigsaw puzzle to create a portrait of the Kentucky Fried Chicken founder. The image took nearly 50 people almost three months to conceive, create and construct, including six days putting the tiles in place.

Until all this, the biggest topic for discussion out here was cows on the road.

MAX WINTHROP

MAX WINTHROP

Rachel—world-famous for UFO speculation.

MAX WINTHROP

Hiko.

Hiko

ON NEVADA HIGHWAY 318 a short distance north of the Extraterrestrial Highway.

An early seat of Lincoln County, Hiko was a short-lived silver camp that attracted heavy investment in 1866, but produced meager returns. The county seat moved to the more successful and substantial Pioche in 1871 and Hiko subsided almost completely. In 1874 the following notice appeared in one of the Pioche newspapers: "The Indians have killed eight persons, including one woman and three children, within the last few days in this county, on the Muddy Reservation and near Hiko. We have no arms and no protection. We wish arms and that the Indians be punished." Today the Post Office is in a private residence and there is nothing visible to suggest the promise of its youth.

Welcome to Hiko

Museums

ALIEN RESEARCH CENTER
100 Extraterrestrial Highway. 775-725-3750
Welcome to the Alien Research Center, the gateway to Area 51, please visit our museum and view the Alien on display and see documents and photos from around the world on extraterrestrial events. You won't be sorry you visited.

NEVADA HISTORICAL SOCIETY

Pioche.

Pioche

NAMED FOR the San Francisco mining promoter who financed development of the ore body, Pioche was at once the richest, roughest, and remotest mining boomcamp of its day. It is still a source of considerable municipal pride that seventy-five (more or less, the figure varies with the source) men were buried in the cemetery before anyone in Pioche had time to die a natural death. According to one reputable source, nearly 60 percent of the homicides reported in Nevada during 1871-72 took place in and around Pioche. A favorite example of the town's bloody character recalls the arrival in 1871 of a young Illinois lawyer and his bride aboard the afternoon stagecoach. As the pair collected their baggage, a flurry of shooting broke out and before they could sprint into the hotel, three men were sprawled dead, still twitching, in the dirt street. The bride didn't even bother to unpack; she hopped right back aboard the stagecoach and was headed back to mother within minutes of her arrival.

PIOCHE	
Caliente	25
Ely	109
Las Vegas	175
Tonopah	215
Virginia City	427

In 1871 The population had reached the thousands and Pioche was the seat of Lincoln County, one of the largest counties in the United States (still including what is now Clark County), when the town was pulverized by the explosion of 300 kegs of powder in a Main Street business house during an exuberant celebration of Mexican Independence. Beams, splinters, and debris mowed through the crowded street like grapeshot, killing thirteen and injuring 47. The accompanying fire left virtually the entire population homeless.

By 1876, despite construction of a narrow gauge railroad to the mills at Bullionville, low grade ore and strangling litigation combined to force suspension of operations at all but the smallest mines. In 1907, activity picked up again with the completion of a spur line from the Union Pacific at Caliente. Mining continued intermittently since.

Delamar. GOLD HILL NEWS ARCHIVES

Pioche Area Ghost Towns

Hiko

5 miles north of Crystal Spring via Nevada Route 318 Lincoln County's seat from 1867 to 1871, Hiko's municipal history is without further distinction. The few remaining stone buildings are now being used by a Pahranaghat Valley rancher. A post office remains open on a part-time schedule, and the old cemetery is preserved. Ask the Postmaster for directions to Logan City if you have a vehicle rugged enough for the twelve miles of rough roads.

Delamar

47 miles southwest of Pioche via US 93 and marked, graded dirt road leading south away from the highway. Discovered in 1890, the gold deposits at Delamar prompted the establishment of Golden City, adjacent to the Monkey Wrench Mine, and Helen, near the Magnolia. Both communities gave way to Delamar when ownership of several of the most productive mines was centralized. By 1879 Delamar was the principal gold mining center in Nevada, supporting a thriving business district of stores, saloons, theaters, and professional offices. As many as 120 mule-drawn freight wagons were ceaselessly employed in importing supplies from the railroad at Milford, Utah. The Delamar cemetery is large. Despite Delamar's terrible reputation for silicosis, miners were glad to get the three-dollar-a-day jobs during the slack times elsewhere in the state. Improper ventilation permitted silica dust to waft continuously through the mines and mills with fatal results for many of the workmen. Three months was enough to kill a man in Delamar, and the town became notorious as a widow-maker. The gravy days were over in 1909, though small-scale activity continued for many years after. The rock remains, crowded as they are into the shallow canyon above the mine dumps, create a picturesque picture, and Delamar in ruins possesses a charm that the living community never managed.

Crystal Spring

On the south side of Nevada 318 at its intersection with Nevada 375 some 42 miles west of Caliente. Originally the site of a Paiute village, Crystal Spring had been used for a decade as a resting place for travelers bound for southern California when it was "permanently" settled in 1865 in consequence of the silver discoveries nearby. Designated as the seat of the newly proposed Lincoln County in 1866, Crystal Spring never had a population of more than a few dozen, most of them transient. Hiko got the county seat in 1867, and nothing now remains at Crystal Spring but the spring itself and a few cottonwoods.

Most recently, an attempt was made in 1969 to put the Number One mine at the head of Main Street back into production. Thirty miners worked two shifts a day retimbering the old shaft and tunnels, driving a new tunnel toward an ore body estimated at 10,000 tons of $100 ore. It didn't pan out, and the ore is still down there, worth more than 20 times what it was worth 40 years ago. One day someone will be opening up that shaft again.

Pioche is a magnificent historic treasure, far enough from the main lines of travel, and the main centers of population to have remained relatively undiscovered and undeveloped. It is a diamond in the rough. If it can escape the fate of other old western towns ruined by sudden prosperity, Pioche

MAX WINTHROP

Downtown Pioche.

will be one of Nevada's greatest attractions in the years ahead. Today Pioche is an uncomfortable mix of old and the older. The thin trickle of prosperity from the mines after 1907 permitted the remodeling of the old buildings along Main Street, with the result that something of the Victorian charm of early Pioche has been lost under coats of stucco and facings of tile and asphalt shingles. The city is a treasure trove of authentic pioneer architecture, though, and restoration of the old Gem Theater and the Thompson Opera House next door is underway.

There is at least a half a day's enjoyable wandering here, but only about 30 rooms for overnight visitors — including the historic Overland Hotel (with bathroom down the hall), so make arrangements early if you intend

NEVADA COMMISSION ON TOURISM

Lincoln County's million dollar courthouse, Pioche.

to stay over. Interestingly, the community supports a free RV overnight park, as well as a couple of full hook-up parks. There's a mini-mart, car repair services are readily available, and visitors are still rare enough to get a friendly welcome as they wander around town. The Silver Cafe on Main Street serves breakfast, lunch and dinner (hint: the sweet potato fries).

Recent efforts by the Chamber of Commerce show up in the information office kept open daily on Main Street, and in the series of historical markers that decorate the historic sites around town.

One that you should visit is the Million Dollar Court House on La Couer Street, a monument to deficit financing, where tours are offered daily.

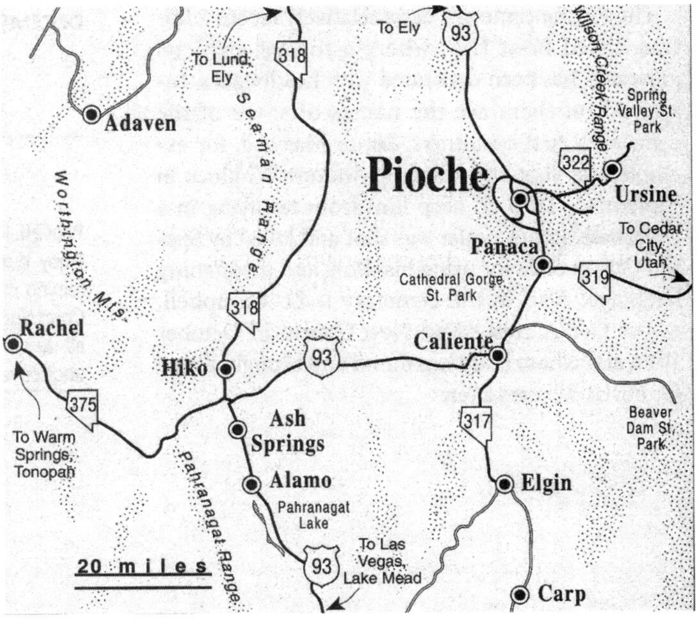

Contracted for at $26,400 after the catastrophe of 1871, the cost had climbed to $88,000 by the time the two story building was completed the following year. Declining tax revenues and corrupt officials forced refinancing of the building several times, and interest continued to accumulate.

In the 1880s the unpaid balance plus interest amounted to $181,000. By 1907 the debt had reached $670,000. When the obligations were at last paid off in 1937, the total had grown to nearly a million dollars, hence the name. By then the court house had been condemned for four years. In 1958 the building and the four lots it sits on were sold at auction for $150.

MAX WINTHROP

Uptown Pioche.

You'll enjoy a visit to the Pioche Historical Museum on the south side of Main Street where a varied collection of early antiques and curiosities are displayed. You'll find mastodon bones and mineral samples among such memorabilia as Lt. Stanley A. Campbell's WWII Army Air Corps uniform and his grandfather's medical case. My favorite occupies a prominent place on the wall: two photographs of an open-air amputation at Delamar, caption reading in part: "Note leg propped up against the box — second picture."

Also of interest on Main Street: Heritage Park is an attractive miniature, a municipal ornament at the top of the street, imaginatively designed, nicely developed, and dedicated to the memory of two beloved citizens. The Alamo Bar, still operating under the oldest extant Nevada liquor license, is thought to be the oldest continuously-operated business of any kind in the state.

The Pioche cemetery has a relatively recent addition called Boot Hill, where a row of artificial gravesites has been decorated with headboards. Inscribed on them are the names of some of the cemetery's first customers. James Maxwell, for example, was shot and killed by Andrew Whitlock in September, 1870, to keep him from testifying in a court case. James Butler was shot and killed by Special Officer Shea for using insulting and threatening language. Also in the cemetery is Lt. Campbell, whose C-47A crashed on New Guinea in October 1944, and whose body was found and brought home for burial 37 years later.

You'll find a recreation center down by the new Court House, with a park and picnic facilities, a swimming pool, tennis and handball courts and a baseball diamond near the local garden club's Memorial Gardens, all available for you to use.

Pioche and Panaca represent a classic Nevada contrast: the rough, roistering mining city in the mountains above and the slow, steady Mormon farming town in the valley below. They are as different in character as any two towns you can imagine, yet as closely dependent on one another as two boys in a three-legged race.

Welcome to Pioche

Area Information

PIOCHE CHAMBER OF COMMERCE
Main Street. 775-962-5544
Visit historic Pioche on U.S. 93, the Great Basin Highway, between Las Vegas and Ely. Take the 5-mile Highway 93 business loop on SR-321. One of the best preserved mining towns in the west, attractions include the Million-dollar Courthouse, Lincoln County Museum, Boot Hill and the Silver State Trail.

MAX WINTHROP

The famous Caliente Railroad depot.

Caliente

CALIENTE IS an almost supernaturally quiet community, shaded by the immense cottonwood trees that forest the residential streets, and decorated by lilacs. Main Street is the exception. It is divided by a broad open space that was once an immense railroad switching yard. Business houses on its opposite sides faced each other through lines of boxcars awaiting shipment to Salt Lake City or the Pacific Coast. This was spectacularly noisy when trains were being made up, and it is now spectacularly quiet. The community is presided over by the city's architectural crown jewel, the immense Mission-style depot built when Caliente was envisioned as a resort destination: "The new Sun Valley."

CALIENTE	
Pioche	25
Ely	134
Las Vegas	150
Denio	504

The structure is occupied now by city offices, an art gallery and the local library. The neat line of railroad cottages with rose gardens lining the highway north is the closest thing we have in Nevada to a street scene in Holland. Caliente has a full complement of services to travelers, with food (including a dinner house, Hansen's), drink, overnight accommodations in several small motels (but the Hot Springs Motel on the north side of town is not accepting casual travelers at press time), two RV Parks, and even a small casino.

You can spend a pleasant interlude exploring the calm little community and its surroundings. You can play the Rainbow Canyon Golf Course, but you

MAX WINTHROP

Rose gardened Railroaers' cottages in Caliente.

MAX WINTHROP

US 93 in southern Nevada has an exotic beauty.

may have to shoo the deer off the fairways if you get there early in the day. There are a surprising number of state parks within a short distance of Caliente, and all the wide open spaces a person can use.

Kershaw Ryan State Park

This beautiful little paradise three miles south of Caliente was washed out by a sudden flood a few years ago and much of what made it so wonderful — the vine-covered cliffs, the little forest of oaks — was severely damaged. The park has been restored to pre-flood perfection and has re-opened with the group use ramada, water system, restrooms and trails all available, but camping is not yet permitted. A $4 entrance fee is charged, and is well worth it for the glimpse of paradise this small area provides.

Welcome to Caliente

Area Information

LINCOLN COUNTY CHAMBER OF COMMERCE

What's there to do in Lincoln County? Check our website, pick up a copy of the Walking & Driving Tours guide at local businesses & the Visitor Center at Cathedral Gorge State Park, and check out the Rock Art Guide on the website (www.lincolncountynevada.com).

Lincoln County Campgrounds

Beaver Dam State Park

35 miles east of Caliente via marked, graded and graveled dirt road, this is probably the loveliest (and most remote) of Nevada's State Parks. This 1,713-acre park hasn't the profound impact of Valley of Fire or Lake Tahoe, but until the spring of 2005 it was so irrepressibly cheerful a place that the long, dusty drive was a small price to pay for a visit. But the failure of the dam has drained the reservoir and eliminated the rainbow trout and crappie fishing. Hiking trails wind through high mountain pine forests, there are picnic facilities and 33 developed campsites, though picnicking and camping are permitted anywhere you find a spot you like. Drinking water is provided, but there are no boating services or facilities, no visitor center, no electricity and no concessions. $4 entrance fee.

Echo Canyon State Park

About 12 miles east of Pioche via Nevada 322 (4 miles) and 86 (8 miles), this is a popular fishing and boating destination. The 65-acre reservoir has a boat launch ramp, and the 33-unit campground is equipped with all facilities including group areas and a sewage dump for RVs. $4 entrance, plus $10 camping fee.

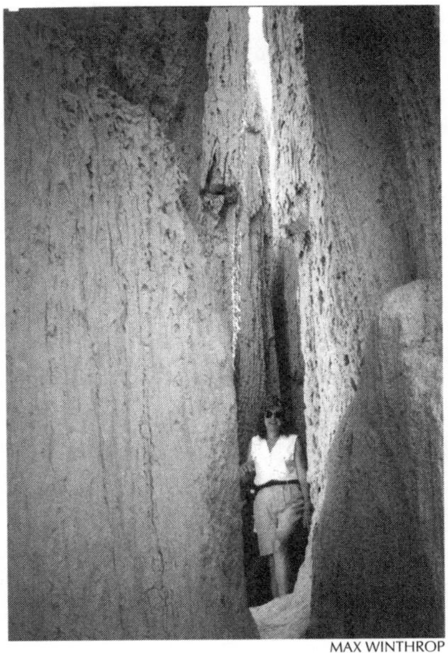

MAX WINTHROP

Exploring at Cathedral Gorge.

Spring Valley State Recreation Area

Some 18 miles east of Pioche at the end of Nevada 322, the Eagle Valley Reservoir is outfitted with a boat launching ramp and a 42-unit campground with water, grills, tables and restrooms. The reservoir is the center of activity here, but you can also enjoy hiking in the surrounding hills, and counting the stars at night.

In 1866, settlers from Eagle Valley, five miles to the south, followed streams to this valley and counted 150 springs in a single day's exploration. Later, 22 families moved to Spring Valley and built a mud-walled fortified village in its center. You can see the remains of these early ranches along the road north of the reservoir. The park is open the year around, but visitors are wise to check road conditions during the winter months. $4 entrance plus $10 camping fee.

Cathedral Gorge State Park

16 miles north of Caliente via US 93 and the park road or 5 miles northwest of Panaca via US 93, this cut in the earth's dry skin is a place to exercise the imagination more than the legs or lungs. What separates this smallish wash from countless others in this wild country is that its walls are made of a chalk-soft suede-textured tan Bentonite clay which has eroded into a fantasyland of intricate shapes. Cathedrals, yes, and wedding cakes; fortresses and hunch-backed men; pillars and dragons; palaces and melting elephants; baroque architectural creations and structures as yet undreamed of — lacy, filigreed, fluted and feathered. There are shaded picnic tables at strategic viewing points, 22 developed campsites with restrooms, showers and a few scenic walking trails. The park comprises 1,608 acres in all, but outside of the gorge itself the countryside is relatively unremarkable. The Regional Information Center at the entrance to the park is open from 9:00 am to 4:00 pm daily, but there are no concessions. Nothing but drinking water and magic. $4 entrance plus $10 camping fee.

Panaca

THIS VENERABLE settlement on the Meadow Valley Wash is another of the early Mormon communities and perhaps the classic example of the genre in Nevada. A historical marker on one of the principal thoroughfares in the town notes that its sleepy appearance has changed only imperceptibly since its establishment in the 1860s. As many business houses in Panaca are boarded up or in ruins as are open for business, and these cater principally to local needs. Cindy Sooz Country Kitchen is open on Main Street and the Pine Tree Inn Bed & Breakfast is at 320 N. Third Street. There is a service station and cafe intended for the convenience of travelers at the junction of US 93 and Nevada 319 a mile west of town.

PANACA	
Pioche	11
Caliente	14
Las Vegas	164
Mesquite	192

So little has Panaca been affected by the passage of time that when the Panaca Centennial Book Committee published "A Century In Meadow Valley" in 1946, the biography of virtually every individual who ever resided in the vicinity, and details of virtually every event of note or interest in the history of the region was contained in fewer than three hundred pages. This interesting volume also effectively dismisses the notion that the Mormon pioneers were dour and humorless folk.

One day, the authors inform us, a stranger stopped in front of a group of men sitting on the porch of the N.J. Wadsworth store. Impressed by the lavish display of greenery in the fields, he asked the group what the precipitation was in the area. One of the natives who was "unlearned but friendly" replied: "I think it's potatoes." Another gathering of Panaca philosophers has been immortalized in the book: a discussion on the porch of the Panaca Co-op regarding wagons. The question was, "Which kind of wagon runs the longest without grease?" Each man seemed to have his favorite kind of wagon, which he defended vehemently until Bert Price ended the argument: "The kind of wagon that will run the longest without grease is a borrowed one."

The sidewalks at Panaca roll up at dark, except when there is a Little League game, or an event at the LDS church, but they have one of the finest swimming holes in the state. The Panaca Warm Springs are on 5th Street slightly more than a mile north of Main Street (Nevada 319), a large pool with easy access and parking. Everyone is welcome, there's no fee, and the water temperature is in the mid-80s — highly enjoyable.

MAX WINTHROP

Panaca warm springs.

Ash Springs

Several years ago I wrote that Ash Springs was "a tragic shadow of its former self." The little resort that had welcomed travelers since pioneer times, with its warm water swimming hole was closed, fenced off and locked away. "The happy shouts of splashing children no longer ring out in the hot dry air," I sniffled. So when I pulled into R-Place for fuel I was startled to hear...the happy shouts of splashing children from across the highway. The chain link fence is still up, and even sports big "No Trespassing" signs. But someone has chopped a hole through the fence, a dozen cars were parked beside this impromptu entrance, and all's right with the world once again.

The R-Place market, cafe and car repair shop across the street provides essential provisions and services to travelers, including RV hookups and helpful information. Its most unusual attraction, though, is gone: the bird's nest in the "O" on the Texaco sign was removed when it became a Shell station.

Welcome to Ash Springs

Shopping

R-Place

US 93 at the north side of town. 775-725-3545.

We're your last-minute convenience store, fishing outfitter and RV overnighter on Highway 93. We stock all the necessities and some luxuries too. Fill your gas tank, your beer chest and your picnic basket. Our deli is a favorite with local folks and travelers too. Come circle your wagons with us.

Alamo

ALAMO IS the traditional social and business center of the rich Pahranaghat Valley, a long, slender ribbon of green with two small sparkling lakes at its southern end. It is a quiet, neighborly town with a beautiful LDS church and appealing atmosphere.

ALAMO	
Ash Springs	7
Rachel	48
Las Vegas	96
Pioche	79
Gold Hill	386

In the early 1860s, though, this valley was prime range for horse thieves who stole stock in

DAVE MAXWELL

Ash Springs is one of the most unexpected delights in southern Nevada.

Utah and Arizona and drove it here to rest up for the long trail across the desert to California. One old-timer reported counting 350 different brands in the valley at one time. The discovery of gold, the establishment of mining towns, and the creation of Lincoln County brought civilization too close to the valley for the comfort of the bandits, but before these unexpected events changed its character, the valley was described by one of the original settlers as "the toughest place I ever saw." So peculiar was its society, and so remote, that in 1862 Dan DeQuille, a leading writer for Virginia Citys Territorial Enterprise, chose it as the locale for one of his elaborate hoaxes.

It was a peculiarity of the valley, he wrote with an air of earnest astonishment, that the stones lying about the valley floor were pulled to its center by some mysterious power, which then reversed and sent them rolling ponderously back to their original places. He advanced a deadpan theory of screwball magnetism to explain the unique phenomenon, and the article was enthusiastically reprinted in other papers throughout the country. Eventually the story, in translation and undoubtedly garbled from passing through so many presses along the way, reached Germany. Scientists working with electromagnetics wrote requesting more details. When DeQuille declined, they furiously demanded that he cease withholding scientific knowledge. P.T. Barnum's reaction to the story was more succinct, if no more perceptive. He offered $10,000 if the stones could be made to perform on stage for his audiences.

A smatter of commercial activity on the highway and an air of small-town simplicity and friendliness have not yet been corrupted by the passage of too many tourists. The Windmill Ridge restaurant and lodging on the highway at the north side of town is the biggest attraction for out-of-towners, and maybe for local residents too.

MAX WINTHROP

Pahranaghat Lake: one of Nevada's most beautiful places.

Nevada Horoscope

On October 31, 1864, President Abraham Lincoln signed the Act which created Nevada a state in the Union. As his pen touched the document the Sun and the Moon were in the sign of Scorpio with her ruling planet Pluto set in midheaven. Thus Nevada is a double Scorpio with Leo ascending.

Scorpio is the most secretive and powerful section of the Zodiac. It merges the spiritual and the material. It is the world, the flesh, the Devil: and also the spirit which seeks to temper them.

It is represented by the Scorpion (death), the Snake (wisdom) and the Eagle (spiritual attainment). Scorpion, snake and eagle, symbols of Scorpio and creatures of Nevada.

Dreams are an important channel between the spiritual and material worlds. Nevada has always been a peddler of dreams, rags to riches, the alluring promise of the gold fields and the green felt tables. In no other sign do the forces of light and freedom so closely approach the forces of darkness and slavery.

The Sun in Scorpio rules Nevada's personality and outward behavior. The Moon in Scorpio rules its dreams and its goals. Nevada, therefore seems capable of living up -or down-to its aspirations.

The whole nature of the state is fiercely independent, quite capable of telling the rest of the world where to get off, and solidly unwilling to let anyone else tell it what to do.

Nevada has always tempted a person to ride the fine line. Anything goes, any time. This state will not be your stern father or your compassionate mother.

Mythologically, Pluto, the rich one, is rule of the Underworld and the underground regions of the earth. He wraps himself in a concealing cape and wears a helmet producing invisibility. Nevada is notorious as being a haven for underworld characters, from "Farmer" Peel in the 1860s to Baby Face Nelson in the 1930s. Well-known for being little-known, Howard Hughes also sought obscurity in the folds of Nevada.

The subterranean occupation of mining is within the domain of Scorpio and Pluto, and the Moon in the fourth house indicates great wealth to back Nevada's independent attitude.

Scorpio: death and sex. Legal prostitution is an unusual facet of our state. We are not yet famous for death or dying, but they're working on it, as the architects of the MX missile system survey the valleys of eastern and southern Nevada.

But Nevada is also the phoenix rising from the ashes. As important within the life cycle as sex, conception and death is the promise of renewal and resurrection.

The rising sign, or ascendant, describes the outward personality and physical appearance of a person or place. Leo is a fire sign, ruled by the Sun, hot and dry like most of Nevada. Leo is a sign annoyed by smallness, ruling grand ideas and large-scale ambitions. The enormous mountains, vast deserts and great valleys of Nevada's 110,000 square miles keep the grand image.

Black and shades of red are kin to Scorpio and Leo. Black and red dominate the motifs of casinos and gaming houses throughout the state. Also the Moon and its node are in conjunction with each other, bringing a great deal of luck. Moreover, this conjunction occurs at the very nadir of the chart, at midnight, between the Sun and the Moon. No wonder that inside the state's casinos midnight and noon are indistinguishable.

On Nevada's chart Pluto is in opposition to the Moon. Pluto shares some of the nature of Mars, and is something of a daredevil. Pluto is in conjunction with Mars in the Midheaven, both of which have a great deal to do with warfare. Thus it is not surprising that Nevada was admitted to the Union during the Civil War ("Battle Born" is the state motto), nor that the nuclear bomb testing facility is here, the ammunition depot at Hawthorne, and the MX is still to come. Our relationship to the rest of the nation is dominated by warfare (and its attendant death) rather than by what we do to support ourselves.

In the third house we see indications of close neighbors and relatives. In Nevada's case, with the Sun, Mercury and Saturn there, the suggestion is of the close ties we have with Utah and California. The Mormon Church and the California tourist both exert profound influences on Nevada life.

Uranus is in conjunction with Mercury, activating our hopes and desires. The position of Uranus also suggests that Nevadans tend to be eccentric and individualistic.

And the conjunction of Mars and Pluto in the midheaven suggests violent action of some kind. The image is of a tidal wave, clearly farfetched in our inland desert state, but the impression remains of a catastrophic event of enormous magnitude in Nevada's future.

Nevada's chart is that of a renegade state, proud and independent, and exemplifying the spirit of the wild West.

Las Vegas Territory

If there were any justice there would be a big statue of Bugsy Siegel in the middle of the Las Vegas Strip, cast out of melted down nickels and ten times life-size. It would look the way people still remember him sitting in the lobby of his fabulous Flamingo: small, dapper, handsome, watching the action out of onyx eyes. It would gleam in the ceaseless glory of the biggest boomtown the world has ever seen, a gaudy universe, all stemming from the inspiration of one man. True, it was Billy Wilkerson, publisher of the Hollywood Reporter, who had the inspiration to build the fabulous Flamingo on the two-lane highway that eventually became the Strip. But it was Bugsy who had the inspiration to muscle Wilkerson out and take over the Flamingo for himself.

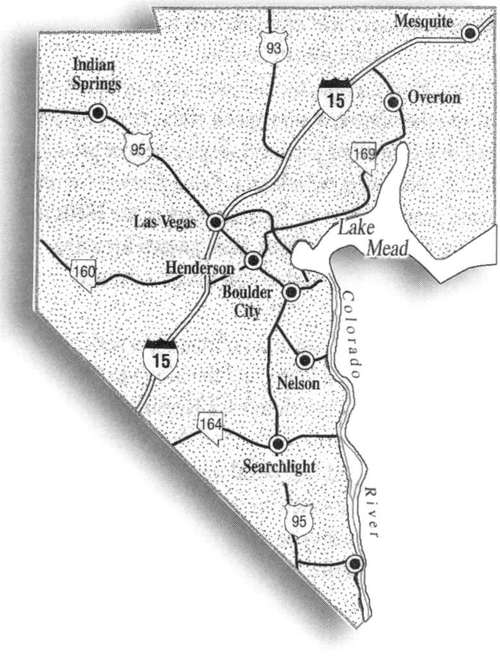

There is no statue, not even a Siegel Street. As a Nevada pioneer he ranks far in front of explorers and trappers like Kit Carson, Jed Smith and Peter Ogden. He makes John Fremont look like a dilletante. Bugsy Siegel claimed Las Vegas for the Mob, yet the school texts do not even mention him in a footnote. Bugsy had been born in Brooklyn in 1905, the same year that Las Vegas had been born in the far western desert. By the time gambling was legalized in Nevada in 1931, Bugsy was living in luxury in a suite at the Waldorf Astoria Hotel and when Boulder Dam was completed 4 years later, Bugsy was associated with some of the very biggest names in the crime business back East.

These men sent Benjamin Siegel — you didn't call him Bugsy to his face — to Los Angeles in 1937 to look after western interests. He came to Las Vegas for the first time in 1942 and saw a railroad town that had prospered from the construction of Hoover Dam but still showed clear signs of its pioneer past.

The ranch property at Las Vegas, long in Gentile hands, was purchased in 1903 by the San Pedro, Los Angeles, and Salt Lake Railroad for a di-

Grand opening of the Excalibur.

MAX WINTHROP

vision point and townsite. This occurred just as the gold and silver strikes at Tonopah and Goldfield were raising two major mining cities on the northern desert and the Searchlight mines to the south, active since 1898, were approaching peak production.

In May, 1905, the railroad conducted a two-day lot auction and disposed of 1200 town lots for a total purchase price of $265,000. Frame structures began to replace the tents in which the first settlers had set up housekeeping, and in 1906 the first through train chuffed into Las Vegas on the Los Angeles-Salt Lake City run. When a second railroad line was extended from Las Vegas to Tonopah the following year, the little place began to bustle in earnest, launched into its first boom as a provincial shipping center and crossroads commercial town. In 1909 the state legislature acknowledged the importance of the new community by lopping off the southern end of Lincoln County and creating Clark County with Las Vegas as its seat.

MAX WINTHROP

The fabulous Moulin Rouge.

But in 1910 the railroad was ripped up by unexpectedly heavy flooding in the Meadow Valley Wash, and rail traffic was suspended for five months. With the additional depressing effect of the Panic of 1907 on the mines, Las Vegas fell into the doldrums. For 15 years Las Vegas remained a fly-blown little hick town in the board-warping

CITY OF LAS VEGAS

Las Vegas City Firemen, 1925.

heat of the desert sun, breathing to the rhythms of the freight trains rattling through. Caliente, some 150 miles to the northeast, was another railroad town and division point, and no more vivacious than Las Vegas. One Mormon who grew up there recalls that when he was a good boy, his dad would take him down to the station to listen to the railroad men eat.

The monotony in Las Vegas ended suddenly when government crews arrived to begin preparations for construction of a huge dam across the Colorado River. The site of construction was at Black Canyon, 31 miles from Las Vegas and only a short distance downstream from the Mormon settlements on the Muddy and Virgin rivers. At once Las Vegas began to swell with arriving engineers, government officials of every weight and stripe, truck drivers, hard rock miners, heavy equipment operators, scalers and laborers. The population of Las Vegas had been 5,165 before the dam was begun. When construction officially commenced on September 17, 1930, there were more than 10,000 people crammed into Las Vegas. The dam was the largest single item ever built by human beings, and with peak employment at 5,218 Las Vegas' quiet times were over for good.

Even so, remainders of the Old West hung on. The renegade Cocopah Quejo, who had been murdering and pillaging at isolated households in the desert southeast of Las Vegas since 1919, was still somewhere out beyond the shimmering horizon. He had been spotted buying a can of peaches in a Fremont Street grocery store in 1930, while a posse was clattering through the fantastic grottoes of the Valley of Fire searching for his tracks. It wasn't until 1940 that his body was found in a cave near the Colorado, partially mummified and apparently the victim of a natural death.

In 1940 Richard Lillard was writing his excellent book about Nevada, Desert Challenge, and describing Las Vegas as "respectable, bumptious, and decadent," where culture consisted in the fact that Rex Bell and Clara Bow had a ranch south of town, and where "a new resident isn't a stranger long. Someone will clap him on the back. 'You're a stranger here, aren't you? Come in and have a drink.' Anywhere else such a greeter might be a 'con man,' but not in Las Vegas. There he is just a citizen who has a town to share." That easy affability began to wane a little during the war when the development of war-related industry, notably the magnesium plants at Pittman (now Hender-

GOLD HILL NEWS ARCHIVE

Las Vegas aerial, 1930s.

son) between Las Vegas and Boulder City, brought thousands more newcomers. Nevertheless, at war's end Las Vegas was still playing a decidedly second fiddle to Reno where some of the "first families" had already made it beyond the second generation, and where the state economic and political power had been concentrated since the decline of Tonopah and Goldfield.

When Bugsy Siegel paid another visit at the beginning of 1946 he found a small town with a well-developed taste for action and ready for anything. War production had nearly ceased and things were slow. The same half-dozen little drinking and gambling places still clustered at the west end of Fremont Street by the railroad depot. Out of town to the south the El Rancho Vegas was a rectangular green compound of gardens and Spanish Colonial architecture through which dance music drifted out under the overhanging trees, and where there was always a little excitement around the tables in the tiny casino. The nearby Last Frontier was a Knott's Berry Farm gambling parlor heavily flavored with an overcooked Old West atmosphere. Far beyond El Rancho Vegas, and well back from the two lanes of pavement that led to Los Angeles 300 miles away, Billy Wilkerson, the prescient owner of Hollywood's Brown Derby Cafe was struggling to complete a luxurious new resort.

But it was a tremendous undertaking in the materials-hungry days at the end of the war, and the project was on the ropes when Bugsy came along. Building materials were not a problem to a man with Bugsy's connections, and as the new owner of the Flamingo, he spent money by the suitcaseful buying the richest carpeting, the most expensive furniture and the most luxurious appointments for the rooms. He staffed the gambling tables with top professionals from Jersey City and Detroit. He hired European chefs to feed his guests and movie stars to entertain them. And he painted the whole thing pink.

Opening night was December 26, 1946. When Bugsy gave the signal the big front doors swung open to reveal the future Las Vegas inside: a splendidly appointed gambling resort where two of the hottest properties in show business, Abbot & Costello and the Xavier Cugat Orchestra, entertained in the spacious theater-restaurant. Outside, at the

GOLD HILL NEWS ARCHIVE

Fremont Street, 1953.

edge of the highway, pink neon bubbles rose hypnotically up the pink cylindrical tower marking the entrance, disappearing at the top into the limitless black desert night.

The resulting boom has been of such enduring magnificence that after all these years the dust hasn't settled because it's still going up.

The effect of the Flamingo on raffish, eager little Las Vegas was about the same as the effect on an Indian village when the Spaniards built a mission next door. It marked the beginning of a new age for Las Vegas and for Nevada.

But even as the new era began, Bugsy's triumph became tragedy. The Flamingo flopped and had to be closed again so that construction could be finished. Worse, the gentlemen back East wanted their money back. In late March, 1947, Bugsy reopened the Flamingo and by May it was running in the black. But in June one evening after dinner in Beverly Hills, Bugsy Siegel was put to death for disobedience: two bullets in his handsome face and two more in his bold heart.

The year after Siegel was murdered Del Webb, who had built the Flamingo, built his own Thunderbird Hotel. Wilbur Clark's Desert Inn opened to

UNLV

Las Vegas loves a publicity stunt.

tremendous publicity in 1950, and when Estes Kefauver's Senate Special Committee to Investigate Organized Crime threw the slot machines out of Elks Clubs all over the country, gamblers showed up by the dozens to pull the legal handles in Las Vegas.

The entente cordiale between eastern gangsters like Siegel and the strait-laced Mormons of southern Nevada was an incongruous alliance. But the underlying realities were like those in other states where a bootlegger-Baptist alliance keeps a county dry. Also, the Mormon population of Southern Nevada had already

LAS VEGAS NEWS BUREAU

Benjamin Siegel.

been severely diluted with Gentiles.

As the mines at Searchlight slowed and failed, many of the residents moved to Las Vegas. Some of the families that had come to build Hoover Dam stayed, as did many of the war workers who had come ten years later. Nevertheless, the Mormons still remain the largest cohesive political force in Clark County.

Fortunately for Siegel and his colleagues, the Mormon faith is long on material achievement and short on broad social involvements outside the church. After Joseph Smith the Mormons have brought forth no theologians or religious philosophers of impact, but they can point to scores of extremely successful businessmen.

Confronted with Bugsy Siegel, the Mormons in Clark County in 1945 adopted about the same attitudes their grandfathers had toward the miners at Hiko and Pioche. They saw the advantages in the presence of a large capital investment, a continuing payroll, and the recurring need for services and supplies. If Siegel had an unsavory reputation, well, that was back East. Out here he wasn't proposing to do anything illegal at all, so why shouldn't he have his chance like everybody else? If he succeeded, everybody in the county would get some of the benefit. If he didn't, it was no skin off their noses.

Thus two business hierarchies have grown up side-by-side in Las Vegas. One is the gambling industry, which dominates the city's political life the way the mining business dominated Virginia City in its heyday, and the other includes everybody else. But the non-gambling business establishment (in which members of the "old" families play a large part) owes its prosperity, if not its very existence, to the growth and well-being of the gambling trade, so business deals are made freely back and forth between men who would never set foot in one another's homes in a social way.

Economic interdependence has not overcome deep philosophical differences on other issues. The Equal Rights Amendment, for instance, was generally supported within the gambling industry but overwhelmingly opposed by the Mormon community and died a slow death in the Nevada legislature.

Siegel himself showed a certain perspicacity in arriving at a good working relationship with the Mormon community by hiring a public relations man with good connections in Las Vegas, and having him quietly change his given name to Brigham.

In the first shuddering years of the great boom the city grew in bucks and bursts. One horrible year money dried up so suddenly and completely that Savings & Loans were forced to repossess whole subdivisions of new houses with tumbleweeds growing in the empty streets. But then the wheel spun again, prosperity kicked in, and everyone was in the chips.

Unlike other famous Nevada boomtowns before it, Las Vegas was not built on a ledge of silver or an outcrop of gold. Its foundations rest instead on the deeper and more yielding soil of human nature, but the immense casino hotels that began to line the Los Angeles highway took on the same unmistakable air of authority as the mines and mills that once dominated Gold Canyon on the Comstock Lode.

To celebrate the opening of the famous Desert Inn in 1950, Wilbur Clark booked three major acts into his showroom: Edgar Bergen & Charlie McCarthy, Vivian Blaine and the Ray Noble Orchestra. The other hotel keepers glumly watched the action from their own sparsely attended gambling rooms and reluctantly joined the bidding for top stars. Casino operating costs went up, but the association between Las Vegas gamblers and show business quickly became very rewarding.

For one thing, the gamblers had found a commodity they could advertise beyond the state line. So energetic was the promotion, and so eager the players, that the old-line gamblers could settle back in the counting rooms, turn the management of their table games and slot machines over to employees, and let the odds grind out their fortunes.

By 1958 there were three miles of casino-hotels up and down the Strip with lots of empty sand between them, celebrities in every showroom, and in every counting room, smiles.

Nevertheless, risk had not been eliminated, it had only been moved from the casino to the showroom. Because the principal casinos were furnished with more or less equal opulence, the public displayed an annoying tendency to follow the most popular entertainers. A headline act of limited appeal became a real liability.

To avoid this problem, the Stardust abandoned its big-name policy, and instead staged an extravaganza review made up of orderly Parisian naughtiness in the shape of topless-costumed showgirls, train wrecks, chariot races, blizzards, and even an erupting volcano. It was a combination of apparently inexhaustible appeal, and as the Lido de Paris played to eager audiences for more than a generation. In 1960 the Tropicana acquired the exclusive American franchise for the Folies Bergere, and four years later the Dunes opened Casino de Paris on a stage — a complex machine, really — which required highly trained specialists to operate and cost a quarter million dollars to construct.

Only about a quarter of the city's population is employed directly in tourism-connected jobs, but there is no question in anyone's mind that the other three-quarters would be out of work in a minute if the tourism industry foundered and the millions of visitors each year stopped coming.

That had always been a worry when men like "Icepick Willie" Alderman, Ruby Kolod, Benny Goffstein, and others with unsavory histories were running Las Vegas casinos. As legal as their Nevada operations were, their past associations made everyone uneasy.

In 1958 the state created a stringent apparatus of control over the gambling industry, aimed at policing it carefully. Incidents of cheating by the house have been few, for with close scrutiny it simply made no sense for a man with a multi-million dollar property to jeopardize it for a few extra thousand. The majority of cheating incidents exposed have been the result of private enterprise on the part of dealers, and they have been cheating the house more often than the customers.

Then Bobby Kennedy, as Attorney General of the United States, began to apply some federal heat. The question he raised was whether all the money coming in over the tables, was being properly counted and reported as income, or whether some of it was being skimmed off the top first. The heat on the Mob was becoming very intense. So spirited, in fact, was the federal effort to obtain evidence of wrongdoing that the executives of the Tropicana were reduced to holding conferences while walking in circles around the big splashing fountain in the parking lot to prevent their conversations being overheard with listening devices. With firm evidence of skimming, the federal government might take action to cripple or even destroy the mainstay of the Nevada economy.

When who should come wandering along but that mad genius of western enterprise, Howard Hughes, his pockets stuffed with million-dollar bills. Hughes took up residence on the ninth floor of the mob-associated Desert Inn for an extended stay, and several pocketfuls later he had bought seven casinos and was the new owner of all the old Mob joints. Everybody was happy.

Especially happy was that large part of Las Vegas that had always yearned for respectability. To them, getting Howard Hughes in place of Moe Dalitz, Gus Greenbaum and the others he displaced, was an enormous improvement over and above the thundershower of greenbacks he was promising to rain down.

But the New Age didn't pan out as expected. Howard Hughes turned out to be a stranger man than anyone had quite understood, and in the end there was no supergiant jetport, not even the 24-hour indoor golf course. There was only an old man wearing Kleenex boxes on his feet to protect against germs, and buying a television station so he

LAS VEGAS NEWS BUREAU

Las Vegas Strip in the '70s; still plenty of room.

could stay up all night watching old movies while his vice-presidents ran the gambling games downstairs.

Nevertheless, the Hughes presence created enormous changes in the gambling business. He influenced the State Gaming Control Board to permit the licensing of corporations as well as individuals. With this change, other corporate owners acquired casino hotels and a new management climate began to predominate.

Also, Hughes spent so much money buying into the action that the ante went way up. Gone was the day when three or four guys could get together on a four or five million dollar shoestring and put together a casino.

Hotels continued to proliferate along the Strip and Las Vegas has continued to prosper and grow. Its population doubled between 1950 and 1960 and doubled again between 1960 and 1964. In the spring of 1990 Nevada's population officially passed one million, with considerably more than half of it residing in the Las Vegas Valley. In 2005 the population of the Las Vegas Valley alone was nearly a million and a half.

For the most part these folks are quite content to make incomes well above the national average and have the option of doing the family shopping at four in the morning if they feel like it. Ask them what Las Vegas is like and they will pause, reflect, and answer, "It's pretty much like anywhere else." But it's not.

By the 1980s the sandy patches between the great resorts had filled with huge hotels and brightened up with neon. But as the operations expanded, the business changed. The high-rollers couldn't support this level of action. Marketing departments broadened their reach.

And as casino gambling began to appear elsewhere, a concern appeared that Las Vegas might be obsolete, unable to compete.

Wasn't little Laughlin blossoming wildly on the riverbank just over the horizon to the south, its boosters promising to out-do Las Vegas in size and brilliance?

WHAM! - Steve Wynn, who had already transformed the downtown Golden Nugget from a gaudy Howdy Podner beer-and-cigarets casino into an elegant international destination, built the Mirage, stocked it with Dolphins and Siberian tigers, hired Seigfried and Roy to entertain and installed a regularly erupting volcano at Stripside.

WHAM! - the 4,032-room Excalibur went up across the Strip from the Tropicana, offering one of the most enjoyable sights in town: the brooding mystery of the Tropicana's Polynesian Aku-Aku Stone Heads with the Toontown architecture of the Excalibur rising behind them.

WHAM! - The MGM Grand created a $1 billion Hollywood-based theme park with 5,009 rooms, eight restaurants, four showrooms and the largest casino in the world, along with the 33-acre amusement park with "theme streets" and attractions like Ghost Coaster and Journey to the Center of the Earth.

WHAM! - Circus Circus built Luxor just south of the Excalibur, a highly reflective bronze Pyramid 30 stories high containing 2,521 guest rooms and an assortment of virtual reality rides and "riverboat" excursions on the Nile riverboats, elevators that slide up and down the 39∞ slope of the pyramid at its corners, and an exact full-scale replica of King Tut's tomb beneath the casino floor.

WHAM! - Steve Wynn built the 3,000-room Treasure Island, an enormous theme casino that would surely astonish Robert Louis Stevenson. Outside, the pirate ship Hispaniola engages in nightly cannonades with the Royal Navy right at Stripside, while inside the internationally acclaimed "Cirque du Soleil" performs.

WHAM! - Circus Circus built Grand Slam Canyon, a relatively modest $75 million 5-acre climate-controlled enclosed scenic theme park adjacent to Circus Circus with water rides and a four-loop roller coaster among numerous attractions.

Suddenly Las Vegas had 12 of the 13 largest hotels in the world, all on the Las Vegas Strip and on nearby Paradise Road (Number ten was the Honolulu Hilton). In the process it endured the strain of filling 15,000 new jobs, and of redistributing the flow of tourists through the city. Inevitably the hot new places attracted the best and the brightest employees and the most discriminating customers from the smaller, older casinos, some

The Strip, looking south, towards Paris.

MAX WINTHROP

of which won't survive the acceleration into the 21st century.

WHAM! The Forum Shops are built on eight acres at Caesar's Palace, just south of the Mirage, where the race track had been. One hundred million dollars later and a Roman street dating from the time of Christ has 70 tenants: Gucci, Guess, Fraterni Warnerius, and Luis Vuitton are here and there's a waiting list to pay the highest retail rents in the city.

WHAM!-WHAM!-WHAM! in a series of aftershocks the Boulevard Mall expands and modernizes, the Fashion Show Mall redoes its face and the Meadows Mall adds a carousel.

WHAM! two sets of Factory Outlet Stores appear way, way south on the Strip and another, huger one at Primm where already the world's tallest roller coaster carries passengers to scenic heights, then sends them screaming down-down-down to earth level far below.

As the Strip became the midway of an intergalactic carnival WHAM! Casinos blossom off the Strip — Palace Station, the Rio, the Orleans, the Santa Fe — a handful of small casinos burst up on the Boulder Highway in Henderson WHAM! Neighborhood casinos — Arizona Charlie's, Texas and the Fiesta, huge new neighbors north on Rancho, Boulder Station. . . .

WHAM! Here comes New York, New York high-rising at the fourth corner of the intersection of Tropicana and the Strip, the richest corner in the American West.

And KA-WHAMMO-BLAMMO! rising up above everything in the Las Vegas Valley, the Stratosphere Tower in 1996 — the everpresent landmark rooted in a $500,000 complex containing 2,500 hotel rooms, an enormous casino and an even more enormous shopping mall.

And from there things started getting really big: Monte Carlo, New York New York, Paris, Bellagio, transformed the Las Vegas Strip from a string resorts tethered like great glowing space ships along both sides of the meteor-stream of traffic into the Street of Dreams, a technicolor hallucination of a movie studio back lot in which we can all be extras or (if sufficiently well-heeled) featured players.

So once again Las Vegas has redefined itself with characteristically vast scale, immense energy and daring, antic style. This is a boomtown no longer — it has achieved critical mass. Hold onto your

MAX WINTHROP

Venice, just downstream from New York New York.

hat, Las Vegas is Boom City, and she's really roaring now.

Now 19 of the world's 25 larg-est hotels are located in Las Vegas, and eight of the ten biggest: the MGM Grand 5,044 rooms), Mandalay Bay 4,752), Luxor (4,408), The Venetian (4,049), Excalibur (4,008),

Bellagio (3,993), Circus Circus (3,774), Flamingo Las Vegas (3,565). Fifth largest is the Ambassador City in Jomtien Thailand (4,210). The biggest hotel in the world is now the First World Hotel Genting Highlands of Malaysia with 6,118 rooms, but before long that will give way to a 6,500-room hotel in Dubai.

Like the mining bonanza cities of the past, Las Vegas has come to dominate the affairs of the state. The 5-story King Tut's Tomb at 555 E. Washington houses state government offices in grand, if chilly style. The blue-carpeted corridors epitomize the bureaucratic maze as more and more state agencies require a presence where the action is.

MAX WINTHROP

City Hall, Las Vegas.

Bugsy's old Flamingo is nothing like the original. Bugsy's pink Flamingo sat back beyond a great green lawn from the two-lane road, a big pink tower happily bubbling neon bubbles at the entrance.

More recent owners have built pink mirrored towers right out to the sidewalk and up to the sky with 3,530 rooms. It's the tenth largest hotel in the world, behind seven other Las Vegas hotels starting with the MGM Grand (5,009 rooms), one in Malaysia (biggest in the world with 6,118 rooms), and one in Thailand with 4,210. A 6,500-room hotel is underway in Dubai.

But as changed as it is, the Flamingo is still every bit as sacred to Nevadans as the old Mormon Fort. This is where Bugsy Seigel first defined the style, the scale and the spirit of the Las Vegas Strip: all the class that money can buy.

Nice going, Bugsy. There is more action going here than in any other city in the world, and in the long run that is a better monument to Nevada's greatest 20th century pioneer than any mere statue could ever be.

INDUSTRIAL PHOTOGRAPHICS/JIMMIE GARRETT

The Stratosphere Tower from above. Are you ready for this?

LAS VEGAS NEWS BUREAU

The Mirage volcano at Stripside, an Old Faithful for a new age.

Las Vegas

THE LAS VEGAS VALLEY is an uneven sweep of gritty brush-tufted desert with ash-heap mountains on every horizon. In three generations a small green smear on this dry desert floor has become Mother Earth's hottest erogenous zone and produced Las Vegas, the greatest boomtown in history, first city of the 21st Century.

LAS VEGAS	
Henderson	13
Hoover Dam	22
Pahrump	70
Tonopah	207
Wendover	400
Carson City	435
Reno	443

Las Vegas is one of the great man-made wonders of the modern world, far more impressive than nearby Hoover Dam. It's an unofficial International Park, privately owned and paid for by the direct, voluntary financial support of citizens from every nation on earth. The Las Vegas Strip is as familiar an American landmark as the Statue of Liberty, and Las Vegas is the best-known city in the world. More than a million people now inhabit the valley, and thousands more arrive every month, creating — with neighboring Henderson and North Las Vegas — the brightest new urban center in the American Southwest.

For more than 60 years Las Vegas has amazed the world with its extravagant ways of entertaining visitors. Entertaining visitors is the industry here, and it is no accident that the iridescent pyramid of the Luxor outshines anything the Pharaohs ever dreamed of, and — say, doesn't the New York skyline look great against the Spring Mountains? — brilliance greets the eye.

In Las Vegas the central nervous system is assaulted by the eager promise of pleasure on every side, and you won't need a book to enjoy yourself in Las Vegas. Everything that money can buy is available here, from primitive excitements to exquisite ecstasies, all at a good price.

So let's get right to the food.

This is one of the world's great cities for dining, always one of Las Vegas' great attractions, for its excellence, variety and affordability. Great chefs are a three-generation tradition now, and the buffet is a local art form. In addition to the fine casino restaurants there are also the many specialty restaurants you would expect to find in any sophis-

The Excalibur, cartoon architecture on a high scale.

MAX WINTHROP

ticated city twice its size. In fact, Las Vegas is now a better town for restaurants than San Francisco, and parking is so much easier. Someone with credentials told me that there are more four-star chefs at the Bellagio than in all of San Francisco.

I don't know if that's literally true, but it expresses a reality that I've had to confront in writing this book: keeping up with the dining options in Las Vegas is a full-time job and I'm only in town part-time. So instead of my behind-the-curve viewpoint, I'm going to give you the best internet sites to guide you. Google "Las Vegas Restaurants" and you'll get 3,270,000 results, which gives you an idea of both the dimension of the topic and the power of the resource. Here are the sites I use:

www.lasvegasrestaurants.com/
las.vegas.diningguide.com/
www.vegas.com/restaurant/
www.gayot.com/travel/guides/nevada.html
(http://www.gayot.com/cityguides/lasvegas/main.html)
www.usmenuguide.com/lasvegas.html
www.ieatvegas.com/
www.tasteofvegas.com/
www.lvrg.com/
www.accessvegas.com/las-vegas-restaurants.htm
www.lasvegas-nv.com/restaur.htm

Each of them has strengths and weaknesses, and the best plan is to visit as many of them as you feel necessary while you're making your choices. If you can't or won't get online, you'll find a handful of printed guides which focus on dining in Las Vegas. The Las Vegas Review-Journal (the big daily) the weekly City Life and the bi-weekly magazine What's On provide a wealth of knowledgable suggestions.

Shopping

The Boulevard Mall at 3528 Maryland Parkway was the first large shopping mall built in Las Vegas, and with its recent expansion it is still the largest in the state. It has been enclosed and beautified, and houses major department stores such as Dillard's, the Broadway and JC Penney as well as a broad cross-section of 140 smaller shops and a 10,000 square foot Food Court to provide nourishment.

The Fashion Show Mall was a glamorous sensation when it opened on the Strip next to the Frontier Hotel, and its has maintained a glittering presence that is the equal of any of its neighbors. Saks Fifth Avenue, Bullock's, Nieman-Marcus and the May Company are the stars of this show.

The Meadows Mall on Valley View is another large shopping mall, anchored by a Dillards and a JC Penney and featuring a magnificent carousel to add a festive aspect to any shopping trip for 50¢ a ride.

MAX WINTHROP

The UNLV flashlight.

Up to this point, the development of Las Vegas shopping malls followed a pattern familiar in other cities. With The Forum Shops, however, something new and wonderful emerged. This collection of upscale shops is the offspring of a marriage between a shopping mall and the first great themed casino on the Strip. It is an arcade of specialty shops, boutiques and cafes built to imitate a sequence of Roman streets and plazas, enclosed and air-conditioned beneath a plaster sky painted with Mediterranean clouds, which imperceptibly change from rosy pink to fleecy white to glowing gold and back again as shoppers troop along the "street" below, and once an hour the statues at the fountain come stunningly to life. It is a major attraction in itself, a new astonishment in this astonishing city.

Back to mundane modernity, enormous shopping complex, Las Vegas Outlet Center has been built far out the Strip at 7400 Las Vegas Boulevard South near the Blue Diamond offramp from I-15. All kinds of new merchandise is available from the brand-name manufacturers — Levi's, Van Huesen, Mikasa, Florsheim et al — at discounted prices. The Las Vegas Premium Outlets, an outdoor shopping mall at 875 S. Grand Central Parkway off Charleston Blvd West at I-15 offers high end brand names such as Armani, Ralph Lauren and others.

As for antiques, there aren't many homegrown ones in a city where the 1970s are ancient history, but several dozen antique dealers offer treasures and intriguing items brought in from elsewhere. Many of them have shops on East Charleston Boulevard between Maryland Parkway and the Boulder Highway, and represent a wide range of interests, from Granny's Nook & Cranny to Fancy That.

Attractions

By the time you have moved around Las Vegas in search of food, drink and the shopping experience, you'll have noticed the valley's distinctive architectural style, highly individualistic, even eccentric or outright screwball, but magnificent in its epic scale, and utterly true to the innovative and individualistic spirit of the city. There are many interesting man-made landmarks in the Las Vegas Valley, and this brief connect-the-dots tour will bring you by some of them.

McCarran International Airport is the first glimpse of Las Vegas for many of the city's visitors, and it is an eyeful, worth a visit even when you're not flying anywhere — and won't have to compete with the crowds of passengers (more than 25 million a year now) hurrying through this deco-retro-futuristic structure, taking robotic shuttles to and from planes at 57 gates on three concourses. A new autobahn provides easy access from the I-15 freeway via a tunnel beneath the runways.

MANDALAY BAY

On the beach in Las Vegas.

The University of Nevada Las Vegas is one of the city's great resources, and an attraction to visitors not only for the multitude of cultural events taking place there, but also for its own sake: this is a college campus unlike any other, and its students are as diverse and as unusual as its architecture. You'll encounter high school valedictorians and high-jumping slam dunkers — both on scholarships — chorus girls attending classes before work and Ph.D. candidates blinking in the bright sun as they emerge from the (round, red) library. A monumental sculpture by Claes Oldenberg, an enormous black flashlight standing on its lens, occupies a prominent place on the campus between the Judy Bayley Theatre and the Artemus W. Ham Concert Hall. The sculpture lighted up a storm of controversy when it was installed, but is now nearly beloved as the signature piece of the campus (along with the Thomas & Mack Center where the Runnin' Rebels play).

Galleries, Theaters & Museums

Access to the Marjorie Barrick Museum of Natural History is around in back via Paradise Road and East Harmon Street. There's a small parking area. The Donna Beam Fine Art Gallery in the Alta Ham Fine Arts Building exhibits work in all media by students and faculty of the UNLV Art Department and nationally recognized artists from the Nevada Institute for Contemporary Art. The Nevada Dance Theatre is Nevada's only professional ballet company and performs at the Judy Bayley Theatre on the UNLV campus.

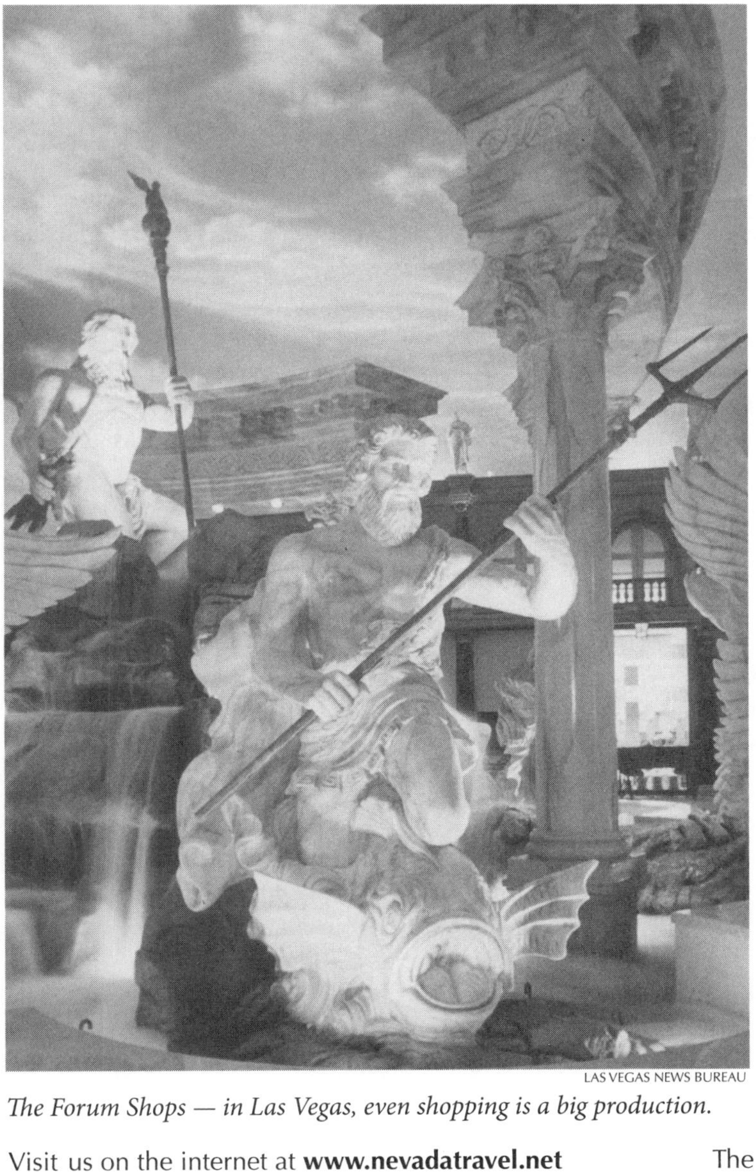

LAS VEGAS NEWS BUREAU

The Forum Shops — in Las Vegas, even shopping is a big production.

The Nevada State Museum and Historical Society is at 700 Twin Lakes Drive, just northwest of the Meadows Mall on Valley View. Exhibit Galleries display aspects of natural history and the regional history of southern Nevada.

A new museum building is under construction at the Spring Preserve, a 180-acre patch of scrub where water came up from beneath the surface to nourish wildlife, early humans, travelers on the Old Spanish Trail, dozens, hundreds, thousands, tens of thousands, and then hundreds of thousands of residents, the railroad, the casinos and other enterprises ˜ until it dried up in 1962.

Now it has been transformed into a rather fabulous campus serving as a teaching facility, art gallery, historical exhibit, performance theater, children's activity center, wildlife habitat and a new Nevada State Museum building under construction (it already has a Wolfang Puck restaurant). Put this on your must-see list; it's at 333 S. Valley View Blvd.

The Liberace Museum at 1775 E. Tropicana at Spencer is a popular cultural shrine, open 10-5 Monday through Saturday, and Sundays 1-5. Proceeds from the modest admission charge support the programs of the Liberace Foundation for the Performing and Creative Arts. The maestro's career was nourished here in the 1940s and '50s before he and television discovered one another, and, as "Mr. Showmanship" he ultimately became the highest paid entertainer in Las Vegas and one of its most famous residents. He has reciprocated by leaving us his treasures to look at, many of which would be prize acquisitions at the finest museums in the world: the beautiful cars (including the red-white-and-blue Rolls Royce), the Chopin piano, the Czar Nicholas desk, the elaborate wardrobe he made famous, and more. You don't have to be a Liberace fan to enjoy his museum. The museum's Gift Shop was once the living room of his hideaway apartment.

The Imperial Palace Auto Collection on the 5th floor of the parking garage of this Strip hotel is an exhibit of Americana that any museum would envy. Here, gleaming like jewelry, are the rides that carried Eddie Cantor, Al Capone, Tom Mix and Elvis to their glamorous destinations. One of Hitler's cars is here, rarities like the 1954 Tucker, and an entire Duesenberg gallery. 9:30 am-11 pm; $6.95; seniors and kids $3; under 3 free.

There are now a number of outside entertainments on the Strip. The first and most enduring of them was the great sign for the Stardust, a mesmerizing marvel when it was erected in the 1970s. But theStardust has been imploded, and the sign is now in storage awaiting a suitable new site. More recent productions are more ambitious. One of them appeared in 1989: the volcano at the Mirage, which still entertains sidewalk passersby with an eruption every 15 minutes from dusk to midnight, and now the fountains at the entrance to Belaggio are getting top reviews.

A "cultural corridor" is being created on Las Vegas Blvd North. The Lied Discovery Children's Museum adjoins the new library at No. 833, and offers kids an hour or more of hands-on enjoyment.

Across the street at No. 900 is The Las Vegas Natural History Museum, with even more to offer kids. The big attractions here are the dinosaurs, with a new 35-foot-long T-Rex poised to attack the Triceratops that ruled the exhibit room for years. Deinonocus, Dimetrodon and Ankylosaurus (with cute little fanged babies just hatching) are also present. There are sharks — models of great whites and some actual (small) sharks in a 3,000-gallon tank.

The Mormon Fort, first permanent intruder outpost in the Las Vegas Valley, is behind the Natural History Museum. You can reach it via the Cashman Field parking lot. The fort is now maintained as a postage stamp-sized State Park. Without the identifying sign, you might mistake the historic fort for the wing of an old motel (under a coat of stucco you can't tell adobe from cinder block), but it is in fact the authentic pioneer structure. Across Washington Street is its modern counterpart, the monstrous new 5-story State Office Building.

Pro Sports

Cashman Field provides exhibit and convention space, and a theater where road show productions ("Les Miz") are staged. Best of all, there's a ball park where the Las Vegas Area 51s play AAA Pacific Coast League baseball, the final step up to the big leagues. This is not only modern Americana, it is one of the best bargains in Las Vegas — bleacher seats with a good view for $8 on a warm evening, and the hot dogs are good too.

The biggest single professional sporting event of the year is the National Finals Rodeo, held at the Thomas & Mack Center each December. Called "the Super Bowl of Rodeo," this is the national competition among champions and attracts aficionados from all parts of North America. A few years back the Runnin' Rebels blew out Navy in front of 20,573 screaming basketball fans to set the arena's attendance record.

The Las Vegas Convention Center is on Paradise Road between Desert Inn and Riviera. It is perhaps Las Vegas' leading attraction for visitors, as hundreds of conventions and trade shows are scheduled in its 1.3 million square feet of exhibit space each year. Its visitor information center inside the front doors, is the best source of current information about Las Vegas and the surrounding territory: 702-892-7576.

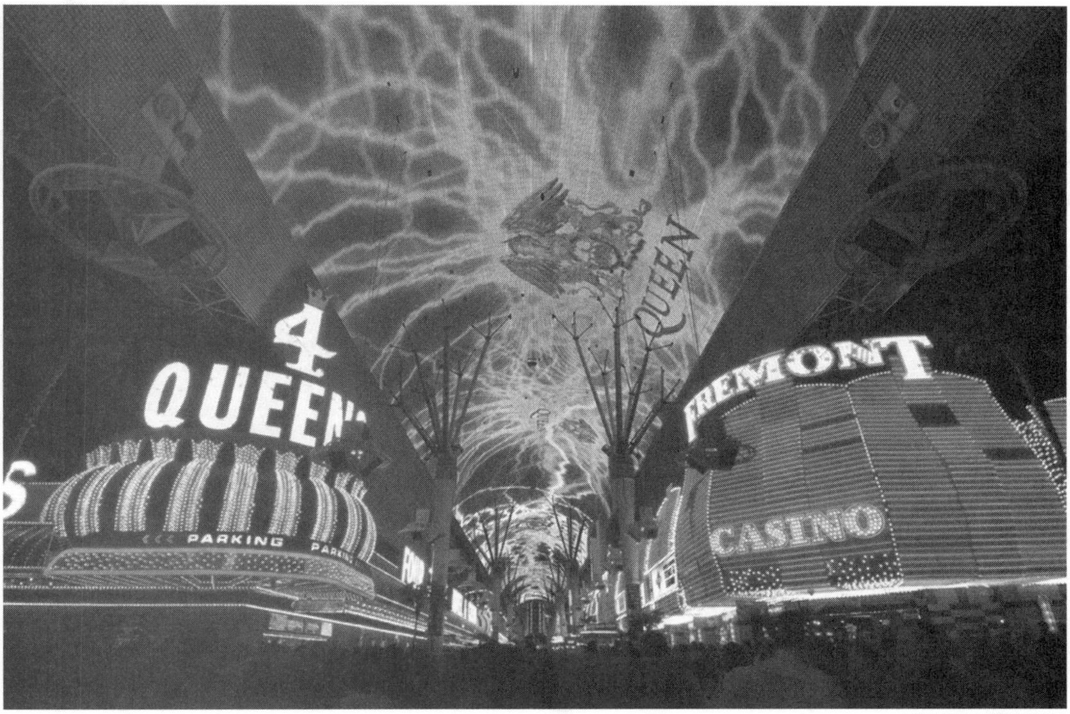

LAS VEGAS NEWS BUREAU

The Fremont Street Experience

Good grief! The most photographed street scene in the American West has been … improved. Glitter Gulch, the little stretch of Fremont Street that was once the whole city, had become such an icon that tampering with it seemed perverse. But as bright as it was, Glitter Gulch was losing ground to the ever-regenerating magnificence of the Strip.

So the City and the owners of the ten downtown casino hotels put up $70 million to create The Fremont Street Experience.

Those endearing scramble-type pedestrian signal lights are gone now. Cross traffic still goes through, but Fremont Street itself is now a pedestrian mall shaded by an electronic canopy called the Space Frame covering four blocks of Fremont Street to a height of nearly 90 feet at its apex and containing more than 12 million led lights. The canopy, about 20 times bigger than the biggest electric sign in the world, encloses the marquee fronts of the Fremont Street casinos. It is the palette on which a team of electronic age artists create — with major music — a "multi-sensory show."

Every hour on the hour beginning at dusk, the marquee lights of the ten great casino hotels snap off, and for a startling moment the famous street of lights goes dark. Then the show begins overhead, as brilliant images dance and swirl to the accompaniment of 550,000 watts of symphonic sound.

Say! Not bad!

Special themed events are scheduled on the street on alternate Thursday evenings, and several major annual events, such as the Holiday Festival with a 50-ft Christmas Tree at one end of the Space Frame and a covey of professional ice skaters at the other. The $70 million project has prompted another $200 million in improvements and expansions of the downtown casino hotels, and has given the old downtown a new look for the 21st century.

The most visible attraction in the city is the Stratosphere Tower, a 1,149 foot tall wonder that tops off a $500 million complex with 2,500 hotel rooms, 97,000 sq ft of casino space and a huge shopping mall at its base. In the bulb at the top of the huge shaft you'll find food, drink and that great view, but those amenities are overshadowed by the rides up here. At 920 ft above the Strip, daring thrill seekers will climb out of the tower and into enclosed roller-coaster cars for a brisk and breezy ride around the outside. Or if that's too tame, you can "ride" the reverse-bungee chairs that rocket straight up 160 feet and then free-fall back down to the roof. That might take the cake if it weren't for the 70-foot model of King Kong that was to climb the tower on the outside with a full complement of passengers in his tummy, losing his grip now and then to increase the fun. But he has yet to make an appearance.

LAS VEGAS NEWS BUREAU

What's new in Las Vegas? Everything. The world's most famous skyline now stands on its most famous street.

Visitors are often surprised to find an actual city spreading out across the valley floor, but Las Vegas is now a ranking sunbelt city with diverse business interests and worldwide connections. It is racing so fast in every direction toward the rim of the valley that it sometimes seems like an oversized petri dish experiment gone out of control.

Its bargains, delights and excitements aside, Las Vegas is its own greatest attraction, the likes of which the world has never seen before and may never see again. It is surrounded by a superb system of parks and lakes, water sports, the Colorado River, near-virgin wilderness — even a ski area — all of it easily accessible by car.

No other American city combines the attitudes of the frontier past with so confident a vision of the future.

But.

There is a dark side to this bright success. Like previous Nevada boomtowns, Las Vegas is full of reckless and violent people. Early in 1996 there was a shoot-out between two sets of bad guys right on the Strip, in front of one of the great resorts. One of them was killed in the street — just like Pioche or Virginia City a century and a half ago, except they were all in cars. The history of teen-aged shootouts over drug deals gone sour goes back two generations now, and drive-by shootings are a daily event. As the valley's population grows by 4,000 new residents every month there's no sign things are getting any better. You probably won't have a problem, but just keep in mind it's not all wonderful here all the time.

It's almost enough to make you nostalgic for the bad old days when the mob guys ran Las Vegas. "We only kill each other," Bugsy Seigel assured Del Webb not very long before he himself was snuffed in his prime by disgruntled business associates.

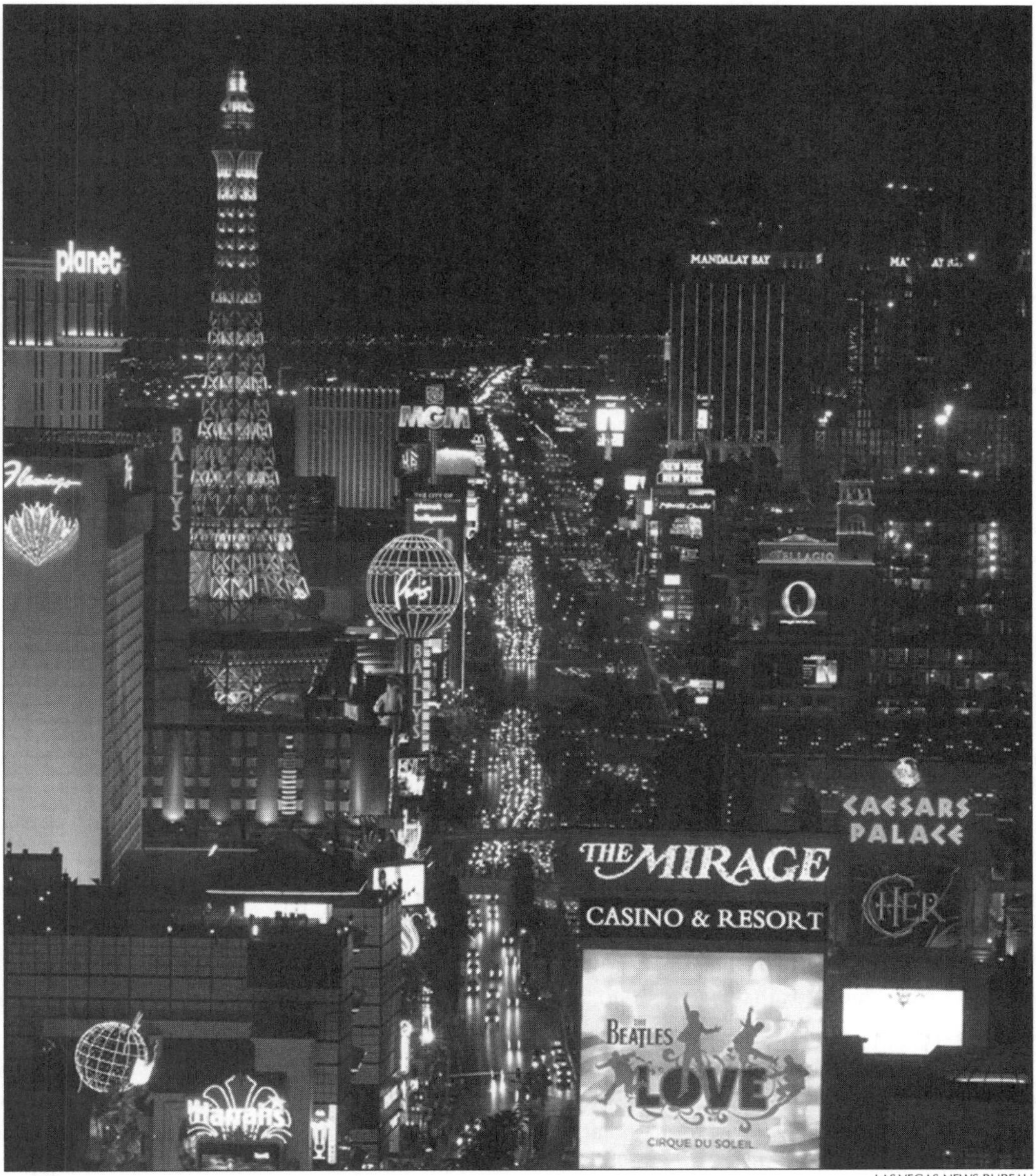

LAS VEGAS NEWS BUREAU

The Las Vegas Strip

THE LAS VEGAS STRIP is America's largest objet d'art (bigger than Mt. Rushmore), and is best viewed at night. My recommendation: start by driving south on I-15 from Sahara. As you glide along the elevated freeway to the west of the Strip you'll pass down its length, seeing each great hotel glowing with light. Some, like the Rio (off the Strip on the west side of the freeway) blaze with neon. Others, like Harrah's, are painted with light. It's quite delicious. Take the Tropicana off-ramp and go east (left), and then north (left again) to progress slowly up the Strip itself. The accumulating impact of the architectural extravaganza — bright and lively music for the eyes — is stunning and stimulating at the same time, overwhelming the rational mind.

Mount Charleston

Mount Charleston is Nevada's third highest mountain, towering nearly 12,000 feet above sea level, and nearly 10,000 feet above the Las Vegas Valley floor. It is the focus for development of Forest Service recreation facilities in the 60,000-acre Las Vegas Ranger District of the Toiyabe National Forest, and the site of the Mount Charleston Wilderness Area.

It is also one of Nevada's hidden treasures, an alpine oasis of forests and craggy summits barely 35 miles from the Las Vegas Strip. It embraces a magnificent pristine wilderness area and a gourmet restaurant. There is a luxurious hotel at its entrance, a scatter of 144 developed campsites and hundreds of picnic tables, miles of hiking and riding trails (with horses conveniently available) and a ski and snowboard area.

To experience the contrast at its most extreme, set out from the frenetic flash of Glitter Gulch in downtown Las Vegas. Go north across the dry valley floor on US 95 to the Kyle Canyon turnoff (Nevada 157), and take it west up into the mountains. As it meanders upward it rises through a continuum of life zones. At 5,000 feet the road leaves creosote bushes and the joshua trees behind to enter the pinyon-juniper woodlands that extend up to about 6,500 feet. There the lowest outposts of the ponderosa pine forest appear. The ponderosa pine belt dominates the mountainsides to about 8,000 feet, where the forest canopy gives way to fir and aspen.

The grand finale to your drive should be the Mt. Charleston Lodge with its inviting deck in warm weather and welcoming fireplace when it's cold. Roads don't go higher than this but trails have been opened high into the summits where subalpine fir and ancient bristlecone pine cling precariously to the crags. You can make a scenic drive of it by taking Deer Creek Road (Nevada 158) north along the mountainside to its intersection with Nevada 156, the Lee Canyon road and then returning to the valley floor, or you can book one of the Lodge's log cabins or make camp at one of the campgrounds.

Or make the modern 62-room Mt. Charleston Hotel your base camp and explore the high country on foot or on horseback. Golf and tennis are available right outside. No more wonderful respite can be imagined from the heat and urban razzamatazz of the Las Vegas Valley far below.

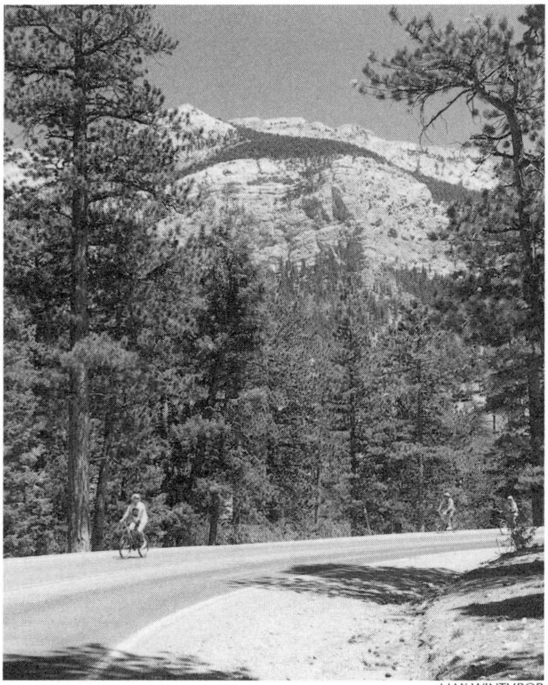

MAX WINTHROP

It's all downhill from here.

There's an easy half-mile stroll from the upper end of the Kyle Canyon Road to Mary Jane Falls, or you can make the 15-mile climb from Cathedral Rock to the summit. From the top you can see parts of four states: Nevada, California, Utah and Arizona, a view that embraces the highest and lowest points in the U.S., Mount Whitney and Death Valley. Any trail you choose will take you into a diverse wildlife habitat, with deer, elk, turkey, fox and mountain lion. In the summer months you will be thrilled by the sight of the hummingbirds that visit the mountains, capering and darting through the air like brilliant sparks (and consuming 25 lbs of sugar a week in the feeders put out for them.)

Some of the highlights of the mountain:

Kyle Canyon Campground 25 family campsites with trailer spaces, toilets, fire pits and firewood.

Less than a half mile southeast of the fire station at Charleston Park, Cathedral Rock dominates a large picnic area. An easy three-quarter mile trail leads to the top of the rock from the picnic ground,

Snow play on Mt. Charleston is just a 45-minute drive from the Strip

and the view it affords of Kyle Canyon makes it worth the hike. The 15-mile trail to Charleston Peak and the sheer west face of Mummy Mountain ends at the picnic ground, and so does the half-mile trail to the head of Little Fall.

Take Forest Service Road 22 three miles north from the end of Kyle Canyon Road and walk a quarter mile to Robbers' Roost Caves. According to local legend these limestone caverns were used as hideouts by Mexican bandits in the middle years of the 19th century while they rested between raids into southern Nevada, western Utah and northern Arizona. Continue on just over a mile to 35-unit Hilltop Campground with its 100-mile view. The Mahogany Grove group picnic area (reservations required) is a little farther on, and Deer Creek picnic area (no reservations required) is right next door. About two miles farther along, a short walk from the road to Desert View Point provides stunning views of the desert sunrise.

Dolomite Campground is at the upper end of the Lee Canyon Road, providing 30 family campsites with drinking water, toilets, tables and firewood provided. At 8,000 feet there are stands of bristlecone pines within a relatively easy walk from your camp. The bristlecone is among the oldest living things on earth, achieving ages of 5,000 years and more. They are recognizable by their preference for rocky, exposed locations at high altitudes, by their weather-whipped twisted trunks and relatively short stature.

The Las Vegas Ski & Snowboard Resort is also at the end of the Lee Canyon Road. For years a relatively little-known local ski slope, the Lee Canyon area has flourished as it has occurred to out of town skiers that Las Vegas may be the greatest apres-ski environment in the world. Development has been steady ever since. Lifts carry skiers from the day lodge to medium and long runs. A pro shop sells and rents ski equipment and private and group lessons are available. Snow-making equipment is on hand in case of good weather.

LAS VEGAS MOTOR SPEEDWAY

The action is fast and furious at the Las Vegas Motor Speedway.

North Las Vegas

NORTH LAS VEGAS	
Las Vegas	4
Lake Mead	20
Hoover Dam	40

NEVADA'S FOURTH largest city is a leading industrial center anchored between its namesake to the south, and Nellis Air Force Base to the north and east. Established in 1946, North Las Vegas has shared in the population boom of the Las Vegas Valley: 1990 population, 48,000; 2006 census projections, 197,567. Long in the shadow of its more glamorous neighbor, North Las Vegas is home to a half-dozen large casino hotels and the $100 million Las Vegas Motor Speedway. The 1,500 acre complex across from the Air Force Base contains 20 racing venues, including a 1.5-mile superspeedway, a 2.5-mile FIA-approved road course, a half-mile dirt oval and a 4,000-ft. drag strip. Seating is provided for 107,000 spectators and parking for 60,000 cars, with 148 VIP suites overlooking the action.

The College of Southern Nevada campus is on Cheyenne Avenue, a busy commercial airport on the east side of Rancho Road, and two large casino hotels, the Texas Station and the Fiesta, are located in North Las Vegas along with a handful of smaller ones. There are two golf courses in the city, the 18-hole Craig Ranch Golf Course and the 9-hole North Las Vegas Community Golf Course.

Apart from the racing schedule, the highlight of the year in North Las Vegas is the autumn BaloonaPalooza, when the skies over the Las Vegas Valley are made beautiful by hot air balloons drifting upward from the Craig Ranch Regional Park like bright bubbles into the tame blue yonder.

MAX WINTHROP

North Las Vegas cityscape.

LAS VEGAS NEWS BUREAU

Red Rock landscape.

Red Rock Canyon

RED ROCK CANYON consists of 195,819 acres (about 130 square miles) of BLM land with a variety of usual and unusual forms of desert vegetation and wildlife including Bighorn Sheep and wild burros, wind sculptured sandstone, picnicking and outdoor camping sites, and the striking Red Rock Escarpment, a 5,000-foot eruption of rainbow-colored pinnacles and boulders jutting up from the canyon floor.

All of this is accessible by scenic drives, hiking trails and on horseback. Take Charleston Boulevard 16 miles west of Las Vegas to the beginning of the scenic loop road. Entrance fee is $5 per car, which admits you to theVisitor Center and the 13-mile scenic drive.

The drive: about two miles along, the first paved turnout is the Calico Hills Vista, a panoramic view of a massive clump of red sandstone hills cross-etched by the wind. A short marked trail takes hikers to the bottom of a wooded and rock-strewn ravine where they can crawl over the same boulders that Paiute Indians called home nearly 900 years ago. A visit after a recent rainfall reveals varied forms of animal life living in the water-filled sandstone potholes or in standing ponds.

A mile farther along the scenic road brings you to the Sandstone Quarry turnoff. One-quarter mile in lies a parking area where you can strike off in several directions to see an area which provided standstone slabs for Las Vegas home construction many years ago. Picnic tables are provided at the quarry area. A climb to the east and north rewards hikers with glimpses of Indian petroglyphs and mescal pits in Brownstone Canyon. Modern day visitors have left their own form of less interesting graffiti here and there.

From the road toward Willow Springs four and a half miles farther on, look south down the canyon and see the rugged backdrop which has been used in movies, television and commercial productions. At Willow Springs picnic tables are provided. Access to the primitive site is by trail through an area known as Rocky Gap, and only campers walked in by state park or federal rangers are allowed. Three paved viewpoints give photographers exceptional angles of massive boulders, rock chimneys and rugged bluffs. All along here, the feeling is of stone giants towering above, ready to come crashing down at the slightest breeze. But rockslides are extremely rare in this area and earthquakes are unknown. Sudden flash floods can occur in Red Rock Canyon, especially from July to September, but the road is well-prepared for these deluges.

After returning to West Charleston Boulevard, continue south one mile to a dirt and rock-studded road leading to Oak Creek Canyon at the base of the escarpment. Picnicking and primitive camping is permitted here. Two miles north via trail is Pine Creek Canyon. Far back in this isolated cranny there is abundant groundwater and cooler temperatures to support such exotic desert plants as Maidenhair Fern, Columbine and the Stream Orchid, a unique climatic condition existing nowhere else in the desert.

BLM

Red Rock Canyon homestead.

The Red Rock area varies in elevation from 3,500 feet to 7,500 feet and is a transition zone for desert and mountain flora — cacti and yucca in the low elevations through joshua trees and agaves in the next zone to oak trees on the lower escarpment slope and Ponderosa pines in the high elevations. Further plans promise more than 100 miles of hiking and horse trails; additional viewpoints; and preservation of the upper elevations in their primitive state.

Red Rock Canyon is open year round, camping at primitive sites is limited to 14 days. There are no developed sites for overnight stays. The area is maintained by the Nevada State Park System and the Bureau of Land Management.

Spring Mountain Ranch is about 2 miles south of the Red Rock entrance. Before becoming a part of the Nevada State Park System in the mid-70s the rambling, country-style ranch and grounds were a seldom-used retreat for the mysterious Howard Hughes and his executives. Before Hughes it was the principal residence of Vera Krupp, widow of the notorious German munitions magnate, Alfred Krupp von Bohlen. Tours of the house are available from 10 to 4, and picnicking under a grove of cool oaks is a pleasant experience. A $5 per vehicle use fee is charged. Outdoor theatrical performances are offered in June, July, and August when the "Theater under the Stars" features musicals and plays for the whole family.

Bonnie Springs Ranch, about a mile farther south, is another pioneer ranch dating back to the 1840s, now doing duty as a western theme park with duck pond, petting zoo, motel, gunfights and hangings in the street, miniature railroad (the weekend shuttle from the parking lot), riding stables with guides and ice cream parlor that kids will enjoy. The grownups, especially on a balmy spring or autumn night, will enjoy the saloon and dinner house.

Cowboy Trail Rides offer hourly, half-day and all-day rides through the red rock country for individuals and groups. Advance booking is suggested, but unreserved customers are accepted most days: 702-249-6686. Or ride in air-conditioned comfort in a Pink Jeep Tours half-day tour: 702-895-6777.

MAX WINTHROP

Sculptures humanize Green Valley, one of Henderson's new neighborhoods.

Henderson

ONCE THE UGLY DUCKLING of southern Nevada, Henderson has quietly transformed itself into a small city of considerable variety, sophistication and interest. With more than 200,000 residents, it is now Nevada's second-largest city, after Las Vegas and ahead of Reno, and is expected to exceed 330,000 by 2010. Henderson's best-known boulevard, the Boulder Highway, has been transformed into something like the Champs Elysee (a la southern Nevada): the center divider is planted with palms, scalloped lawns and pleasantly shady trees; treated, recycled water keeps everything green, and the engineering is in place to extend the effect step-by-step from the northern end of the city to the southern end. Once the main line of travel from Las Vegas to Needles, Kingman and the Dam, Boulder Highway is losing its World War II landmarks as places like the Swanky Club have given way at last to new development (don't worry, there's still some funky stuff left). What was once a two-lane stretch of bumpy asphalt across a landscape of grit is now an urban greenbelt boulevard through a new age metropolis — an appropriate symbol of Henderson's transformation.

HENDERSON	
Laughlin	82
Hoover Dam	18
Lake Mead	15
Lost City	48

Henderson's traditional "main street" is Water Street, a recently made-over relic of Harry Truman's America. Until trees and landscaping were added it was a four-block time capsule, with only the modern municipal buildings at the top of the street to spoil the illusion of 1950. On Thursday afternoons a block of Water Street is closed to vehicles to allow booths to be set up for the Farmer's Market. Hours are 4 - 8 pm April - October and 3 - 7 pm from November through March. Fresh produce from nearby farms, barbecue and other treats, fresh-baked bread, crafts and entertainment make this a popular event for Henderson.

A product of World War II when its landmark Basic Magnesium Incorporated plant (nearly a square mile in floor area) worked at full throttle to equip the war machine, Henderson rapidly became one of Nevada's largest and busiest cities. The plant was closed in 1944, and Henderson's jobs disappeared. In a bold and brilliant stroke of Economic Development, the state of Nevada acquired the facility. Rather than allow Henderson to become another ghost town, the state found permanent tenants for the huge structure and today the original facility, much modified over the years, is home to major industrial companies whose products are shipped all over the world.

The urgency with which it was built, the transience of its early residents and the dominance of heavy industry gave Henderson a hard-working blue collar reputation which persisted into the 1950s and 60s. In the 1970s a second wave of industrial development began with the arrival of Artex International, a manufacturer of linen table cloths for restaurants, hotels and airlines. After Artex came Levi's, GTE-Sylvania, L'Eggs, Gold Bond Ice Cream, Berry Plastics and many others, capitalizing on low land and labor costs, easy access to western markets, agreeable climate and co-operative government.

This industrial diversification fueled the transformation of Henderson, which began in earnest with the development of the immense Green Valley development in the late 1970s, the first large-scale master-planned community in the Las Vegas Valley, and the first one in southern Nevada since Boulder City. It is a vast, self-sufficient suburb to the west of the old city center, developed with style and, incredibly enough, wit: the delightful J. Seward Johnson, Jr. sculptures that punctuate the public parkways are a wonderful touch and worth the trip to Henderson all by themselves. More recent residential development has brought half-million dollar mini-mansions to Henderson hillsides, contrasting with the flat-roofed boxes built 60 years ago in the workingmen's neighborhoods below. The Galleria, Henderson's first covered mall, opened on Sunset Road with indoor waterfalls, topiaries and 110 stores.

Henderson occupies 94 square miles at the southern end of the Las Vegas Valley, almost twice the area of San Francisco (stretching from the east across Boulder Highway and the original Basic Townsite all the way west to I-15). Much of it is still undeveloped, but heavy equipment is accelerating

MAX WINTHROP

Heritage Street,Southern Nevada Museum on the Boulder Highway in Henderson.

LAS VEGAS NEWS BUREAU

Sunset Station in Henderson.

Henderson's transformation. The freeway is extending south toward the rim of the valley, changing raw hillsides and eroded slopes, sparsely grown with stringy brush, into new mega-neighborhoods, whole seas of red tile roofs and mazes of carefully curved streets. The most impressive of the new developments is Lake Las Vegas, a $3.5 billion — that's right, with a B — project incorporating 3,000 residential units, commercial centers, five golf courses and six resort-casinos that adds more than 11,000 rooms to the regional inventory. At the center of all this is Lake Las Vegas itself, a 2-mile by 3/4-mile body of water behind a 4,800-foot earthen dam with a four-lane boulevard on top. Planning and construction of the dam and the associated infrastructure was the largest civil engineering project underway in America when it was built.

Entertainment & Nightlife

Until recently, neighborhood bars and two long-established downtown casinos provided Henderson's nightlife. New gambling houses have sprouted on the downhill reaches of Boulder Highway and elsewhere in Henderson, but it is the exceptional new Sunset Station that puts Henderson in the major leagues of the themed casino world.

This is not New York New York, Hollywood or never-never-land, this is Spain. A Spanish village occupies the ground floor, with exceptional restaurants and the fabulous Gaudi Bar, a Gordon Biersch brewery restaurant and an oyster bar.

Dining Out

Ciao is at 2855 N. Green Valley Parkway, serving northern Italian food California style and providing music after dark. Also in Green Valley, Samuele's Deli, 2724 Green Valley Parkway, is a New York kosher deli with an extensive list of delicious sandwiches and fresh pastries. DiMartino's Che Pasta, 2801 Athenia Drive, provides a pleasantly intimate setting for a dinner chosen from an enormous variety of pasta dishes. Coyote's Cafe & Cantina is just a few doors away, offering a traditional Mexican menu with innovative touches. Barley's in the Green Valley Center at 4500 Sunset Road, is a casino-brewery with all the trimmings and the next-door Crocodile Cafe is across the road from Alley Gators Sportz Grille.

Attractions

There is an easy half day's touring to do here, which the kids will especially enjoy. You can start at Henderson's main
attraction for visitors, the Southern Nevada Museum beside the Boulder Highway.

Displays in the new exhibit gallery include Na-

MAX WINTHROP

The Pyramid House, Henderson.

tive American materials and relics of pioneer life in the area, and there is a small gift shop offering Native American-made and other goods, books and other items of interest.

Outside, part of the 25-acre site is now Heritage Street, a collection of early structures from various southern Nevada communities. This gravel "street" has one of the thousand Basic Townsite houses built in Henderson for the workers at the magnesium plant, across from a house built in Las Vegas in 1912, when Fourth Street was a prime residential address. Another Las Vegas residence, "an Americanized fantasy based on a Swiss chalet" has been restored to represent Las Vegas in the 1950s, across from an 1890 printer's shop. There's also a 1933 Boulder City house, and the house across the street was built in Goldfield in 1906. All these structures are open for visitors — like little Goldilocks you can open any front door and go inside. The lights are on, clothes hang in the closets, the air conditioning is keeping everything cool, but there's no one home. There's no porridge to eat, though, and signs asking that you not sit on the furniture.

There is also a nature stroll and an Indian village. A Ghost Town exhibit is made up of fragile structures, lifted gently up onto trucks and driven in from around the southern part of the state to be maintained here in classic delapidation.

Fascinating from a different perspective is the Ethel M Chocolate Factory with its views of the candy factory and its unusual 2.5-acre cactus garden. Free tours 8:30-5:30 daily with a taste of chocolate at the end. You'll find more than 350 varieties of cactus, succulents and rare plants from the deserts of the world.

To get there, take the Tropicana exit from the 93/95 freeway, and go south two miles on Mountain Vista. Turn left on Sunset Way to enter the Green Valley Business Park and left again on Cactus Garden Drive. From Boulder City take the Boulder Highway and turn left on Sunset Way. Proceed four miles to the Green Valley Business Park and go left on Cactus Garden Drive. Ethel M is at number 2.

Take Sunset east across Boulder Highway to Moser Drive and turn left to enter the Henderson Bird Viewing Preserve, a 147-acre collection of basins, lagoons and ponds that attracts nearly 200 species of waterfowl, wading birds and birds of prey. Mapped trails and a small gift shop.

Higher up the valley's rim from here you can look out across the valley to the north, and on a clear day — increasingly rare as the low-lying pollution cloud becomes a familiar feature of life in the Valley — you'll see the faraway resorts of the strip, and the downtown cluster of high-rise casinos very small in the distance. The huge scale of the valley becomes more apparent, and the magnitude of the development more impressive. This valley holds more than half of Nevada's population, wealth and political power.

From the high ground at Henderson you can see where the Spaniards came into the valley from the east, plodding along on horseback and on foot, making camp about where the Union Plaza stands, their tiny campfires the only light. The trail was used from 1830 until the California Gold Rush, when everything in the west changed forever. Since then the valley has been transforming constantly, and if you watch for even a short time, you can see it happen: U-Haul trucks rolling in from someplace where the jobs dried up or went overseas, unloading furniture into houses so new the paint is still drying, in neighborhoods that didn't even exist last week.

The Gold Strike Casino at Jean.

MAX WINTHROP

Jean

25 miles southwest of Las Vegas and 12 miles from the California line on I-15, Jean is a former railroad siding that has attracted a plastics factory, a prison, and a large casino hotel. The Gold Strike Hotel & Gambling Hall is a western-themed property with RV parking and an Auto Plaza. The Nevada Landing across I-15 is being demolished to make way for non-gaming commercial development.

JEAN	
Las Vegas	43
Goodsprings	7
Primm	13

Goodsprings

Goodsprings dates back to a lead silver discovery in 1868, but it was 20 years before development began in earnest. A gold discovery in 1892 accelerated the pace, as did the railroad siding at Jean and the discovery of large bodies of zinc in 1906. In 1912 production from the mines totalled $1.2 million, and in 1913 the Pioneer Saloon opened, with a Brunswick back bar from the 1860s brought from Rhyolite. The 20-room Fayle Hotel opened three years later and Goodsprings was flying high with a population of 800 and as many as 50 small mines in operation. The mines continued to produce until 1952. The hotel burned in 1966, but the Pioneer Saloon endures. When you stop in for a cold refreshment, take note of the bullet holes beside the juke box and hope the locals are telling Papa Don Hedrick stories. This colorful man, wild-haired and bearded, bought the saloon in 1965, serving for many years as volunteer ambulance driver and for two terms as Constable.

MAX WINTHROP

Goodsprings street scene.

MAX WINTHROP

Another extravagant experience in the middle of nowhere.

Primm

PRIMM, 43 MILES south of Las Vegas on I-15, is a curious byproduct of the California-Nevada state line. It is a cluster of three large casino hotels, all operated by Terrible Herbst, an outlet mall, two gas stations, a McDonald's, and a 100-store factory outlet mall on the Nevada side of the line and a small convenience store selling lottery tickets on the California side. Free transportation between the resorts is provided by Monorail or shuttle bus.

PRIMM	
Jean	13
Goodsprings	20
Las Vegas	56

At Whiskey Pete's you used to be able to inspect the bullet-riddled Ford the bandits Bonnie Parker and Clyde Barrow drove to their deaths. The "Death Car" was an attraction in the lobby, along with other Bonnie & Clyde relics, including the bullet-tattered shirt worn by Clyde Barrow on the day they were ambushed by the FBI on May 23, 1934. But now the car is only occasionally on the premises. With the acquisition of Whiskey Pete's by Herbst Gaming Corporation, it is on tour at Terrible's Casinos all around the USA.

There was an actual Whiskey Pete who operated a gas station here when the highway was two-lane. He also peddled the whiskey he made in a nearby cave, and kept a sharp eye on the traffic passing by. According to legend he is buried standing up where he can watch the road.

Buffalo Bill's has one of the world's tallest and fastest roller coasters, the "Desperado." Other amusements include the 5-6 minute Adventure Canyon Water Flume Logride, the 170-foot-high Turbo Drop, first run movies, and a Buffalo-shaped swimming pool with a spiraling water slide and an outdoor spa. Oh, and 1,723 slot machines.

At the 660-room Primm Valley Resort & Casino the theme is golf. When a second championship golf course was added a few years ago, the casino, conference area and all of the public areas including the bars, restaurants and buffet were renovated with a golf theme.

Boulder City

BY ALL MEANS get to Hoover Dam, get to Lake Mead, don't miss them! But don't be so tightly focused on the Great Artifact that you miss Boulder City on the way. Anywhere else on the state map, Boulder City would be a 5-star wonder. Here, between the mega-attractions of Las Vegas and Hoover Dam it sometimes goes unrecognized as the exceptionally inviting city it is.

BOULDER CITY	
Hoover Dam	9
Goodsprings	20
Las Vegas	56

Boulder City was built by the federal govermment to house the workers who built Hoover Dam, and was the first planned community developed in the U.S. After more than 70 years it still stands in such pronounced contrast to the higgledy-piggledy aspect of other Nevada towns that it seems an exotic flower indeed to have grown from the gritty desert soil.

For many years Boulder City was a federal reservation; homes could not be purchased, only leased; gambling and liquor were prohibited. This tradition ran so deep in the community that it was nearly ten years after the feds gave up ownership (in 1960) before laws were relaxed enough to allow liquor licenses (casino gambling is still outlawed). To this day the Chamber of Commerce gets calls inquiring if FBI background checks are required before newcomers can move into town.

They're not of course, but a controlled growth ordinance enacted in 1979 limits the number of new building permits each year, so that the population increase here — so close to the fastest-growing city in America — is barely 400 people a year.

That's part of the reason the pace is so much slower here, and the atmosphere so much calmer than in Las Vegas. This more relaxed environment is one of Boulder City's characteristic attractions, but there are a jillion things to do here, with plenty of comfortable accommodations and a varied selection of dining choices.

To explore Boulder City, park at the center of town and walk to the Boulder Dam Hotel. You will be transported effortlessly to 1933 when this was the most luxurious hotel in Nevada, catering to guests like Shirley Temple and the Prince and Princess of Norway.

The hotel's more recent history has been less lofty, and it was recently acquired by a consortium of local non-profits for an ambitious program of restoration. About 20 of the upstairs rooms (each one dedicated to a famous patron) are being refurbished for guests, and Matteo's Restaurant adjoins the almost-exactly original lobby.

Begin a pleasant stroll at the 728-seat Boulder City Theater, the largest in Nevada when it opened

MAX WINTHROP

The Boulder Dam Hotel.

MAX WINTHROP

The Boulder Dam Brewing Company in Boulder City.

public setting dedicated to art and reflection, was the inspiration of '31er ('31ers are Boulder City's version of the '49ers) Teddy Fenton and the creation of community volunteers.

Take Railroad Avenue and turn left on Birch or Cherry Streets to stroll through the first planned neighborhood in the first fully-developed planned city in America. A map and suggestions for exploration are available at the Chamber of Commerce, 465 Nevada Way, conveniently next door to the new Boulder Dam Brewing Company.

The Historic District is still the center of interest but there are other attractions.

Drive west on the Nevada Highway to Buchanan Street and turn south. The boulevard passes the popular Boulder City Municipal Golf Course and the recently created Veterans' Cemetery en route to the airport. There is a small rodeo arena on B Hill — take Avenue K south to Corral Road — where you are likely to see ropers working themselves and their critters most any afternoon. This is the only part of Boulder City where horses are allowed to reside, and they are here in force.

Bootleg Canyon is a world-famous mountain bike park with both cross-country and downhill trails, and shuttles available to take you and your bike (rentals available) back to the top after you've made it to the bottom.

You'll find great shady, lawned public parks all over the city and you are welcome to enjoy them, but the locals use different names for them than the mapmakers. If you can't find Wilbur Square, ask for Government Park, and if Bicentennial Park eludes you, try Gazebo Park.

Hemenway Valley is one of the fabulous sights in Southern Nevada. It lies to the north of the city

in 1932. Walk west along Arizona street past the hotel, taking in the characteristic "Southwestern" architecture of the commercial buildings and indulging your interests and curiosity as you go.

You'll notice that the Backstop Sports Pub still honors a famous local guarantee: "Free Drink to Anyone Any Day the Sun Doesn't Shine in Boulder City." Cross the Nevada Highway, and walk southwest along Boulder City's original commercial block. The Happy Days Diner is a 50's-style cafe and the Coffee Cup Cafe on the corner of Ash was built in 1931 and is the oldest surviving business structure. Evan's Grill a few steps from the Hotel, Milo's Cellar with its sidewalk cafe on the main boulevard, and the Bistro on the western approach to town are recommended. The Pit Stop, 802 Buchanan Blvd # D at the Nevada Highway, is notable for classic burgers and malts.

Boulder City's downtown commerce today is geared to Dam tourists and other travelers, with an emphasis on antiques and southwestern art. The galleries display a great variety of exceptional work (yes, there's junk and kitsch too).

Turn right on Ash Street and walk up to its intersection with Railroad and Colorado Streets, where, next to the old water treatment plant, you will find the extraordinary Reflections Center. This

proper, a wide, rocky barranca spilling down toward the broad blue expanse of Lake Mead. Near the top of the Valley the St. Jude's Ranch for Children welcomes visitors. The highway to Hoover Dam follows the steep slope of the valley and overlooks the stunning architectural free-for-all that is taking place on this expensive real estate. The immense homes here are all very new, and most of them are built with eager new money and an unrestrained exuberance, the absolute antithesis to the carefully planned, trim and tidy government houses on the other side of the hill. If you are lucky, you'll also find a band of mountain sheep grazing on the broad lawns of Hemenway Park.

A brief digression from the highway to tour this magnificent neighborhood is highly recommended, and at Christmas when these mansions are elaborately decorated, it is mandatory.

LAS VEGAS NEWS BUREAU

Daily raft trips on the Colorado River below Hoover Dam.

It is seven miles to Hoover Dam and the Lake Mead Recreation Area from downtown Boulder City.

MAX WINTHROP

Boulder City's Toilet Paper Man.

Welcome to Boulder City

Area Information

BOULDER CITY CHAMBER OF COMMERCE
465 Nevada Way. 702-293-2034
Located in the beautiful historic district, we'll supply you with the information you need to make your stop a pleasure. Boulder City offers many activities and attractions. Gateway to Hoover Dam and breath-taking Lake Mead, we are rich in recreation and home for varied wildlife. A World Away For A Day!

Lodgings

EL RANCHO BOULDER MOTEL
725 Nevada Highway. 702-293-1085
The El Rancho Boulder Motel is Locally, American and Family owned and operated. We have been in operation for over 50 years and still believe in real Customer Service. Please check out our website or give us a call. The price we quote, plus tax is the price you pay.

Museums

NEVADA STATE RAILROAD MUSEUM
600 Yucca Street. 702-486-5933
Nevada State Railroad Museum, Boulder City offers excursion train rides along the historic Boulder Branch between Boulder City and Railroad Pass aboard classic Pullman Coaches dating to 1911. While you ride, learn about the rich history of the railroad and the role it played in the construction of Hoover Dam.

Valley of Fire State Park

12 miles south and west of Overton, Nevada, via Nevada 169 and Park road; 50 miles northeast of Las Vegas via Interstate 15. Twenty-six thousand acres of brilliantly colored sandstone contorted into a maze of spectacular spires, domes, beehives, and more fanciful forms, the valley undergoes a subtle transformation with each moment that the sun moves across the metallic blue sky above. Stare at any given point for a minute and you will see no change. Glance away and back again, and the landscape has shifted: it is a different shade of red; shadows have slithered out from hidden crevices; shapes have been imperceptibly altered by the changing angle of the sun's rays. It is as if the landscape were in surreptitious molten movement. That, and the unutterable silence, make this an unforgettable place. Gregarious folk may find themselves uneasy here, and chatterers hear their gabble gulped up by the ancient redrock walls: this is no place for "touring" in the usual sense, despite the remarkable scenery.

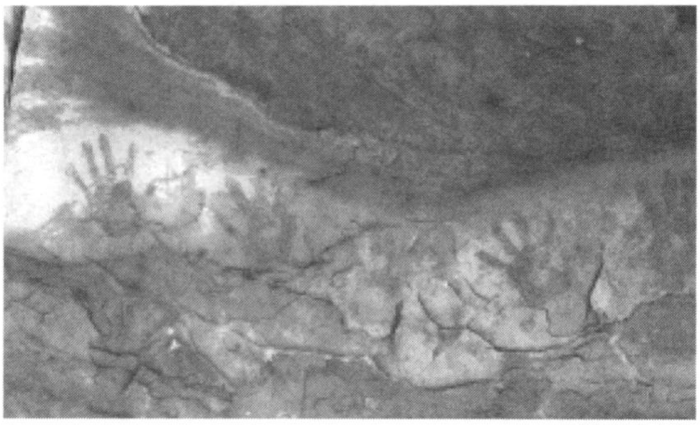

MAX WINTHROP

Ancient travelers passed through the Valley of Fire.

You might as well "see" the Grand Canyon from an airliner as try to take in the Valley of Fire from a moving car. Stop. Turn off the radio. Get out. Sit for a while, and don't talk. Look. Feel the heat, gaze through the shimmering air. Listen. Men came into this valley more than two thousand years ago and have left plentiful evidence of their presence. They built no permanent villages, only rough rock shelters at temporary campsites. Anasazi ventured here from their village at Lost City; hunters and gatherers from Utah; Mogollon people. None of them stayed. The only natural sources of water in the valley are the tanks scoured into the rock by the centuries of wind and rain, in which water collects during infrequent rains. One of these, called Mouse's Tank, is now accessible by self-guided tour from the roadside. Mouse, a Paiute renegade who raided isolated homesites in the region at the turn of the century, kept himself alive between forays with the water collected in this stone bowl. There are numerous petroglyphs in the valley and many of them are identified for visitors.

MAX WINTHROP

Valley of Fire State Park

The park is open throughout the year, and there is a ranger-staffed visitor center where complete information is available regarding all park facilities. Bring all supplies you'll need with you, including drinking water. The developed campsites, and most of the picnic areas, have water available, but there is virtually no water elsewhere in the park. Automotive breakdown, while not likely to prove fatal with hundreds of thousands of people a year visiting the park, could provide some uncomfortable hours without a little water to sip. Development of the park has been aimed toward promoting ecological and esthetic values. There is nothing to buy. No soda pop, no popsicles, nothing. Merely the opportunity to observe the majestic unconcern of the centuries in the solitude of remarkable scenic surroundings.

MOAPA VALLEY

Overton

ONE OF THE EARLY Mormon settlements in the Muddy (now Moapa) Valley, Overton was the site of the first grocery store in this region. Development has been slow, but the favorable conditions made this a major agricultural producer in the 19th and early 20th centuries.

OVERTON	
Mesquite	41
Hoover Dam	45
Las Vegas	61
Pioche	156

So superior were the vegetables, melons and other fruit grown here, in fact, that in the 1920s a local farmer sold his produce by mail. Four heads of lettuce, four bunches of green onions, two bunches of spinach or beet greens, two bunches of asparagus, two bunches of carrots, one batch of garden cress or parsley and, as a graceful touch, a rose or a small bouquet of sweet peas. Price, postpaid as far as Los Angeles or Salt Lake City: one dollar. No more, alas.

Overton received a heavy influx of population when the residents of St. Thomas were forced to flee the rising flood waters of Lake Mead in the 1930s, but these industrious Mormon farmers weren't the first agrarian settlers here.

This region was once a westernmost outpost of the Pueblo people called the Anasazi, the ancient ones. Their thriving settlements were thick along the river courses where they farmed. They built irrigation canals, and homes like hives of mud and sticks. Most of their houses were modest, but some were immense and complex. The largest found at El Pueblo Grande de Nevada — Lost City — had 94 rooms. Their villages stretched up the Virgin and the Muddy rivers, with El Pueblo Grande de Nevada dominating the peninsula at the joining of the rivers.

Twelve hundred years ago they flourished here. Five hundred years later they had abandoned their homes and farms and gone. Many of their settlements, like Lost City itself, were submerged beneath Lake Mead, but many more survive, including some near Logandale.

The Lost City Museum occupies a little knoll

MAX WINTHROP

Lost City Museum, Overton.

just south of Overton. Its cool interior contains one of the most complete collections of artifacts of the early Pueblo Indians in the Southwest. Beginning with the mammoth hunters of the Desert Culture 10,000 years ago, through the different phases of Pueblo culture as they acclimated themselves to agriculture and developed their intricate villages, until they vanished. In addition to the exhibits inside, a small Pueblo residence cluster was constructed on original foundations as a CCC project during the 1930s. It is as exact a replica as governmental hands can build, and as long as you don't climb on the fragile tops of the structures, you can crawl inside and see life from the Anasazi perspective for a few moments. Admission is $2 for adults over 18 and the gift shop is a good source of authentic Native American goods.

Overton is also the provisioning point for fishermen on the Overton arm of Lake Mead. The Overton Beach resort area is 12 miles from town, and the drive in provides a magnificent view of the bright blue lake set in the dull red rock of the desert like turquoise in brick. Driving out you'll see the red rock of the Valley of Fire a few miles to the west, as bright and as brilliant as a sunset at noontime. Because it is surrounded by well-known attractions of such interest, Overton itself is sometimes overlooked by travelers. Take at least five minutes for a detour from the highway to idle through Overton's quiet, comfortable streets. It's a modest advance over the Anasazi, perhaps, and a major advance over life in any modern city. All services are available, and lodgings choices include the recently restored 1955 Plaza Motel.

Welcome to Overton

Area Information

LOST CITY MUSEUM
721 South Moapa Valley Bloulevard. 702-397-2193
Located on an actual site of Pueblo Grande de Nevada, the large Ancestral Puebloan complex known as Lost City, the museum interprets this great civilization with exhibits of artifacts including pottery, stone tools and jewelry. Open daily 8:30 a.m. to 4:30 p.m., the museum store features local and Nevada items.

Mesquite

ONE OF A HANDFUL OF PIONEER farming communities established by the Mormons on the Muddy and Virgin rivers, Mesquite was first settled in 1880 and then abandoned, then occupied permanently in 1894.

MESQUITE	
Las Vegas	82
Lost City	45
Laughlin	164
Beatty	196

For its first century Mesquite was a hard-working farm town of considerable reputation in agricultural circles, unknown otherwise.Then in 1980 this attractive town two miles west of the Arizona line began to sprout neon, add asphalt and show other signs of becoming a new Nevada boomtown. Now, after more than a century of hardscrabble farming and more than two decades in the resort business, Mesquite is proclaiming itself the new — no, not Las Vegas — Palm Springs!

You'll find casino games and slot machines galore in four large casinos, but in Mesquite the name of the game is golf. Six major league golf courses (so far), one designed by Arnold Palmer, draw golfers from St. George and the rest of southwestern Utah, southern Colorado and western Arizona . Add to them the Las Vegans who enjoy a respite from the supercharged atmosphere of their city, and you've got some serious golfing going on.

The Oasis Resort Hotel Casino, occupies the old Pulsipher Ranch property at the site of a once-famous truck stop, and was for a decade the major casino presence in town, developed by the gambling industry pioneer Si Redd. Then the Virgin River Casino (where you can also catch a first-run movie) was built at the eastern freeway exit and the boom began to build. In 1995 Players' Island appeared, a 500-room resort with a tropical theme and a full-service spa with mineral water pools, and Merv Griffin as an owner. Merv's gone and it's called The Casablanca now, but the property is even more elegant than before. The Eureka is the fourth of Mesquite's Casino resorts, on the north side of the life-giving freeway, and there are numerous modern motels and two RV Parks, as well as the Falcon Ridge Hotel, a non-gambling property overlooking the new Wal-Mart.

MAX WINTHROP

Mesquite is an inviting little city on the I-15 at the Arizona border.

With the casinos, the golf courses and the spas, Mesquite offers an easy and inviting escape from humdrum routine and the vexations of daily life. You can keep a hectic schedule of relaxation here: take the morning to play golf, linger over an afternoon in the spa, spend an exciting hour or two at the gaming tables in the evening, sleep late, have a leisurely breakfast, and then hit the trail for an afternoon on horseback. Even without the modern facilities this is a pleasant oasis, free of big-city madness. There are more than a dozen restaurants in the casinos alone, and you'll find plenty to choose from outside the casinos too. Locals like Los Lupes for Mexican food, the Panda Garden for Chinese, and Playoffs for ribs and sports on tv. All of these and more are on Mesquite Boulevard, as is El Rancho Market, an excellent source of picnic provisions.

It's all so easy and enjoyable in Mesquite now that it's hard to realize what a struggle life was for the first settlers here. It was so hard, with a miles-long irrigation ditch to be dug by hand, and croplands to be cleared, that after 15 years only one family remained: Dudley Leavitt, his five wives and 51 children. In 1897 five newly-wed couples from Bunkerville joined the Leavitts at Mesquite, erecting a tent to serve as school, church and town hall, with three more long years before the first frame buildings were built.

At the wonderful Desert Valley Museum, on Main Street, you can get a sense of how it was before golf. The small stone building, which has been entered on the National Register of Historic Places, was contructed by the National Youth Administration in 1941, first used as a library, then a hospital, and finally dedicated as the new City of Mesquite's historical museum in 1985. It is something of a community attic, displaying a wide variety of pioneer implements and accoutrements ranging from a Paiute rabbit fur cloak to a 1945 television set, including oddities such as the petrified tree stump with an "egg" in it. What sets the museum apart, though, is the collection of local reminiscence, memoirs, clips and quotes on local history encouraged, collected and maintained by the volunteer staff. They have accumulated a magnificent archive of the pioneer experience, sorted into volumes, and you can browse through it to find stories, some of them typed and pasted in, some of them written out by hand, like these from the volume titled Folklore:

MAX WINTHROP

Mesquite street scene.

A large man with a small high voice stayed at the Abbott Motel. Early in the morning the man saddled his horse, adjusted his bedroll across his shoulder and climbed into the saddle. People standing around asked why he didn't just tie the bedroll behind the saddle. "Oh, no," he replied, "My poor little mare has enough to do carrying me without having to carry my bedroll too."

Soon after I came from my mission the town decided to move the cemetery from the corner of Tobler's field to its present location because of the farmland and ditch. There were three crews working — one digging up the bodies, one hauling by team and wagon, and one digging new graves and burying the bodies. It took us about three days. My sister Clarissa had twin boys that died at birth and they selected a place in the new cemetery; those were the first graves. Right after that we started moving the bodies from the old cemetery. This experience made me know that the saying "Dust thou art and unto dust shalt thou return" is true. One child had been buried for a couple of years and inside there wasn't a thing but dark fine dust; you could see the print of lace where the hood had been. The child's father felt through the dust and there were no bones. I helped bury that child, so I know it returned to dust. Another father opened the casket of his daughter who had been dead a few months and she looked perfectly normal but when the air hit her she turned dark as coal. He shrank back and said, "Cover it quickly." One boy who had been dead a couple of years had long fingernails and whiskers and hair. One child was just a skeleton, no flesh at all. I had always wondered about the dead, but I saw them in every stage from flesh to dust and I saw all I wanted.

Charles Arthur Hughes, 1905

In 1890 after Heber Hardy had been courting Betsy Leavitt for a few months, he got up enough courage to ask Grandpa Dudley. He said, "Brother Leavitt, I would like to marry one of your daughters."

Dudley answered, "All right, Heber, I'll bring a load of them back from town with me on my next mail run and you can take your pick."

Heber said, "I've already chosen Betsy! She's the one I want!"

These remembrances help anchor the luxuries and pleasures of the resorts and the gambling houses in the reality of human experience, and this unpretentious little museum is as wonderful in its way as the big resorts. The Mesquite Arts Center next door offers another opportunity to explore Mesquite's inner world. There's a 500 seat Concert Hall, Black Box Theatre and the Main & Chamber Galleries presenting the work of local and regional artists.

Take the Bunkerville loop road for a short scenic excursion along the Virgin River. Bunkerville was settled a few years before Mesquite, but you won't find much accessible antiquity here, just a pretty country drive with a dairy farm and enjoyable views of the river.

NATIONAL PARK SERVICE

The fishing is great on Lake Mead.

Lake Mead

AT ITS FARTHEST reach upriver from Hoover Dam, Lake Mead is 115 miles long. Its deepest point is 589 feet below the surface, which has a total area of 229 square miles, making it the largest man-made body of water in the western hemisphere. There are 550 miles of shoreline, much of it sandy beach and most of it accessible only by boat.

Those figures are historical datum points, but at press time many years of drought beginning in 1999 have combined to reduce the lake volume to less than half of maximum, lower the lake level 115 feet and reduce the surface area from 162,700 acres to 95,000. Below-average snowfall in the Colorado Rockies has decreased the amount of runoff into the Colorado River, and Lake Mead is now more than three trillion gallons below capacity.

The disruption of lake shore activities has been considerable as marinas and other shore installations have been forced to move. Drought is common in the history and pre-history of the southwest. Decades of drought dominated this part of the world in the 16th century, and other drought cycles have occurred in centuries past. Water levels returned to normal within a year after a drought in the late 1950s but it took almost ten years for the lake to recover from the record low levels in the next decade.

Nevertheless, freshwater pleasures abound at Lake Mead — active pleasures on the water, and calmer, drier ones such as sunbathing or sipping martinis aboard a floating saloon.

Fishermen take largemouth and striped bass — 20-lb. stripers are common and you're allowed five per day — as well as channel catfish, black crappie and bluegill. The lake's modern marinas offer all services and amenities. You can launch your own boat or rent one here, anything from a skiff for a couple of hours to a luxury houseboat for a couple of weeks. Overnight accommodations and campsites are also available on shore.

The National Park Service manages the Lake and has overseen the development of a large complex of

GOLD HILL NEWS ARCHIVE

The distinctive wildlife of southern Nevada is a part of the attraction here.

concessions, campgrounds and all recreation facilities. A Visitors Center on US 93 at Lakeshore Road offers maps, advice and current information about enjoying the lake, as well as exhibits, narrated slide presentations and a short movie.

Boulder Beach

Two miles northwest of the Visitors Center at the lake shore, Boulder Beach is almost urban in its concentration of services. Campgrounds afford a vast number of individual campsites, densely

MAX WINTHROP

Housboat vacationers at Lake Mead.

LAS VEGAS NEWS BUREAU

The Desert Princess makes lake cruises from its new dock near the Lake Mead Marina to the Dam.

developed but separated by a luxurious growth of oleanders for privacy. Tables and fire grates are provided at each campsite, with water and restrooms in abundance. A swimming beach is roped off and supervised during the hot — very hot — summer months, and the water is pleasantly warm. Picnic shelters, a boat launching ramp and a dock are available for free use and the ranger station is a source of current information.

Lake Mead Marina (702-565-9111)

Three miles farther along the lake shore is a large marina where houseboats and cruisers may be rented or chartered by the hour or for overnight sightseeing and fishing. Water-skis and equipment are also available in case you left your own at home. You'll also find a small country grocery store, moderately priced accommodations in a modern motel, and a floating coffee shop, cocktail lounge and dining room.

Las Vegas Bay Marina (702-293-1191)

Moved from its previous location to Hemenway Harbor, this long-time family-owned business is now acquiring its next-door neighbor, the Lake Mead Marina.

Lake Mead Cruises (702-293-6180)

Scheduled lake tours and excursions depart Hemenway Harbor daily for scheduled tours with special cocktail/dinner cruises, sunset dinner/dance cruises and breakfast cruises available. Recommended as the easiest way for a casual visitor to get a good look at the lake with an informative narration accompaniment.

Echo Bay (702-394-4000)

49 miles from the Visitor Center; about 46 miles northeast of Las Vegas, beyond Callville Bay. All boating and fishing needs are provided for, as well as 166 campsites, a privately operated trailer park with complete hookup facilities, and a modern resort hotel with restaurant and bar. Min-fee $4. 30 day limit.

Rogers Spring

5 miles north of Echo Bay. A developed picnic site and popular family swimming hole. Shaded by a large tamarack tree and fed by a warm spring, the pool tends to get crowded on weekends.

Overton Beach (702-394-4040)

14 miles beyond Echo Bay; 9 miles south of Overton. No developed campsites, but drinking

water is provided. A full range of boating and fishing services including a small store and overnight accommodations are available.

St. Thomas

This pioneer Mormon settlement at the junction of the Virgin and Muddy rivers, dates from 1865 and had achieved a population of nearly 300 people, mostly farm families. When Hoover Dam was completed the residents had to move, as the rising waters of Lake Mead slowly flooded their homes. After 65 years under water the town's remnants have re-emerged, one of the few happy consequences of the drought afflicting the southwestern US, and some trees have taken root in the old townsite. It's about a 1½ mile walk from St. Thomas Point, which you can reach via the dirt road leaving Nevada Highway 169 opposite the east entrance to Valley of Fire State Park. The trail is marked and as long as it's dry and not too hot you'll have an easy stroll to the ruins and back.

Las Vegas Bay (702-565-9111)

10 miles northwest of the Visitor Center 9 miles northeast of Henderson via Nevada 147. Facilities as at Boulder Beach, except no trailer court or overnight accommodations. 89 campsites but no hookups; small grocery store and cafe, boat launching ramp and marine supplies are available. The marina has been relocated to Hemenway Harbor. 30 day limit.

Callville Bay (702-565-8958) 800-255-5561

On North Shore Drive 27 miles from the Visitor Center and 23 miles from Henderson. 30 developed campsites with showers and toilets, laundry and store, boat launching ramp and marine supplies as well as houseboat rentals are available. The Mormon community of Callville, established in 1864 as a freighting center for Colorado River traffic, lies submerged in the warm waters of Lake Mead near here. The sternwheelers Esmeralda and Nina Tilden made the difficult and dangerous ascent of the rapids in Black Canyonãduring the few months of the year when there was enough flow through the canyon to allow passage at all — by winching to ring bolts driven into the bedrock along the banks. Downriver terminus was Fort Yuma.

LAS VEGAS NEWS BUREAU

Hemenway Harbor is home to many of Lake Mead's pleasure boats as well as the Desert Princess.

LAS VEGAS NEWS BUREAU

The mighty dam.

Hoover Dam

31 MILES SOUTHEAST of Las Vegas, 8 miles from Boulder City via U.S. 93. When it was built, Hoover Dam was the largest thing ever made by human beings. Every statistic is awesome, even in our mega-number world. In 1931 it seemed incredible: more than 1,000,000 cubic yards of river fill were excavated. Enough rock was excavated, about nine million tons, to build 2,500 miles of masonry wall. Enough digging to dig a hole 100 feet long by 60 feet wide and one mile deep. Enough concrete to lay a strip of pavement twenty feet wide from California to Florida or to build a solid tower 2,100 feet high on a base 300 feet square.

As much structural and reinforcing steel as in the Empire State Building, 1000 miles of steel pipe, 165,000 railroad cars of sand, gravel and cobbles, 900 cars of hydraulic machinery. If you assembled all these materials and loaded them aboard a single train, the locomotive would be entering Boulder City just as the caboose left Kansas City, Missouri.

According to Herodotus the Great Pyramid of Egypt required 100,000 men 20 years to build. Hoover Dam was bigger, and with the largest collection of specialized equipment ever assembled at any project, it took 1,200 men less than two years to build.

It gave Depression-bound, baffled America something to be enthusiastic about, something tangible to point to and say, "Well, if we can build a dam that big, things must be getting better."

Minimum wage at the project was $4 a day, to laborers and helpers. Truck drivers made up to 75 cents an hour, and so did carpenters and electricians. Cat-skinners made 62.5 cents, and the shovel operators were kings at $1.25 an hour. Even without overtime that came to $10 per day.

Total cash receipts for the project amounted to $51,950,000. That didn't include nearly half a million dollars the government paid to acquire 154 tracts of land totalling 6,287 acres, including the villages of Kaolin and St. Thomas and 6.5 miles of the Los Angeles-Salt Lake railroad. All this real estate is now at the bottom of 115-mile Lake Mead. Still more money went into the building of Boulder City, the most meticulously planned community in the world at that time.

It was a great show and it continued from July, 1930, when the first work officially began, through September, 1935, when President Roosevelt dedicated the completed structure. It was a landmark before the first shovelful of earth was ever turned, and it remains a landmark today, even in this era of mammoth projects.

The structure rises more than 725 feet from bedrock, and plugs Black Canyon. It is 660 feet thick at its base, tapering to 45 feet at the top. The sec-

The mighty Colorado near Black Canyon.

MAX WINTHROP

tion of two-lane highway along the crest of the dam connecting Nevada and Arizona is 1,244 feet long. Three and a quarter million cubic yards of concrete were used to build it.

In the summer of 1983 flooding on the Colorado and its upriver tributaries brought the waters of Lake Mead to the overflow level for the first time in its history (other than a test of the spillway system 42 years before).

These and other facts are amplified and illuminated by the guides who lead 25-minute tours through the dam, its hydroelectric generating facilities, and the spillways and penstocks of the water distribution system.

Tours begin in the marvelous new Visitor Center on the Nevada side of the Dam. Built to harmonize with both the rugged canyon and the enormous dam, the structure offers a fabulous view of the dam from the observation level. Perhaps just as wonderful on an August afternoon, there is covered parking for 450 cars ($7) from 8 am to 6 pm with escalator access to the exhibit area from which the tours depart.

Tour ticket sales begin at 9 am and end at 4:15 pm daily except Thanksgiving and Christmas. The visitor center closes at 5 pm so to see it all, you should arrive by 3 pm for tours. Power Plant Tour: Adults (17-61) $11, Seniors (62+) $9, Juniors (7-16) $9, Military and Dependents (adults & seniors) $9, Military in uniform Free, Children (6 and under) Free. Dam Tour: $25 for everyone, no children under 8. For entrance to the Visitor Center only: $8. America the Beautiful, Golden Eagle or Golden Age Passports/discounts are not accepted for admission to the Hoover Dam Visitor Center or tours.

It is best to take the Dam tour early in the day, especially during the summer months when temperatures regularly rise above 110 degrees during the afternoon, resulting in seats and steering wheels too hot to touch after a few minutes in the sun. The guides, too, are weary by late afternoon. It is not only the heat but that they have answered every conceivable question about the Dam eight million times already, and they are pretty sure you are going to ask one of them again.

Oskar Hansen's Winged Figures of the Republic pause eternally balanced on each side of the star map and universal calendar. These magnificent sculptures are the most obvious of the many works of art that embellish the great dam. There are bas-reliefs on two elevator towers, eagles inlaid in the bronze elevator doors and tile motifs in the tunnel floors within.

The lake cruiser Desert Princess provides a lake-side view of the Dam and you can't ask for a finer touristic experience than the rugged landscape, the glittering water, the boat and the dam combine to provide.

Because of security concerns after the terrorist attack on the Twin Towers, no pedestrians are allowed on the dam after dark, and 18-wheelers are being detoured via Laughlin and US 95 while a spectacular new composite concrete deck arch bridge is being constructed a short distance south of the great dam, expected to open to traffic in 2010. At that time, dam-top traffic will be limited to visitors.

MAX WINTHROP

Lake Mohave is a bright blue jewel in a brown earthen setting.

Lake Mohave

AFTER FUNNELING through the penstocks, tunnels and tubes to spin the immense turbine generators within Hoover Dam, the Colorado River resumes its flow downriver. This new lease on life is only temporary, however. A few miles farther along the current slows again and stops as the river enters Lake Mohave, a long, slender body of water bulging out of the old riverbed upstream from Davis Dam. Lake Mohave is a part of the Lake Mead Recreation Area, and like Lake Mead has been developed under the supervision of the National Park Service. Immediately below Hoover Dam, where there is some current, rainbow trout are large and willing, especially in the five months beginning in October. In the warmer lake waters farther down, channel bass, channel catfish and crappie are the principal game fish, especially active from March through May. Fishing remains good through the summer and peaks again in the autumn months.

Eldorado Canyon

34 miles southeast of Boulder City, via U.S. 95 and Nevada 165, on the Nevada shore of Lake Mohave. Trailer hookups, a small store, and cafe were washed away by a flash flood some years ago. No developed campsites.

This canyon was the scene of intensive mining operations beginning in 1857, when soldiers from Fort Mohave discovered placer gold. Legends of previous Indian and Spanish mining in the region are plentiful, and Nelson's Landing became a busy port of call for the stern-wheeled steamers on the Yuma-Callville run. Rich silver deposits were uncovered in 1861, and lode mines were active despite the incredible isolation which required six months to freight supplies and equipment from the Pacific Coast.

Remote from even the rough camps at Hiko and Pioche, Eldorado Canyon was so lawless a place that not even a killing was sufficient inducement for law officers to make the difficult journey there. Mining continued until 1890, revived again in 1905, lurched on through the early decades of the century, and bottomed out for good in 1941 after producing a total of some $10 million, principally from the Techatticup Mine. The townsite and mills of Eldorado are submerged beneath Lake Mohave, though mining ruins, including aging structures housing a population of about 50, remain at Nelson.

The town of Nelson is totally residential, the residents must drive to Boulder City, Henderson or Las Vegas for all their needs. You're welcome to visit on your way to view the lake and the mining relics, but remember, these are people's home and there's nothing to buy.

MAX WINTHROP

The Searchlight Nugget.

Searchlight

A MINING town that grew up around a rich gold strike in 1897, Searchlight succeeded Pioche as the principal city of southern Nevada when production began in earnest in 1902. In 1907, when Las Vegas was still a village of tents and shanties, Searchlight's population was nudging 1,500 and it had business streets, newspapers, telephones and a chamber of commerce. There were more than 300 claims and nearly 50 mines in production, with a dozen mills and a through rail connection with the Santa Fe at Needles, California to the south.

SEARCHLIGHT	
Laughlin	39
Boulder City	37
Las Vegas	61
Gerlach	611

The origin of the town's unusual name is explained in an exhibit at the small museum a short distance east on the Cottonwood Cove road. It says the Mining District (and therefore the town that grew up there) was named for a brand of wooden matches. The display includes a piece of the wooden box they came in. It's big enough to serve as a small 'writing-desk' (the original laptop!) and I can picture a group of elated miners searching their excited minds for a name to give their discovery, and nobody accepting another's favorite ("Let's call it the Bonnie Sue!") until finally an eye falls on the box. One more note of interest about the name: Scott Joplin wrote "The Searchlight Rag" for friends who'd invested in mines here. Other mines were the Spotted Horse and the rich Duplex.

By 1910 Searchlight's glow had dimmed — due to the simultaneous catastrophes of the Panic of 1907 and the depletion of high-grade ore. Mining continued, but at a much reduced pace. By 1927 there were barely 50 residents remaining, deriving their livelihoods as much from the highway traffic and the surrounding ranches as from the mines. One of these ranches, the Walking Box, became the residence of movie stars Rex Bell and Clara Bow, giving Searchlight a modest grandeur during the quiet '30s and '40s. The great costume designer Edith Head spent some of her girlhood in Searchlight, and doubtless dressed her dolls here. One of Nevada's U.S. Senators, Harry Reid, was born here.

These days Searchlight is basking in a new prosperity derived from the Las Vegas - Laughlin traffic on US 95. Main Street has been widened to four lanes, and it's considerably brighter than it was, with new enterprise clamoring for attention.

Laughlin

LAUGHLIN MIGHT AS WELL have been named Fun City — no-one comes here for business unless they are in the fun business. We come for the food, the drink, the easy-going atmosphere, the gambling, the fishing, and the golf in the unique Colorado River setting.

LAUGHLIN	
Las Vegas	95
Tonopah	302
Ely	408
Jackpot	582
Denio	660

Laughlin is like a fond memory of long-ago Las Vegas — resorts instead of megaresorts — all the luxury and razamataz of the big casino hotels but without the traffic jams. There are ten of these palaces now, nine clustered along the Colorado River near Don Laughlin's original Riverside and the tenth, The Avi, 16 miles south on the Fort Mohave Tribal Reservation.

The natural attraction provided by the Colorado River and the surrounding desert landscapes still captivates visitors as much as the bright and busy casino hotels along Casino Drive. It's a unique combination of harsh with lush, and just the right balance between Monaco and Mayberry, a gambling resort with fishing privileges, a calm, friendly and undemanding.

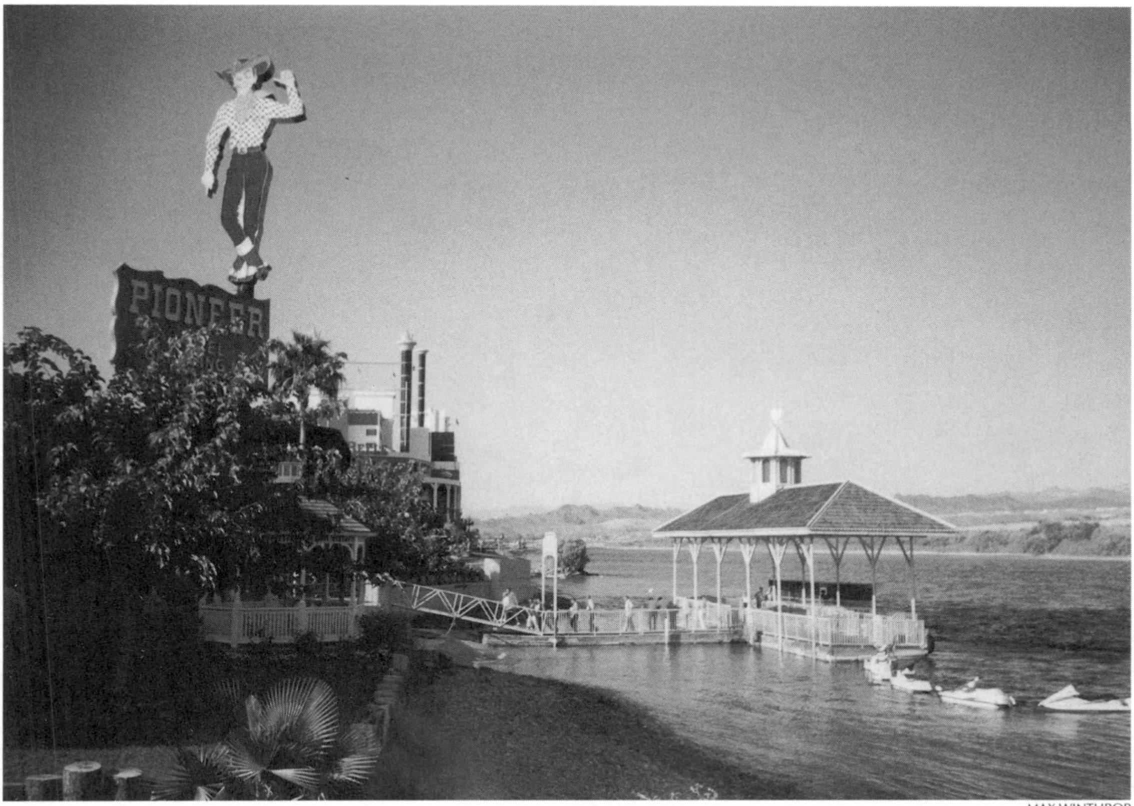

MAX WINTHROP

Laughlin's gaudy greeting welcomes constantly arriving visitors all year around.

In 1966 an enterprising fellow named Don Laughlin bought a rundown bait shack with six stools, a beer bar license and 10 slot machines

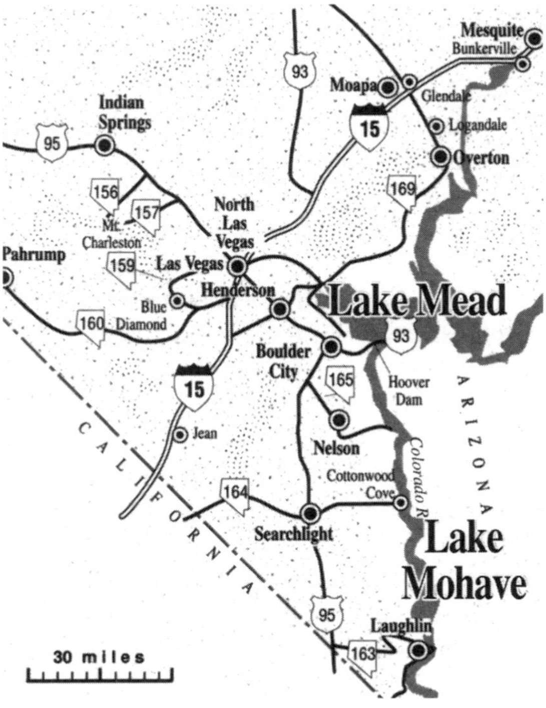

across the Colorado River from Bullhead City, Arizona. He persuaded the post office to open a substation at his isolated outpost, and set to work. Fifteen years later the Wall Street Journal reported: "Mr. Laughlin's red brick, colonial-style casino is the biggest in town, with some 700 slot machines and 28 gaming tables." In 1982 his gambling operations grossed more than $20 million.

By then, "town" was seven casinos lining the bank of the river, five of them with hotels totaling 600 rooms. There were 3,200 employees dealing the cards, mixing the drinks and making the beds, but only 92 of them could find places to live in Laughlin. Most of the rest rode to work on the water taxis flitting constantly back and forth across the river from Bullhead City. The customers they served came mostly from southern California (via Needles or Nipton) and from Arizona. They drove to Bullhead City from the interior of the state and then parked their cars and RVs on one of the great asphalt pads on the Arizona side of the river to catch water taxis bound for the casinos on the Nevada side.

In those days Laughlin seemed destined to rival

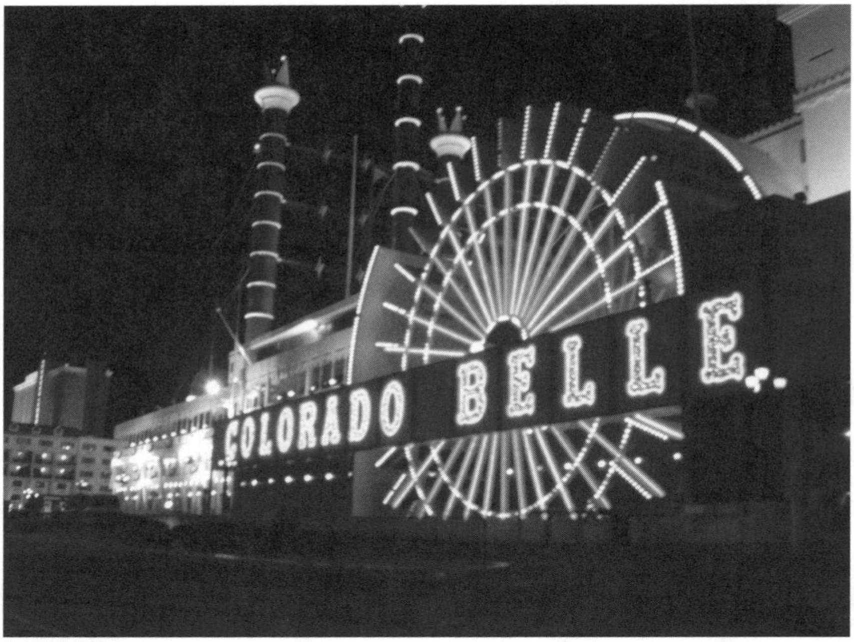

MAX WINTHROP

Laughlin's Colorado Belle lights up the night.

Las Vegas for splash and excitement. Don Laughlin's dinky little bar and motel had grown into Don Laughlin's mighty Riverside Hotel Casino. The Colorado Hotel (now the Pioneer Club), the Regency and the Colorado Belle were built. The Edgewater Hotel went up in 1979. Twenty years ago Circus Circus made the Colorado Belle the most photogenic casino on the river. With the addition of the Ramada Express (now the Tropicana Express), Harrah's and Flamingo Hilton, the buoyant municipal mood was predicting a newer, younger, brighter and bigger Las Vegas taking shape along the Colorado.

It didn't happen. The existing properties have multiplied their their rooms with new towers, and occasionally a new resort was built, but growth has been sedate in comparison with the magnificent madness of Las Vegas. In 1996 the Fort Mohave Indian tribe built the Avi Casino Resort 16 miles south of town.

There are now 10 casino resorts with more than 9,000 rooms for guests, and talk of overtaking Las Vegas has ended. In fact Laughlin presents itself as a serene alternative to Las Vegas overload. The River Walk is now being extended upriver with a trail from the new bridge all the way to Davis Dam, and one of the recent improvements was the addition of a fishing platform.

Laughlin had to wait for nearly 20 years after Don Laughlin's arrival before there were 100 residents — the first house wasn't built until 1985 - most of the early community development took place on the Arizona side of the river. There are more than 10,000 residents in Laughlin now (a 22% growth rate since 2000, most of it around the corner and out of sight from Casino Drive), and growth is expected to increase another 16% over the next five years.

Bullhead City has grown even faster and larger, and now there's a comet's tail of suburban sprawl on the Arizona side extending all the way to Needles, California, with a Target store, a Kohl's, a Bed, Bath & Beyond and other national chain stores. "We're part of the big world now," a local resident told me happily.

The resorts here have been changing hands — the old Flamingo is now the new Aquarius and the Ramada Express is now the Tropicana Express — and gently renovating and upgrading in the process. The outlet mall that opened ten years ago has new owners who have added three new stores and are bringing 28 new stores, more high-end than before.

Laughlin still doesn't have a cemetery, and its church congregations hold services in hotel meeting rooms, but it has its own supermarket-anchored shopping center, pizza places and Chinese cafe.

Gnat's Landing, in another little shopping plaza, was the first non-casino bar in town. Almost all the attributes of a mainstream American town, in other words, except that everything is brand new. There has certainly never been a neater, cleaner boomtown in Nevada.

For a fascinating half-hour driving tour, take the main boulevard downriver from the casinos. You'll pass the long, skinny Emerald River Golf Course and, looming like a ghost above the sparkling waters of the Colorado, a haunting monument to greed and bad judgment: the skeleton of the 4,000-room Emerald River Casino Hotel, financed with junk bonds and abandoned before completion.

Turn right at the Needles Highway to tour the residential part of town and return to the casinos, or go left and visit the newest and most surprising casino attraction on the River — the Avi, an enterprise of the Mohave Tribe adding to the prosperity of far southern Nevada.

Be sure to visit the strange and wonderful state of Arizona, directly across the river and accessible by water taxi, the 6-mile scenic route via Davis Dam, or directly across on the new bridge. This bridge, with the river flowing slowly and serenely beneath it, and the profoundly barren mountains reared up against the sky above, is the supreme symbol of Laughlin. A bridge was long overdue to relieve both the car traffic forced to take the long-way-around via the dam and the too-heavy pressure on the water-taxi system, but neither Nevada nor Arizona could afford to build it. Even if they could, the process might take years. So the ever-enterprising Don Laughlin built the $3 million bridge himself and donated it to the states. As you stand on a warm evening in the light of the neon, watch the endless stream of cars cruising back and forth between Nevada and Arizona and pay tribute to Don Laughlin's pioneering spirit. Wretched excess? Of course, it's a Nevada specialty. But would anyone seriously want to go back to a bait shack with six stools and a beer cooler?

There are some big events in Laughlin each year. Laughlin Winter Break is an elder version of the college students' Spring Break, and the Laughlin Desert Challenge is held in January. The Laughlin River Run is an ear-shaking motorcycle rendezvous held each spring, and Rockets Over the River just after dusk on July 4th, is a 20-minute fireworks display that brings spectators viewing along the River Walk.

Apart from the casinos, Laughlin's main attraction is the Colorado River. On a recent visit in late August, afternoon temperature 112∞, the river was a busy playground, with swimmers, sunbathers and babies playing patty-cake at the Harrah's beach, little water-skeeters zipping up and down the river, water taxis buzzing from one hotel to another, water-skiers bouncing behind sleek boats and sending up rooster-tails behind them, and the Little Belle gliding grandly on its sight-seeing cruises.

For many visitors, the trout fishing is as great a lure as the gambling games, and many of Laughlin's visitors bunk up in their RVs, enjoy the fishing and the mild winter temperatures, and only enter the casinos for an early breakfast before heading off to catch lunch and dinner.

The countryside around Laughlin is inviting to the backroad explorer; temperatures are most comfortable from late fall through early spring, and in March and April the wildflowers make a brilliant display.

There's an inviting detour I recommend to anyone making the drive from Laughlin to Las Vegas. As you make the climb up from the river west toward US 95 you'll see a marked road on the right: Christmas Tree Pass. Take it for a pleasant 16-mile meander (maybe an hour's drive if you've brought your camera, more if you're wearing your hiking boots) that's easy enough for the family car. You'll climb as you follow the graded gravel road north into highly picturesque landscapes and over the spine of the ridge and back down west again to US 95.

Welcome to Laughlin

Activities

DESERT RIVER KAYAK
1034 Highway 95, Bullhead City. 928-754-5320

Kayak or canoe the beautiful Colorado River past the casinos of Laughlin and the riverfront homes of Bullhead City, the Black Canyon at the base of Hoover Dam or the stunning Topock Gorge. Trips from 1 hour to multiday. Casino pick ups available. Year round fun on a beautiful river. 888-529-2533

Ten Essential Titles for your Nevada Book Shelf

1. ***The Thompson & West History of Nevada***. This weighty volume was written by a skillful journalist named Myron Angel when the pioneer experience was still fresh in Nevada. When Thompson and West originally issued the 680-page book, the Territorial Enterprise greeted it with enthusiasm. The new book, it predicted, "will either take its place as a standard work of reference, or will serve as the basis at some future time for the history which is to be written after the present generation passes away." Right on both counts.

2. ***Roughing It***, by Mark Twain. This is Twain's brilliant telling of his Nevada adventures, a great book by any standard. It is a classic of the American West, and it should be on everyone's bookshelf, not just yours and mine. It was written in 1872, a little more than 10 years after Sam Clemens deserted his Confederate militia unit and headed out for Nevada with his brother Orion.

3. ***Nevada Ghost Towns & Mining Camps***, by Stanley Paher. Forty years ago Paher traveled throughout Nevada pestering people for a look at the family photo albums they kept as monuments to the time when they and Nevada were young. He prowled the courthouses of the state, poring through bales of records, documents and maps and managed to pinpoint the locations and histories of more than 600 mining towns, logging camps, ranching villages, railroad shipping points, military posts, trading posts, Pony Express stations, stagecoach depots, way stations and spas in Nevada and the adjacent parts of Oregon, Arizona and California. The encyclopedia which emerged from his prodigious researches is illustrated with over 700 photographs of pioneer settlements in Nevada, and was an undisputed classic the moment is appeared.

4. ***Martha & the Doctor*** by Marvin A. Lewis. This is the powerful depiction of the experiences of James and Martha Gally and their two children in and around Austin during the ten years beginning in 1864. Their struggle to maintain themselves on the far frontier with no other resources than their courage and determination makes for dreadful, absorbing reading. It is a harrowing picture of family life in the desert wilderness of early Nevada, and of the courage and devotion required simply to endure. The story has a happy ending (more or less), but its great lesson for the modern reader is its unvarnished and highly personal depiction of the frontier reality. This is a fine book about very real people.

5. `***Nevada, The Great Rotten Borough***, by Gilman M. Ostrander. As one reviewer puts it, "Gilman Ostrander was very angry with the Founding Fathers for creating the U.S. Senate and argues that Nevada makes his case." Whether you agree with his conclusions or not, you'll learn a lot from this carefully researched political history of our beloved but imperfect state.

6. ***Any book by Walter Van Tilburg Clark***. My own preference is for his ***Collected Stories***, but you may prefer ***The Ox-Bow Incident, Track of the Cat***, or ***City of Trembling Leaves***. Whatever your preference, Clark's loving and lyrical responses to the Nevada environment are unforgettable. He was one of the first Western American novelists to achieve national recognition, redefining Western history and geography in the public mind and created a distinctly Nevada literature with national stature.

7. ***I Want to Quit Winners***, by Harold Smith. This is the Harold for whom Reno's famous Harold's Club was named, and for whom it made millions. It is rare that anyone writes so frank and thoughtful an autobiography. Even rarer that it be a businessman, and rarest of all that it be a man who played a crucial role in developing casino gambling from a back room saloon sideline into the state's premiere industry.

8. ***Fear & Loathing in Las Vegas***, by Hunter S. Thompson. Originally published in The Rolling Stone, this was the birth of Gonzo Journalism, and stems from a faraway time (1971) before what happened in Vegas stayed in Vegas. Thompson wrote, "There was madness in any direction, at any hour. . . . You could strike sparks anywhere. There was a fantastic universal sense that whatever we were doing was right, that we were winning. . . . And that, I think, was the handle — that sense of inevitable victory over the forces of Old and Evil. Not in any mean or military sense; we didnít need that. Our energy would simply prevail. There was no point in fighting — on our side or theirs. We had all the momentum; we were riding the crest of a high and beautiful wave. . . . So now, less than five years later, you can go up on a steep hill in Las Vegas and look West, and with the right kind of eyes you can almost see the high-water mark — that place where the wave finally broke and rolled back."

9. ***Complete Nevada Traveler***, by my humble self. This is "the affectionate and intimately detailed guidebook to the most interesting state in America" and introduces you to all of our 110,000 square mile theme park. Perhaps modesty should forbid including this book on the list, but . . . it doesn't.

10. ***Your Choice*** at the bookstore. This is the one you pick out for yourself at the book store or online, where you can find out-of-print books as well as more recent titles. You might pick An ***Editor on the Comstock Lode*** by Wells Drury, ***My Adventures with Your Money*** by the early 20th century mining stock promoter George Graham Rice, ***My Memories of the Comstock*** by Harry Gorham or Sally Zanjani's ***Devils Will Reign***, about the earliest beginnings of Nevada history. Follow your interests and you may end up with 11 or 12 books on your shelf.

Nevada Visitors Centers and Chambers of Commerce

Southern
Las Vegas Territory

Boulder City Chamber of Commerce
702-293-2034
bouldercitychamber.com

Boulder City State of Nevada
Welcome Center
702-294-1252
visitlasvegas.com

Henderson Convention Center
and Visitors Bureau
877-775-5252, 702-267-2171
visithenderson.com

Las Vegas Convention and Visitors Authority
877-VISIT-LV
visitlasvegas.com
Las Vegas Territory
lvterritory.com

Laughlin Chamber of Commerce
702-298-2214
laughlinchamber.com

Laughlin Visitors Information Center
800-452-8445, 702-298-3321
visitlaughlin.com

Mesquite Area Chamber of Commerce
702-346-2902
mesquite-chamber.com

Mesquite State of Nevada
Welcome Center
702-346-2702, 877-MESQUITE
visitmesquite.com

Moapa Valley Chamber of Commerce
702-398-7160 Logandale
moapavalley.com

North Las Vegas Chamber of Commerce
702-642-9595
northlasvegaschamber.com

Primm State of Nevada Welcome Center
702-874-1360
visitlasvegas.com

Searchlight Community Center
702-297-1682

Central
Pioneer Territory

Amargosa Valley Chamber of Commerce
775-372-1515 avnv.us

Beatty Chamber of Commerce
775-553-2424, 866-736-3716 beattynevada.org
Caliente Chamber of Commerce
lincolncountynevada.com

Dayton Area Chamber of Commerce
775-246-7909
daytonnvchamber.org

Death Valley Chamber of Commerce
760-786-3200 Shoshone
deathvalleychamber.org

Death Valley National Park Info Center
775-553-3200 Beatty nps.gov/deva

Death Valley Natural History Association
Death Valley Morning Report
800-478-8564 dvnha.org

Furnace Creek & Death Valley
National Park Visitor Center
760-786-3200 nps.gov/deva

Goldfield Chamber of Commerce
775-485-3560
geocities.com/goldfieldchamber

Greater Lincoln County Chamber of
Commerce Panaca
lincolncountynevada.com

Greater Smoky Valley
Chamber of Commerce
775-377-2830 Round Mountain
bigsmokyvalley.com

Mason Valley Chamber of Commerce
775-463-2245 Yerington
masonvalleychamber.org

Mineral County Chamber of Commerce
775-945-2507 Hawthorne
mineralcountychamber.com

Pahrump Valley Chamber of Commerce
775-727-5800, 866-722-5800
pahrumpchamber.com

Pioche Chamber of Commerce
775-962-5544 piochenevada.com
Pioneer Territory
877-848-5800
thesolitudes.com

Tonopah Convention Center &
Visitors Authority
775-482-3558
tonopahnevada.com

Statewide

Indian Territory

Grimes Point Archaeological Site
775-885-6000 Fallon
nv.blm.gov/carson/Recreation/
Rec_grimes_pt.htm

Hidden Cave /Churchill County Museum
775-423-3677 Fallon ccmuseum.org

Indian Territory
800-NEVADA-8 travelnevada.com

Lost City Museum
702-397-2193 Overton
moapavalley.com, nevadaculture.org

Nevada State Museum
775-687-4810 Carson City
nevadaculture.org

Numana Hatchery Visitors Center
775-574-0290 Nixon
plpt.nsn.us

Wellington Station Museum
775-465-2314

Wigwam Native American Museum
775-575-2573 Fernley

Walker River Paiute Tribe
775-773-2306

North Western

Reno/Tahoe Territory

Carson City Chamber of Commerce
775-882-1565 carsoncitychamber.com

Carson City Convention and Visitors Bureau
775-687-7410, 800-NEVADA-1 visitcarsoncity.com

Carson Valley Chamber of Commerce &
Visitors Authority
800-727-7677, 775-782-8144
Gardnerville visitcarsonvalley.org,
carsonvalleynv.org

Lake Tahoe Incline Village/
Crystal Bay Visitors Bureau
775-832-1606, 800-GO-TAHOE
Incline Village gotahoenorth.com

Lake Tahoe South Shore
Chamber of Commerce
775-588-1728 Lake Tahoe
tahoechamber.org

Lake Tahoe Visitors Authority
530-544-5050, 800-AT-TAHOE
South Lake Tahoe bluelaketahoe.com

Reno Sparks Chamber of Commerce
775-337-3030
reno-sparkschamber.org

Reno/Sparks Convention and
Visitors Bureau
775-827-7600, 800-FOR-RENO
visitrenotahoe.com

Reno-Tahoe Territory
775-687-7410 renotahoe.com

Ski Lake Tahoe
(for a free Skiers & Boarders Guide)
888-TAHOE-38 skilaketahoe.com

Sparks Chamber of Commerce
775-358-1976 sparkschamber.org

South Lake Tahoe Wedding Association
tahoeweddings.org

Town of Genoa
775-782-8696 genoanevada.org

Virginia City Convention & Tourism
Authority
775-847-4386, 800-718-7587
visitvirginiacitynv.com

Northern

Cowboy Country

Battle Mountain Chamber of Commerce
775-635-8245
shopbattlemountain.com,
battlemountainchamber.org

City of Carlin
775-754-6354 explorecarlinnv.com

Cowboy Country
877-626-9269 cowboycountry.org

Elko Convention & Visitors Authority
775-738-4091, 800-248-3556
exploreelko.com
Jackpot Recreation & Tourism Center
775-755-2653

Jarbidge Community Association
775-488-2311

Lander County Convention &
Tourism Authority
775-635-1112
battlemountaintourism.com

Lovelock/Pershing County
Chamber of Commerce
775-273-7213 loverslock.com

McDermitt Information
775-532-8742

Wells Chamber of Commerce
775-752-3540
wellsnevada.com

West Wendover Tourism &
Convention Bureau
775-664-3138, 866-299-2489
westwendovercity.com

Winnemucca Convention &
Visitors Authority
775-623-5071, 800-962-2638
winnemucca.com

North Central

Pony Express Territory

Greater Austin Chamber of Commerce
775-964-2200
austinnevada.com

Bristlecone Convention Center
775-289-3720, 800-496-9350 Ely
elynevada.net

Eureka Opera House
775-237-6006 co.eureka.nv.us

Fallon Chamber of Commerce
775-423-2544 fallonchamber.com

Fallon Convention & Tourism Authority
775-423-4556, 800-874-0903
fallontourism.com

Fernley Chamber of Commerce
775-575-4459
fernleychamber.org

Great Basin National Park
775-234-7331 nps.gov/grba

Great Basin Tourism Council Baker
greatbasinpark.com

Pony Express Territory
888-359-9449 ponyexpressnevada.com

Silver Springs Chamber of Commerce
775-577-4336 silverspringsnevada.com

White Pine Chamber of Commerce
775-289-8877 whitepinechamber.com